BEYOND THE ELITE

A volume in the series

Medieval Societies, Religions, and Cultures

Edited by M. Cecilia Gaposchkin and Anne E. Lester

A list of titles in this series is available at
cornellpress.cornell.edu

BEYOND THE ELITE

EVERYDAY JEWISH LIVES IN
MEDIEVAL NORTHERN EUROPE

EDITED BY
ELISHEVA BAUMGARTEN

CORNELL UNIVERSITY PRESS
Ithaca and London

Copyright © Cornell University, 2026

All rights reserved. Except for brief quotations in a review, this book, or parts thereof, must not be reproduced in any form without permission in writing from the publisher. For information, address Cornell University Press, Sage House, 512 East State Street, Ithaca, New York 14850. Visit our website at cornellpress.cornell.edu.

First published 2026 by Cornell University Press

Librarians: A CIP catalog record for this book is available from the Library of Congress.

ISBN 978-1-5017-8537-5 (hardcover)
ISBN 978-1-5017-8538-2 (paperback)
ISBN 978-1-5017-8539-9 (pdf)
ISBN 978-1-5017-8540-5 (epub)

GPSR EU contact: Sam Thornton, Mare Nostrum Group B.V, Doelen 72, 4831 GR Breda, NL, gpsr@mare-nostrum.co.uk.

*For Audrey Fingherman,
with gratitude and appreciation*

Contents

Introduction: Beyond the Elite:
Everyday Jewish Lives in Medieval
Northern Europe   Elisheva Baumgarten   1

Part I: People

1. Exclusion and Reconciliation:
   Excommunication in Medieval
   Jewish Communities   Miri Fenton   31

2. Jewish Orphanhood and Orphans
   in Medieval Ashkenaz: Cultural
   Conceptions and Everyday Life
   Andreas Lehnertz and Eyal Levinson   49

3. Everyday Disruptions: The
   Negotiation of Local Power Struggles
   by the Jews of Münzenberg and
   Assenheim   Annika Funke   74

Part II: Spaces

4. Rivers, Tolls, and Ships: The
   Movement and Communication
   of Medieval German Jews
   Tzafrir Barzilay   103

5. Jews and Lombards in
   Fourteenth-Century Paris:
   A Comparative Look   Nureet Dermer   125

6. Between Inns, Hospices, and
   Homes: Jewish Travel and
   Communal Hospitality in Medieval
   Ashkenaz   Albert Evan Kohn   145

CONTENTS

PART III: OBJECTS

7. The Medieval Stone Revolution Reflected in Hebrew Inscriptions from Worms and Mainz
   NETA BODNER AND ARIELLA LEHMANN   175

8. The Objects of Others: The Risks of Non-Elite Debtors in Jewish-Christian Credit Exchange
   AVIYA DORON   208

9. Beyond Kiddushin: The Medieval Ashkenazic Betrothal Ring IDO NOY   226

PART IV: RITUALS

10. Not Only for the Learned: *Piyyutim* as Part of Public Prayer
    EREZ SHAHAR ROCHMAN   259

11. Curing Fevers, Sharing Prayers: Jews, Christians, and Conjurations
    ELISHEVA BAUMGARTEN AND AMIT SHAFRAN   279

12. To See and Be Seen: The Role of Jews in Medieval Urban Processions
    HANNAH TEDDY SCHACHTER   304

    Afterword: Beyond the Elite, and Much More MIRI RUBIN   328

Acknowledgments 337
List of Contributors 341
Index 345

BEYOND THE ELITE

Introduction
Beyond the Elite: Everyday Jewish Lives in Medieval Northern Europe

Elisheva Baumgarten

An early fifteenth-century manuscript contains a quote attributed to Solomon son of Samson, who was active in the early twelfth century, describing events that he himself did not witness.[1]

> When we first came to Speyer, it was with the hope that we pitch our tents forever, never having to uproot its stakes. We settled there because of the fire in Mainz—the city of Mainz, our birthplace, the place of our fathers, that ancient community famed and praised beyond all communities of the realm. The entire Jewish section and their street [that of the Gentiles] in Mainz were burned and we were in great fear of the townspeople. At that time, Meir Cohen

---

My thanks to Judah Galinsky and Eyal Levinson for their comments on this introduction and to the readers for the press who helped me improve it. A special thanks to all the team members of the Beyond the Elite project, throughout the years. This article was written under the auspices of the Beyond the Elite: Jewish Daily Life in Medieval Europe Project, PI Elisheva Baumgarten, from the European Research Council (ERC) under the European Union's Horizon 2020 research and innovation program, grant agreement No. 681507, and prepared for publication with funding from the Israel Science Foundation Grant 2850/22, Contending with Crises: The Jews of XIVth Century Europe, PI Elisheva Baumgarten.

1. Haverkamp, *Hebräische Berichte über die Judenverfolgungen während des Ersten Kreuzzugs*, 54–56.

arrived from Worms bearing the book of Leviticus (*torat kohanim*). Persons thinking that it was gold or silver slew him. According to the order of Creation, it was the year of "Shall the priest and the prophet be slain in the sanctuary of the Lord?" Our master, R. Meshulam said to them [the Jews]: "Now you need not fear, for his death overweighs and atones for our transgressions."[2]

We then decided to leave and seek settlement in a fortified city. . . . He [the bishop][3] received us kindly and dispatched his officers and horsemen to accompany us [into town]. He then gave us quarters in the city and said that he would build a wall around us with a bolted gate so as to protect us from oppressors. It would thus be a fortress built for us. He was compassionate to us like a father to his son.[4]

This passage appears within his narrative concerning the inauguration of a new synagogue in Speyer in the wake of the attacks of the First Crusade (1096), and describes how the Jews settled in Speyer two decades earlier (1084). While the attention of most scholars has been drawn to his description of the attack on the Jewish community in 1096,[5] this quotation, which has been determined to be a later addition, focuses on the period before and after the Crusade and on the ways the foundations for everyday life were set up.

Solomon recounts that the Jews moved to Speyer, by invitation,[6] after two traumatic events. The first was a fire in Mainz that destroyed the Jewish residences and their street,[7] and the second was the murder of

---

2. About Meir Cohen and Meshulam, see Avraham Grossman, *The Early Sages of Germany: Their Lives, Leadership and Works (900–1096)* (Jerusalem: Magnes Press, 1981), 178 and 385–93.

3. This refers to Rudiger of Speyer, see below, note 6.

4. This passage has been discussed and edited by Shlomo Eidelberg, ed., *The Jews and the Crusaders: The Hebrew Chronicles of the First and Second Crusades* (Madison: University of Wisconsin Press, 1977), 71–72; Avraham M. Haberman, *Gezerot Tzarfat VeAshkenaz* (Jerusalem: Tarshish, 1946), 59–60; Eva Haverkamp, ed., *Hebräische Berichte über die Judenverfolgungen während des Ersten Kreuzzugs* (Hannover: Hahn, 2005), 490–93.

5. See for example, Ivan G. Marcus, "From Politics to Martyrdom : Shifting Paradigms in the Hebrew Narratives of the 1096 Crusade Riots," *Prooftexts* 2 (1982): 40–52; Robert Chazan, "The Facticity of Medieval Narrative: A Case Study of the Hebrew First Crusade Narratives," *AJS Review* 16 (1991): 31–56; Robert Chazan, *European Jewry and the First Crusade*, First paperback printing (Berkeley: University of California Press, 1996), 40–43.

6. This corresponds with the privilege granted by Rudiger, bishop of Speyer. See https://sourcebooks.fordham.edu/source/1084landjews.asp.

7. Siegmund Salfeld and A. Bein, "Mainz," *Germania Judaica: Von den ältesten Zeiten bis 1238*, ed. I. Elbogen, Abraham Freimann, and H. Tykocinski (Breslau: M. & H. Marcus, 1936), I: 174–225, see 176.

R. Meir Cohen who came from Worms to Mainz, where he was killed.[8] In many ways, these short lines provide a snapshot of the complexity of Jewish existence and belonging in medieval Europe, in this case, specifically medieval Germany. On the one hand, these lines describe the suspicion and violence to which Jews were subject and portrays the sense of anxiety and apprehension they experienced. The Jews were reluctant to stay in Mainz after the fire because of their fear "from the other burgers" (*hayinu bepahad gadol meha'ironim*).[9] They were also fearful because of the incident described above, in which their Christian neighbors mistook the volume that R. Meir was carrying for a treasure worth robbing.[10] On the other hand, in the same breath, the author states that the Jews pitched their tents in Speyer, never to be removed. He also acclaims the community in Mainz as the oldest, most praiseworthy, and finest community in the entire kingdom, exhibiting impressive local pride, stating, "Our birthplace, the place of our fathers, that ancient community famed and praised beyond all communities of the realm."[11]

These two, somewhat contradictory, sentiments conveyed by the author are indicative of medieval realities. Jewish existence in medieval Christian Europe was precarious, with Jews recurrently threatened by local Christians and requiring the protection of local leadership, of the Church, and of the rulers of the territories within which they dwelled. However, the towns along the Rhineland were also home, and the Jews living in them saw themselves there for the long term. This understanding was true also on the part of the Christian officials and neighbors who welcomed and cooperated with them. For example, Rudiger of Speyer, who, as described in the text above, invited the Jews

---

8. Haverkamp, *Hebräische Berichte über die Judenverfolgungen während des Ersten Kreuzzugs*, 491, lines 11–13.

9. Haverkamp, *Hebräische Berichte über die Judenverfolgungen*, 491n1.

10. This description of an interreligious misunderstanding is worthy of further exploration as demonstrated by Israel Yuval; see Israel Jacob Yuval, *Two Nations in Your Womb: Perceptions of Jews and Christians in Late Antiquity*, trans. Barbara Harshav and Jonathan Chipman (Berkeley: University of California Press, 2006). See also Miri Rubin, *Gentile Tales: The Narrative Assault on Late Medieval Jews* (Philadelphia: University of Pennsylvania Press, 2004).

11. For examples of local pride, see Lucia Raspe, "Between Judengasse and the City: Jews, Urban Space and Local Tradition in Early Modern Worms," *Journal of Jewish Studies* 67 (2016): 225–48; Elisheva Baumgarten and Judah D. Galinsky, eds., *Jews and Christians in Thirteenth-Century France* (New York: Palgrave Macmillan, 2015); Eva Haverkamp, "Martyrs in Rivalry: The 1096 Jewish Martyrs and the Thebean Legion," *Jewish History* 23, no. 4 (2009): 319–42. For an early twentieth-century discussion of this phenomenon, see Abraham Berliner, *Aus dem Leben der deutschen Juden im Mittelalter: Zugleich ein Beitrag für deutsche Culturgeschichte* (Berlin: M. Poppelauer, 1900), chapter 1. For a more recent discussion, see Nureet Dermer, "Between Expulsions": Jews and Christians in Fourteenth-Century Northern France" (PhD diss., Jerusalem, Hebrew University of Jerusalem, 2024).

to Speyer, declared that he did so because they would bring prestige to his town. His privilege states: "When I made the villa of Speyer into a town, I thought I would increase the honor I was bestowing on the place if I brought in the Jews." At the same time, he acknowledges the tension: "Lest they should be too easily disturbed by the insolence of the citizens, I surrounded them with a wall."[12]

This tension between the peril Jews experienced and their sense of belonging, or conversely, of the integration of Jews by Christians who also viewed them with suspicion and animosity, is one that modern scholars have sought to express, oftentimes emphasizing one side of the equation over the other.[13] Articulating this tension is particularly challenging in light of the nature of the historical record, which favors disruption over harmonious day-to-day existence, and tends to set down and remember those events underscored by unrest and violence. Modern historical events, most markedly the Holocaust, have also made the religious enmity that was part of medieval Jewish life loom even larger.[14] As a result, moments of crisis and attack, such as the events of 1096 that the above quotation is appended to, have featured far more regularly in historical accounts than the mundane activities they disrupted.

It is the mundane that is at the heart of this book of collected essays, *Beyond the Elite: Everyday Jewish Lives in Medieval Northern Europe*, which is the product of a research group funded by the European Research Council from 2016 to 2022.[15] This book is premised on the idea that crises, such as the one described above, which have often been the focal points for studying the history of medieval Jews, as impactful as they

---

12. See note 6.
13. See for example the discussion by Ivan G. Marcus, *Rituals of Childhood: Jewish Acculturation in Medieval Europe* (New Haven, CT: Yale University Press, 1996); Ivan G. Marcus, "A Jewish-Christian Symbiosis: The Culture of Early Ashkenaz," in *Cultures of the Jews: A New History*, ed. David Biale, 1st ed (New York: Schocken Books, 2002), 449–516; Robert Chazan, *Reassessing Jewish Life in Medieval Europe* (New York: Cambridge University Press, 2010); Kenneth R Stow, *Alienated Minority: The Jews of Medieval Latin Europe* (Cambridge, MA: Harvard University Press, 1992); Jonathan M. Elukin, *Living Together, Living Apart: Rethinking Jewish-Christian Relations in the Middle Ages* (Princeton: Princeton University Press, 2007). To a large extent, these late twentieth and early twenty-first century discussions echo nineteenth-century and early twentieth-century emphases, as well as some of the differences between Salo Baron's approach and those of Zionist historians. See the articles by Israel Yuval and David N. Myers in David N. Myers and David B. Ruderman, *The Jewish Past Revisited Reflections on Modern Jewish Historians* (New Haven, CT: Yale University Press, 1998).
14. See David Engel, *Historians of the Jews and the Holocaust* (Stanford, CA: Stanford University Press, 2022); Tzafrir Barzilay, "The Term 'Antisemitism' as a Category for the Study of the History of Jews in the Middle Ages Zion," *Zion* 85 (2020): 195–207.
15. https://beyond-the-elite.huji.ac.il.

were, were only part, and not necessarily the most important part, of the story. This volume is our final joint publication, and this introduction articulates some of the goals and methods that have served us during the course of our work together and also serves as an introduction to the specific studies that appear here.

The Jews of Medieval Ashkenaz

Most days and years of Jewish life in the High Middle Ages were not a "valley of tears," despite the tensions and animosity that were part of their lives as a minority among a Christian majority.[16] Although during the course of the Middle Ages Jews ultimately settled in towns and cities throughout Europe, our work focuses specifically on the communities of today's Germany and northern France, a region that is part of a larger area in Jewish culture that came to be referred to as "Ashkenaz," The use of the term *Ashkenaz* expresses the shared ritual practices that characterized the Jews living in these regions in contrast to those in other geographies, for example the Jews in southern France, in Provence and in Iberia, or in North Africa.[17]

Following their initial settlement in Paris and northern France, and in the Rhineland during the last centuries of the first millennium, Ashkenazic Jews soon expanded outward, moving westward across the Channel to England and eastward into Central Europe. As they did, they developed alliances and ongoing relationships with the ruling authorities and with their neighbors in each location.[18] The communities dis-

---

16. I am referring here to the biblical term based on Psalms 84:7 that was used by the early modern historian Joseph ha-Cohen, see Joseph ha-Cohen, *Sefer Emeq ha-Bakha* (*The Vale of Tears*), ed. Robert Bonfil (Jerusalem: Magnes Press, 2020).

17. See Israel M. Ta-Shma, *Early Franco-German Ritual* (Jerusalem: Magnes Press, 1992), 14–16; 22-27; Avraham Grossman, *Pious and Rebellious: Jewish Women in Medieval Europe*, trans. Jonathan Chipman (Hanover, NH: Brandeis University Press, 2004); Ephraim Kanarfogel, *The Intellectual History and Rabbinic Culture of Medieval Ashkenaz* (Detroit: Wayne State University Press, 2013). Others have argued for greater differentiation: Haym Soloveitchik, "Piety, Pietism, and German Pietism: Sefer Hasidim I and the Influence of Haside Ashkenaz," *Jewish Quarterly Review* 92 (2002): 455–93; Eric Zimmer, *Society and Its Customs* (Jerusalem: Merkaz Zalman Shazar, 1996).

18. See the survey, Robert Chazan, *The Jews of Medieval Western Christendom, 1000–1500*, Cambridge Medieval Textbooks (Cambridge: Cambridge University Press, 2006), as well as the two volumes edited by Cluse that survey a large number of communities: Christoph Cluse, ed., *The Jews of Europe in the Middle Ages (Tenth to Fifteenth Centuries): Proceedings of the International Symposium Held at Speyer, 20–25 October 2002* (Turnhout: Brepols, 2004); Christoph Cluse and Lukas Clemens, eds. *The Jews of Europe around 1400: Disruption, Crisis, and Resilience* (Wiesbaden: Harrassowitz Verlag, 2018). For England, see Robin R. Mundill, *England's Jewish*

cussed in the various chapters herein are, among others, those of the Rhineland, the city of Paris and its environs, following the route taken by many Jewish families, further East to Thuringia, Bavaria, and Franconia, with some sources coming from as far east as today's Poland. The examples in this book are just snapshots of some of the areas in Ashkenaz where medieval Jews lived. Other studies we have conducted have included England, other areas in Germany as well Moravia, Bohemia, and parts of northern Italy.[19] This book and the work of the scholars within it joins recent studies that seek to focus on the range of experiences of medieval Jews, in Ashkenaz, broadly defined, during the High Middle Ages, especially the period spanning from the end of the eleventh century (after the First Crusade) until the mid-fourteenth century, using a traditional terminus ad quem in the field, that of the onset of the Black Death.[20] Undoubtedly, many of the issues we address are pertinent for other geographies, including the Jewish communities of Iberia, Italy, and Eastern Europe, as well as those on other continents, and we hope our work will inspire future research on these geographies.

Daily Life

Our focus in this volume is on daily life and mundane activities. Daily life is by no means antithetical to times of crisis or tension. A variety of pressures, including religious animosity, were present in these ongoing

---

Solution: Experiment and Expulsion, 1262–1290 (Cambridge: Cambridge: Cambridge University Press, 1998); Robin R. Mundill, *The King's Jews: Money, Massacre, and Exodus in Medieval England* (London: Continuum, 2010); John Tolan, *England's Jews: Finance, Violence, and the Crown in the Thirteenth Century* (Philadelphia: University of Pennsylvania Press, 2023). For France, see William C. Jordan, *The French Monarchy and the Jews: From Philip Augustus to the Last Capetians* (Philadelphia: University of Pennsylvania Press, 1989); Roger Kohn, *Les Juifs de la France du nord dans la seconde moitié du XIVe siècle* (Louvain: Peeters, 1988).

19. See our joint publications: https://beyond-the-elite.huji.ac.il/publications.

20. This is a fairly standard terminus ad quem, as the Black Death was a landmark event in medieval Europe and many studies follow this pattern. See for example Alfred Haverkamp and Friedhelm Burgard, "Die Judenverfolgungen Zur Zeit Des Schwarzen Todes 1m Gesellschaftsgefüge Deutscher Städte," in *Verfassung, Kultur, Lebensform: Beiträge Zur Italienischen, Deutschen Und Jüdischen Geschichte Im Europäischen Mittelalter* (Mainz am Rhein: von Zabern [u.a.], 1997), 223–97; Beatrice Gottlieb, *The Family in the Western World from the Black Death to the Industrial Age* (New York: Oxford University Press, 1993); Anna Foa, *The Jews of Europe after the Black Death* (Berkeley: University of California Press, 2000); Elisheva Baumgarten, *Mothers and Children: Jewish Family Life in Medieval Europe* (Princeton: Princeton University Press, 2004); Katherine L. French, *The Good Women of the Parish: Gender and Religion after the Black Death* (Philadelphia: University of Pennsylvania Press, 2008); Susan L. Einbinder, *After the Black Death: Plague and Commemoration among Iberian Jews* (Philadelphia: University of Pennsylvania Press, 2018).

and repetitive interactions. Yet, in contrast to times of crises or attack, these tensions were sustained and contained,[21] resulting in ongoing tensions that rose and ebbed, alongside mundane exchanges.[22] Understanding the social institutions and mechanisms that enabled the continuation of individual and communal activities was one of the issues at the heart of our investigation. As scholars, we sought to understand Jewish life as it was led, first and foremost, in urban centers; the daily routines of these communities; and their engagement with each other and with their Christian neighbors, business associates, and local ruling elites. We were interested in understanding the ways they preserved their distinct Jewish identity by choice and/or out of necessity but also in the ways they were part of their localities, and conducted their lives similarly to their neighbors. When did interreligious tensions play an important role and when were they of less consequence?

Daily life allows for multiple, often recurring, opportunities, as medieval people, like modern ones, have set annual and diurnal routines. Understanding these mundane routines is an important stage in an even larger project of connecting the everyday lives of Jews to their experiences during specific crises, such as the Crusades, blood libels, host accusations, or expulsion. Ultimately, it is likely that the same patterns and means of contending with tensions were typical of both the unremarkable moments and crises, yet without understanding both, it is harder to make sense of the complexity that was part of medieval Jewish daily life. Some of the methods we used are presented in greater detail below. This volume also contains some comparisons between the Jews of Ashkenaz and those in other communities. Further comparisons between Ashkenaz and other areas in Europe will help underline local sensibilities and are needed for future research.

---

21. For the importance of everyday life, see Michel de Certeau, *The Practice of Everyday Life* (Berkeley: University of California Press, 1984); Ben Highmore, *Everyday Life and Cultural Theory: An Introduction* (London: Routledge, 2002); Alf Lüdtke, ed., *The History of Everyday Life: Reconstructing Historical Experiences and Ways of Life*, Princeton Studies in Culture/Power/History (Princeton: Princeton University Press, 1995); Pierre Riché, *La vie quotidienne dans l'Empire Carolingien* (Paris: Hachette, 1973).

22. Alfred Haverkamp has called this "concivilitas"; see Alfred Haverkamp, "Jews and Urban Life: Bonds and Relationships," in *The Jews of Europe in the Middle Ages (Tenth to Fifteenth Centuries)*, ed. Karin Birk, Werner Transier, and Markus Wener (Ostfildern: Hatje Cantz, 2004), 55–69; David Nirenberg, *Communities of Violence: Persecution of Minorities in the Middle Ages* (Princeton: Princeton University Press, 1996).

"Beyond the Elite"

Our work in this book and throughout the project sought a shift of focus from the learned individuals, the rabbis, who have been the central heroes of most studies of Ashkenazic Jewry to date, to the myriad others who comprised the Jewish communities of the period.[23] The rabbis, who were the leaders of their communities' religious lives, penned most of the Hebrew sources that have survived from medieval Europe. Their writings, rabbinic responses, exegetical commentaries, custom books, belles-lettres, poetry, and prayers are valuable sources for daily life and have been mined as such by other scholars primarily within the purview of the history of Jewish law (*halakhah*). Oftentimes, these writings have been read as descriptive rather than prescriptive, with the assumption that all medieval Jews followed these exact guidelines.[24] This is, at least to some extent, a fallacy, as the writing themselves abound with cases in which Jews transgressed rabbinic prescriptions, with this very action often being the trigger for the record that has reached us. This is not to say that many Jews did not observe Jewish rituals and practices, but still cautions one against using the rabbinic materials as a reflection of overall practice.[25]

---

23. For example, Ephraim Elimelech Urbach, *The Tosaphists: Their History, Writings, and Methods*, 4th ed. (Jerusalem: Bialik Institute, 1980); Haym Soloveitchik, "Pawnbroking: A Study in Ribbit and of the Halakah in Exile," *Proceedings of the American Academy for Jewish Research* 38 (1970): 203; Grossman, *The Early Sages of Germany*; Ivan G. Marcus, *Piety and Society: The Jewish Pietists of Medieval Germany* (Leiden: Brill, 1981); Yedidya Alter Dinari, *The Rabbis of Germany and Austria at the Close of the Middle Ages* (Jerusalem: Mossad Bialik, 1984); Israel Jacob Yuval, *Scholars in Their Time: The Religious Leadership of German Jewry in the Late Middle Ages* (Jerusalem: Magnes Press, 1988); Avraham Grossman, *The Early Sages of France: Their Lives, Leadership, and Works* (Jerusalem: Magnes Press, 1995); Kanarfogel, *The Intellectual History and Rabbinic Culture of Medieval Ashkenaz*; Simcha Emanuel, *Fragments of the Tablets: The Lost Library of Ba'alei ha-Tosafot* (Jerusalem: Magnes Press, 2007); Avraham (Rami) Reiner, *Rabbenu Tam: Interpretation, Halakhah, Controversy* (Ramat Gan: Bar-Ilan University Press, 2021); Judah D. Galinsky, *The Making of a Medieval Bestseller: Rabbi Isaac of Corbeil's Pillars of Exile and Its Readers* (Oxford: Oxford University Press, forthcoming). This was also the emphasis in the entries in *Germania Judaica*, see for example note 7; and Henri Gross, *Gallia Judaica: Dictionnaire geographique de la France d'apres les sources rabbiniques*, ed. Simon Schwartzfuchs (Amsterdam: Philo Press, 1969).

24. See for example in the works of Israel Ta-Shma, Ta-Shma, *Early Franco-German Ritual*; Israel M. Ta-Shma, *Ritual, Custom and Reality in Franco-Germany, 1000–1350* (Jerusalem: Magnes, 2000²); Grossman, *Pious and Rebellious*; David Joshua Malkiel, *Reconstructing Ashkenaz: The Human Face of Franco-German Jewry, 1000–1250* (Stanford, CA: Stanford University Press, 2009); Jeffrey R. Woolf, *The Fabric of Religious Life in Medieval Ashkenaz (1000–1300): Creating Sacred Communities* (Leiden: Brill, 2015).

25. For some thoughts on this matter see: Adiel Schremer, "History, Halakha, and Religious Identity in the Halakhic Discourse of Rabbinic Sages in Medieval Ashkenaz," *Zion* 81 (2016): 31–65.

Importantly, prior to the fourteenth century there were few professional rabbis, and thus most of the well-known rabbinic leaders were also business people, moneylenders, craftsman, and service providers, and some held agricultural interests. As a result, their communal standing was not just the result of their erudition but also due to the roles they played within the financial and intellectual complexities of daily life.[26] The vast majority of Jews in Ashkenaz were not, however, part of the learned and/or wealthy elite. This is clear from data gleaned from the surviving tombstones from a variety of medieval communities, which indicate that rabbis constituted less than 5 percent of those buried in the cemetery.[27] Even if this number is doubled or tripled to include their family members and nonlearned yet wealthy families, it is clear that the Jewish elite was only a small minority. Unfortunately, as opposed to the rabbis who left behind written materials bearing their names in Hebrew, most members of the community remain anonymous, and even those for whom we have epitaphs or whose names appear in various lists, lack the detail often available with regards to the learned men.[28] This is why this goal was phrased as "beyond the elite" rather than as "the non-elite," as learning about people who left behind few written records and are often unnamed is a daunting task.[29]

---

26. See for example Yuval, *Scholars in Their Time*.

27. Avraham (Rami) Reiner, "'A Tombstone Inscribed': Titles Used to Describe the Deceased in Tombstones from Würzburg between 1147-1148 and 1346," *Tarbiz* 78 (2009): 123-52; Karlheinz Müller et al., eds., *Die Grabsteine vom jüdischen Friedhof in Würzburg aus der Zeit vor dem Schwarzen Tod (1147–1346)* (Würzburg: Gesellschaft für Fränkische Geschichte, 2011).

28. Müller et al., eds., *Die Grabsteine vom jüdischen Friedhof in Würzburg aus der Zeit vor dem Schwarzen Tod (1147–1346)* (Würzburg: Gesellschaft für Fränkische Geschichte, 2011); Elisheva Baumgarten, "Reflections of Everyday Jewish Life: Evidence from Medieval Cemeteries," in *Les vivants et les morts dans les sociétés médiévales: XLVIIIe Congrès de la SHMESP (Jérusalem, 4–7 mai 2017)*, ed. Congrés de la SHMESP, Histoire ancienne et médiévale 158 (Paris: Éditions de la Sorbonne, 2018), 95–104.

29. See the early work by Eric Robert Wolf, *Europe and the People without History* (Berkeley: University of California Press, 1982); Aron Gurevich, *Categories of Medieval Culture* (London: Routledge and Kegan Paul, 1985); Peter Burke, *History and Social Theory* (Ithaca: Cornell University Press, 2005²); Pierre Boglioni, Robert Delort, and Claude Gauvard, eds., *Le petit peuple dans l'Occident médiéval. Terminologies, perceptions, réalités* (Paris: Publications de la Sorbonne, 2002); Robert Bonfil, *Jewish Life in Renaissance Italy* (Berkeley: University of California Press, 1994). This is one of the central challenges of social history and a problem our group has given some thought too as is reflected in the different essays in the book. Recent databases are also trying to provide a variety of answers to this problem. See for example https://medievallondoners.ace.fordham.edu/. The database of women's letters, Epistolae, tries to showcase known and less-known women in a different way. In the medieval Jewish context the website of tombstones, epidat, allows some such work, and see for example Elisheva Baumgarten,

To what extent were these unnamed people like their leaders and to what extent were they different? Addressing this question with awareness of the research done over the past decades, which has often blurred the borders between leaders—intellectual, political, financial, or other—and the communities within which they lived, we have not assumed that the communal elites, particularly the erudite scholars, were always so different from their fellow Jews, but we also have sought to remember that they were not necessarily the same. Although, in the religiously defined reality of medieval Europe, Jews were first and foremost Jews, they were also members of their localities, professionals, and individuals. Some were rich and some were poor, and they all had their own networks of family and contacts within their societies. Our approach was that despite known categories, we had to acknowledge and seek out unexpected affiliations alongside those that were self-evident.

In this respect the question of the similarities that existed or did not exist between the elite and the rest of the Jewish community, posed a variety of challenges. Much research to date has outlined Jewish identity and changing self-perceptions within the medieval Jewish community, assuming that the community as a whole shared the stance of the elite rabbis who led them.[30] This leads to a positivistic interpretation of their writings. In our work we asked to what extent the ideas and beliefs of the scholars were held by all and ultimately questioned the degree to which many of these ideas were prominent in everyday activities. In fact, specific studies undertaken by team members are excellent examples of the multiplicity of identities that characterized the lives of the community, including the intellectual elite. Thus, for example, archival documents were found that contradict the activities that scholars

---

"Who Was a Ḥasid or Ḥasidah in Medieval Ashkenaz? Reassessing the Social Implications of a Term," *Jewish History* 34, no. 1–3 (2021): 125–54.

30. Kanarfogel, *The Intellectual History and Rabbinic Culture of Medieval Ashkenaz*; Malkiel, *Reconstructing Ashkenaz*; Ephraim Shoham-Steiner, *On the Margins of a Minority: Leprosy, Madness, and Disability among the Jews of Medieval Europe* (Detroit: Wayne State University Press, 2014); Ephraim Shoham-Steiner, *Jews and Crime in Medieval Europe* (Detroit: Wayne State University Press, 2021). For a different approach, see Elisheva Baumgarten, *Practicing Piety in Medieval Ashkenaz: Men, Women, and Everyday Religious Observance*, Jewish Culture and Contexts (Philadelphia: University of Pennsylvania Press, 2014); Elisheva Baumgarten, *Biblical Women and Jewish Daily Life in the Middle Ages*, 1st ed., Jewish Culture and Contexts (Philadelphia: University of Pennsylvania Press, 2021); Eyal Levinson, *Gender and Sexuality in Ashkenaz in the Middle Ages* (Jerusalem: Merkaz Zalman Shazar, 2022).

themselves promoted or forbade, in which the scholar himself appears to be acting against his own instructions.[31]

One of the ways to address and challenge the extent to which there was or was not a distinction between the learned members of the Jewish communities about whom we know more and those who left less written documentation was to see if they were treated in similar ways by the Christian elites and/or neighbors among whom they lived as well as to compare them in general to their Christian neighbors and the ways they led their daily lives. Such a comparison underlines differences and similarities between Jews and Christians and helps define distinctions that may have existed among Jews as well.

Sources

To address both of these foci: daily life and those who were "beyond the elite," we relied on existing sources and sought to expand our source base and the methodologies we employed. For example, the quote with which this introduction opened is from a Hebrew chronicle, few of which have survived. Most Hebrew sources are halakhic (legal), liturgical, and exegetical, while chronicles are significantly more widespread, first in Latin and later in vernacular languages as political authorities sought to provide narratives of the realms they controlled. This is but one example of the disparity of the sources that have reached us. What is true, however, of all medieval sources, whether Hebrew, Latin, or vernacular; whether textual, material, or visual, is that they were written, on the whole, by the learned, political, and financial elites.[32] As a result, Jews (and Christians) who were not part of the elite remain in the shadows of history; their perspectives, thoughts, actions, and beliefs lost to time. This poses an acute challenge to historians attempting to understand their lives, and one that speaks to the heart of our efforts.[33]

---

31. Aviya Doron, "Into the Market and Back Again: Jews, Trust and the Medieval Marketplace," *Jewish Studies Quarterly* 28, no. 4 (2021): 349, https://doi.org/10.1628/jsq-2021-0020.

32. See the discussion of this matter by Arnold Esch, "Überlieferungs-Chance und Überlieferungs-Zufall als Methodisches Problem des Historikers," *Historische Zeitschrift* 240 (1985): 529–70. My thanks to Andreas Lehnertz for this reference.

33. This is a topic that has been tackled by many historians of everyday life: Robert Fossier, *The Axe and the Oath: Ordinary Life in the Middle Ages* (Princeton: Princeton University Press, 2010); Hans-Werner Goetz and Steven W. Rowan, *Life in the Middle Ages: From the Seventh to the Thirteenth Century* (Notre Dame: University of Notre Dame Press, 1993). This was also a central concern of the Annales School; see Peter Burke, *The French Historical Revolution: The Annales School, 1929–2014* (Cambridge: Cambridge Polity, 2015); André Burguière, *The Annales*

To contend with this challenge, members of our research team used a variety of surviving texts in Latin, Hebrew, and local vernaculars.[34] These included legal and economic sources, such as court records, charters, notarial books, tax lists, rabbinic responsa, and custom books, as well as chronicles, poems, necrologies, epitaphs, stories and fables, moral literature, and exempla. In addition, art and architecture, as well as material objects including wax seals and items found in medieval "treasures" or illustrated in manuscripts all served as sources for daily life and practice. It is a key premise of our work that the use of this multiplicity of sources, genres, and languages was the most effective way to glean evidence about daily life and those beyond the elite.

Defining multigenre and multilinguistic research as one of our goals was an important step for three reasons. Studies of medieval society, Jewish and non-Jewish alike, tend to stick to one category or another of sources. Within Jewish studies, for example, some scholars specialize in Hebrew sources, written by the Jews themselves, meaning, primarily, the writings of the elite that are often closely related to halakhic and liturgical matters.[35] Others study Latin and vernacular sources in which Jews appear, whether as part of the affairs of the city as a whole or in documents specifically dealing with the Jewish community.[36]

School: An Intellectual History (Ithaca, NY: Cornell University Press, 2009); Peter Schöttler, *Die "Annales" Historiker und die Deutsche Geschichtswissenschaft* (Tübingen: Mohr Siebeck, 2015).

34. See examples of our group publications: Elisheva Baumgarten and Ido Noy, eds., *In and Out, Between and Beyond: Jewish Daily Life in Medieval Europe* (Jerusalem: The Hebrew University of Jerusalem, 2021); Elisheva Baumgarten, ed. *Jewish Space and Place in Medieval Ashkenaz: A Special Issue of Jewish Studies Quarterly* 28, nos. 3-4 (2021).

35. Jacob Katz and his students championed the use of response literature. See for example Jacob Katz, *Exclusiveness and Tolerance: Studies in Jewish-Gentile Relations in Medieval and Modern Times* (New York: Behrman House, 1961); Jacob Katz, *Tradition and Crisis: Jewish Society at the End of the Middle Ages* (New York: Schocken Books, 1993); and the work of his students, for example, Haym Soloveitchik, *The Use of Responsa as Historical Source* (Jerusalem: Merkaz Zalman Shazar, 1990). Others have focused on other genres; see for example Marcus, *Piety and Society*; Eli Yassif, *The Book of Memory That Is The Chronicle of Jerahme'el* (Tel Aviv: Tel Aviv University Press, 2001); Eli Yassif, *Ninety-Nine Tales: The Jerusalem Manuscript Cycle of Legends in Medieval Jewish Folklore* (Tel Aviv: Tel Aviv University, 2013); Rella Kushelevsky, *Tales in Context: Sefer ha-Ma'asim in Medieval Northern France*, 1st ed., Raphael Patai Series in Jewish Folklore and Anthropology (Detroit: Wayne State University Press, 2017); Jeremy Cohen, *Sanctifying the Name of God: Jewish Martyrs and Jewish Memories of the First Crusade*, Jewish Culture and Contexts (Philadelphia: University of Pennsylvania Press, 2004); Rainer Josef Barzen, ed., *Taqqanot Qehillot Šum: die Rechtssatzungen der jüdischen Gemeinden Mainz, Worms und Speyer im hohen und späten Mittelalter* (Wiesbaden: Harrassowitz Verlag, 2019).

36. See for example the series of studies produced by the Arye Maimon Institute at Trier University under the direction of Alfred Haverkamp, and the database they created: https://www.medieval-ashkenaz.org/ or the earlier exemplar: Julius Aronius, *Regesten zur Geschichte der Juden im fränkischen und deutschen Reiche bis zum Jahre 1273* (Berlin: Berlin : L. Simon, 1902).

Combining these various genres and languages enables the creation of a broader and much more expansive picture.

Were we working alone, this approach would be constrained by the limitations of each scholar's experience and training. However, by working together as a research group we were able to provide each other with whatever knowledge and training others were lacking. The many coauthored chapters in the volume are proof of the fruitfulness of this collaboration. Finally, multilinguistic and multigenre discussions are a more accurate reflection of everyday life. No person, past or present, functions within only one context or genre. The Jews of medieval Europe spoke local vernaculars and read Hebrew; they went to the market and to the synagogue. Their surviving writings in Hebrew thus reflect only one part of their daily interactions. For this reason, seeking everyday life across genres and languages proved especially rewarding.[37]

By regularly referencing sources in multiple languages, and moving between texts and visual and material sources, as well as between genres, additional criteria were introduced to the quest to understand what specific sources present and represent. If a common thread appeared in all the sources, or conversely, the sources presented different interpretative possibilities, these all contributed to understanding daily routines and tensions. The simultaneous use of different genres brought to the fore repetitive phenomena and, at the same time, enabled the identification of exceptions to the rule. Such distinctions are especially challenging as people in the past, like people today, tend to describe and analyze extraordinary events rather than the ordinary. In situating daily routines as the heart of our inquiry, the ability to understand what was common and what was unusual was all the more important.

Austrian-based scholars have gathered all the vernacular and Latin material concerning the Jews in Austria in multiple volumes: Eveline Brugger, Birgit Wiedl, and Manfred Anselgruber, *Regesten Zur Geschichte Der Juden in Österreich Im Mittelalter* (Innsbruck: StudienVerlag, 2005). For England, collections exist from the early nineteenth century through recent years, see Judith Olszowy-Schlanger, *Hebrew and Hebrew-Latin Charters and Tallies from Medieval England* (Turnhout: Brepols, 2015); Bernhard Blumenkranz, *Les auteurs chretiens latins du moyen age sur les Juifs et le Judaisme* (Paris: Mouton, 1963); Gérard Nahon, *"Inscriptions hébraïques et Juives de France médiévale"* (Paris: Belles Lettres, 1986).

37. See for example the sourcebook we produced: Elisheva Baumgarten, Tzafrir Barzilay, and Eyal Levinson, eds., *Jewish Everyday Life in Medieval Northern Europe, 1080–1350: A Sourcebook*, Teams: Documents of Practice (Kalamazoo: Medieval Institute Publications, Western Michigan University, 2022).

14   INTRODUCTION

Methods: Prisms and Practice-Based Research

Our research group read the wealth of sources described above using a wide variety of methodologies, some traditionally associated with specific genres and other that are more general. To genre-specific methods, from narrative theory to codicology and paleography, and economic theories, one can add methods that by now have become part of the work of all social historians such as quantitative methods, the study of objects and things (material culture), the use of anthropological ritual and spatial theories, and a quest to read "against the grain" that has become an important component for understanding culture.

Incorporating this plethora of methods, the members of the Beyond the Elite research team sought to examine aspects of the everyday lives of medieval Jews and their communities in various locations by engaging with sources related to Jewish life as well as those related to the specific place where they lived. We determined that our work would be constructed around the intersection of four prisms we believe are key aspects of daily life: rituals, spaces, objects, and people. This separation was heuristic rather than substantive, as none of these prisms exist in a vacuum and elements of each overlap. Below I offer a short explanation of each.

People

Although one of our prime goals was expanding our knowledge of the different people who were part of the medieval Jewish communities, this proved, to some extent, ironically, to be the most elusive prism. In many cases, all we had to work with were names that appeared on tax lists, court records, property records, seals on documents, lists of charitable donations, or lists of the dead, without further details.[38]

---

38. A first attempt to identify different sorts of people can be attributed to the pioneering work of Eileen Power, *Medieval People* (London: Methuen, 1924). Most of the people who have been described at length are people who left written evidence. For a different kind of pioneering example, see Carlo Ginzburg, *The Cheese and the Worms: The Cosmos of a Sixteenth-Century Miller* (Baltimore: Johns Hopkins University Press, 2013). See also two illustrative examples based on wills and charity lists: Steven Epstein, *Wills and Wealth in Medieval Genoa, 1150–1250*, Harvard Historical Studies, vol. 103 (Cambridge, MA: Harvard University Press, 1984); Charlotte A. Stanford, *Commemorating the Dead in Late Medieval Strasbourg the Cathedral's Book of Donors and Its Use (1320–1521)*, Church, Faith, and Culture in the Medieval West (Farnham, Surrey, UK: Ashgate, 2011) as well as the website https://scholar.harvard.edu/smail/

Tombstones, which tend to reveal little about the dead, besides, at best, a trite description of their outstanding pious traits, were also examined.[39] In some cases, by looking at all these different sources together, we were able to find individuals and present their stories.[40] Furthermore, as the chapters in this volume demonstrate, even without knowing the names of specific people, it is possible to trace their everyday practice, whether treating a sick family member, attending prayer services, traveling on the local rivers, or greeting rulers when they came to town. Given the minimal nature of the information, quantitative and digital methods proved especially useful in this sphere, as demonstrated in this book.

Understanding medieval Jews as individuals is important because being a Jew in medieval Europe could mean many different things depending on gender, economic status, profession, family background, and more; and there was clearly much variation within and between communities. In addition, we sought to explore the different kinds of daily contact between Jews and Christians. Did the frequency and intensity depend on personal traits or on profession? When did Jews and Christians see each other and when were they within their own religious communities and how did this vary based on space, objects, and rituals?

---

dalme. For work using charity lists and lists of dead among medieval Jews, see for example Müller et al., *Die Grabsteine vom jüdischen Friedhof in Würzburg aus der Zeit vor dem Schwarzen Tod (1147–1346)*; Baumgarten, *Practicing Piety in Medieval Ashkenaz*; Debra Kaplan, *The Patrons and Their Poor: Jewish Community and Public Charity in Early Modern Germany* (Philadelphia: University of Pennsylvania Press, 2020).

39. Another topic that seems worthy of reexamination is names, as Jews, especially men, often had two names, a Hebrew name and a name they used for everyday business. See Leopold Zunz, *Namen Der Juden* (Hildesheim: Gerstenberg, 1971); Lilach Assaf, "Lovely Women and Sweet Men: Gendering the Name and Naming Practices in German-Jewish Communities (Thirteenth and Fourteenth Centuries)," in *Intricate Interfaith Networks in the Middle Ages: Quotidian Jewish-Christian Contacts* (Turnhout: Brepols, 2016), 231–50.

40. See for example the article published by team member Nureet Dermer, "Between Foreigners, Strangers and Jews: The Changing Perception of Parisian Jews on the Eve of the 1306 Expulsion," *Medieval Encounters* 27, nos. 4–5 (2021): 308–34, https://doi.org/10.1163/15700674-12340110.

Space

The spatial turn in recent historiography[41] has unique implications for medieval Jewish history and historiography.[42] Dilemmas regarding how to understand the spaces of Jewish existence in medieval Europe, alongside assumptions, or, perhaps more accurately, presumptions, have long been part of historiographical debates. Were Jews closed off from their neighbors, physically and/or figuratively? To what extent did Jews move about freely in the urban spaces that were, first and foremost, Christian spaces? Recent research suggests that the Jews were far more intertwined in the urban fabric of the locations in which they lived than has been supposed by earlier generations of scholars.[43] Christians were present in Jewish homes, whether as servants, business accomplices, or neighbors, and Jews were present in Christian homes, mainly as part

---

41. Martha C. Howell and Walter Prevenier, *From Reliable Sources: An Introduction to Historical Methods* (Ithaca, NY: Cornell University Press, 2001); Peter Arnade, Martha C. Howell, and Walter Simons, "Fertile Spaces: The Productivity of Urban Space in Northern Europe," *Journal of Interdisciplinary History* 32, no. 4 (2002): 515-48, https://doi.org/10.1162/002219502317345493; Marc Boone and Martha C. Howell, *The Power of Space in Late Medieval and Early Modern Europe: The Cities of Italy, Northern France, and the Low Countries* (Turnhout : Brepols, 2013); Barbara Hanawalt and Michal Kobialka, eds., *Medieval Practices of Space*, Medieval Cultures, vol. 23 (Minneapolis: University of Minnesota Press, 2000); Caroline Goodson, Anne Elisabeth Lester, and Carol Symes, eds., *Cities, Texts, and Social Networks, 400–1500: Experiences and Perceptions of Medieval Urban Space* (Farnham, Surrey, UK: Ashgate, 2010); Meredith Cohen, "Metropolitan Architecture, Demographics and the Urban Identity of Paris in the Thirteenth Century," in *Cities, Texts, and Social Networks, 400–1500: Experiences and Perceptions of Medieval Urban Space*, eds. Caroline Goodson, Anne Elisabeth Lester, and Carol Symes (Farnham, Surrey, UK: Ashgate, 2010), 65–101; Albrecht Classen, *Urban Space in the Middle Ages and the Early Modern Age* (Berlin: De Gruyter, 2009), https://www.degruyter.com/view/product/42987.

42. See for example the work of Charlotte Fonrobert and Vered Shemtov, eds., *Jewish Conceptions and Practice of Space*, vol. 11.3 (Special Edition of *Jewish Social Studies* 11, no. 3 (2005); Debra Kaplan, *The Patrons and Their Poor: Jewish Community and Public Charity in Early Modern Germany* (Philadelphia: University of Pennsylvania Press, 2020).

43. This point has been reassessed in different ways since the nineteenth century. See Moritz Güdemann, *Geschichte des Erziehungswesens und der Cultur der Juden in Deutschland während des XIV und XV Jahrhunderts* (Vienna: Hölder, 1888); Alfred Haverkamp, "The Jewish Quarters in German Towns during the Late Middle Ages," in *In and out of the Ghetto: Jewish-Gentile Relations in Late Medieval and Early Modern Germany*, eds. Hartmut Lehmann and R. Po-Chia Hsia (Cambridge: Cambridge University Press, 1995), 13–28; Alfred Haverkamp, "Jews and Urban Life: Bonds and Relationships," in *The Jews of Europe in the Middle Ages (Tenth to Fifteenth Centuries)*, ed. Christoph Cluse (Ostfildern: Hatje Cantz, 2004), 55–69; David Nirenberg, *Communities of Violence: Persecution of Minorities in the Middle Ages* (Princeton: Princeton University Press, 1996); Raspe, "Between Judengasse and the City"; Baumgarten, ed., *Jewish Space and Place in Medieval Ashkenaz*.

of business or neighborly interactions.⁴⁴ No less important, Jews and Christians were in daily contact outside the home, on the streets, in markets, and also in each other's holy spaces, such as churches and synagogues.⁴⁵ Our studies as a whole demonstrate the extent to which Jews were simultaneously both insular and integrated. Under such circumstances our challenge has been to understand the functioning of this dynamic of being at once entangled and distinct, and how this was expressed in the daily lives of the communities.

Objects

Everyone possessed objects, from learned rabbis and their families to paupers who had no right of residence. Objects are thus instruments to "getting beyond the elite." Although not many of these physical objects have survived, we know about them from descriptions and depictions in a variety of medieval texts.⁴⁶ Furthermore, while there were objects that were specifically identified with Christianity or Judaism, many more were mundane and used by all. As such, objects not only provide an additional path to examining Jewish entanglement within the medieval world but also offer a sense of the daily activities themselves.⁴⁷ In

---

44. This point has been made again and again. See for example Jacob Katz, *The "Shabbes Goy": A Study in Halakhic Flexibility* (Philadelphia: Jewish Publication Society, 1989); Elliott S. Horowitz, Israel Bartal, and Isaiah Gafni, "Between Masters and Maidservants in the Jewish Society of Europe in Late Medieval and Early Modern Times," in *Sexuality and the Family in History: Collected Essays* (Jerusalem: Zalman Shazar Center, 1998), 193–211; Bonfil, *Jewish Life in Renaissance Italy*; Baumgarten, *Mothers and Children: Jewish Family Life in Medieval Europe*; Joseph Shatzmiller, *Cultural Exchange : Jews, Christians, and Art in the Medieval Marketplace*, Jews, Christians, and Muslims from the Ancient to the Modern World (Princeton: Princeton University Press, 2013); Aviya Doron, "Into the Market and Back Again: Jews, Trust, and the Medieval Marketplace," *Jewish Studies Quarterly* 28 (2021): 349.

45. Shatzmiller, *Cultural Exchange* ; Doron, "Into the Market and Back Again."

46. On objects, see the now-classic discussions by Arjun Appadurai, ed., *The Social Life of Things: Commodities in Cultural Perspective* (Cambridge: Cambridge University Press, 1986); Bruno Latour, *Reassembling the Social an Introduction to Actor-Network-Theory* (Oxford: Oxford University Press, 2005). On objects in religious contexts, see Caroline Walker Bynum, *Christian Materiality: An Essay on Religion in Late Medieval Europe*, 1st paperback ed. (New York: Zone Books, 2011); Sara Lipton, "Images and Objects as Sources for Medieval History," in *Primary Sources: Using Historical Sources to Discover Medieval Europe*, ed. Joel T Rosenthal (London: Routledge, 2012), 225–42.

47. See for example Ruth Mellinkoff, *Outcasts : Signs of Otherness in Northern European Art of the Late Middle Ages* (Berkeley: University of California Press, 1993); Flora Cassen, *Marking the Jews in Renaissance Italy: Politics, Religion, and the Power of Symbols* (Cambridge: Cambridge University Press, 2017); Sara Lipton, *Dark Mirror: The Medieval Origins of Anti-Jewish Iconography*, 1st ed. (New York: Metropolitan Books/Henry Holt, 2014); Baumgarten, *Practicing Piety in Medieval Ashkenaz*.

addition, many studies of religious difference, and more important, of the legal framework of Jewish existence in medieval Europe, have focused on laws that include detailed descriptions of a variety of objects.[48] By making objects an important focus of inquiry, we were able to get closer to the medieval Jews and their practices. This applies to objects both small and large, such as buildings and architectural design, which can tell us about the ways Jews blended in to their surroundings and crafted a separate identity. Thus bringing together space and objects, our studies have sought to take the landscape and its design into consideration as part of the contours of everyday life.

Rituals

Whether carried out on a daily, monthly, or annual basis, rituals were part and parcel of the daily lives of all medieval Jews, much like they were important components in the lives of the Christians among whom they lived.[49] A ritual might be performed by a group or by a single individual,[50] and rituals encompass all aspects of life, through a variety of distinct arenas: economic, political, civic, communal, and urban.

---

48. For example, the Fourth Lateran Council included references to Jewish clothing, but also many loan agreements refer to pawns and objects. Attention to what these objects were has only recently come into the focus of scholars. See Daniel Lord Smail, *Legal Plunder: Households and Debt Collection in Late Medieval Europe* (Cambridge, MA: Harvard University Press, 2016); Daniel Lord Smail, "Interactions between Jews and Christians in Later Medieval Provence," *Medieval Encounters* 27 (2021): 410–33; Aviya Doron, "Pawned Horses: Risk and Liability in Fourteenth Century German Small-Credit Market," *Medieval Encounters* 27 (2021): 387–409; Nureet Dermer, "Between Foreigners, Strangers and Jews: The Changing Perception of Parisian Jews on the Eve of the 1306 Expulsion," *Medieval Encounters* 27 (2021): 308–34; Andreas Lehnertz, "Dismantling a Monopoly: Jews, Christians, and the Production of Shofarot in Fifteenth-Century Germany," *Medieval Encounters* 27 (2021): 360–86.

49. Recent projects have studied rituals within Jewish culture, some using ritual theory and others focusing on the many rituals that appear in legal literature and their history. See for example Marcus, *Rituals of Childhood*; Baumgarten, "Annual Cycle and Life Cycle"; David I. Shyovitz, "'You Have Saved Me from the Judgment of Gehenna': The Origins of the Mourner's Kaddish in Medieval Ashkenaz," *AJS Review* 39 (2015): 49–73; Simha Goldin, *The Ways of Jewish Martyrdom* (Turnhout: Brepols, 2008).

50. For an excellent survey of ritual theory, see Catherine Bell, *Ritual Theory, Ritual Practice* (New York: Oxford University Press, 1992). More recently, see Gerhard Jaritz, ed., *Ritual, Images, and Daily Life: The Medieval Perspective* (Vienna: Lit Verlag GmbH, 2012); Edward Bailey, *Rituals: Past, Present, and Future Perspectives*, Focus on Civilizations and Cultures (New York: Nova Publishers, 2017). Some scholars have protested the extensive use historians have made of ritual theory; see Philippe Buc, *The Dangers of Ritual : Between Early Medieval Texts and Social Scientific Theory* (Princeton: Princeton University Press, 2001); Adam B. Seligman and Robert P. Weller, *Rethinking Pluralism Ritual, Experience, and Ambiguity* (New York: Oxford University Press, 2012).

Despite the already existing focus on the study of rituals among medieval Jews, and especially of life-cycle rituals, there were multiple daily rituals that were part of Jewish practice and of their interactions with their Christian neighbors that have gone unnoticed and unexplored. We aimed to trace and define these rituals. Every member of the Jewish community took part in some rituals, but there were others that were unique to specific classes, genders, and professions. Understanding these basic activities, from the way a loan was made and processed to the ways the sick were cared for, allows for further insight into the beliefs and norms of medieval Jews and the range of actions associated with them. In this context, anthropological theory that looks at the participants in rituals, at continuous elements alongside innovations, and at tensions that are reflected in the ritual were all central to this prism.

Practice-Based Research

These four prisms and the intersections between them enabled us to examine as many practices as possible, with the daily actions and activities of medieval Jews and their embeddedness and distinction from their Christian neighbors at the heart of our analysis of everyday life. The result is a series of studies, of which this book is but one, that highlights practice and action rather than ideas.[51] This is an important departure from most research on medieval Jews, which tends to emphasize beliefs and ideology over practice. While we are in no way suggesting that beliefs and ideas are inconsequential (practice would be incomprehensible without them), our focus on practice afforded more agency and presence to those who left no written record.[52]

Our interest in practice underlines our methodological point of departure, which is that of social history, broadly defined.[53] Gender studies methods were also at the foundation of our work, as we sought to create a more inclusive, and by definition, less elite-male portrait of

---

51. See note 19.
52. For a discussion of practice and the importance of focusing on practice, see Roberto Gronda et al., "Histoires Pragmatiques: A Conversation with Simona Cerutti and Yves Cohen," *European Journal of Pragmatism and American Philosophy* 8, no. 2 (2016), https://doi.org/10.4000/ejpap.654. My thanks to Aviad Markovitch for this reference. See also Baumgarten, *Practicing Piety in Medieval Ashkenaz*, 1–21.
53. See Burke, *History and Social Theory*.

Jewish life in the past.[54] Scholarship on cultural history, in some ways an extension of some of the social-historical approaches we undertook, was also of great import, although, as a rule, we saw ourselves more as social than as cultural historians.[55] These methods are evident in the different chapters in this collection and would require more space than is available in a short introductory chapter.

Nevertheless, I want to briefly underline methods that provided us with guidelines for our joint work. One is that of everyday culture (*Alltagsgeschichte*). The insight that daily and repetitive rituals define religious, ethnic, and social identity, no less than unique and extraordinary milestones, has informed the thinking of European historians in particular, and, in a more limited fashion, of scholars of medieval Jewish life.[56] The work of theorists and scholars such as De Certeau, Goetz, Ludtke, Roux, and others provided a confirmation of the productivity of looking at daily life, as well as examples for comparison and emulation.[57] No less important was the work pertaining to medieval Jews in other geographies, first and foremost S. D. Goitein's monumental study on the Jews of medieval North Africa, and the academic tradition he inspired.[58] At the same time, our emphasis on the centrality of religious difference and similarity made our work different from that

---

54. For a recent exploration of gender methods and Jewish history, see the plethora of examples explored in Federica Francesconi and Rebecca Lynn Winer, eds., *Jewish Women's History from Antiquity to the Present* (Detroit: Wayne State University Press, 2021). Gender studies has been a relative latecomer to Jewish Studies despite pioneering studies such as those by Judith Baskin, Paula Hyman, and others.

55. For difference between social and cultural history, see Peter Burke, *What Is Cultural History?* 2nd ed., What Is History? (Malden, MA: Polity, 2008). See also the special issue of the *Journal of Social History* 37 (2003) and especially the article by Paula Fass, "Cultural History/Social History: Some Reflections on a Continuing Dialogue," 39-46.

56. For some examples in some cases, from more than one hundred years ago, see Israel Abrahams, *Jewish Life in the Middle Ages* (Philadelphia: Jewish Publication Society, 1917); Adolf Berliner, *Aus dem Leben der deutschen Juden im Mittelalter: Zugleich ein Beitrag für deutsche Culturgeschichte* (Berlin: M. Poopelauer, 1900); Moritz Güdemann, *Geschichte des Erziehungswesens und der Cultur der Juden in Deutschland während des XIV und XV Jahrhunderts*, 3 vols (Vienna: Hölder, 1888); Herman Pollack, *Jewish Folkways in Germanic Lands (1648-1806): Studies in Aspects of Daily Life* (Cambridge: MIT Press, 1971), as well as Shlomo Dov Goitein, *Daily Life*, vol. 4 of *A Mediterranean Society: The Jewish Communities of the Arab World as Portrayed in the Documents of the Cairo Geniza* (Berkeley: University of California Press, 1999).

57. De Certeau, *The Practice of Everyday Life*; Goetz and Rowen, *Life in the Middle Ages: From the Seventh to the Thirteenth Century*; Alf Lüdtke, ed., *The History of Everyday Life: Reconstructing Historical Experiences and Ways of Life* (Princeton: Princeton University Press, 1995); Pierre Riché, *La vie quotidienne dans l'Empire carolingien* (Paris: Hachette, 1973); Simone Roux, *Paris in the Middle Ages* (Philadelphia: University of Pennsylvania Press, 2008).

58. Goitein, *A Mediterranean Society*.

of the theorists mentioned above or the approach undertaken by scholars of the Geniza.[59] Each member of our research team used different methods that were appropriate to their specific case study.

Belonging in Medieval Europe

The distinction between Jews and Christians allows for a comparative perspective but also poses a fundamental challenge. One of our points of departure, as demonstrated in the opening quotation of this introduction, is the assumption that the medieval Ashkenazic Jews shared a sense of belonging to the places where they lived. This basic sentiment did not preclude expulsion, peril, or threats they may have felt as part of their daily lives but it expresses our understanding that they also felt part of their surroundings and were proud members/citizens of the locations in which they resided.[60] Jewish presence in the towns and countryside grew exponentially throughout the High Middle Ages, with numbers falling only in the mid-fourteenth century, when many communities were expelled and some were completely annihilated as the plague approached or as part of other attacks on the Jewish communities.[61] There were additional significant changes with regards to anti-Jewish rhetoric, violence, and accusations, which intensified throughout the thirteenth century.[62] Yet, at the same time, even during this period, everyday practices were in place to ensure continued Jewish life and trade in these localities.

---

59. Geniza studies have paid less attention to religious practice as part of daily practice, whereas scholars of medieval Ashkenaz have focused far more on religious practice than on daily activities.

60. This understanding is in some ways in contrast to scholars who have described Jews as "strangers"; see for example Stow, *Alienated Minority: The Jews of Medieval Latin Europe*, but does not preclude the idea that at times they felt and were treated as foreign. This complexity merits further investigation; see Nureet Dermer's dissertation.

61. For the lack of sources on Jews outside urban centers, see Rainer Josef Barzen, "Ländliche Jüdische Siedlungen Und Niederlassungen in Aschkenas. Vom Hochmittelalter Bis Ins 16. Jahrhundert. Typologie, Struktur Und Vernetzung," *Aschkenas* 21, nos. 1–2 (2013), https://doi.org/10.1515/asch-2013-0002; Debra Kaplan, *Beyond Expulsion: Jews, Christians, and Reformation Strasbourg* (Stanford, CA: Stanford University Press, 2011), 49–68.

62. See the now-classic Solomon Grayzel, *The Church and the Jews in the XIIIth Century: A Study of Their Relations during the Years 1198–1254, Based on the Papal Letters and the Conciliar Decrees of the Period*, Dropsie College (Philadelphia, Hermon Press, 1933); Rowan Dorin, *No Return: Jews, Christian Usurers, and the Spread of Mass Expulsion in Medieval Europe* (Princeton: Princeton University Press, 2023); Tzafrir Barzilay, *Poisoned Wells: Accusations, Persecution, and Minorities in Medieval Europe, 1321–1422* (Philadelphia: University of Pennsylvania Press, 2021).

Regional and local culture were important considerations. We sought to explore the place of all five senses within urban settings, emphasizing what urban dwellers saw, heard, touched, tasted, and smelled.[63] These urban dynamics, as well as the different activities conducted in cityscapes, are mentioned within medieval Hebrew sources as well as vernacular and Latin sources from the period. The comparison between the representation of the Jews in these sources and the depiction of belonging and exclusion that emerge from them, are all of import to daily life. Our decision to focus only on medieval Ashkenaz rather than include work on other diasporas (with small comparative sections in specific chapters), stems from our conviction that understanding the contexts within which medieval Ashkenazic Jews lived and their sense of belonging is paramount.

This line of thought, the quest to understand how Jews fit into their local landscapes, stands in contrast to earlier historiography that saw all Jews as more connected and affiliated with their fellow communities than with the loci in which they lived.[64] Such studies attributed greater weight to diachronic connections between Jews, with an emphasis on how current medieval ideas and beliefs departed from or adhered to more ancient formulations found in Hebrew texts from previous centuries or other diasporas. Finding a balanced approach between the similarities of Jewish life resulting from the power of shared textual, cultural, and practical heritage and the importance of local features of daily life is a difficult task, and this matter is assessed and reassessed in the different chapters.

All in all, the work presented here strives to present complex and nuanced analyses of daily life. Medieval Jews, like all medieval people, lived under multiple sources of power. For Jews this included, at the very least, the leadership of both the Jewish community and municipal and ecclesiastical establishments, to which, sometimes, further layers of competing authority were added. Their daily lives mirrored these

---

63. Goodson, Lester, and Symes, *Cities, Texts, and Social Networks, 400–1500*; Sarit Shalev-Eyni, "The Aural-Visual Experience in the Ashkenazi Ritual Domain of the Middle Ages," in *Resounding Images: Medieval Intersections of Art, Music, and Sound*, eds. Susan Boynton and Diane J. Reilly, Medieval Intersections of Art, Music, and Sound (Turnhout: Brepols, 2015), 189–204.

64. In contrast to Abraham Berliner, *Aus dem Leben der deutschen Juden im Mittelalter*, for example. In contrast the work of those who belonged to the so-called "Jerusalem school" saw Jews as much closer to all Jews wherever they may be. See, for example, David N. Myers, *Re-Inventing the Jewish Past: European Jewish Intellectuals and the Zionist Return to History*, Studies in Jewish History (New York: Oxford University Press, 1995).

multiple affiliations. Therefore, we are not asking to what extent Jews were part of their surroundings and to what extent they were a discrete entity. Rather, we are positing that they were both. This was not an undesired "marriage of convenience" serving Jews and Christians, replete with ideological and theological tensions. This was the reality within which medieval Jews lived, and these were the localities with which they identified, concurrent with the contrasting understanding of them as strangers or foreigners.[65]

It is our hope that this emphasis on the ways Jews belonged and were different will provide new insights not just for scholars interested in Jews qua Jews but also for scholars of medieval Europe at large. As integral parts of local markets, were the dealings of Jews so different from those of their neighbors? Can the information we have about them serve as examples of trade at large? As the sections of the book show, many of their daily practices were identical to those of their neighbors. When was their identity as Jews of import and when can they be seen as examples of medieval people and practice at large, and specifically of medieval urban inhabitants?[66] Even when considering religious practice, a topic that has been the focus of many studies on medieval Ashkenaz, when Jews adapt features from the practices of their neighbors, how can the similarities be assessed together with the difference?[67] Medieval Jews have often been "othered" more than included. Finding a new balance between these two impulses, remains a desideratum but one that we hope we have helped to reconsider.

This volume is the final joint publication of the Beyond the Elite: Jewish Daily Life in Medieval Europe research group. It is organized according to the four prisms described above: People (Miri Fenton, Eyal Levinson and Andreas Lehnertz, and Annika Funke); Spaces (Tzafrir Barzilay, Nureet Dermer and Albert Kohn); Objects (Neta Bodner and Ariella Lehmann, Aviya Doron, and Ido Noy); and Rituals (Erez Shahar Rochman,

---

65. Dermer, "Between Foreigners, Strangers and Jews"; Miri Rubin, *Cities of Strangers: Making Lives in Medieval Europe* (Cambridge: Cambridge University Press, 2020).
66. I refer back here to Goitein's *Mediterranean Society* where he does just that—namely, he sees Jewish evidence as relevant for Mediterranean peoples at large.
67. David Berger, "A Generation of Scholarship on Jewish-Christian Interaction in the Medieval World," *Tradition: A Journal of Orthodox Jewish Thought* 38 (2004): 4–14; Elisheva Baumgarten, "Appropriation and Differentiation: Jewish Identity in Medieval Ashkenaz," *AJS Review* 42 (2018): 39–63.

24   INTRODUCTION

Elisheva Baumgarten and Amit Shafran, and Hannah Teddy Schachter). Each section is prefaced by a methodological reflection that introduces the chapters within it and reviews some of the guiding principles girding their research. The assorted chapters include examinations of a wide variety of aspects of medieval life: economy, governance and law, life within the home and the family, medicine, liturgy, communal institutions, and mobility. The volume concludes with a reflection by Miri Rubin.

Taken as a whole, this volume highlights the importance of the study of daily life and shows how the exploration of the seemingly mundane or "ordinary" creates a historical picture that exceeds the exceptional. The minutiae of the everyday were as much a central component of life in the past as they are in the present, and their study fills a lacuna that has hardly been addressed, and in fact has been rather taken for granted or treated anachronistically to date. Above all, the chapters in this volume take the historical actors it presents—men, women, and children, rich and poor, Jewish and Christian, and their daily lives—seriously.[68] Social history as a field developed from the understanding that history cannot be fully understood by looking only top-down. The power of any individual and any authority, no matter how potent, did not, alone, determine the course of the past, and thus the view from the "bottom up" is equally crucial to a robust understanding of events.

An everyday perspective that focuses on the routine and repetition does not omit change over time. I began this chapter with a quote from a text that chronicles the rebuilding of the Speyer synagogue after the first one was destroyed during the First Crusade. The Jews of Speyer were attacked numerous times throughout the twelfth and thirteenth century, only to be totally destroyed in 1349.[69] This pattern of rebuilding and destruction was to repeat itself over and over again throughout the late Middle Ages and up to the modern period.[70] Specific events preceded and evolved during each chapter of Jewish history in the city. The mundane details of these events: where people lived, who was involved, how they manifested their presence in the city, and how they were received, are of significant import to understanding the history of this community over time. This is true not only for Speyer but for many communities that experienced similar, albeit not identical, fates. When

---

68. See Gronda et al., "Histoires Pragmatiques," 3, for a useful formulation.
69. See "Speyer," *Germania Judaica* (Tübingen: J.C.B. Mohr, 1963).
70. For a survey of select locations, see Cluse and Clemens, *The Jews of Europe around 1400*.

did the Jews feel that they had "pitched their tents forever"? When didn't they? Did this feeling change over time and how did it influence everyday activities? These are questions worth exploring, and they are questions with which this volume only begins to contend.

Further Readings

Arnade, Peter, Martha C. Howell, and Walter Simons. "Fertile Spaces: The Productivity of Urban Space in Northern Europe." *Journal of Interdisciplinary History* 32 (2002): 515–48, https://doi.org/10.1162/002219502317345493.
Baumgarten, Elisheva, ed. *Jewish Space and Place in Medieval Ashkenaz: A Special Issue of Jewish Studies Quarterly* 28 (2021).
Bonfil, Robert. *Jewish Life in Renaissance Italy.* Berkeley: University of California Press, 1994.
Bynum, Caroline Walker. *Christian Materiality: An Essay on Religion in Late Medieval Europe.* New York: Zone Books, 2011.
Cluse, Christoph, ed. *The Jews of Europe in the Middle Ages (Tenth to Fifteenth Centuries).* Turnhout: Brepols, 2004.
Cluse, Christoph, and Lukas Clemens, eds. *The Jews of Europe around 1400: Disruption, Crisis, and Resilience.* Wiesbaden: Harrassowitz Verlag, 2018.
De Certeau, Michel. *The Practice of Everyday Life.* Berkeley: University of California Press, 1984.
Dorin, Rowan. *No Return: Jews, Christian Usurers, and the Spread of Mass Expulsion in Medieval Europe.* Princeton: Princeton University Press, 2023.
Einbinder, Susan L. *After the Black Death: Plague and Commemoration among Iberian Jews.* Philadelphia: University of Pennsylvania Press, 2018.
Engel, David. *Historians of the Jews and the Holocaust.* Stanford, CA: Stanford University Press, 2022.
Francesconi, Federica, and Rebecca Lynn Winer, eds. *Jewish Women's History from Antiquity to the Present.* Detroit: Wayne State University Press, 2021.
Gronda, Roberto, et al. "Histoires Pragmatiques: A Conversation with Simona Cerutti and Yves Cohen." *European Journal of Pragmatism and American Philosophy* 8 (2016): 1-13. doi.org/10.4000/ejpap.654.
Grossman, Avraham. *Pious and Rebellious: Jewish Women in Medieval Europe*, trans. Jonathan Chipman. Waltham, MA: Brandeis University Press, 2004.
Güdemann, Moritz. *Geschichte des Erziehungswesens und der Cultur der Juden in Deutschland während des XIV und XV Jahrhunderts.* Vienna: Hölder, 1888.
Gurevich, Aron. *Categories of Medieval Culture.* London: Routledge and Kegan Paul, 1985.
Hanawalt, Barbara, and Michal Kobialka, eds. *Medieval Practices of Space.* Minneapolis: University of Minnesota Press, 2000.
Jordan, William C. *The French Monarchy and the Jews: From Philip Augustus to the Last Capetians.* Philadelphia: University of Pennsylvania Press, 1989.
Kaplan, Debra. *Beyond Expulsion: Jews, Christians, and Reformation Strasbourg.* Stanford, CA: Stanford University Press, 2011.

Katz, Jacob. *Exclusiveness and Tolerance: Studies in Jewish-Gentile Relations in Medieval and Modern Times*. New York: Behrman House, 1961.

Kohn, Roger. *Les Juifs de la France du nord dans la seconde moitié du XIVe siècle*. Louvain: Peeters, 1988.

Lipton, Sara. *Dark Mirror: The Medieval Origins of Anti-Jewish Iconography*. New York: Metropolitan Books/Henry Holt and Company, 2014.

Lüdtke, Alf, ed. *The History of Everyday Life: Reconstructing Historical Experiences and Ways of Life*. Princeton: Princeton University Press, 1995.

Marcus, Ivan G. *Rituals of Childhood: Jewish Acculturation in Medieval Europe*. New Haven, CT: Yale University Press, 1996.

Nirenberg, David. *Communities of Violence: Persecution of Minorities in the Middle Ages*. Princeton: Princeton University Press, 1996.

Rubin, Miri. *Cities of Strangers: Making Lives in Medieval Europe*. Cambridge: Cambridge University Press, 2020.

Rubin, Miri. *Gentile Tales: The Narrative Assault on Late Medieval Jews*. Philadelphia: University of Pennsylvania Press, 2004.

Shatzmiller, Joseph. *Cultural Exchange: Jews, Christians, and Art in the Medieval Marketplace*. Princeton: Princeton University Press, 2013.

Smail, Daniel Lord. "Interactions between Jews and Christians in Later Medieval Provence." *Medieval Encounters* 27 (2021): 410–33.

Ta-Shma, Israel M. *Ritual, Custom and Reality in Franco-Germany, 1000–1350*. Jerusalem: Magnes, 2000. (Hebrew).

Yuval, Israel Jacob. *Two Nations in Your Womb: Perceptions of Jews and Christians in Late Antiquity*, trans. Barbara Harshav and Jonathan Chipman. Berkeley: University of California Press, 2006.

Part I

People

Andreas Lehnertz, Eyal Levinson, Miri Fenton, and Annika Funke

This section focuses on *people* as active participants in shaping their own destinies; as individuals who have a sense of agency, who express their desires and goals, who make plans and carry them out, who are engaged with the social structure and who, to some extent, are capable of influencing the outcome of events in the world around them. There is, however, an intricate connection between agency and power. When individuals act (exercise their agency), they are utilizing whatever power they have, whether that power is personal (such as knowledge or skill) or structural (a position of authority). When individuals or groups are disenfranchised or marginalized, this capacity to act autonomously is often diminished.

The three chapters in this section illustrate the deep connection between personal agency and power structures, whether these were political, communal, or familial. The concept of excommunication, the subject of Miri Fenton's essay, is a first example of the complex relationships between agency and power for medieval Jews. Excommunication was a time for negotiating communal affiliation and could also provide individuals with a space for resistance. Fenton shows that excommunication was not a blanket legal mechanism with easily enforced consequences. Instead, it was a legal tool encompassing a spectrum of actions, ranging from the more to the less impactful, rather than a clear and immediate cutting off of ties with, or the exclusion of, an individual. In addition, excommunication was a legal strategy employed in the framework of both conflict prevention and conflict resolution, relying on the prior consent of all parties. Mapping out the nuanced operation of different manifestations of excommunication in medieval Ashkenaz, Fenton demonstrates how it served as a powerful but complex and locally specific tool for social regulation that enabled people to express intentional agency in the hope of bettering their situation.

The orphans studied by Andreas Lehnertz and Eyal Levinson also confronted differing power systems that sought to determine their fate. Orphans, especially those from affluent families, had to negotiate both familial and communal power structures and sometimes enlisted local authorities to help them achieve their desired aims. In doing so, they sometimes went against their own family members and defied communal norms and boundaries. While a child's agency is more difficult to assert, and their ability to influence events disputable, sociologists, such as Emma Sorbring and Leon Kuczynski, have argued that "the idea that children are actors and agents who contribute positively to family and other social processes is well accepted at a theoretical level," and that children are able to express their resistance "despite their difference in power in an asymmetrical but interdependent close relationship."[1] Arising from the sources explored by Lehnertz and Levinson, quarrels between orphans and their stepparents and stepsiblings were a known phenomenon, driving some widows and widowers to question whether to remarry at all. It becomes clear that at least some orphans actively challenged coercive powers, while manifesting autonomous intentional agency.

Like the individuals who were or were not excommunicated studied by Fenton, and the orphans studied by Lehnertz and Levinson, Annika Funke tells the story of an individual and his dealings with the different power structures in his life. The hero of her article is Anschel of Münzenberg, who in 1512 asked the Count of Hanau to wave the cost of his protection. In exploring his story, Funke poses a fundamental question regarding the political agency of late medieval Ashkenazic Jews, namely: Were the Jews simply pawns in the hands of powerful leaders? A question she then goes on to answer by focusing on the political actions

---

1. Emma Sorbring and Leon Kuczynski, "Children's Agency in the Family, in School and in Society: Implications for Health and Well-Being," *International Journal of Qualitative Studies on Health and Well-being* 13 (2019): 1–3, https://doi.org/10.1080/17482631.2019.1634414.

of the Jewish population of Münzenberg and Assenheim, highlighting their active role in the diplomatic exchange between the town lords during the first half of the sixteenth century. By examining letters written by the Jews of Münzenberg and Assenheim to their patron between 1502 until 1557, Funke underlines confrontational maneuvers, shedding light on the mechanics of political influence and the scope of action available to these rural Jewish communities.

All three chapters examine a variety of sources, but first and foremost, legal sources and letters. It is typical of these genres, that what gets noted and handed down are moments of disruption and discord, when events, whether on the individual or communal level, lead to familial ruptures and the destabilization of communal norms and boundaries. We must therefore bear in mind that threats of excommunication were in fact rare occurrences, not all orphans suffered from uncompassionate guardians, and Jews in Ashkenaz also enjoyed peaceful times and fruitful cooperation with their Christian neighbors. Nonetheless, these were instances that enabled individuals to express their agency and contest coercive powers, while hoping to influence the course of events to their own benefit. As such, they shed valuable light on the broader medieval Jewish communities of Ashkenaz and on the surrounding Christian majority culture.

In sum, the chapters in this section offer a nuanced exploration of the interplay between individual agency and power within medieval Ashkenazic communities. By examining the ways in which people—whether marginalized Jews, excommunicated individuals, or orphans—engaged with and sometimes resisted the forces that sought to control their lives, these studies illuminate the complex dynamics of power and autonomy in medieval society. The disruptions and conflicts that are highlighted, while not representative of everyday life, reveal crucial moments where the exercise of agency came to the fore. Though exceptional, they provide us with deeper insights into the social fabric of medieval Ashkenaz, revealing how individuals and communities navigated their circumstances to assert their will and influence the world around them. Agency is therefore as much at the heart of these articles as the powerlessness to exercise it.

CHAPTER 1

Exclusion and Reconciliation
Excommunication in Medieval Jewish Communities

Miri Fenton

For medieval Jews, excommunication was one of the most definitive moments for negotiating communal affiliation. It was a strategy for enforcing normative behavior and determining the boundaries of acceptable conduct by excluding an individual from the community, for the benefit of others. Yet, in practice, individuals could resist attempts to excommunicate them by appealing to their fellow Jews or to local authorities. Neighbors could continue interacting with excommunicated people, thus undermining the excommunication order. Neither easy to enforce nor a blanket legal mechanism, excommunication in medieval Ashkenaz constituted a spectrum of more or less impactful instances of using a legal tool in a range of locally specific ways.

There were many different forms of medieval excommunication, including famous bans on rabbis or scholars and/or their philosophical approaches,[1] bans on settlement,[2] bans on whole communities,[3] and bans on specific goods, all of which shared the same terminology.[4] This heterogeneity is reflected in the inconsistency of the terms used: *herem* (usually translated as ban), *nidui* (usually translated as excommunication), and *gezerah* (usually translated as an imprecation oath but which in some instances functioned as an ordinance).[5] In high medieval

---

1. Rabbis enacted bans against each other, against their students, and against methods or subjects of study. These sorts of excommunications were often motivated by a desire to maintain uniformity in halakhic rulings and practice, and so local political factors played a central role in these sorts of excommunications of particular individuals or whole communities. As such, these actions did not have substantial implications for the vast majority of medieval Jews. See Ram Ben-Shalom, "The Ban Placed by the Community of Barcelona on the Study of Philosophy and Allegorical Preaching—A New Study," *Revue des etudes Juives* 159, no. 3-4 (2002): 397; Gregg Stern, *Philosophy and Rabbinic Culture: Jewish Interpretation and Controversy in Medieval Languedoc*, Routledge Jewish Studies (New York: Routledge, 2009), 204. R. Meir of Rothenburg argued that a teacher always had the right to excommunicate his student, so the student had to accept all the regulations and ordinances passed by the teacher or accept censure. See R. N. Rabinowitz, ed., *She'elot u-Teshuvot Maharam Bar Barukh*, Lvov ed. (Lemberg, 1850), §77.

2. See the pro forma declaration of *herem ha-yishuv* from Bibl. National Paris Heb. 1293 in A. Gulak, *Otzar ha-Shtarot ha-Nehugim b'Israel* (Jerusalem: ha-Poalim, 1926), 21. R. Solomon b. Adret argued that it was not possible to place a ban on people coming to reside in a certain city, implicitly because those rights are contingent on paying royal taxes, which anyone might do. See Rashba I, 664. See also Louis Rabinowitz, *The Herem Hayyishub: A Contribution to the Medieval Economic History of the Jews* (London: E. Goldston, 1945); Simon Schwarzfuchs, "Herem ha-Yishuv (Ban on Settlement)," in *Medieval Jewish Civilization: An Encyclopedia*, ed. Norman Roth (New York: Routledge, 2003).

3. Despite sporadic attempts by rabbis or communal leaders to excommunicate whole communities (see Irving A. Agus, *Teshuvot Ba'alei ha-Tosafot* [New York: Yeshiva University Press, 1954], §1. See also Aharon Zelzenik, ed. *She'elot u-Teshuvot ha-Rashba* (Jerusalem: Makhon Yerushalayim, 1997), §474, and the de jure plausibility of doing so (see I. J. Vidavsky, ed., *Sefer Kol Bo* [Jerusalem: Makhon Even Yisrael, 1997], §142), the ability of one community to impose an ordinance on pain of excommunication on another community without their agreement or consent was not accepted in Ashkenaz or the Crown of Aragon during the high Middle Ages.

4. This was primarily successful in the Crown of Aragon, where there were some successful attempts to enact boycotts against particular goods from another region, though these disputes seem to have resolved quickly. See Yom Tov Assis, *The Golden Age of Aragonese Jewry: Community and Society 1213-1327* (London: Littman Library of Jewish Civilization, 1997), 173.

5. The term *shamta* does not feature in the high medieval European sources discussing excommunication of ordinary people. Gideon Libson, *Jewish and Islamic Law: A Comparative Study of Custom during the Geonic Period*, Harvard Series in Islamic Law (Cambridge, MA: Harvard University Press, 2003), 1:134. Gideon Libson's discussion of different sorts of bans during the Geonic period indicate many terms and widely divergent local customs. To avoid taking God's name in vain in a perjurious oath, the Geonim developed the *gezerta* (imprecation oath) and *herem stam* (a judicial imprecation inviting herem on anyone who made a false claim in court, with the aim of intimidating litigants to tell the truth), which did not use God's name. Though the use of the *gezerta* oath diminished in the twelfth and thirteenth centuries, Rachel Furst demonstrated that these *gezerta* oaths were still in use throughout high medieval Ashkenaz. See Gideon Libson, "The Gezerta in the Gaonic and Early Medieval

Europe, the terms *herem* and *nidui* were often used similarly, and sometimes interchangeably, to refer to excluding people from communal life, either post facto or as a threat.[6] Though this chapter will treat the term *excommunication* as a spectrum of exclusion mechanisms from nidui to herem, exploring several examples indicates that blurred lines between the terms represented inconsistencies in their application in practice.

Offenses warranting excommunication ranged from breaking the terms of a private contract, through public violation of communal ordinances on charity, to crimes like murder or theft. Excommunication could be pronounced as a threat, usually to coerce people to behave in a certain way or abide by an agreement, or as a punishment for crimes already committed. By exploring how excommunication was used both as a threat and as a punishment, this chapter demonstrates its usefulness as a tool for conflict prevention and resolution in medieval Jewish communities.

Mid-twentieth-century scholarship on medieval excommunication in Ashkenaz argued that the fear of being placed under the ban was so great that obedience to law and local ordinances was almost guaranteed by virtue of its presence as a punishment in legal texts.[7] Jeffrey Woolf summed up the view of historians when he wrote that "excommunication (herem or nidui), which was originally a judicial penalty, was the heaviest weapon in the communal arsenal . . . [it] possessed sufficient weight to instill fear into the stoutest heart . . . [and] transformed its object into a non-person."[8] As it is impossible to measure this fear, we can only evaluate the ways in which excommunication actually operated. Louis Finklestein argued that "excommunication was so effective a punishment that there was no need of police power or physical force

---

Period," *Shenaton ha-Mishpat ha-Ivri: Annual of the Institute for Research in Jewish Law* 5 (1978): 147–52.

6. There is some evidence that nidui involved a shorter period of social isolation, in contrast to herem which was stricter and longer in duration. See Archive of the Crown of Aragon, Barcelona (from now on, ACA), Reg. 71 f.55v. See also Assis, *The Golden Age of Aragonese Jewry: Community and Society 1213–1327*, 157. This difference in terms varied across sources and regions.

7. For example, see also Agus's statement that "community decrees were obeyed religiously," Irving A. Agus, *Urban Civilisation in Pre-Crusade Europe: A Study of Organised Town-Life in North-Western Europe during the Tenth and Eleventh Centuries Based on Responsa Literature* (New York: Yeshiva University Press, 1965), 61.

8. Jeffrey Woolf, *The Fabric of Religious Life in Medieval Ashkenaz (1000–1300): Creating Sacred Communities* (Leiden: Brill, 2015), 71–73.

of any kind," as he compared the power to excommunicate with the power of popes over kings in the twelfth century.⁹

Historians' focus on this fear factor stemmed from the fact that excommunication separated someone from the community and cursed the person during its imposition. A herem formula, appearing in the fourteenth-century *Sefer Kolbo*, includes cursing, decreeing, and oath taking: "We excommunicate and forswear, anathemize and ban, curse and imprecate, by the will of the people and on the torah scroll, on the 613 commandments written therein . . . [the excommunicate shall be] cursed by the mouth of God . . . Lord, God of all spirits of flesh, destroy him and annihilate him."¹⁰ Not only did the formulation of the herem include curses, but curses could be proscribed on top of a herem in order to attempt to enforce compliance.¹¹ Yet, despite the use of curses, excommunication as a punishment was less effective than the levying of fines. As Ephraim Kanarfogel demonstrated, fines were central to resolving cases of violence between community members.¹²

Prescriptive texts certainly support the understanding of the power of excommunication as residing in the fear it instilled. *Sefer ha-Rokeah* outlines the details of a murderer's three-year exile: "On entering a new town, he should say 'I am a murderer,' and he should not eat meat or drink wine or shave his beard or head. He should wash his clothes, body, and beard only once a month . . . and walk barefoot . . . Once the term of his exile has ended, he should fast on Mondays and Thursdays for a year . . . and not engage people in conversation." As the text

---

9. Finklestein argued that "excommunication was so effective a punishment that there was no need of police power or physical force of any kind in the execution of the order of the court. For the excommunicated person was not only forbidden to take part in the religious life of his people, which in itself would have been a serious blow to anyone in those days of piety and observance, but he was socially ostracized. The possession of the power of excommunication gave the rabbi and the community as great an advantage in dealing with recalcitrant individuals as the similar power exercised by the popes gave them over the kings of the twelfth and thirteenth centuries." Louis Finklestein, *Jewish Self Government in the Middle Ages* (New York: The Jewish Theological Seminary of America, 1924), 7. Though there is an argument to be made that the second half of the quoted analogy also breaks down, that subject is beyond the scope of the current volume.

10. *Nusah Herem, Sefer Kolbo* §139.

11. R. Meir of Rothenburg, *Shut Maharam b. R. Barukh*, Prague ed., ed. M. A. Bloch (Budapest, 1895), §251. Curses were also a part of excommunication liturgy in Church rites. See Lester K. Little, *Benedictine Maledictions: Liturgical Cursing in Romanesque France* (Ithaca, NY: Cornell University Press, 1996), 30–43.

12. Ephraim Kanarfogel, "The Adjudication of Fines in Ashkenaz during the Medieval and Early Modern Periods and the Preservation of Communal Decorum," *Dine Israel* 32 (2018): 159–87.

stipulates, this de jure strict exile continued even after the murderer was allowed to return home, reminding the community at every opportunity (on Mondays and Thursdays—days of communal Torah reading) of the crime committed. Moreover, *Sefer Hasidim* clearly states that the only sanctions available to Jews at the time are "the oath and excommunication" and that "there is no greater punishment than breaking a *herem*."[13]

Thus, at least in theory, excommunication was a severe punishment. Contact with an excommunicate was severely limited: "Do not walk alongside them ... do not associate with them in public, in business, or in writing." By outlining the severity of excommunication as a punishment, rabbinic leadership may have attempted to dissuade community members from committing the crimes or actions that might lead to their own excommunication and thereby prevent, rather than resolve, conflict. Simultaneously, by stressing the significance of being cut off from one's community, these threats were likely to have strengthened feelings of communal affiliation in at least some community members, though the extent of this impact is impossible to measure. Yet, *Sefer Hasidim* here also provides a built-in exemption, stating, "Even [communication] through writing is forbidden *without the permission of the community leaders*."[14]

Another example of a similar type of exemption indicates the importance *Sefer Hasidim* placed on contact between communities. In one exemplum, the excommunicated person pleads: if "exiled among the gentiles, I will break [the laws of the] sabbath." In order to avoid this fate, he "made a belt of iron that caused him great distress so that he would not eat gentile bread or break the sabbath."[15] The impetus to both exile and maintain the boundaries of acceptable contact indicates the assumption that exiled community members will travel between other centers of Jewish life and that they will, eventually return. The length of an excommunication depended on an individual's marital and family status—if married with children the term of "his wandering [while excommunicated] is three years." *Sefer Hasidim* certainly stressed the importance of maintaining strong links between families and maintaining affiliation to Jewish practice and observance. It repeatedly

---

13. *Sefer Hasidim* (Parma), ed. Jacob Wistenetski (Frankfurt: Mekize Nirdamim, 1924), Parma §1386.
14. *Sefer Hasidim* (Parma), §1234.
15. *Sefer Hasidim* (Parma), §176.

advocated for repentance, rather than punishment by excommunication in the face of wrongdoing.

The desire to prevent conflict within the community pre-dated *Sefer Hasidim* in Ashkenazic communities. One passage from the twelfth-century *takkanot* of Rabeinu Tam, where the threat of excommunication was the driving force of the regulations, indicates the hesitancy to actually impose excommunication as a punishment and instead emphasizes local community affiliation and reconciliation: "A *herem* concerning one who strikes his neighbour: the community must not release him so that he may be counted for a *minyan* until he has agreed to perform whatever the court may enjoin upon him. That is provided that the assailed person makes a claim, otherwise the community may suspend the *herem* of their own accord."[16] Unless the person harmed by the excommunicate makes a claim, it is possible for the community to suspend the herem in order to maintain the ordinary functions of community life, in this instance of praying in a quorum (*minyan*). In this ordinance, the community played a central role in the resolution of a conflict between individuals. Community leaders and rabbinic officials thus provided a general framework that local communities could deploy, or not, toward that end.

Conflicts could also be resolved through the culprit's repentance. One thirteenth-century responsum of R. Meir of Rothenburg regarding a murder case states that "we should have pity on [the murderer's] soul, for he has deviated from the righteous path, and he needs penance. Indeed, the God-fearing people should be zealous about this and abstain from any contact with this murderer and punish him and suppress him by any means of oppression, until his heart surrenders and he repent his evil deeds. . . . I call upon the murderer and say: Be gone, you man of blood, one so full of defilement. But if he submits to this admonishment he will be redeemed and will receive penance."[17] In this case, not only was the excommunication voluntary (the community was invited to exclude, and the murderer was called on to accept excommunication) but, by consenting to excommunication, the murderer secured penance instead of exclusion. Thus, excommunication

---

16. Finklestein, *Jewish Self Government in the Middle Ages*, 199.
17. Simcha Emanuel, *Responsa of Rabbi Meir of Rothenburg and His Colleagues* (Jerusalem: World Union Jewish Studies, 2012), 1:566–67, §255. See Ephraim Shoham-Steiner, *Jews and Crime in Medieval Europe* (Detroit: Wayne State University Press, 2020), 153–54.

functioned primarily as a means to achieve penance, repentance, and reacceptance into the local community.

Prioritizing reacceptance over punishment can be seen in other responsa as well. One, written by R. Isaac b. Avraham of Dampierre (the Ritzba) (twelfth-century northern France), attests to the custom in some communities of excommunicating violent offenders as a punishment, rather than just threatening excommunication. He was asked how a town should respond when one person hit another. R. Isaac argued that excommunicating the aggressor would not be effective. Instead, the townspeople should compel the aggressor to "conduct himself according to the law" and ask forgiveness from his victim. The victim should openly accept this apology and forgive him. However, in this actual recommendation (rather than prescriptive description), the accused remained in the local community for the duration of the term of excommunication, enabling the victim to forgive the perpetrator. The responsum even states that "the victim . . . should not be cruel to the person seeking forgiveness."[18]

The hesitancy toward excommunication is also apparent in a responsum that refers to a *takkanah* allowing the community to excommunicate anyone who accuses a fellow community member of being careless with fire in their home, stating that "even though our rabbis wrote to impose excommunication on one who accuses his fellow of a conflagration. . . it seems to me that everything depends on the case and on what they foresee, for if they are too insistent on this and force excommunication on him, there is fear that he will flee and leave his fellow, with his entire household, in mortal danger. For if a fire breaks out, they will cast them into the fire."[19] It goes on to state that only a known slanderer should be excommunicated. Emanuel argues that as it is unlikely that an established community member would flee the town over a three days' excommunication: "The communities were concerned about . . . beggars and vagabonds," who could flee with little material consequence.[20] Given the danger posed by fire in medieval cities, the

---

18. Emanuel, *Responsa of Rabbi Meir of Rothenburg and his Colleagues*, 2:730 §367.

19. Emanuel, ed., *Responsa of Rabbi Meir of Rothenburg and His Colleagues*, vol. 2, §393, 65–67. See Simcha Emanuel, "Conflagrations and Crimes in the Late Middle Ages: Some Attestations from Halakhic Literature," in *Medieval Ashkenaz: Papers in Honour of Alfred Haverkamp Presented at the 17th World Congress of Jewish Studies, Jerusalem 2017*, eds. Christoph Cluse and Jörg Müller (Wiesbaden: Harrassowitz Verlag, 2021), 283.

20. Emanuel, "Conflagrations and Crimes in the Late Middle Ages: Some Attestations from Halakhic Literature," 282.

hesitancy to impose excommunication on all townspeople is significant in and of itself, and likely indicates the difficulty of enforcing this punishment. In addition, excommunicating one Jew, who had made a complaint to local authorities about another Jew, could leave the first exposed to serious repercussions from local authorities and no recourse. In Ashkenaz, the fact that excommunication was primarily a Jewish punishment meant that communal considerations had to balance the conflict between Jewish parties, on the one hand, with the relationship between the Jewish community and local authorities, on the other.

Thus, hesitancy to excommunicate reflected both the importance of maintaining community affiliation and the inability to enforce excommunication. Responding to a complex murder case in which other community members were slandering the perpetrators, Haim Or Zaru'a argued: "It is appropriate to castigate all those who call R. Moshe and his father-in-law 'murderers' with regard to this terrible episode, and so too, to clear their names, that they did not tell that villain to do it . . . Nonetheless, to ban and excommunicate [herem and nidui] those who open their mouths against them on this matter, without constraint—this is not possible due to [the prohibition] 'Do not place a stumbling-block before the blind,' for it is clear they will transgress."[21] The point Or Zaru'a is making here is clear: do not impose excommunication because it is impossible to excommunicate everyone who gossiped about a complicated and scandalous murder.

This ambivalence toward imposing excommunication may be rooted in a sense that it had to be supported by community consent. R. Meir of Rothenburg went so far as to state that if someone violates an excommunication imposed on them, they can only be punished for doing so if they had consented to the herem in the first place.[22] However, even

---

21. Isaac b. Moses of Vienna, *Sefer Or Zaru'a*, ed. Yakov Farbstein (Jerusalem: Makhon Yerushalayim, 2010), §25.

22. R. Isaac of Corbeil, *Semak: Sefer Mitzvot Katan (Amude golah)* (Jerusalem: Yerid ha-Sefarim, 2005), §81. Irving Agus argued that R. Meir of Rothenburg held so tightly to the idea of individual freedom that he rejected the notion that someone could be cursed against his will. Because of this, "the curse [as ḥerem was accompanied by curses, as discussed below] can only be construed as the invocation of the anger of God and his punishment on the perpetrator of a particular forbidden act. If the person did not consent to the enactment of the particular rule, [they were] not bound by this rule and committed no sin in breaking it. So, God had no right to punish [them], and the curse was of no avail. R. Meir therefore was forced to adopt the principle that a *herem* must be voluntarily accepted before it becomes binding on the individual." Irving A. Agus, *Rabbi Meir of Rothenburg: His Life and His Works as Sources for the*

when formulated as a punishment, reports of excommunication in responsa literature are overwhelmingly prescriptive rather than descriptive. It was ruled that married women who reported fellow Jews to non-Jewish authorities should be excommunicated, just like men, and had to pay a fine.[23] A man who married a woman within three months of her husband's death should be excommunicated, as the paternity of the child who might be born thereafter would be in doubt.[24] A *levir* who refused to perform *yibum* or *halitzah* with or for his sister-in-law, and thereby release her from her obligation to marry him following the death of his brother, was considered a recalcitrant husband, and was threatened with both excommunication and corporal punishment.[25] In addition, a man who refuses to pay for his wife's maintenance, especially if she had made a complaint against him, can be excommunicated.[26] In all these instances, the practical import of these threats seems to have been to foster the communal affiliation of vulnerable women, in many instances to protect them, and most clearly to prevent intracommunal conflicts.

The same concerns motivated the instances of recommended excommunication threatened in responsa. In one example, one man had been ordered by the court to divorce his wife following violent behavior, but failed to do so. He was threatened with prolonged excommunication (herem), unless his behavior changed substantially.[27] In the case of a man who refused to marry his fiancée, a responsum proposed excommunication (nidui) as a reasonable punishment for breaking this agreement.[28] However, excommunication was only one of the possible responses to such behavior—R. Meir of Rothenburg also threatened physical punishment for violent husbands.[29] It is important to note that in Ashkenaz, neither party in these domestic disputes had an alternative legal authority to turn to. On the one hand, this lack of alternative avenues for redress effectively put more weight on the potential

---

Religious, Legal, and Social History of the Jews of Germany in the Thirteenth Century (Jersey City, NJ: KTAV Publishing House, 1970), 1:111n197.

23. Emanuel, *Responsa of Rabbi Meir of Rothenburg and His Colleagues* §84. See also *Shut Maharam b. R. Barukh*, Prague, §599.

24. See Agus, *Rabbi Meir of Rothenburg: His Life and His Works as Sources for the Religious, Legal, and Social History of the Jews of Germany in the Thirteenth Century*, vol. 1. doc no.247, 285-86.

25. Finklestein, *Jewish Self Government in the Middle Ages*, 230. English translation, 247.

26. V. Conti, ed., *Sefer She'elot u-Teshuvot Maharam*, Cremona ed. (Cremona, 1557), §291.

27. *Shut Maharam b. R. Barukh*, Prague, §927.

28. *Shut Maharam b. R. Barukh*, Prague, §203.

29. *Shut Maharam b. R. Barukh*, Prague, §81.

threat of excommunication as a punishment against which there was appeal. On the other hand, it also meant that there were few enforcement mechanisms for ensuring that a man threatened with excommunication would in fact be barred from communal life.

From fire safety to domestic abuse, excommunication thus functioned as an internal Jewish punishment. This internal dynamic and in principle consent to excommunication also gave weight to the use of excommunication in other circumstances: as a penalty for disobeying communal ordinances (takkanot), as a predetermined penalty for a broken oath or sworn agreement, and as a threat to compel witness testimony. This chapter will address each in turn.

Communal ordinances, takkanot, were regulations enacted by scholars to modify, update, or supplement preestablished Talmudic laws.[30] Many takkanot were promulgated on pain of excommunication, which is to say that a certain action or practice was forbidden, and the consequence of transgression was excommunication. One of the earliest sets of takkanot, issued with the agreement of the elders and scholars of many Ashkenazic communities on pain of excommunication (herem and nidui),[31] was reissued as *Takkanot Shum* when representatives convened at Mainz to institute a series of new taxation regulations.[32] The use of the threat of excommunication as an enforcement mechanism in these ordinances was therefore primarily a legal tool that enabled relevant regulations to be enforced in principle. Their authority and validity rested on references to the "ordinances of the elders" as well as the signed agreement of leaders and representatives of a wide range of communities.[33]

In many instances, ordinances drew on preexisting customs. For example, in ruling about the disposition of marital property if one spouse died shortly after marriage, R. Meir of Rothenburg stated that

---

30. See Avraham Reiner, "Rabbenu Tam's Ordinance for the Return of the Dowry: Between Talmudic Exegesis and an Ordinance That Contradicts the Talmud," *Dine Israel* 33 (2019): 71–98.

31. Vidavsky, *Sefer Kol Bo*, §117.

32. Rainer Barzen, *Taqqanot Qehillot Šum. Die Rechtssatzungen der Jüdischen Gemeinden von Mainz, Worms und Speyer im hohen und späten Mittelalter* (Wiesbaden: Harrassowitz Verlag, 2019).

33. For example, the takkanot of the Rhine communities in 1220: "All these *takkanot* were made by the *herem*. We have renewed now in the year 4980, what our ancestors ordained previously many years ago, here at Mayence by a severe *herem*; except for the ordinances of the great light, R. Gershom, the light of the Dispersion, b. R. Judah, where are very many and are well known, and did not need renewal." Finklestein, *Jewish Self Government in the Middle Ages*, 222. See *Shut Maharam b. R. Barukh*, Prague, §1022.

"I found [a] *herem* of the elders" regarding the property of a woman if she died within a year of her marriage without children.[34] Other such ordinances of elders include a herem on villagers who passed through a town two weeks before Purim, requiring them to give Purim-related charity (*matanot l'evyonim*) to the poor if requested. One ordinance, and a herem to leave the remaining portions of large candles lit for Yom Kippur in the synagogue after the end of the holiday,[35] and another to subject oneself to the beit din of the town in whose cemetery you plan to be buried or bury your dead, are also punishable by herem.[36] In these instances, the threat of excommunication was, in principle, a legal sanction. They also illustrate substantive attempts to prevent conflict from emerging in the first place. The threat of excommunication had to be sufficiently severe to make this conflict prevention strategy effective.

In Ashkenaz there was an emphasis on the need for assent to an ordinance, and thereby to the enforcement mechanism of the threat of excommunication. An exemplum from *Sefer Hasidim* recalls, "A community instituted [an ordinance on pain of] excommunication to give charity, and a minority of the wealthy community members left the synagogue [at the time the threat of excommunication was proclaimed], and they protest the ordinance [applying to them] as they had left [the synagogue when it was proclaimed] and so [claim] that the penalty of excommunication does not apply to them."[37] In this instance it seems that conflict prevention was key—without having assented to the ordinance to give charity, there was no way to force the rich community members to do so by using the threat of excommunication.

In other instances, by using the language of ostensibly reaffirming a preexisting ordinance, later ordinances implied that the members of communities had, at least in principle, already assented to them. This meant that the attendant penalties, including excommunication, could be imposed. For example, the takkanot of R. Jacob Meir Tam state that "we have voted, decreed, ordained, and declared under the herem, that

---

34. *Shut Maharam b. R. Barukh*, Prague, § 483. This might be contrasted with the practice in Toledo, where the dowry of a woman who died without children was split between her husband and her parents without any time limit. See A. Zaleznik, *She'elot u-Teshuvot ha-Rashba ha-Hadashot mi-Ketav Yad* (Jerusalem: Mekhon 'Or ha-Mizrah, 2005), § 325.
35. *Shut Maharam b. R. Barukh*, Prague, § 153.
36. *Shut Maharam b. R. Barukh*, Prague, §1022.
37. *Sefer Hasidim* (Parma), §1713. See also *Sefer Hasidim* (Parma), §1294, §1295. This Ashkenazi approach to assenting to a *herem* in order for it to be enforceable might be contrasted with the approach detailed in Mishpat ha-Herem of the Ramban. See Vidavsky, *Sefer Kol Bo*, §148 (*Mishpat ha-herem l'Ramban*).

no man or woman may bring a fellow Jew before Gentile courts or exert compulsion on him through Gentiles, whether by a prince or a common man, a ruler or an inferior official, except by mutual agreement made in the presence of proper witnesses."[38] This was reinforced by a later ordinance signed by R. Haim b. Yehiel "Hefetz Zahav" of Cologne, R. Isaac b. Meir of Dura, R. Isaac b. Judah ha-Levi of Mainz, and the communities of Worms, Speyer, and Würzburg, and states that "no man is allowed to testify about his fellow [Jew] in non-Jewish courts."[39] In this instance, too, the threat of herem was imposed in order to prevent conflict within local Jewish communities, and the way in which it was imposed deterred certain people from rejecting the ordinance. Thus, excommunication was a local legal strategy that enabled rabbis to double down on conflict prevention.

Communal ordinances in Ashkenaz could also foster communal affiliation. For example, R. Meir of Rothenburg was asked: "In a case where some members of the community seek to pronounce a *herem* for a certain purpose while others openly protest against it, are the former permitted to pronounce the *herem*, and when pronounced, will it be binding on the latter group?" To which he replied:

> If the decree for which the pronouncement of the ban is sought, is designed for the public benefit or to fill a great need in the community, while without such a decree the existence of the community will be jeopardized, the members of the community are permitted to coerce one another to adopt the required resolution and to abide by its provisions. A *herem*, however, cannot be effectively invoked upon those who protest against its being pronounced, since a *herem* must first be accepted voluntarily by a person before it becomes binding on him.[40]

This ability to accept or reject an ordinance, as well as the inability to enforce a herem agreed to under duress, is predicated on being able to enact communal ordinances and then punish people who, having agreed to these ordinances, then disobeyed them.[41] In theory, the practical upshot of this consent-based approach was that community

---

38. Finklestein, *Jewish Self Government in the Middle Ages*, 153 (Hebrew text), 155–56 (translation). See also *Shut Maharam b. R. Barukh*, Prague, §1022.
39. Emanuel, *Responsa of Rabbi Meir of Rothenburg and His Colleagues*, §454.
40. R. Isaac of Corbeil, *Semak: Sefer Mitzvot Katan (Amudei golah)*, §81.
41. See *Shut Maharam b. R. Barukh*, Prague, § 968.

members had a high degree of ownership over the rules that governed them and were therefore more deeply committed to them and their enforcement.

Widely promulgated communal ordinances played such an important role in Ashkenaz because they were thought to be essential to enforcing the rules of the community and creating cohesion and affiliation among its members. Thus, when questioned about how to resolve intracommunal strife, R. Meir of Rothenburg answered that "all the heads of households should be assembled, and each take it upon himself, under the threat of the ban, to give his opinion only for the sake of heaven and the common good."[42] The threat of excommunication here prompts adherence to upright behavior in resolving a communal dispute, rather than as a legal mechanism to enforce a particular rule. Thus, excommunication in communal ordinances in Ashkenaz functioned both to prevent conflict and to foster communal affiliation.

In addition, the threat of excommunication was considered to be an effective tool in enforcing a variety of interpersonal agreements. By including the threat of excommunication should it be broken, the agreement was strengthened by the additional guarantee of the social pressure of local community members, who as witnesses of the original agreement, could, presumably, be relied on to ostracize and excommunicate the relevant party should this become necessary.

There are several examples of people during this period agreeing to particular things under pain of excommunication, and then breaking that agreement. In one example, "Reuven's wife took upon herself, by force of *herem*, in the presence of people of the city, and wrote a document regarding the *herem* and witnesses [signed the document], and she transgressed two or three times."[43] A longer version of the same responsum states that "all the people of the city signed the document." A follow up question indicates that the husband, Reuven, had also undertaken a, presumably similar, agreement on pain of herem, though the same detail of his consent to the herem is not provided. Both Reuven and his wife were able to bring witnesses that it was the other who had transgressed their agreement and should be placed

---

42. M. A. Bloch, ed., *Sefer Sha'arei Teshuvot Maharam Bar Barukh*, Berlin ed. (Berlin, 1891), §865. See Christoph Cluse, "Jewish Community and Civic Commune in the High Middle Ages," in *Strangers and Poor People: Changing Patterns of Inclusion and Exclusion in Europe and the Mediterranean World from Classical Antiquity to the Present Day*, eds. A. Gestrich, L. Raphael, and H. Uerlings (Frankfurt: Peter Lang, 2010), 182.

43. *Sefer She'elot u-Teshuvot Maharam*, Cremona, §185.

under herem. In this instance, keeping agreements on pain of herem did not just involve the two individuals between whom an agreement had been made but also all the people who provided their initial consent to this bilateral agreement on pain of herem, that is, namely the people who witnessed the original agreement and those who saw the actions of the parties thereafter. The threat of excommunication meant that the social cost of not keeping agreements was higher than it might otherwise have been.

Agreements contracted under penalty of herem played an important social and legal role. When in court, enabling a woman to swear an oath on pain of herem that she was telling the truth allowed her to avoid the potential penalties associated with swearing a false oath. According to the French Tosafot, this excommunication order was less easily enforceable, as indicated by one thirteenth-century responsum by R. Isaac b. Elijah in which he stated that "our teachers in France were accustomed to issuing a *herem* so that she might speak the truth, for [then] it is not so serious if she subsequently transgresses." This seems to be in contrast to the practice in German lands, where oaths taken by women were not on pain of herem, and may indicate that herem was taken more seriously and was more of a threat in Germany than in northern France.

Bilateral agreements made under penalty of herem could also be used to prevent conflict. The thirteenth-century *Sefer Mordekhai* relates a case in which two people were engaged to be married under penalty of herem. Subsequently, however, "the man apostatised [converted to Christianity] and later returned [to Judaism]." Once Jewish again, the man refused to marry the woman with whom he had made the original agreement. In this instance, the question arose as to whether the woman was bound by the original threat of herem if she did not marry him. The responsum ruled that it depends on whether or not she sought to be released from the herem when he was an apostate, at which point it would have been granted automatically, or only after he returned to Judaism. In the latter case, she "had to seek release from the *herem* [from the man]." This indicates that intracommunal conflict prevention was certainly one goal of building the threat of herem into a bilateral agreement—the woman could be released from the herem during the man's phase of apostacy. However, after renouncing his apostacy, they both had to agree to her release.

In addition, swearing agreements on pain of herem could also be used to facilitate information gathering for other community members. We learn in one responsum that a known thief had sworn, on pain of excommunication, to redeem a pledged horse but had failed to do so, which was evidence of his untrustworthiness. *Mahzor Vitry* attests to debtors agreeing with creditors in writing to be placed under excommunication (nidui in this instance) in the event of defaulting on a loan. Here the threat of excommunication served to prevent and mitigate conflict rather than resolve it.

The final situation in which excommunication was used as a threat was to compel and ensure testimony. In BT Yevamot 52a it states that Rav used to strike "anyone who was under the ban for refusing to swear an oath in court for thirty days without coming to court to challenge the verdict."[44] Gideon Libson demonstrated that the main purpose of the *herem stam* (anonymous ban) in the Geonic period was "to intimidate litigants and bring out the truth."[45]

In high medieval Ashkenaz, communal leaders issued a herem stam in an attempt to prevent conflicts from escalating, or to resolve them, by prompting witness testimony in a particular case.[46] Even R. Eliezer b. Joel ha-Levi, who disparaged the frequency of using oaths in general, was not opposed to using the herem stam or compelling testimony on pain of excommunication.[47] Herem stam was pronounced in the synagogue in order to encourage witnesses to come forward so that a

---

44. Zev Farber, "Extra-Legal Punishments in Medieval Jewish Courts," in *Mishpetei Shalom—A Jubilee Volume in Honor of Rabbi Saul (Shalom) Berman* (New York: KTAV Publishing House, 2010), 191–231; Bar Belinitzky and Yakir Paz, "Bound and Banned: Aphrahaṭ and Excommunication in the Sasanian Empire," in *Jews and Syriac Christians: Intersections across the First Millennium*, eds. Aaron Michael Butts and Simcha Gross (Tübingen: Mohr Siebeck, 2020), 67–88.

45. Libson, *Jewish and Islamic Law*, 114. Libson demonstrates that the herem stam derived from interaction with contemporaneous Muslim legal treatment of oaths.

46. *Herem stam* is not the same as *herem beit din*. The latter ensured the jurisdiction of the local beit din in a particular case, and their concurrent ability to summon specific persons to testify in a relevant case. This avoided people refusing to have their cases be decided in the local beit din or gaining some legal or financial advantage by taking their case to a different one, either their home beit din, somewhere inaccessible to the other parties in the case, or somewhere they would have another advantage. For analysis and contextualization of the procedure of herem beit din as described by Samson b. Abraham of Sens, see Moshe Greenberg et al., "Herem," in *Encyclopaedia Judaica*, eds. Fred Skolnik and Michael Berenbaum, 2nd ed., vol. 9 (Detroit: Macmillan Reference USA in association with the Keter Pub. House, 2007), 16. For a description of herem beit din in takkanot Rabbeinu Tam in *Shut Maharam b. R. Barukh*, Prague, §1022. See also S. Frankel, ed., *Sefer Mishneh Torah Hu ha-Yad ha-Hazakah le-Rabenu Moshe b. R. Maimon* (Jerusalem: Shabtai Frankel, 1975), Shoftim §2 (last paragraph); Mordekhai b Hillel ha-Cohen, *Sefer Mordekhai ha-Shalem*, ed. A. Halpern (Jerusalem: Makhon Yerushalayim, 1992), Sanhedrin, chap. Zeh Borer.

47. Eliezer b. Joel ha-Levi, *Sefer Ra'aviah*, vol. 4, ed. David Deblytski (Bnei Brak: n.p., 2005), § 919, 306. See also *Shibolei ha-Leket* p.129: citing passage from *Sha'arei Shevu'ot*: "But if his neighbours should testify that he has means, he should be compelled by a thorn that does

wide range of conflicts could be resolved.⁴⁸ In one case, when a woman borrowed a silver key and then lost it, the responsum claimed that: "A *herem stam* should be pronounced in the synagogue against the persons who have the silver key and do not return it, and against those who may not return it in the future."⁴⁹ It was widely accepted and seems to have been applied equally to women as well as men, even though some rabbinic authorities ruled that married women could not individually swear oaths in the beit din.⁵⁰

Herem stam could also act as a legal mechanism for gathering information. R. Meir of Rothenburg documented the custom across Ashkenaz, in which a herem was pronounced in synagogue against anyone who had a claim to property being sold and did not report it before leaving the synagogue. Once all the claims had been examined and were found to be baseless, a document was written attesting to the process of the herem and the fact that there were no other viable claims to the property. If thereafter a claim were raised by someone who was there when the herem was pronounced, it would be null and void.⁵¹ Though not referred to as herem stam, it functioned in an almost identical way. In one instance, the threat of herem was used as a tool to uncover the location of a property that a woman had promised to the community, then reneged on her promise and hid.⁵² Herem stam functioned to resolve disputes by pressuring people to give evidence. Though it could have been used to bolster the social power of the elites, as it could only be pronounced by the leaders of the local beit din, it also relied on the social standing of the people involved and the extent to which community members felt that, if it were revealed that they knew something and did not give testimony, they might face repercussions.

As revealed in this chapter, excommunication was a legal tool for both the prevention and the resolution of conflict. It was brought to bear at challenging and often potentially precarious moments in people's lives. The threat of excommunication served to prevent conflict by adding an extra layer of pressure and compulsion to people's commitments to each other. At the same time, by overriding excommunication through

---

not draw blood [i.e. excommunication], and he should not blaspheme in public by taking an oath."

48. Finklestein, *Jewish Self Government in the Middle Ages*, 33.
49. *Shut Maharam*, Lvov, §206.
50. Mordekhai b Hillel ha-Cohen, *Sefer Mordekhai ha-Shalem*, Bava Kama, 208–9.
51. *Sefer She'elot u-Teshuvot Maharam*, Cremona, §362.
52. *Shut Maharam b. R. Barukh*, Prague, §998.

repentance, penance, and readmission to the community, rabbinic texts indicate the prioritizing of community ties over the commitment to legal norms or mechanisms of exclusion. This tension surrounding excommunication, whether threatened or enforced, was informed by the lack of a cohesive local legal system to enforce restricted contact between Jews in Ashkenaz, rendering excommunication all but unenforceable. In theory, excommunication in Ashkenaz relied on the prior consent of all parties and functioned as a tool for conflict prevention. In practice it relied on sociocultural buy-in and collective coercion for enforcement. Mapping out the nuanced operation of different sorts of excommunication in medieval Ashkenaz indicates that it was a powerful, but complex, locally specific tool for social regulation.

Further Readings

Agus, Irving A. *Rabbi Meir of Rothenburg: His Life and His Works as Sources for the Religious, Legal, and Social History of the Jews of Germany in the Thirteenth Century*. 2 vols. Jersey City, NJ: KTAV Publishing House, 1970.

Agus, Irving A. *Teshuvot Ba'alei ha-Tosafot*. New York: Yeshiva University Press, 1954.

Agus, Irving A. *Urban Civilisation in Pre-Crusade Europe: A Study of Organised Town-Life in North-Western Europe during the Tenth and Eleventh Centuries Based on Responsa Literature*. 2 vols. New York: Yeshiva University Press, 1965.

Assis, Yom Tov. *The Golden Age of Aragonese Jewry: Community and Society 1213–1327*. London: Littman Library of Jewish Civilization, 1997.

Barzen, Rainer. *Taqqanot Qehillot Šum. Die Rechtssatzungen der Jüdischen Gemeinden von Mainz, Worms und Speyer im hohen und späten Mittelalter*. Wiesbaden: Harrassowitz Verlag, 2019.

Belinitzky, Bar, and Yakir Paz. "Bound and Banned: Aphrahaṭ and Excommunication in the Sasanian Empire." In *Jews and Syriac Christians: Intersections across the First Millennium*, edited by Aaron Michael Butts and Simcha Gross, 67–88. Tübingen: Mohr Siebeck, 2020.

Ben-Shalom, Ram. "The Ban Placed by the Community of Barcelona on the Study of Philosophy and Allegorical Preaching—A New Study." *Revue des études juives* 159 (2002): 387–404.

Cluse, Christoph. "Jewish Community and Civic Commune in the High Middle Ages." In *Strangers and Poor People: Changing Patterns of Inclusion and Exclusion in Europe and the Mediterranean World from Classical Antiquity to the Present Day*, edited by A. Gestrich, L. Raphael, and H. Uerlings, 165–192. Frankfurt: Peter Lang, 2010.

Emanuel, Simcha. "Conflagrations and Crimes in the Late Middle Ages: Some Attestations from Halakhic Literature." In *Medieval Ashkenaz: Papers in Honour of Alfred Haverkamp Presented at the 17th World Congress of Jewish Studies,* Jerusalem 2017, edited by Christoph Cluse and Jörg Müller, 276–84. Wiesbaden: Harrassowitz Verlag, 2021.

Farber, Zev. "Extra-Legal Punishments in Medieval Jewish Courts." In *Mishpetei Shalom—A Jubilee Volume in Honor of Rabbi Saul (Shalom) Berman*, 191–231. New York: Ktav Publishing House, 2010.

Finkelstein, Louis. *Jewish Self Government in the Middle Ages*. New York: Jewish Theological Seminary, 1924.

Kanarfogel, Ephraim. "The Adjudication of Fines in Ashkenaz during the Medieval and Early Modern Periods and the Preservation of Communal Decorum." *Dine Israel* 32 (2018): 159–87.

Libson, Gideon. "The Gezerta in the Gaonic and Early Medieval Period." *Shenaton ha-Mishpat ha-Ivri: Annual of the Institute for Research in Jewish Law* 5 (1978): 147–52.

Libson, Gideon. *Jewish and Islamic Law: A Comparative Study of Custom during the Geonic Period*. Harvard Series in Islamic Law. Cambridge, MA: Harvard University Press, 2003.

Little, Lester K. *Benedictine Maledictions: Liturgical Cursing in Romanesque France*. Ithaca, NY: Cornell University Press, 1996.

Rabinowitz, Louis. *The Herem Hayyishub: A Contribution to the Medieval Economic History of the Jews*. London: E. Goldston, 1945.

Reiner, Avraham. "Rabbenu Tam's Ordinance for the Return of the Dowry: Between Talmudic Exegesis and an Ordinance That Contradicts the Talmud." *Dine Israel* 33 (2019): 71–98.

Shoham-Steiner, Ephraim. *Jews and Crime in Medieval Europe*. Detroit: Wayne State University Press, 2020.

Stern, Gregg. *Philosophy and Rabbinic Culture: Jewish Interpretation and Controversy in Medieval Languedoc*. New York: Routledge, 2009.

Woolf, Jeffrey. *The Fabric of Religious Life in Medieval Ashkenaz (1000–1300): Creating Sacred Communities*. Leiden: Brill, 2015.

CHAPTER 2

Jewish Orphanhood and Orphans in Medieval Ashkenaz

Cultural Conceptions and Everyday Life

Andreas Lehnertz and Eyal Levinson

Jacob ben Moses Moellin (d. 1427), an early fifteenth-century Ashkenazic rabbi, proclaimed that "there is no greater commandment than to raise an orphan . . . because they are abandoned and very miserable [*me'od shfelim*]."[1] This perception of orphans as an acutely disadvantaged group, particularly deserving of special attention, protection, and care, is a well-established theme in Western societies among both Christians and Jews. However, as we argue in this chapter, reality was more complex than the statement quoted above suggests.

This chapter was written under the auspices of the Beyond the Elite: Jewish Daily Life in Medieval Europe Project, PI Elisheva Baumgarten, from the European Research Council (ERC) under the European Union's Horizon 2020 research and innovation program, grant agreement No. 681507, and prepared for publication with funding from the Israel Science Foundation Grant 2850/22, Contending with Crises: The Jews of 14th Century Europe, PI Elisheva Baumgarten. Andreas Lehnertz also had a postdoc fellowship in the Martin Buber Society of Fellows in the Humanities and Social Sciences. We thank Birgit Wiedl, Gerd Mentgen, Markus Wenninger, Elisheva Baumgarten, Hannah Teddy Schachter, Ido Noy, and the two anonymous reviewers for their comments.

1. Yitzhak Satz, ed., *She'elot u-Teshuvot Maharil* (Jerusalem: Makhon Yerushalaym, 1980), 32, § 37. According to canon law, Christians also viewed orphans as being among the *miserabiles personae*; see Richard H. Helmholz, "Children's Rights and the Canon Law: Law and Practice in Later Medieval England," *Jurist: Studies in Church Law and Ministry* 67 (2007): 39–57, at 41.

CHAPTER 2

Like other social phenomena, the definition of orphanhood and what it means to be an orphan varies over time and between cultures, reflective of dominant ideologies and socioeconomic realities. Answers to questions such as: Who is considered an orphan, who should care for them, how they should be treated, and up to what age, is connected, among other factors, to the organization of the family (kinship, nuclear, matrilocal, single parent, and extended family), existing communal institutions (e.g., orphanages or other types of institutions), and how members of the group relate to their dead.

In this chapter we examine orphanhood among the medieval Jewish communities of the Holy Roman Empire and northern France, between the twelfth to the early sixteenth centuries. We focus on both girls and boys, who lost either one parent or both and needed guardians to manage their affairs. This chapter seeks to shed light on questions such as: What do the sources reveal regarding the daily lives of Jewish orphans? Given that Jewish orphanages were not established until the seventeenth century, it is clear that most Jewish orphans were cared for by their families, relatives, or communities. What was their status in these adoptive families? Were they treated the same as the biological or stepchildren? Were they taken advantage of by adults and foster parents? Did orphanhood lead to sibling rivalries and conflicts with parents and stepparents? And what can we learn from these documents about an orphan's personal agency?

We argue that the repeated cultural emphasis on the religious merits gained by raising orphans and underlining their vulnerability indicate that attempts by relatives and other community members to benefit from their misfortune was not a negligible social phenomenon among Ashkenazic Jews. So problematic was the treatment of orphans that some, particularly the more affluent members of the communities, attempted to preemptively forestall any future difficulties by writing halakhically binding wills before their death or by publicly expressing their wishes in the presence of at least two male witnesses. But even such measures did not always prevent disruptive familial disputes following the death of the head of a household, as indicated by the final case study presented in this chapter.

Households during the High and Late Middle Ages were complex sociological constructs headed by a paterfamilias that often included biological, step-, and adopted children.[2] It is therefore likely that the

---

2. For the differences between a family and a household, see Tovah Bender, "The Family and the Household," in *A Cultural History of the Home in the Medieval Ages*, ed. Katherine L.

vast majority of Jewish orphans during this period were under the authority of such a patriarchal figure, whether as adopted children of the family, apprentices, or servants. Examples of this type of extended family are found, among other sources, in privileges of settlement from German cities between the thirteenth and fifteenth centuries. Take, for example, the story of the Jewish paterfamilias Mathis and his family, who came to the city of Landau in 1445:

> By the grace of God, I Reinhard [von Helmstatt], Bishop of Speyer, declare publicly with this record that Mathis the Jew reached an agreement with us that he together with his wife, three children, a maid, and a little orphan, and he may also have another Jew with him—all together eight persons in this household, who eat his bread ... they can live and settle in our city for the next two years.[3]

Such family constellations created by relatively high mortality rates and the dangers of the period—wars, expulsions, plagues, and the like—were by no means rare, among either Jews or Christians.

Orphans who lost their fathers were not only bereft of the person charged with protecting and sustaining them, providing for their education, and ensuring they made a good marriage, but also of the male head of their household, who represented them in legal matters. In addition to family rupture, this loss also caused legal, social, and economic problems that medieval societies dealt with in different ways. In this sense, orphans occupied the same social category as widows. The situation was not entirely analogous, however, given that for widows the death of their husbands also represented an opportunity to exert their authority over their own households or even over the workshops of their deceased husbands, run their financial affairs as they wished, and decide to whom to bequeath their goods, assets, and possessions. Underage orphans, by way of contrast, were always placed under the

---

French (London: Bloomsbury, 2021), 31–48 (with further bibliography). See also Eyal Levinson, "The Family," in *Encyclopedia of Jewish-Christian Relations*, ed. Walter Homolka, Rainer Kampling, Amy-Jill Levine, Christoph Markschies, Peter Schäfer, and Martin Thurner (Berlin: De Gruyter, 2023), https://doi.org/10.1515/ejcro.27412038.

3. Karlsruhe, Generallandesarchiv, Best. 67, no. 291, fol. 216v. See Franz-Josef Ziwes, *Studien zur Geschichte der Juden im mittleren Rheingebiet während des hohen und späten Mittelalters.* Forschungen zur Geschichte der Juden, A 1 (Hanover Hahnsche Buchhandlung, 1995), 311. It is undetermined if the fact that the "little orphan" is mentioned after the maid had a hierarchical significance indicating that the maid had a better social position than the orphan in this household.

supervision of guardians and were largely dependent on their goodwill.[4] Furthermore, while orphaned boys could eventually expect to gain legal autonomy once they came of age, orphaned girls were often married off by their guardians as soon as possible and were always dependent on an adult male to represent them in legal matters. Our chapter thus reveals different attitudes toward orphaned boys and girls and demonstrates the gender biases at work in the pursuit of justice.

Orphanhood in Medieval Europe

Orphanhood was a widespread social phenomenon in the cities of medieval Europe. Orphans were commonly cared for by the remaining parent or by other family members.[5] When this was not an option, guardians were appointed by the local urban administration. Among Christians, cultural norms during this period dictated that Christian orphans were under the protection of the church, the king, the nobles, and the local municipalities. Every respectable knight was expected to treat orphans with empathy and offer them their protection. However, studies indicate that at times historical reality was far removed from these cultural ideals, and orphans were also among the most oppressed and wretched groups in medieval society.[6] Since orphanages did not yet exist, the fate of these children was in the hands of relatives, communal dignitaries, Church authorities and institutions, and even strangers.[7]

---

4. For Jewish widows, see Etelle Kalaora, "Jewish Widows' Homes in Ashkenaz in the 12th and 13th Centuries," *JSQ* 28, no. 3 (2021): 315–30.

5. Barbara Hanawalt, *Growing up in Medieval London: The Experience of Childhood in History* (Oxford: Oxford University Press, 1993), 89. See also Susan Scott, ed. *Orphans, Widows, and Guardians in Medieval and Early Modern Bristol: The Register of Recognizances, 1333–1594*, vol. 73 (Bristol Record Society, 2020). In Bristol and London, for example, between 1300 and 1424 more than nine hundred Christian boys and girls are listed as orphans—and these are only the ones who were economically well-off, because they inherited a significant amount of money and/or property. See Elaine Clark, "City Orphans and Custody Laws in Medieval London," *American Journal of Legal History* 34 (1990): 168–87, https://doi.org/10.2307/845520. See also Miriam Müller, *Childhood, Orphans, and Underage Heirs in Medieval Rural England: Growing up in the Village* (Cham, Switzerland: Palgrave Macmillan, 2019). As for Christian children, the *Saxon Mirror* states that all had a guardian to represent them in legal cases; see Maria Dobozy, ed. and trans., *The Saxon Mirror: A Sachsenspiegel of the Fourteenth Century*, Book I (Philadelphia: University of Pennsylvania Press, 1999), 11, 23, 32.

6. Shulamit Shahar, *Childhood in the Middle Ages* (New York: Routledge, 1992).

7. It was only in the late fifteenth century that the first Christian orphanage was opened on the continent, in Strasbourg (1482), in Lübeck (1546), and then in Augsburg (1572). In London, Christ's Hospital was established in 1552 to care for the fatherless children of the freemen of London. Kazmierczak Manzione, *Christ's Hospital of London*. The first Jewish boy's orphanage, *Avi Yetomin*, was opened in Amsterdam in 1648 by the local Portuguese

For their part, orphans were obligated to pray for their parents, and it was a well-known phenomenon during this period that the deceased mothers and fathers appeared to their children in dreams or visions asking for their assistance in the afterworld.[8]

Our knowledge of Jewish orphanhood during the Middle Ages is still very limited, although this topic provides valuable information on the attitudes of the communities toward their less fortunate members and on family life, and especially on how families contended with crises. One of the few studies shedding some light on this topic is Rebecca Lynn Winer's exploration of widowed mothers in thirteenth-century Perpignan.[9] Winer convincingly demonstrates that widowed Jewish mothers frequently served as guardians for their children, supported by a broader network of guardians, often consisting of wealthy and respected community members who took on the responsibility of overseeing the financial affairs and guarding the legal rights of orphaned children. Similar to what was common among the Christian population, the Jewish communities took responsibility for finding guardians for orphans or appointing one for them by order of the (Jewish) court. Winer concluded that "the care of fatherless children was both a familial and a communal duty, but family members were more important in fulfilling this responsibility than outsiders."[10] Like their Christian counterparts, Jewish orphans in Ashkenaz were expected to pray for their deceased parents, reciting a special prayer for the dead called the Mourner's Kaddish.[11] In addition, among Spanish Jewry during the

---

(Sephardic) Jewish community. See no ed., *Sha'are Orah ve-Avi Yetomim: Laws of the Spanish and Portuguese Jews' Orphan Society for Educating, Maintaining, Clothing, and Apprenticing Orphan Children* (London: Wertheimer, Lea and Co., 1885). See also Gérard Nahon, "The Portuguese Jewish Community of Amsterdam as Reflected in the Memoirs of Abraham Haim Lopez Arias, 1752," *Dutch Jews as Perceived by Themselves and by Others*, ed. Chaya Brasz and Yosef Kaplan (Leiden: Brill, 2001), 69-78; Tali M. Berner, *In Their Own Way: Children and Childhood in Early Modern Ashkenaz* (Jerusalem: The Zalman Shazar Center, 2018), 196-201. The Jewish orphanage in Fürth, established in 1763, was the first of its kind in Germany. See "Fuerth," *Jewish Encyclopedia*, https://www.jewishvirtuallibrary.org/fuerth (Hebrew).

8. Jean-Claude Schmitt, "Les rêves de Guibert de Nogent," in *Le corps, les rites, les rêves, le temps. Essais d'anthropologie médievale*, ed. Jean-Claude Schmitt Bibliothèque des histoires (Paris: Gallimard, 2001), 263-94.

9. Rebecca Lynn Winer, "Family, Community, and Motherhood: Caring for Fatherless Children in the Jewish Community of Thirteenth-Century Perpignan," *Jewish History* 16, no. 1 (2002): 15-48, https://www.jstor.org/stable/i20101456.

10. Winer, "Family," 23.

11. The Mourner's Kaddish is an Aramaic prayer said at funerals by orphans and recited during every traditional prayer service, when a *minyan* (a quorum of ten male attendees) is present. See David Shyovitz, "'You Have Saved Me from the Judgement of Gehennah': The

thirteenth century, the poor and the orphaned were the preferred recipients of communal charitable funds.[12]

There are numerous mentions of Jewish orphans in medieval Hebrew, Latin, and vernacular sources from the medieval Holy Roman Empire and northern France, revolving predominantly around issues of inheritance and the responsibilities of the guardians. The death of a parent, especially the father, was a time of family crisis and could lead to significant family conflicts. Thus, it comes as no surprise that the documents provide information on sibling rivalry, disputes between orphans and their grandparents, and orphans challenging their mothers in court for their share of their fathers' inheritance.[13] Underage orphans with assets were naturally the most likely to be subject to legal regulations and were in the most danger of being exploited by greedy relatives or guardians. Other issues also come to the fore, such as the relationships between orphans and stepparents, appreciation for guardians who take on themselves the task of caring for orphans, and issues relating to orphans who converted to Christianity. We should bear in mind that due to the nature of these sources they tend to reveal more about tensions and disputes than about routine interactions or the presumably numerous orphans treated compassionately by their relatives, guardians, and communities.

In addition, medieval Hebrew literature rarely discusses the formative years of orphans nor offers an opportunity for their voices to be heard, but rather presents scattered pieces of information that must be pieced together to present a coherent historical picture of orphanhood. Hence, our access to what orphans thought or felt is severely limited.

Origins of the Mourner's Kaddish in Medieval Ashkenaz," *AJS Review* 39, no. 1 (2015): 49–73, https://doi.org/10.1017/S0364009414000646. Recently, Javier Castaño presented cases of orphans from the Portuguese Jewish community in Miranda do Douro in 1490, concluding that the topic has "not yet been properly studied for this time and region." Javier Castaño, "The Orphan's Portion and the Jews of Miranda do Douro in 1490," in *Portuguese Jews, New Christians, and "New Jews": A Tribute to Roberto Bachmann*, ed. Claude B. Stucynski and Bruno Feitler (Leiden: Brill, 2018), 102–21, at 113.

12. Judah Galinsky, "Jewish Charitable Bequests and the Hekdesh Trust in Thirteenth-Century Spain," *Journal of Interdisciplinary History* 35, no. 3 (2005): 423–40, https://doi.org/10.1111/hic3.12207.

13. This is paralleled to some degree in the sources on Christian orphans. See Barbara Megson, "Life Expectations of the Widows and Orphans of Freemen in London 1375-1399," *Local Population Studies* 57 (1996): 18–29. Clark, "City Orphans; Maryanne Kowaleski, "The History of Urban Families in Medieval England," *Journal of Medieval History* 14 (1998): 47–63, esp. 53.

The Yiddish letter presented at the close of this chapter is quite unique in providing a rare opportunity for such a voice to be heard.

Studies of early modern Jewish orphans reveal that the communal treatment of orphans, the institution of guardianship, the management of orphans' assets, and the religious and social merits gained by those who raised orphans were mainly social/cultural constructs that originated in the Middle Ages or even in Late Antiquity.[14] For example, one study shows that even in eighteenth-century Germany, orphaned Jewish girls from poor families were ensured of being able to marry by being provided with a dowry in exchange for working as domestic servants: "The communities proposed to establish a period of service, often within the households of distinguished members of the community, at the end of which time (usually three years), the girl would receive a sum sufficient for a modest dowry."[15] Arranging marriages for orphaned girls was also a major communal concern for medieval Ashkenazic Jews, although it seems that early modern communities played a more significant role in these cases than their medieval predecessors: for example, by regulating the period of service an orphaned girl served in her new household, while raising the sum for her dowry.[16]

For the purposes of this chapter, we examined a variety of sources, including halakhic discussions and responsa (legal rabbinic) literature, as well as books of customs, moral compendiums, exempla, vernacular administrative sources, and an ego-document in Yiddish that was probably written in 1518 by a male orphan after he reached adulthood. It was this wide-ranging methodological approach that enabled us to develop a broad cultural understanding of orphanhood in medieval Ashkenaz.

---

14. Berner, *In Their Own Way*, 196–201.

15. Two additional studies deserve our attention, both of which are beyond the scope of our timeframe but enhance our understanding of Jewish orphans in Germany in premodern times: Elisheva Carlebach's examination of Jewish domestic servants in eighteenth-century Altona, Hamburg, and Wandsbek; and Tali Berner's study of children and childhood in early modern Ashkenaz. Elisheva Carlebach, "Fallen Women and Fatherless Children: Jewish Domestic Servants in Eighteenth-Century Altona," *Jewish History* 24, no. 3-4 (2010): 295-308, http://www.jstor.org/stable/40864855. Berner, *In Their Own Way*, 196–201. Also, see Debra Kaplan, *The Patrons and Their Poor: Jewish Community and Public Charity in Early Modern Germany*, Jewish Culture and Contexts (Philadelphia: University of Pennsylvania Press, 2020).

16. Surprisingly, this matter is not mentioned anywhere in the *Takkanot Shum*, the ordinances issued by medieval Rhineland Jewry. For the new edition, see Rainer J. Barzen, *Taqqanot Qehillot Šum: Die Rechtssatzungen der jüdischen Gemeinden Mainz, Worms und Speyer im hohen und späten Mittelalter*, Monumenta Germaniae Historica. Hebräische Texte aus dem mittelalterlichen Deutschland, 2,2 (Wiesbaden: Harrassowitz Verlag, 2019).

Raising Jewish Orphans as an Act of Piety

The vulnerability of orphans is repeatedly emphasized in medieval sources, which often quote or paraphrase the Hebrew Bible as the authoritative text warning against their mistreatment, usually together with admonitions against the exploitation of widows.[17] However, apart from these exhortations to treat orphans with compassion, the Bible is silent when it comes to aspects regarding their lives and welfare, including issues of guardianship, the management of their assets, and securing their marriages. Such concerns were addressed by the rabbinic scholars of Late Antiquity and elaborated on by medieval rabbis, who often sought to negotiate between Jewish law (*halakhah*) and customs (*minhagim*), and local customary laws.[18]

Rabbis in Late Antiquity highlighted the religious merit gained by those who take in orphans, writing, "Anyone who raises an orphan boy or girl in his house, the verse ascribes him credit as if he gave birth to him."[19] Centuries later, in thirteenth-century Germany, R. Meir ben Barukh of Rothenburg (d. 1293), reiterated this teaching and added: "Because one who raises an orphan, the orphan is called 'his son,' so also the orphan deserves to call the one who raises him 'my father' and his wife 'my mother.'"[20] We cannot determine from these words if there were orphans who actually called their adopted parents "mother" or "father." However, we do know from the opening of this responsum that there were stepparents who referred to their adopted orphans as "my son" or "my daughter." In this specific case, a man who married a widow referred to her son (from a previous marriage) in a legal deed as "our son," and Meir ruled that this did not invalidate the deed. We also learn from this short query that some medieval Ashkenazic rabbis thought, like their Talmudic predecessors, that raising adopted orphans bestowed equal religious merits as raising biological children.

The virtue associated with raising orphans and ensuring their marriages is further elaborated in the fourteenth century by the author of *Sefer ha-Aggudah*, R. Alexander Süslin of Frankfurt: " [As for the quote of BT Ket. 50a] 'And his righteousness stands forever'—this refers to

---

17. See, for example, Ex. 22:21; Deut. 10:18; Jos. 1:17; Jer. 7:6; Ez. 22:7; Ps. 68:6.
18. See among other places, Mish. Git. 4:3, 5:2, 5:4, Pes. 8:1, Ket. 11:1, Yev. 13:7–9; BT Ket. 67b, Pes. 31a, Meg. 13a, Yev. 110a, Ket. 67a. See also Yaakov K. Reinitz, "Orphans Boarding with the Householder." *Bar-Ilan Studies* 1 (1980): 219–50.
19. BT Meg. 13a, Trans. *Sefaria*. See also BT San. 19b.
20. Meir ben Barukh of Rothenburg, *She'elot u-Teshuvot* (Lvov, 1860), 242, §270.

one who raises an orphan boy or an orphan girl and marries them off."²¹ Praise for those who took it on themselves to raise orphans is also apparent in a story, told by Shalom of Neustadt (d. 1413), of a man named Moshel "who acted very piously."²² Among Moshel's virtues, according to the rabbi, was the fact that he raised in his house two orphaned brothers from Krems an der Donau in Austria.

The emphasis on the merit gained by raising orphans is also evident in more popular literature, such as the thirteenth-century *Sefer ha-Ma'asim*, a compilation of sixty-nine moral tales, probably originating from northern France. One tale, entitled *The Three Treasures*, tells the story of a pious man:

> Once there was a *hasid* [a pious man] who used to give charity and perform numerous favors and benevolent acts for Torah students and ordinary people. . . . And he had three treasures: one of gold coins, one of silver, and one of pennies. When he came to his students, he would give them of the gold coins; to orphans and widows, he would give the silver coins; and he would support orphans who did not study with the pennies. And how would he support them? He would give five gold coins to whomever had five souls in his home. And that was his practice every day.²³

Evidently, widows and orphans were not on the top of the author's list of charitable donations, but rather "Torah students," those few young men affiliated with the learned hegemony, as was the author himself. Interestingly, although there is no mention of giving charity to the poor and needy, orphans are mentioned twice in this list, once together with widows (possibly their mothers), as the recipients of the silver coins, and once as those who do not study Torah. In this case it seems clear that the author is referring only to male orphans, as only males could study Torah. This then raises the question, however, of whether the second category, "orphans and widows," refers to both male and female children. What is the difference between the orphans who received the silver coins and those who received the pennies? Are we to assume that

---

21. Eleazar Brizel, ed., *Sefer ha-Agudah le-Seder Nashim* (Jerusalem, 1979), 103, § 50.
22. Shlomo Spitzer, ed., *Hilkhot u-Minhagei Rabeinu Shalom Me-Neustadt* (Jerusalem: Makhon Yerushalayim, 1997), 53, § 148. See also Martha Keil, "Ein Zentrum der Frömmigkeit und Gelehrsamkeit—die jüdische Gemeinde der Neustadt im Mittelalter," *Unser Neustadt. Blätter des Wiener Neustädter Denkmalschutzvereins* 1/2 (2020): 2–10, at 8.
23. Rella Kushelevsky, ed., *Tales in Context: Sefer ha-Ma'asim in Medieval Northern France* (Detroit: Wayne State University Press, 2024), 110 (English) and 111 (Hebrew).

the former also studied Torah on some level while the latter did not study at all? The letter presented later on in this chapter, written by the Jewish orphan Götz from Regensburg, sheds some light on this matter. In any case, despite the bias toward Torah students, the appearance of orphans in two out of the three categories is indicative of the cultural attention they received as a special social group in need of community support.

Although the raising of orphans was undoubtedly touted as a virtuous deed that received high praise,[24] one wonders if perhaps the reason for this repeated emphasis was that in fact the reality faced by many orphans was far different, as noted by one thirteenth-century Ashkenazic rabbi who acknowledged that orphans were "commonly mistreated."[25] This picture is further complicated by discussions in the sources that focus on the opposite situation—on those guardians who, at least according to some leading rabbis, were too compassionate in their treatment of orphans, an attitude that continued into the early modern era.[26]

"How Could I Hit an Orphan?"

The importance of raising orphans and treating them compassionately, and the religious merit gained by such acts, is expressed in *Sefer Hasidim*, an early thirteenth-century compilation of moral advice written primarily by Judah son of Samuel the Hasid (d. 1217):

> A righteous man was very sick, and when he cried, they asked him: "Why do you cry? Is it for your little children? But your brothers would replace you." He replied: "My brothers would take care of their needs in this world. I cry because if I lived, I would reproach and chasten them [the children] to bring them to the world to come, to guide them in the right path." The guardian, appointed to care for his children, told him: "I would replace you." The man replied: "You would only care when they would harm you and would steal from you. Then you would hit them so they would refrain from doing it again. Likewise, [as you would replace me as

---

24. Yet another deed was that of hospitality. See Albert Kohn, chapter 6 in the present volume.
25. *Sefer Mitzvot Gadol. The Complete Edition*, vol. 1 (Jerusalem: Makhon Yerushalayim, 2003), 46, § 8.
26. See Berner, *In Their Own Way*, 188.

their educator] you should replace God and educate them to fulfill the commandments, and if they sin against God, you should chasten them, and you should not say: 'How could I hit an orphan?' And if they would say: 'If our father would have been alive, he would pity us and would not hit us.' You should then reply to them: 'Your father would have hit you even harder and this is what he ordered me to do' . . . this is what you should do to my children, give them food and chasten them and make them fear you when they sin, and give them your love when they abide by the will of God, as you instruct them."[27]

R. Judah's main concern in this passage is the religious education of orphans and ensuring that compassionate feelings will not stand in the way of proper religious education. Although, to modern readers, a guardian who acts according to Judah's instructions would likely not be considered as acting compassionately, we should bear in mind that during the Middle Ages, Jews and Christians alike encouraged stern disciplining of children, particularly sons, including corporal punishment and confinement, albeit refraining from excessive cruelty. They often justified their actions by quoting the known biblical saying: "He who spares the rod hates his son, but he who loves him disciplines him early" (Proverbs 13:24).[28] In the eleventh century, Rashi (Solomon ben Isaac of Troyes; ca. 1040-1105) taught that rebuking young children should be done gently with pleasant words, and only as they grow older (twelve years and above) should they be beaten with a belt and prevented from having food.[29] Still, it would appear that Judah's encouragement to hit delinquent orphans who behaved contrary to his pietistic worldview does seem to contradict a biblical warning to refrain from hitting orphans (Job 31:21-23). Thus, in another exemplum in *Sefer Hasidim*, Judah explains why his insistence on beating misbehaving orphans does not in fact contradict the biblical prohibition:

> He who raises orphans and sees that they misbehave and says: "They are orphans. How could I hit them?" His [religious] merit [gained by raising them] is lost. And that which is written [in the book of Job 31:21-23]—"If I raised my hand against an

---

27. *Sefer Hasidim* (Parma), ed. Jacob Wistenetski (Frankfurt: Mekize Nirdamim, 1924), § 302.
28. Eyal Levinson, "Situated Fathering in Medieval Ashkenaz," *JSQ* 28 (2021): 278-96.
29. Rashi, Ketubbot 50a, s.v. "megalgel 'im bno".

orphan"—this refers to one who hit them for no reason, but to scourge them as one does to his own son, it is a commandment to hit them, so they would not go astray.[30]

Once again, we see that raising orphans was considered a religious virtue, and that educating them to behave correctly by hitting them was understood to be a necessity, as it was for biological children who misbehaved.[31]

Judah's harsh attitude toward delinquent orphans and his justification for such acts is echoed in the writings of the thirteenth-century rabbi, Moses ben Jacob of Coucy. Moses also argued that corporal punishment is permissible for the right reasons, and only forbidden if resulting from selfish motivations. However, unlike R. Judah, R. Moses adopted the Maimonidean approach (*Mishneh Torah, De'ot* 6:10), arguing that orphans deserve more compassion than any others:

> A person should not mistreat an orphan and a widow because their soul is very lowly, and their spirit humble. And even though they may be wealthy . . . we are still warned against mistreating them . . . because they are helpless and commonly mistreated. . . . This is true if he mistreated them out of a selfish motive, but if he caused them suffering to correct their ways, then it is permitted, and yet one should handle them more compassionately than any other person. And this is true for anyone who lost his father or lost his mother, and he is considered an orphan until he grows up and does not need an adult to care for him, when he is able to conduct his own affairs like all grownups.[32]

Moses stresses here that the social status of orphans should not influence the way they are treated, since every orphan deserves to be treated compassionately. The author of the anonymous fourteenth-century ethical treatise *Orhot Tzadikim* from Ashkenaz agrees with Moses, writing that "it is a commandment to hit him [the orphan] to ensure he follows the correct path. And yet, one is obliged to handle an orphan with mercy more than any other person, but he must not let him [the orphan] behave according to his own whims."[33]

---

30. Judah Wistinetzki and Jacob Freiman, ed., *Sefer Hasidim* (Frankfurt: Wahrmann, 1924), § 1967.
31. See for example Wistinetzki and Freiman, ed., *Sefer Hasidim*, § 1773.
32. *Sefer Mitzvot Gadol*, 46, § 8.
33. *Orhot Tzadikim*, 45–46.

Taking advantage of vulnerable orphans was clearly a cultural phenomenon that manifested itself in various ways. Most of the cases discussed in the sources involve attempts to profit from their inheritance. One example, from twelfth-century Germany, concerns a man who was accused of trying to take over a house belonging to two underage orphans. After being a tenant for several years in the house, the lodger refused to pay rent and claimed that the house belonged to his wife. The case was brought before a rabbinical court (*beit din*) by the guardian of one of the orphans, who claimed that the tenant had already deceived the other orphan and convinced him to sell his half of the house to him.[34] It is impossible to determine from this source how old the orphan was when the guardian filed the complaint against the lodger, and whether the orphan demonstrated any personal agency. Perhaps the guardian initiated the claim on behalf of the orphan, with or without the orphan's knowledge. However, the following case study is a good example of an orphan demonstrating a strong personal agency, someone who expresses her desires and goals, who makes plans and carries them out, engages with the social structure, and acts intentionally to improve her situation.

A Sense of Strong Personal Agency

Consider the following story about a young woman and her sister who lost both parents. This case, involving four Jewish German communities—Würzburg, Speyer, Worms, and Mainz—took place sometime during the first half of the thirteenth century. It continued for several years and involved two orphaned sisters, who had lost both parents and were being raised by the local rabbi, Barukh ben Samuel.[35] One sister was already a widow when the dispute broke out, while the other was not yet married, and is referred to in the source as "the virgin" (*ha-betulah*). Although it is probably safe to assume that the widowed orphan was the older sister, she could still have been only in her late teens or early twenties, since the marriageable age in these communities was quite young (especially for women) and there is no mention of her

---

34. Eliezer ben Nathan, *Sefer Ra'avan*, Ehrenreich edition (Simleul, 1927), 297.
35. Simcha Emanuel, "Rabbi Baruch of Mainz," *Publications of the Israel Academy of Sciences and Humanities, Issues in Talmudic Research, Conference, 2 December 1996*, Jerusalem 2001, 125–63.

being a mother.[36] The terse source reveals little information about the two sisters, their family, or their circumstances. We do not know, for instance, what caused the death of the parents, how old the sisters were when they became orphans, or how long they were under the guardianship of R. Barukh. It is also unclear why the rabbi decided to raise them or what the relationship was between him and the orphans. But as the story unfolds, we realize that Rabbi Barukh assisted them financially and pursued legal avenues to help them, seeking the opinion of another legal authority, R. David ben She'altiel, regarding this matter.[37] What follows is the question sent by R. David to his colleague on behalf of R. Barukh:

> Here, among us, there is a widow who is an orphan from both father and mother, and I accepted her into my home. And she had in her possession one mark [*zakuk*] and borrowed from me three marks. Moreover, she sent a messenger to her relatives and to other generous people, and she eventually collected 30 marks and gave them to her orphaned and virgin sister and married her off in Würzburg. When she brought the virgin [to Würzburg], she [the virgin] was sick, and after the marriage her situation deteriorated. The bridegroom said that the marriage was a mistake [*mekah ta'ut*, that is a mistaken bargain], and she left his house and was brought here. The poor one took care of her sick sister and spent a lot of money on medicines and then on her [sister's] burial, because she died within two years from her marriage. The widow went to Würzburg to receive her sister's dowry from the hands of her husband, and they did not want to give her anything . . . and they sent from Würzburg [a message] to us in Mainz and to the Speyer community and to the Worms community and we were puzzled about this bad conduct. The Worms community did not reply because the man is related to some of them. The Speyer community, however, ordered him to return half of what the widow gave him [her sister's dowry].[38]

---

36. On the age for marriage, see Jacob Katz, "Marriage and Sexual Life among the Jews at the Close of the Middle Ages," *Zion* 10 (1945): 21–54 (Hebrew); Elisheva Baumgarten, "The Family," *Cambridge History of Judaism*, vol. 6, ed. Robert Chazan (Cambridge: Cambridge University Press, 2018), 440–62.

37. The signatures of both David ben She'altiel and Barukh ben Samuel appear on the ordinances of the Rhineland *ShUM* communities of 1220. Barzen, *Taqqanot Qehillot Šum*, 163.

38. Meir ha-Kohen of Rothenburg, *Teshuvot Maimoniyot*, Tractate Nashim, § 35. This can also be found in: Budapest, Library of the Hungarian Academy of Sciences, Mishne Torah, Northern France, 1296, Ms. A77, VI, fol. 150r.

This legal query reveals a young woman with a strong sense of personal agency, who struggled to raise a sufficient dowry to marry off her sister. A woman who cared for her younger sister, spent what she could to purchase medicine for her when she grew ill, and later, when her sister died less than two years after her marriage, this orphaned widow covered her funeral expenses. Moreover, following the death of her sister, the widow sued her late sister's husband in a Jewish court hoping to receive what belonged to her according to local Jewish ordinances, which maintained that "a man and woman who got married and one of them died within two years, half of the dowry should be returned to the inheritors of the dead person," something that our source acknowledges was well-established by the mid-thirteenth century.[39]

While the commitment of the older sister toward her younger sibling in this source was exemplary, other cases indicate that a less positive relationship was also possible. There is ample documentation of inheritance disputes, made worse by the demands of local lords claiming part or all of the inheritance of "their" Jews, as well as quarrels between orphans and their new stepparents and stepsiblings, driving some widows and widowers to question whether it was worth remarrying at all.[40] A fifteenth-century Hebrew legal document deals with this dilemma:

> A question: Reuben already fulfilled the commandment to be fruitful and multiply and became a widower. Now he wants to marry another woman, but he is afraid that a quarrel would erupt between his new wife and his children [from the former marriage]. Therefore, he decided to marry a woman who is known to everyone as a woman who does not tend to fight. However, she cannot beget children. If he would not find this type of a woman, he would prefer not to marry at all.[41]

Responding to this question, the Austrian rabbi Israel Isserlein (d. 1460), maintained the pronatalist attitude characteristic of Jewish law, but nevertheless permitted the man to marry the infertile and amiable woman. Avoiding quarrels and disputes between the stepmother and the orphaned children, argued Isserlein, takes precedence over the

---

39. Meir of Rothenburg, *Sefer Shut Maharam b. R. Barukh* (Prague, 1608), § 934. On this ordinance see Barzen, *Taqqanot Qehillot Šum*, 239–47.

40. See, for example, Andreas Lehnertz, "Margarete, Reynette and Meide: Three Jewish Women from Koblenz in the 14th Century," *JSQ* 28 (2021): 388–405, DOI 10.1628/jsq-2021-0022. However, such lords would make similar claims, known as *mortuarium*, on their Christian subjects as well.

41. Samuel Avitan, ed., *Trumat ha-Deshen* (Jerusalem, 1991), § 263.

rabbinic commandment to be fruitful and multiply, particularly in this instance.

Disputes over inheritance occurred not only between orphans and their stepparents, but also between orphaned siblings, and between orphans and the remaining parent. An early example of one such dispute between biological brothers appears in *Sefer ha-Dinim* by R. Judah ha-Cohen of Mainz, who was active during the first half of the eleventh century. In this case, a man who fathered several children died after marrying off his eldest son. The remaining orphans argued that their brother should not receive his share of the inheritance, since he already received some money before his wedding, and later, also a book, then considered a precious commodity. The rabbi, however, rejected their plea.[42] It is impossible to decipher what motivated the brothers' action against their eldest sibling. Was it simply avarice and/or jealousy? Regrettably, the source does not reveal the feelings and thoughts of those involved or any other information that might shed light on the family relations prior to and after the death of the father. However, the actions taken by the siblings against their brother do indicate an attempt to obtain what they believed was justifiably theirs.

Another family dispute, this time between an orphaned son and his mother, occurred in an unspecified location in thirteenth-century Ashkenaz and is reported in a legal correspondence.[43] Here too, while the source imparts only minimal information, it does provide a glimpse into the familial tension that resulted from the death of a parent. In this case, the father of the family passed away and left behind a wife and two children—a son and a daughter. The widow opted not to swear the Widow's Oath, which would have awarded her the equivalent of her marriage contract (*ketubbah*).[44] Instead, she reached an agreement with

---

42. Simcha Emanuel, ed., *Responsa of Rabbi Meir of Rothenburg and his Colleagues*, vol. 1 (Jerusalem: The World Union of Jewish Studies, 2012), § 262, 576.

43. Meir of Rothenburg, *Sefer Shut Maharam b. R. Barukh* (Prague, 1608), § 860.

44. Cheryl Tallan explains that: "Widows' claims were prior liens on their late husbands' estates and had to be paid, if they so demanded, before estates were divided among the heirs. It was often to the widow's advantage to choose maintenance over the marriage contract. First, it constituted a continual lien on the estate until her death, although there is some evidence that some widows were not provided with maintenance indefinitely if the heirs objected. Second, according to Jewish law, the widow was to be maintained in the style to which she was accustomed. Third, if she claimed her maintenance, but not her ketubbah, she did not have to swear an oath. Jewish widows, like the rest of the medieval population, were reluctant to swear oaths and often went to great lengths to refrain from having to do so." Cheryl Tallan, "Medieval Jewish Widows: Their Control of Resources," *Jewish History* 5, no. 1 (1991): 63–74, https://www.jstor.org/stable/20101096 (last accessed 1 December 2024).

her late husband's inheritors to receive annual maintenance to support herself and her children. The agreement further specified that she was responsible to feed and sustain the children until they reach a certain (unspecified) age. However, the daughter died before reaching that age and the son sued his mother hoping to receive whatever she would have spent on the maintenance of his sister had she survived. Meir ben Barukh, deliberating on this matter, concluded that the son had no claim against his mother. We assume that the son was of legal age when he sued his mother, since there is no mention of a guardian acting on his behalf. If this was the case, then the son's actions demonstrate his attempt to financially benefit from the death of his sister. In many sources, however, as in the above-mentioned case of the guardian who sued the lodger on behalf of the orphan, and as the following story of Isaac shows, the information about the lives of the orphans come from other people involved in their case, and we have no way of inferring the involvement of the orphans themselves in these cases.

The Story of Isaac the Orphan

Although attempts were often made by the dying to prevent family disputes after their death, as the following fifteenth-century incident demonstrates, these attempts were not always successful. In 1470, Isaac was an underage orphan being raised by his grandmother, Rycke, an affluent Jewish woman from Frankfurt who had been widowed in 1461. A prominent member of the Jewish community of the city, Rycke was a charitable woman who cared for the poor and foreign Jews in her town.[45] All we know about Isaac, however, is that when his grandmother fell sick, she wanted to ensure a prosperous future for him. Rycke had her will drawn up "when [she already had] a weak body, but [was] still at good reason" (*als ich itzunt swaches lijbes und doch guder vernomfft bin*)—a prerequisite for the substantiation of the will according to both German common law and Jewish religious law.[46] Her will, written in German and dated November 9, 1470, can be found in the

---

45. In addition to the fact that Rycke was the only Jewish person with an entry in the *Minor-Währschaftsbücher*, she also owned a personal seal, which is now lost. See Andreas Lehnertz, *Judensiegel im spätmittelalterlichen Reichsgebiet. Beglaubigungstätigkeit und Selbstrepräsentation von Jüdinnen und Juden*. 2 Vols. Forschungen zur Geschichte der Juden, A 30 (Wiesbaden: Harrassowitz Verlag, 2020), 821 and 927.

46. Isidor Kracauer, "Ein jüdisches Testament aus dem Jahre 1470," *Monatsschrift für Geschichte und Wissenschaft des Judentums* 60 (1916): 295–301.

Minor-Währschaftsbücher, a series of municipal books documenting wills, real estate transactions, sureties, and other businesses transactions important to the municipal council. Rycke's will is the only Jewish will amid many Christian ones in this compendium, testifying to her high social and economic position.[47]

The will discloses that Rycke appointed two guardians, a woman, Fromut, Isaac's other grandmother, and a man, Shimon Katz of Mainz.[48] She undertook to pay them a yearly wage to ensure that Isaac receive everything he needed from the time of her death until he reached maturity. The guardians were to appoint a third guardian from Frankfurt or Worms, and Isaac was to live and grow up in the house of one of them, "and in no other house" (*und in keynem andern huse*). In addition, Isaac was to receive a Jewish education (*lernen lassen*), and this is perhaps one of the reasons why Rycke appointed the rabbi as one of Isaac's guardians. The appointment of Fromut and the rabbi was in line with what Rebecca Lynn Winer concluded regarding thirteenth-century Perpignan, namely, that networks of guardians oversaw an orphan's well-being and that often these networks incorporated members of the extended family. Rycke herself was part of this network. Finally, the guardians were also instructed to find Isaac a wife when he reached marriageable age.

Despite all her precautions, however, even determining in her will that, in the case of a legal disputes, all costs of a trial would be paid from her money, after her death in 1473, a family quarrel over her inheritance occurred. A Jewish woman and relative of Rycke named Pewrlin of Kadolzburg appeared before the municipal council in Frankfurt and sued Shimon Katz for payment of her share of Rycke's inheritance. Her claims were even supported by Elector Albrecht of Brandenburg, who had the Frankfurt city council confiscate the entire inheritance until the court decided the matter. Unfortunately, we have no knowledge of the

---

47. There is another regulation regarding two Jewish orphans documented in a law court book in Rothenburg for the years 1345 and 1346, although this was not a will. Claudia Steffes-Maus, "Juden vor dem Rothenburger Landgericht während der ersten Hälfte des 14. Jahrhunderts," *Verschriftlichung und Quellenüberlieferung. Beiträge zur Geschichte der Juden und der christlich-jüdischen Beziehungen im spätmittelalterlichen Reich (13./14. Jahrhundert)*, ed. Jörg R. Müller and Alfred Haverkamp. Forschungen zur Geschichte der Juden, A 25 (Peine: Hahnsche Buchhandlung, 2014), 173–215. The second text was written in Latin and Hebrew; however, both are not entirely concordant.

48. Israel J. Yuval, *Scholars in Their Time: The Religious Leadership of German Jewry in the Late Middle Ages* (Jerusalem: Magnes Press, 1988), 145–46 (Hebrew).

outcome of this dispute.⁴⁹ Rycke's will provides important historical insights into orphanhood among affluent Jewish families in Ashkenaz during this period, particularly regarding how the institution of guardianship functioned: the appointment of two trusted guardians, possibly relatives of the orphan or friends of the family, who then jointly selected a third person to assist them. This will, however, does not reveal any information about the orphan's thoughts, wishes, feelings, and aspirations. The concluding case study, on the other hand, does provide a firsthand glimpse into the experiences of an orphan, who reveals his feelings of disappointment and anger toward the one entrusted to care for him, and whose actions point toward a strong sense of personal agency.

The Story of Götz

Although regulations regarding, and disputes over, inheritance among Ashkenazic Jews are attested to in both rabbinic legal sources as well as in Latin or German municipal documents, the voices of the orphans themselves were seldom recorded during the Middle Ages. We are fortunate, however, to have a rare letter written in Yiddish by a male orphan called Götz von Fuderholz. The letter, likely composed on February 12, 1518, is addressed to Wenzel, the sexton (*shamash*) of the Regensburg Jewish community; to the entire community; and to the city of Regensburg.⁵⁰ In his letter, Götz emphasizes that he speaks only for himself (*doch red ich vur mikh alein*), perhaps in an attempt not to drag his siblings into his disputes with the Jewish community as well as the municipality of Regensburg.

Götz's family lived in Altdorf, and when his father, whom he describes as "a rich man" (*ein reich man*), passed away, his widowed mother married a man named Mendel, and the family moved to Regensburg. Götz calls Mendel his "stepfather" (*stif vater*). With part of her 600 gulden dowry, Götz's mother bought a house for 250 gulden, in which Mendel was currently living with the other children.⁵¹ Götz explains that

---

49. Yuval, *Scholars in Their Time*, 146.
50. Raphael Straus, ed., *Urkunden und Aktenstücke zur Geschichte der Juden in Regensburg 1453–1738* (Munich: Beck, 1960), no. 957. All quotations are from the Yiddish original. Many thanks to Eva-Maria Cersovsky, Julia Bruch, Sabine von Heusinger and Adrian Kammerer for discussing this source with us.
51. Clark, "City Orphans," 178. The law courts would usually decide about the inheritance and guardians of well-to-do orphans, while those from poor families with no (significant) property evoked little interest; Clark, "City Orphans," 170.

according to his mother's will, the house was left to the orphaned children, and Mendel was only given the right to live there so long as his mother was alive. Mendel, Götz insisted, gained rights over this house through "betrayal and treason" (*mit verreter rei und mit buberei*).

He further argued that the remaining part of the dowry, some 350 gulden, was meant to supply him and his orphaned siblings with food, drink, clothes, and a Jewish education (*lernen noch dem judischen orden*) and that their mother gave Mendel money to ensure that he cared for them properly. This is another example demonstrating that the education of Jewish orphans was a major concern, at least among the wealthier families, as both Rycke, Isaac's grandmother, and Götz's mother mentioned this explicitly in their wills. Götz's stepfather was supposed to pay for the orphans' education, possibly by employing a teacher (*melamed*) in their house or sending them to a local tutor.[52] Thus, Götz was accusing his stepfather of denying him the education he deserved.

In his letter, Götz calls his stepfather Mendel a traitor and a villain (*ein verreter und bozwikht*), harsh language revealing the orphan's anger and sense of betrayal at the hands of his stepfather and legal guardian. Moreover, Götz expresses his fear that he would suffer the same fate as his brother Moses, "who was pushed underwater in a dew pond [by Mendel] who was assisted by some evil people" (*den hot er under tochert in einem trunk und boz loit der tzu geholfen haben*).

Mendel broke his agreement and took advantage of his orphaned stepchildren, and Götz left the house within a year, presumably going to one of his other guardians. He now claimed his inheritance and some money as well as pawns from his stepfather. Obviously, Götz was at this point clearly no longer a minor and was already involved in some small-scale moneylending. His siblings, on the other hand, stayed with Mendel, either because they were much younger or because they got

---

52. From a source dating to the late fifteenth-century Nuremberg, for example, we know that most Jewish households employed private tutors; see Michael Toch, "Die soziale und demographische Struktur der jüdischen Gemeinde Nürnbergs im Jahr 1489," *Wirtschaftskräfte und Wirtschaftswege*, vol. 5, ed. Jürgen Schneider (Stuttgart: Klett-Cotta, 181), 79–92. The thirteenth-century *Sefer ha-Ma'asim* we quoted earlier gives another such idealized story, "Torah Saves from Death," where a "father would go out every day, and any poor orphan or beggar he saw, he would take him in and bring him to his son and say: 'My son, teach them, and he [the son] would sit and teach them." Kushelevsky, *Tales in Context*, 262–65 (English and Hebrew). The common perception that all boys, including orphans, should receive at least some basic Jewish education was well-ingrained in this minority culture, although in fact many lacked such education.

along well enough with their stepfather. Let us recall here that Götz explicitly stated that he spoke only for himself.

The goods and money Götz demanded repeatedly from Mendel now that he was mature were not given to him. "Mendel made fun of me" (*er meiner gespot hot*), he protested. While Mendel claimed he was poor and had no money, he had in fact accumulated significant wealth—presumably through moneylending—and when the three years he had to take care of Götz's remaining siblings were over, he suddenly had the huge sum of 1,600 gulden, "which he had won with [their] money" (*das hot er gewunen mit unserem gelt*). Eventually, Götz came to Regensburg and had R. Meir—the oldest rabbi in town—send a letter to Mendel to claim Götz's goods and money. Götz further described how Mendel had betrayed him and his brother Moses, and he promised to fight for his goods and rights in a knightly fashion (*riterlikh*).[53]

Götz, with a somewhat haughty attitude, declared "and I let him [Mendel] know that I renounce [all ties with] my stepfather Mendel of Regensburg, his body and his goods, and the whole Jewish community and also the whole community of the city of Regensburg, that they shall not expect anything good from my part" (*und tu im tzu wisn, das ich im ab zag, meinem stif vater Mendel tzu Regenspurg, zeinem leib und zeinem gut und einer gantzen gemein yudish heit, und auch einer gantzen gemein stat Regenspurg, das zi zikh nikhs darfen gutz tzu mir vor zehen*). This formulation seems to be a declaration of a feud, a very serious threat bearing legal consequences.[54]

The city council of Regensburg was annoyed by the letter and decided to investigate further. Two facts point to this investigation. First, that the letter has been preserved in the Munich State Archives, where many of the municipal records from Regensburg are now stored, meaning that, at some point, the city council took possession of this

---

53. It also seems that Götz was assisted by other people (so-called feud helpers) whom he wanted to repay with a silver cup. See Markus J. Wenninger, "Bearing and Use of Weapons by Jews in the (Late) Middle Ages," *Jewish Studies* 41 (2002): 83–92, https://www.jstor.org/stable/23382824.

54. See Andreas Lehnertz and Birgit Wiedl, "How to Get out of Prison: Imprisoned Jews and Their *Hafturfehden* from the Medieval and Early Modern Holy Roman Empire (Fourteenth through Sixteenth Centuries)," *Incarceration and Slavery in the Middle Ages and the Early Modern Age. A Cultural-Historical Investigation of the Dark Side in the Pre-Modern World*, ed. Albrecht Classen. Studies in Medieval Literature (London: Lexington Books, 2021), 361–413. Many thanks to Hillay Zmora, who confirmed this interpretation and sent us similar wordings from noble feuds. See also his book *The Feud in Early Modern Germany* (Cambridge, MA: Cambridge University Press, 2011).

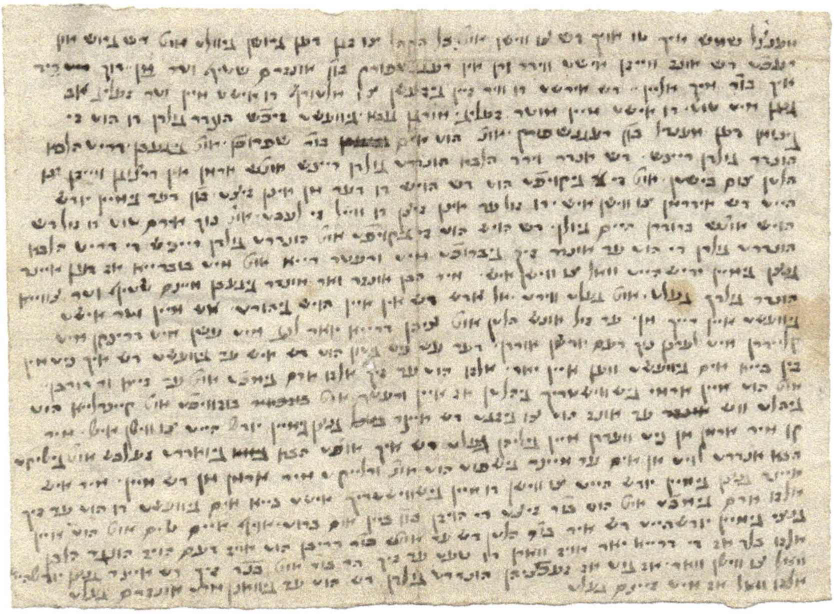

FIGURE 2.1. The first page of Götz's Yiddish letter to the sexton of the Jewish community in Regensburg from 1518. Munich, BHStA, Generalregistratur, Fasz. 1260, Nr. 18r.

Yiddish letter. The second is that the letter was translated—or better, transliterated—into contemporary German and was then sent to at least one Regensburg patrician, by the name of Sigmund Schwebel. The translation was done by Balthasar Hubmair, "doctor of the Holy Scriptures" and *concionator ecclesiae cathedralis* (*thumprediger*) of Regensburg, "as good as it was possible [for him]" (*als vill mir muglich geweset vß*). We can therefore assume that Götz caused a spot of trouble to the city of Regensburg and possibly also to the local Jewish community. In the end, the case was resolved by Mendel paying reparations to Götz.[55] Apparently, Götz's furious letter and the pressure he put on the Jewish community, his stepfather, and the city of Regensburg paid off. Götz the orphan fought for his rights and received justice.

The challenging conditions of life in medieval Europe made orphanhood a common phenomenon. Before orphanages were established, families, relatives, and the communities were the only options for

---

55. Straus, *Urkunden und Aktenstücke*, nos. 988 and 993.

caring for Jewish orphans, unlike Christian orphans who, in addition to being cared for by their families, relatives or communities, could be sent to monasteries and convents. As we have argued in this chapter, various factors motivated people to take in orphans, including family responsibilities, financial benefits, and religious piety. A late tenth-century responsum, attributed to R. Meshulam ben Kalonymus, gives yet another reason why some medieval Jews adopted orphans: "In my house lived Judah, Simon's brother, [who was related to me] through my father. I reared him in my house; I supported him in accordance with my means, and I paid [a teacher] who taught him; I brought him up as a son, since I had no son of my own and no daughter except for the sister of the mother of this orphan, his aunt."[56] This man, so we are told, decided to raise an orphan because he had no child of his own. Perhaps he also pitied his young orphaned relative, and maybe he was also religiously motivated, like others discussed above. However, the attitude toward orphans, as we demonstrated in this chapter, was not always so empathetic and not everyone who adopted, raised, or who was appointed a guardian of orphans did so benevolently.

The cultural emphasis on orphans as an acutely disadvantaged group, particularly deserving of special attention, protection, and care, reflects the often bleak reality faced by many of these children. The wills drawn by parents and guardians of means, which sought to prevent the mistreatment, exploitation, or manipulations of their sons and daughters by people entrusted to ensure their prosperity and well-being, are likely indicative of a fear that this could potentially be the case and thus suggests that such negative outcomes were not unusual. What, then, about those who were less fortunate? Does the emphasis on the religious merits gained by raising orphans imply that in cases where underprivileged orphans were involved people were less motivated to welcome them into their families? Unfortunately, since the sources focus on disputations surrounding inheritance and reflect the social situation of mostly affluent orphans, we know very little of the fate of those who were less privileged. What emerges from the materials studied, however, is a clearer understanding of the sense of personal agency possessed by some medieval Jewish orphans, both male and female. Despite their losses, they actively used all legal avenues available

---

56. Louis Ginzberg, ed., *Genizah Studies, In Memory of Doctor Solomon Schechter, Vol. VII, Geonic and Early Karaitic Halakah* (New York: The Jewish Theological Seminary of America, 1929), 216.

to them to challenge the injustices inflicted by guardians and others who sought to exploit their misfortune. Further studies are required to continue to expand our knowledge of this topic, and to determine, for example, the extent to which the gender of the orphans, and that of the guardians, played a role in determining their lives. Finally, while the available sources do not reflect any major changes in the treatment of orphans throughout the entire period under consideration, further research is required to determine the veracity of this impression and shed light on such changes as occurred.

Further Readings

Baumgarten, Elisheva. "The Family." *Cambridge History of Judaism*. Vol. 6, edited by Robert Chazan, 440-62. Cambridge: Cambridge University Press, 2018.

Bender, Tovah. "The Family and the Household." In *A Cultural History of the Home in the Medieval Ages*, edited by Katherine L. French, 31-48. London: Bloomsbury, 2021.

Berner, Tali M. *In Their Own Way: Children and Childhood in Early Modern Ashkenaz*. Jerusalem: Zalman Shazar Center, 2018 (Hebrew).

Clark, Elaine. "City Orphans and Custody Laws in Medieval London." *American Journal of Legal History* 3 (1990): 168-87. doi.org/10.2307/845520.

Hanawalt, Barbara. *Growing up in Medieval London: The Experience of Childhood in History*. Oxford: Oxford University Press, 1993.

Helmholz, Richard H. "Children's Rights and the Canon Law: Law and Practice in Later Medieval England." *Jurist: Studies in Church Law and Ministry* 67 (2007): 39-57. doi.org/10.1353/jur.2007.0047.

Kalaora, Etelle. "Jewish Widows' Homes in Ashkenaz in the 12th and 13th Centuries." *Jewish Studies Quarterly* 28 (2021): 315-30. doi:10.1628/jsq-2021-0017

Katz, Jacob. "Marriage and Sexual Life among the Jews at the Close of the Middle Ages." *Zion* 10 (1945): 21-54 (Hebrew).

Lehnertz, Andreas. "Margarete, Reynette and Meide: Three Jewish Women from Koblenz in the 14th Century." *Jewish Studies Quarterly* 28 (2021): 388-405. doi:10.1628/jsq-2021-0022.

Levinson, Eyal. "Situated Fathering in Medieval Ashkenaz." *Jewish Studies Quarterly* 28 (2021): 278-96. doi:10.1628/jsq-2021-0015

Megson, Barbara. "Life Expectations of the Widows and Orphans of Freemen in London 1375-1399." *Local Population Studies* 57 (1996): 18-29.

Müller, Miriam. *Childhood, Orphans, and Underage Heirs in Medieval Rural England: Growing up in the Village*. Cham, Switzerland: Palgrave Macmillan, 2019.

Reinitz, Yaakov K. "Orphans Boarding with the Householder." *Bar-Ilan Studies* 1 (1980): 219-50 (Hebrew).

Scott, Susan, ed. *Orphans, Widows, and Guardians in Medieval and Early Modern Bristol: The Register of Recognizances, 1333–1594*. Bristol: Bristol Record Society, 2020.

Sha'are Orah ve-Avi Yetomim: Laws of the Spanish and Portuguese Jews' Orphan Society for Educating, Maintaining, Clothing, and Apprenticing Orphan Children. London: Wertheimer, Lea and Co., 1885.

Shahar, Shulamit. *Childhood in the Middle Ages*. New York: Routledge, 1992.

Tallan, Cheryl. "Medieval Jewish Widows: Their Control of Resources." *Jewish History* 5 (1991): 63–74. https://www.jstor.org/stable/20101096.

Winer, Rebecca Lynn. "Family, Community, and Motherhood: Caring for Fatherless Children in the Jewish Community of Thirteenth-Century Perpignan." *Jewish History* 16 (2002): 15–48. https://www.jstor.org/stable/20101459.

CHAPTER 3

Everyday Disruptions

The Negotiation of Local Power Struggles by the Jews of Münzenberg and Assenheim

Annika Funke

In 1512, a Jewish man named Anschel of Münzenberg asked the Count of Hanau to waive the cost of his protection. Citing financial hardship, Anschel presented a list of erroneous charges levied against him by a variety of competing local authorities in his home region of Wetterau, next to the fair-trade city of Frankfurt. Included on the list of the names of those who extorted Anschel is not only Count Philipp of Solms-Lich, the Count of Hanau's appointed official in Münzenberg and Gambach, and his son Reinhard I, but also the lords of Isenburg and Königstein, and Bernhard III of the neighboring Solms-Braunfels.[1]

Jews in Condominial Territories

Anschel's struggle as an involuntary taxpayer to a whole range of different noblemen illustrates the process of the territorialization of the

---

1. Hessian State Archives in Marburg (HStAM). *Auseinandersetzung zwischen der Herrschaft Hanau und den Mitherren zu Münzenberg wegen deren Forderungen an die Juden in Münzenberg* 86, no. 5925, fol. 4r-v (end 1512); Uta Löwenstein, ed., *Quellen zur Geschichte der Juden im Hessischen Staatsarchiv Marburg: 1267–1600* (Wiesbaden: Kommission für die Geschichte der Juden in Hessen, 1989), vol. 3 no. N 63, wrongly references HStAM 86, no. 5912.

patronage of the Jews toward the end of the Middle Ages. In earlier times, when they lived predominantly in free and imperial cities, Jews were the direct subjects of the Holy Roman Emperor. When disputes arose, the Jewish community representatives, calling on widespread existing diplomatic networks, appealed to the city government and municipal courts, and in cases where the conflict could not to be resolved on the local level, to the emperor himself. These clearly defined realms of responsibility make it easy to comprehend how deeply involved Jews were in the political decision-making and conflict resolution of their cities on a daily basis.[2]

However, in the fifteenth century, increasing numbers of Jews migrated from these cities to the more rural periphery, where they became dependent on territorial rulers and subject to the mercy of their often complex and overlapping claims to power.[3] Those territories where multiple rulers shared governing rights based on various legal sources, such as inheritance, fiefs, and privileges, were called condominiums.[4] Another formal construct of the period was the *Judenregal*,

---

2. David Schnur traced the increasing fragmentation of authorities in medieval Frankfurt: Before the Black Death Jews held permanent citizenship and reported directly to the emperor as *servi camerea regis*, servants of the royal chamber. After it, they fell under the authority of the city itself as an imperial fief. Although their status within the city community became weakened, and they lost their permanent citizenship in favor of limited residency, they were still subject to a linear power structure and fought for their needs in front of the civic council and court, as many recorded supplications and protocols prove. Unlike most of the Jewish communities in free and imperial cities, the community of Frankfurt survived throughout the fifteenth and sixteenth century but became intertwined with a multitude of regional territorial and ecclesiastical rulers. While the city itself still held authority over their Jewish residents, these now had to defend themselves against foreign access as well, making taxation, mobility, and general political participation a hardly assessable topic. For a detailed account of the Jewry of Frankfurt and the community's increasing entanglement with the surrounding territories in the Late Middle Ages, see David Schnur, *Die Juden in Frankfurt am Main und in der Wetterau im Mittelalter. Christlich-jüdische Beziehungen, Gemeinden, Recht und Wirtschaft von den Anfängen bis um 1400* (Wiesbaden: Kommission für die Geschichte der Juden in Hessen, 2017). See especially pp. 253–55, where Schnur demonstrates how Jews were able to use this increasingly complex and fragmented political landscape to their advantage.

3. Friedrich Battenberg, "Aus der Stadt auf das Land: Zur Vertreibung und Neuansiedlung der Juden im Heiligen Römischen Reich," in *Jüdisches Leben auf dem Lande: Studien zur deutsch-jüdischen Geschichte*, ed. Monika Richarz and Reinhard Rürup (Tübingen: Mohr Siebeck, 1997), 9–35; Markus J. Wenninger, "Geleit, Geleitsrecht und Juden im Mittelalter," *Aschkenas* 31, no. 1 (2021): 29–77, here 31, https://doi.org/10.1515/asch-2021-0007.

4. For a more detailed account on condominial government and its role in late medieval and early modern Europe, see Torben Stretz, *Juden in Franken zwischen Mittelalter und Früher Neuzeit: Die Grafschaften Castell und Wertheim im regionalen Kontext* (Wiesbaden: Harrassowitz Verlag, 2016), 331–43; Alexander Jendorff, "Gemeinsam herrschen: Das ateuropäische Kondominat und das Herrschaftsverhältnis der Moderne," *Zeitschrift für Historische Forschung* 34,

the imperial privilege to regulate the settlement and business activity of Jews in a certain area, and to set, collect, and utilize their taxes. Considered a separate legal field, distinct from territorial government, the Judenregal was a privilege granted by the emperor to his allies as part of his role as patron of German Jewry.[5] Consequently, the territorial government and the patronage of the Jews in a condominial space were not necessarily in the hands of the same authority, turning the Judenregal into a frequent object of dispute.

Seeking to expand and unify their authority, territorial lords fought tirelessly against holders of imperial rights to bring the Jews in their lands under their rule. By the Early Modern period, their claims began to prevail over the medieval Judenregal, making it more difficult for the Jews living under them to follow the by now well-established and well-trodden paths of Jewish diplomacy.[6] What recourse was available to these Jews? To whom did they appeal when seeking redress and how did they achieve change in a scattered political landscape characterized by coinciding rights of authority? This is the situation explored in this chapter.

In Anschel's hometown, Münzenberg, we see the effects of condominial governance in a particularly remarkable way. From the end of the fifteenth century, the Jewish residents there were subjected to recurrent acts of blackmail, burglary, and seizures committed by the servants of the local authorities, whose express purpose was to force them

---

no. 2 (2007): 215–42, https://search.ebscohost.com/login.aspx?direct=true&scope=site&db=nlebk&db=nlabk&AN=1462162.

5. In the political constitution of the Holy Roman Empire, Jews were separated from the rest of the population as so-called "Kammerknechte," direct servants of the emperor. They reported to the emperor as their first and foremost authority and were therefore subject to a different legal sphere than their Christian neighbors. Over the course of the High and Late Middle Ages, the German emperors, in order to gain wealth and ensure the support of the territorial lords of the German lands, increasingly distributed their special claim over the Jews to the latter, causing a complex and often conflicting parallelism of territorial and imperial rights. Friedrich Battenberg, "Des Kaisers Kammerknechte: Gedanken zur rechtlich-sozialen Situation der Juden in Spätmittelalter und Früher Neuzeit," *Historische Zeitschrift* 245, no. 3 (1987): 545–99, elaborates on the development of the institution of Kammerknechtschaft at the end of the Middle Ages.

6. Friedrich Battenberg, "Assenheimer Judenpogrome vor dem Reichskammergericht: Die Prozesse der Grafschaften Hanau, Isenburg und Solms um die Ausübung des Judenregals 1567–1573," in *Neunhundert Jahre Geschichte der Juden in Hessen: Beiträge zum politischen, wirtschaftlichen und kulturellen Leben*, ed. Christiane Heinemann (Wiesbaden: Kommission für die Geschichte der Juden in Hessen, 1983), 123–49, 141–42.

to accept territorial rule.⁷ This abuse became a point of contention between the lords sharing the Münzenberg town government and other neighboring condominiums for the entirety of the following century, as is clear from the numerous unsuccessful attempts to reconcile the conflicting interests of all parties involved.⁸ The Jews were thus subjected to more than seventy years of systemic violence against them, until, finally, in 1567, when the failure of regional diplomacy became undeniable, the counts of Hanau obtained mandates from the imperial court to stop the attacks on the Judenregal by Solms and Isenburg. This in turn led to a prolonged trial, during which the conflict between territorial versus imperial rights was fiercely debated, as Battenberg depicted so comprehensively in his study of the Jews of Assenheim.⁹

At first glance, the Jews of Münzenberg and Assenheim appear to be defenseless victims in this power struggle, which was unrelated to their conduct within the town communities and thus offered little political leverage for them to apply. However, a closer look at the sources reveals a significant level of political engagement on the part of the Jews in both towns. They issued letters to all ruling parties on a regular basis in order to promote their case and to urge their patron, the Count of Hanau, to counteract his political rivals.

Correspondingly, researchers such as Stretz and Treue have pointed out that conflicting claims to the government were at times beneficial to Jewish settlers and encouraged and secured their presence in condominial spaces.¹⁰ For example, for an expulsion to be carried out,

---

7. Wolfgang Treue examines the daily lives of Jews under condominial rule in Assenheim, Münzenberg, and Ortenheim, highlighting the unique forms of violence that emerged from contested claims to power. Wolfgang Treue, "Diener dreier Herren: Möglichkeiten und Unmöglichkeiten jüdischen Lebens in der frühen Neuzeit," in *Campana pulsante convocati: Festschrift anläßlich der Emeritierung von Prof. Dr. Alfred Haverkamp*, ed. Frank G. Hirschmann and Gerd Mentgen (Trier: Kliomedia, 2005), 563-97.

8. Correspondence between the condominial lords expressive of conflict over the authority over the Jews begins in the middle of the fifteenth century (see, e.g., Friedrich Battenberg, ed., *Judaica im Staatsarchiv Darmstadt*, vol. 1: *Urkunden 1275-1650* [Darmstadt: Hessisches Staatsarchiv, 1981], nos. 648-49 [July 23, 1453; August 20, 1453]), and continues throughout the sixteenth century, as will be shown in the discussion to follow.

9. Battenberg coherently depicted the process of territorialization and its impact on the Jewish community by analyzing its political structure and development on the cusp of the early modern state. Friedrich Battenberg, *Assenheimer Judenpogrome* (Wiesbaden: Kommission für die Geschichte der Juden in Hessen, 1983), 133-41.

10. Torben Stretz describes the division of power in Franken as a guarantor for the development and continuity of Jewish communities; see Stretz, *Juden in Franken*, 332-37. Multiple other researchers made similar observations, such as Johannes Mordstein, *Selbstbewußte Untertänigkeit: Obrigkeit und Judengemeinden im Spiegel der Judenschutzbriefe der Grafschaft Oettingen*

multiple political actors had to collaborate and agree to this drastic change of policy. Jews were able to play the various sides against each other by offering political and financial incentives to the different lords and thus prevent their collaboration and avert the impending catastrophe. They were able to appeal to the ruler they perceived as being best able to meet their needs and even to profit from the inherent political weakness and failed conflict resolution between the competing powers.

This chapter explores this phenomenon by analyzing argumentative patterns within the numerous supplications of the Jewries of Münzenberg and Assenheim between 1502 and 1557. It highlights the early engagement of Jews in diplomatic exchanges between the town lords in the first half of the sixteenth century, showing that they reacted with nimble flexibility and in an organized communal fashion to the changing political landscape.

Jewish Diplomacy in Münzenberg and Assenheim

In the sixteenth century, the region of Wetterau, home to many small towns and villages with Jewish inhabitants, was split between a large number of counts and knights, each holding rights to small portions of the land and its subjects. The right of inheritance of multiple sons of one noble family often led to further division of the territory, leaving a scattered and politically heterogeneous landscape of minor significance to the imperial federation. The towns of Münzenberg and Assenheim are excellent examples of this complexity. They had been condominiums since the middle of the thirteenth century, when Ulrich II of Münzenberg died without a male heir and his lands were divided between his six sisters. While the house of Falkenstein succeeded in uniting most of the shares of the town government under their authority over the course of century, their line eventually became extinct as well, and their inheritance was bequeathed to the noble houses of Solms, Eppstein, and Isenburg. These noblemen were connected by a broad network of family ties and by their membership in the Wetterauer Grafenverein,[11] an association of regional lords that facilitated and formalized their cooperation

---

1637–1806 (Epfendorf: Bibliotheca-Academica-Verlag, 2005), 200–201, and Battenberg, "Aus der Stadt auf das Land." For example, Treue, in "Diener dreier Herren," 563–64, 570, mentions bribery as a method to gain the support of one ruler against another.

11. Klaus-Peter Decker, "Herrschaften in der Wetterau," in *Handbuch der hessischen Geschichte*, vol. 3, ed. Winfried Speitkamp (Marburg: Historische Kommission für Hessen, 2014), 275–326, 314; Jürgen Rainer Wolf, "Grafschaft Solms," in *Handbuch der hessischen Geschichte*, vol. 3,

in ensuring peace, provided representation in the Imperial Diets, and prevented further expansion on the part of more powerful monarchs.[12] From the administrative seat in the castles of the two towns, the noble families managed the shared estate in collaboration with each other. This type of ownership, in which different nobilities shared a property without meticulous division of rights, was called *Ganerbschaft*, coin-heritance. As Schneider explains, the involved parties did not govern distinct parts of the territory independently, but rather ruled over its entirety together and had to negotiate policies and responsibilities with each other.[13] While governance was complicated by this arrangement, it allowed a number of small noble families to simultaneously profit from the prestige and the resources of the estate.

With only one-sixth of a share in this condominium, the counts of Hanau held the smallest part of the government in Münzenberg and Assenheim. This fraction entered into Reinhard I of Hanau's possession through his wife Adelheid of Münzenberg, sister of Ulrich II, and was successfully held until the eighteenth century without ever being extended to a size large enough to participate extensively in the town government.[14] However, the counts of Hanau possessed another asset. The Judenregal granted to them by Charles IV in the fourteenth century gave them the right to rule over and profit from the prosperous

---

ed. Winfried Speitkamp (Marburg: Historische Kommission für Hessen, 2014), 377–402, 384; Treue, "Diener dreier Herren," 565–66; Battenberg, *Assenheimer Judenpogrome*, 125–26.

12. Georg Schmidt, "Wetterauer Grafenverein," in *Handbuch der hessischen Geschichte*, vol. 3, ed. Winfried Speitkamp (Marburg: Historische Kommission für Hessen, 2014), 327–46, 330–31; Schmidt, *Der Wetterauer Grafenverein: Organisation und Politik einer Reichskorporation zwischen Reformation und Westfälischem Frieden* (Marburg: N. G. Elwert Verlag, 1989), 23, 476.

13. Compare Joachim Schneider, "*Ganerbschaft*en und Burgfrieden in der Frühen Neuzeit: Relikte oder funktionale Adaptionen?" in *Adel in Hessen: Herrschaft, Selbstverständnis und Lebensführung vom 15. bis ins 20. Jahrhundert*, ed. Eckart Conze, Alexander Jendorff, and Heide Wunder (Marburg: Historische Kommission für Hessen, 2010), 129–48, 131; Friedrich Battenberg, "Die Judenschaft der Ganerbschaft Buseckertal zwischen Reich und Territorium," in *Kaiser und Reich in der jüdischen Lokalgeschichte*, ed. Stefan Ehrenpreis, Andreas Gutzmann, and Stephan Wendehorst (Berlin: De Gruyter, 2013), 147–77, 149–50.

14. Uta Löwenstein, "Grafschaft Hanau," in *Handbuch der hessischen Geschichte*, vol. 3, ed. Winfried Speitkamp (Marburg: Historische Kommission für Hessen, 2014), 197–232, 205. Christian Ottersbach points out the insufficient connections through regional marriages that led Hanau to be disadvantaged in the redistribution of land in this period. Christian Ottersbach, *Die Burgen der Herren und Grafen von Hanau (1166–1642): Studien zur Burgenpolitik und Burgenarchitektur eines Adelshauses* (Neustadt an der Aisch: Verlag Ph. C. W. Schmidt, 2018), 35, 43. A document from the seventeenth century names the number of acres attributed to each lord, revealing tremendous differences between the lord of Solms and Isenburg on the one hand, and that of Hanau on the other, who held only one single acre in his possession. See Battenberg, *Assenheimer Judenpogrome*, 126.

Jewish minority of both towns.¹⁵ Hanau's minimal but not insignificant claims to power caused tension even before the end of the noble house of Falkenstein, and this conflict was then inherited by the counts of Solms and Isenburg.¹⁶ These argued that contrary to Hanau's imperial rights, the Jews should be treated as part of the general population of the territory and thus mainly as their own subjects. They referenced a pawnage that they supposedly inherited from the lords of Falkenstein and claimed partial jurisdiction and taxation of the Jews in Münzenberg and Assenheim, in effect pushing the counts of Hanau out of the condominium.¹⁷ Anschel's above-mentioned list of the financial demands of various noble men highlights the consequences of this blending of diverging legal principals and is characteristic of the end of the medieval period during which power was negotiated between multiple territorial lords as well as between them and the weakening imperial government.

The lords of Solms and Isenburg-Büdingen attempted to assert their claim on the Jews by extorting taxes, breaking their safe conduct in- and outside the towns, and in general encouraging acts of violence against them. It became standard procedure for the lords and their servants to enter houses inhabited by Jews and to seize their belongings, whenever the victims refused or were unable to pay desired levies. In addition, they obstructed the administration of justice and punishment

---

15. The counts of Hanau, to whom the Jewish taxes of both towns had been pledged since 1277, came into possession of the Judenregal in 1310, which was fully confirmed as an imperial fief in 1351. For a more detailed depiction of the development of the Münzenberg and Assenheim government, see Wolfgang Treue, "Komplexität auf kleinem Raum: Judenpolitik in der Grafschaft Hanau-Münzenberg vom Ausgang des Mittelalters bis zum Ende des Dreißigjährigen Krieges," in *Juden und ländliche Gesellschaft in Europa zwischen Mittelalter und Früher Neuzeit (15.–17. Jahrhundert): Kontinuität und Krise, Inklusion und Exklusion in einer Zeit des Übergangs*, ed. Sigrid Hirbodian and Torben Stretz (Wiesbaden: Harrassowitz, 2016), 73–96, 75; Eckhard Meise, "Kurzer Überblick über die Geschichte der Hanauer Juden und ihrer Synagogen," *Neues Magazin für Hanauische Geschichte* (2010): 46–127, 45–46, https://doi.org/10.1177/09719458241263464; Eckhard Meise, "Toleranz: Philipp Ludwig II. Graf von Hanau-Münzenberg und die Juden," *Neues Magazin für Hanauische Geschichte* (2007): 3–57, 18–20; Battenberg, *Assenheimer Judenpogrome*, 126–29; Ludwig Rosenthal, *Zur Geschichte der Juden im Gebiet der ehemaligen Grafschaft Hanau unter besonderer Berücksichtigung der Juden in Bergen bei Frankfurt am Main und der dortigen Vorfahren des Verfassers vom 17. bis 19. Jahrhundert: Ein Beitrag zur Geschichte der deutschen Juden* (Hanau: Hanauer Geschichtsverein e.V., 1963), 25.

16. Decker, "Grafschaften in der Wetterau," 310–11; Ottersbach, *Burgen der Herren und Grafen von Hanau*, 43

17. Treue, "Komplexität auf kleinem Raum," 573–74. Battenberg, "Assenheimer Judenpogrome," 128; vgl. Battenberg, *Judaica*, no. 648–49, no. 654, no. 658. Battenberg, "Kammerknechte," 576–78; Hans-Jürgen Löwenstein, "Münzenberg," in *Germania Judaica*, vol. 3, 2, ed. Arye Maimon (Tübingen: Mohr Siebeck, 1995), 914–19, 915.

of offenses against the Jews,[18] thwarted the purchase and renting of houses,[19] and continually lobbied the Count of Hanau for the expulsion of the hard-pressed Jewish minority.[20] The overarching goal was not merely to usurp the Judenregal, but to extinguish the exception of Jews from the territorial rule altogether.

In light of this process of territorialization and the back and forth between the competing powers in the joint estate, Jews opted to actively support the accustomed system of protection, that is, the imperial privilege held by the counts of Hanau. The Jewry of Münzenberg and Assenheim addressed numerous requests to their patrons in an attempt to put a stop to the systematic violence they were facing. While they tackled the issue by negotiation with all the involved authorities, most of the surviving correspondence was directed to the county of Hanau and is now located in the Hessian State Archives in Marburg within a corpus of documents relating to the chamber of Hanau. Documentation of the interaction of Jews with other rulers within the Ganerbschaft is much scarcer, leaving many questions about their diplomatic strategies unanswered. However, drawing from the available resources, two strategies of Jewish diplomacy are apparent. First, the petitioners delegitimized the seizures as being in contradiction to imperial rights and ascribed to them attributes of common criminality. Second, they appealed to the Count of Hanau's self-interest in enforcing his power by positioning their defense as integral to the preservation of his prestige and wealth. Below, I explore the arguments presented in letters signed by Jews from

---

18. The Jews of Münzenberg and Assenheim reported repeated breaches of the common judicial district and the escape of perpetrators despite their known identities: see for example HStAM 86 no. 6000, fol. 30r-v (May 1502); HStAM 86, no. 28548, fol. 2r-3v (November 2-3, 1536) and others. In addition to not pursuing crimes against Jews, the court of the territorial lords also charged disproportionally high penalties from Jewish offenders to maximize its profit: see Treue, "Diener dreier Herren," 568. The Count of Hanau demanded in August 20, 1485, from his co-rulers that they guarantee the proper conducting of court procedures according to the Burgfrieden (further elaboration on page 12), see Löwenstein, *Quellen zur Geschichte der Juden*, vol. 1 no. 430.

19. In 1502 Count Philipp of Solms claimed that the Jews stole real estate from the Christian citizens of Münzenberg, see Hanau's reply to this allegation: HStAM 86, no. 6000, fol. 27r-29r (May 10, 1502). In 1543 the Count of Hanau indeed forbade the Jews to own real estate, see Löwenstein, *Quellen zur Geschichte der Juden*, vol. 3 no. N 115. For more information about this complex issue see Treue, "Diener dreier Herren," 567-70.

20. Löwenstein, *Quellen zur Geschichte der Juden* 1, no. 706 (before December 29, 1508); Löwenstein, *Quellen zur Geschichte der Juden* 1, no. 748 (April 27-August 22, 1511); and other examples.

both towns during the first half of the sixteenth century as expressions of these two diplomatic strategies.[21]

Seizure or Burglary?

In his monograph *Legal Plunder*, Smail wrote about the humiliating character of public seizure authorized through courts.[22] Using both legal and physical force to make the economic circumstances of a debtor visible to the town community was a traumatic event. The seizures conducted by servants of Solms and Isenburg in Jewish houses were no exception. In supplications to their patrons, the victims described their existential fear in the face of the breaches of peace in their own homes, writing that they felt "not safe in [their] houses with [their] wives and children, neither [of their] bodies nor of [their] goods."[23] The description of the seizures followed the same narrative pattern for decades, as displayed for example in a complaint of the Jews of Münzenberg to the Count of Hanau, in 1502: "Also, now almost four weeks ago it was broken into someone's house by night and by fog and four geese were taken and . . . great violence has been committed."[24]

The legal and economic background of the attacks was initially put aside and only the unnecessary and excessive cruelty of the attackers was emphasized. The phrase "by night and by fog" was used in most of the descriptions of trespassing in Jewish houses and taken up by responsible officials of the county and the noble family as well. In June 1509, the councilors of Hanau reported to Count Reinhard IV about a complaint of the Assenheim community: "If they would not give [to the lords of Isenburg] . . . they kicked open the doors which was done by night and fog, and they take what is theirs by force and carry it away."[25]

---

21. In this chapter, I focus on the following letters of the Jewries of Münzenberg and Assenheim to the Count of Hanau: HStAM 86, no. 6000, fol. 30r-v (May 1502, Münzenberg); HStAM 86, no. 19989, fol. 7r (September 19, 1513, Assenheim); HStAM 86, no. 25949, fol. 1r-2v (May 4, 1552, Assenheim); HStAM 86, no. 5925, fol. 8r-9v (October 6, 1557; Münzenberg). A variety of other sources, particularly correspondence between the different territorial lords, will supplement the analysis.

22. Daniel Lord Smail, *Legal Plunder: Households and Debt Collection in Late Medieval Europe* (Cambridge, MA: Harvard University Press, 2016), 242–43.

23. HStAM 86, no. 28548, fol. 2r-v (November 2, 1536). Also May 1502, HStAM 86, no. 6000, fol. 30r.

24. HStAM 86, no. 6000, fol. 30r (May 1502).

25. HStAM 86, no. 19989, fol. 5r (June 29, 1513): *"at night"*; fol. 7r-8r (September 19–20, 1513): *"by night and fog," "by nighttime"*; fol. 3r (June 1509); HStAM 86 no. 5925, fol. 8r-9v (October 6, 1557): *"during the night."*

Four years later, the widowed Countess Katharina repeated in a similar manner that "at nighttime the houses [of the Jews of Assenheim] were broken into, their chests and coffers broken open, and what was theirs was taken and stolen according to [the perpetrators'] own estimation and with violence."[26]

Seeing the words of Jewish supplicants being taken up by their authorities speaks for their success in creating a narrative befitting their argumentative strategy. In emphasizing the evening and night hours, implying the violation of the resting time of the victims of these raids, the act of trespassing is portrayed as particularly disturbing, illegitimate, and criminally motivated. As opposed to the seizures described by Smail, which had the legal backing of court orders and expressed their legitimacy through their purposefully visible conduct, Jews portrayed the seizures by the lords of Solms and Isenburg as a robbery, carried out under cover of darkness in the deviant secrecy of the night.[27]

Indeed, from the perspective of the Jews of Münzenberg and Assenheim there was no legal justification for the trespassing, as it was based on unpaid levies for which the lords had no imperial authorization. As the subjects of the Count of Hanau, they had no legal obligations toward other co-rulers of the condominium. In response to these accusations the lords of Solms and Isenburg pursued a two-part strategy. On the one hand, they regularly denied knowledge of the violence committed in their names,[28] and thus avoided being held accountable by their contestant and the imperial court.[29] On the other, they presented a counterargument, namely that the Jews must report to them as inhabitants of their territory, thus in effect saying that *if* there had been seizures (of which they presumably denied all knowledge), this would have been within their rights as rulers of the territory.

To bring an end to their exploitation, the Jews had to demonstrate that the acts of trespassing that had been committed were both mandated by the *Ganerben*, the co-rulers of their towns, and constituted criminal conduct. To achieve this aim, they used descriptions similar to those they employed when reporting on raids committed against them by members of the town's population whose only goal was

---

26. HStAM 86, no. 19989, fol. 6r (September 2, 1513).
27. Smail, *Legal Plunder*, 172–73.
28. For example HStAM 86, no. 6000, fol. 34r–v (July 7, 1502); HStAM 86, no. 19989, fol. 12r (August 18, 1525).
29. Battenberg, "Assenheimer Judenpogrome," 133–41, describes how Hanau utilized the imperial court to resolve the power struggle.

indiscriminate destruction and violence. For example, the Jews of Assenheim described an assault "in the evening of Sunday after Galli" (October 22, 1536), when their windows and shutters were smashed, their houses forcefully entered, and a young woman severely injured by "several citizens' sons and servants." After Hanau's district administrator failed to bring the perpetrators to justice, they begged the count to take action against the violent townspeople.[30] The recurrent use of force by figures of authority such as the servants of Solms and Isenburg and the lack of law enforcement encouraged acts of civil violence by decreasing the fear of punishment on the part of the offenders.

Other than the authorities, who enforced what they considered their right of governance, civil resentments against the Jews did not follow an articulated agenda. While the political implication of these two types of violence within the urban community was very different, the Jews portrayed them in a parallel manner as a strategy of delegitimization. Both the blindly raging townspeople and the strategically operating servants of the town lords were, in the eyes of their Jewish victims, simply criminals. The legal judgment of Solms's and Isenburg's course of action against the Jews became a question of terminology: does one acknowledge the argument of territorial lordship by speaking about "seizure"—or support the traditional Judenregal as uncontested by calling the incidents "burglary"? To understand the internal logic of the home invasions we need to take a closer look at the unpaid taxes that gave rise to them.

Tax Receivables as a Display of Lordship

The most well-established charge levied by the lords of Solms and Isenburg was the so-called *Trinkgeld*, a toll that Jews were required to pay whenever noble men passed through the town.[31] Demanding provisions and lodging from Jews was a common feature of displaying

---

30. Löwenstein, *Quellen zur Geschichte der Juden*, 3 no. N 108 (May 5–June 30, 1539); HStAM 86, no. 28548, fol. 2r-3v (November 2-3, 1536): "A little while ago, on Sunday evening after Galli [October 22, 1536], we were sitting in our houses in Assenheim, when several citizens' sons and servants, specifically Gangolff's son, the servant of Rüppel's son, and Michel Conrad's servant, out of sheer malice and wantonness, ran violently and unlawfully against our houses, threw a stone through the window of one, hitting a maiden on the head and making a hole in her skull down to the brain, broke the windows of another, and struck the shutters of the third, tearing them apart." See Treue, "Diener dreier Herren," 568.

31. Treue, "Diener dreier Herren," 569; Battenberg, "Assenheimer Judenpogrome," 129-30, 142.

lordship when traveling, serving as a reminder of their power to those living in towns without a ruler in permanent residence. Despite the illegitimacy of this homage to the Ganerben from the perspective of the Jews of Münzenberg and Assenheim, who did not consider them a proper authority, they themselves had committed to pay the Trinkgeld in 1528 as a way to avoid the arbitrary extortion of money. In 1551 the Jews of Assenheim reported that for the past one generation (equivalent to twenty-five years) there had been an agreement between them and the lords of Isenburg, according to which the Jews committed to pay one guilder to him each time he, or one of his servants, rode through the town.[32] Recently, however, they reported, the horsemen claimed the same fee for the way back, causing the Jewish community considerable additional expenses. Family members of the Isenburg town lord demanded the same allowance. Because of this the Jews had paid three guilders a day, three days in a row. In the year 1551 they had already paid twenty guilders.[33] Count Friedrich Magnus even demanded one guilder per horseman in July 1540 and crossed the town of Assenheim with six servants.[34] Hoping to stop this arbitrariness through binding regulations, the Jews asked to pay the levy only to the ruling count himself. Their petition was denied.[35]

The Count of Hanau saw these acknowledgments of the authority of Solms and Isenburg as undermining his own position and consequently forbade the Jews to pay this tax. However, he was unable to provide the Jews with any effective protection against it and those who refused to pay had their property seized by force by the tax collectors. As a result, obeying Hanau's orders was not a sustainable strategy. The

---

32. The commitment by the Jews was supposedly given in 1528, the announced proof, however, is missing from the records of the Imperial Chamber Court, see Battenberg, "Assenheimer Judenpogrome," 130-31. In September of the same year the Jews of Assenheim complained about the levy to Count Reinhard of Solms, see Löwenstein, *Quellen zur Geschichte der Juden*, vol. 3 no. 82 (September 19, 1528).

33. Löwenstein, *Quellen zur Geschichte der Juden* 1, no. 1407 (September 22, 1551); Treue, "Diener dreier Herren," 569-71. Six years later the Jews confirmed that they accepted paying the Trinkgeld, but to a more limited scale than it was interpreted by the lords of Isenburg and Solms: "But, gracious lord, since such a custom has existed for many years, that we and the Jews who were before us have voluntarily and willingly given the tip to the servants of Münzenberg, whenever the counts come to Münzenberg, and no such demand as if it were a right has been made of us. And yet now and repeatedly, we must give such money to the servants of our gracious lord of Solms, as has never happened before," HStAM 86, no. 5925, fol. 8r-9v (October 6, 1557).

34. HStAM 86, no. 5925, fol. 5r (July 12, 1540); Treue, "Diener dreier Herren," 569.

35. Löwenstein, *Quellen zur Geschichte der Juden*, vol. 1 no. 1407 (February 3, 1552).

Jews eventually asked their patron for permission to pay the levy in order to avoid retaliation.[36] Thus, over the course of the sixteenth century, this levy became anchored in customary law, and was in effect a significant setback to Hanau's claim to power.[37]

While the income obtained by the collection of the Trinkgeld was certainly an appreciated addition to the treasury of Solms and Isenburg, the Jews of Münzenberg and Wetterau were not particularly wealthy. This is clear from the lists of goods seized from them, which name objects of daily use, some books,[38] some objects with precious metal or other ornaments,[39] and merchandise.[40] Taken as a whole, it seems implausible that the seizure of these items was able to procure a high fiscal return. In fact, the tax revenue the Jewish community was expected to contribute to Hanau's treasury was marginal and yet could still often not be raised from these impoverished rural Jews, as the example of Anschel of Münzenberg demonstrates.[41] The scope of money lending carried out by the Jews in these two towns was likely very small due to the limited capacity of the rural market, so that abundance was out of reach for most of the businessmen. The Jews of Wetterau adapted better to the agricultural economy but were still not able to establish an outstanding financial elite within the small-town community.

In their supplications to the Count of Hanau, Jews emphasized the nature of the looted goods in order to contextualize their (lack of) supposed wealth and to point out the long-term negative effects not only for themselves, but for the region as a whole. The settlers, who were mainly pawnbrokers, kept a large amount of pawn in their houses, which, accordingly, was not, strictly speaking, their personal property. An inventory of a Jewish household in the nearby town of Windecken

---

36. HStAM 86, no. 25949, fol. 1r-2v (May 4, 1552). In December 1554 the Jews repeatedly apologize for their disobedience to the order of the Count of Hanaus, pointing out their lack of alternatives in the face of violence, see Löwenstein, *Quellen zur Geschichte der Juden*, vol. 1 no. 1420 (December 31, 1554).

37. Treue, "Komplexität auf kleinem Raum," 77-78; Treue, "Diener dreier Herren," 571-72; Battenberg, Assenheimer Judenpogrome, 130.

38. Löwenstein, *Quellen zur Geschichte der Juden* 1, no. 633 (May 10, 1502). Löwenstein, "Münzenberg," 916.

39. Löwenstein, *Quellen zur Geschichte der Juden* 1, no. 1073 (November 21, 1532).

40. Löwenstein, *Quellen zur Geschichte der Juden* 1, no. 769 (June 29, 1513), fabric.

41. HStAM 86, no. 5925, fol. 4r-v (End 1512). By the end of the sixteenth century the financial situation of the Jews had not improved, as continuous struggles to pay for their protection show; see Treue, "Diener dreier Herren," 592. Battenberg, however, still considered the fiscal value of the seizures to be a central motive despite the doubts raised above. See Battenberg, "Assenheimer Judenpogrome," 131.

includes a debt register and a great number of forfeited pawns that show the scope of this rural pawnbroking. While the items pawned were mostly of simple quality, such as tin vessels, lamps, and cloths, these objects were a substantial part of the resident's stock and were kept in his private chambers.[42] Demands for the return of these pawns, sent by the Count of Hanau to his co-lords on behalf of the victims, testify to the omnipresent threat to Jewish business life.[43] Unable to bring the commercial transaction to a conclusion, they feared further acts of violence would enforce the claims of the pledgers after the lord's monetary claims had been satisfied. The Jews of Assenheim wrote on September 19, 1513, to Countess Katharina: "If these pawns are not restored to us . . . when our Lord of Solms' servants next come to Assenheim, they will perhaps seize the Jews much worse than they have ever been seized, so that they would not be able to bear it and would be ruined."[44]

Still, it would appear that monetary reasons were not the main incentive for the acts of violence and blackmail committed, as the seizures brought only negligible financial gains, prevented the commercial recovery of the Jews, damaged the economy of the whole town, and caused conflict with the Christian population. Instead, the lords of Solms and Isenburg seem to have been actively seeking to build a case for the expulsion of the Jewish minority.[45] To convince the counts of Hanau of the need for expulsion, they pointed out the lack of income generated by the Jews. They argued that the tax of twelve guilders each per town

---

42. Löwenstein, *Quellen zur Geschichte der Juden* 1, no. 1073 (November 21, 1532). Compare inventories of the pawned items kept by the Regensburg Jews: Wilhelm Volkert, "Das Regensburger Judenregister von 1476," in *Festschrift für Andreas Kraus zum 60. Geburtstag*, eds. Pankraz Fried and Andreas Kraus (Kallmünz: Lassleben, 1982), 115-41, 118-20. As opposed to the Jews in rural Wetterau, the wealthy townspeople of Regensburg had pawns and belongings of high value, attesting to much more profitable business activity.

43. Löwenstein, *Quellen zur Geschichte der Juden* 1, no. 598 (November 17, 1499), no. 704 (November 15, 1508), no. 771 (September 2, 1513), vol. 3 no. N 121 (January 9, 1553).

44. HStAM 86, no. 19989, fol. 7r (September 19, 1513); compare HStAM 86, no. 25949, fol. 1r-2v (May 4, 1552). Löwenstein, *Quellen zur Geschichte der Juden* 1, no. 772; Treue, "Diener dreier Herren," 566-67.

45. Gerhard Rechter, "Judenschutz als reichsritterschaftliche Statuspolitik: Die Familien Crailsheim und Seckendorff als Fallbeispiele," in *Kaiser und Reich in der jüdischen Lokalgeschichte*, ed. Stefan Ehrenpreis, Andreas Gutzmann, and Stephan Wendehorst (Berlin: De Gruyter, 2013), 179-93, uses the example of the small territory of the knightly family of Crailsheim and Seckendorf to demonstrate that although the income they obtained was small, there was ongoing interest in holding onto the prestige connected to the patronage over the Jews. While his data refers mostly to the seventeenth and eighteenth centuries, the observation is valid for the proceeding centuries as well. For instance, Smail, *Legal Plunder*, 235, describes seizure as a way to generate sovereignty in the Late Middle Ages.

did not justify the damage the Jews were causing to the local society, and even offered to compensate for half of this tax income from their own resources if Hanau agreed to expel the Jews.[46] Therefore, the goal was not to profit financially, but to make the Jewish community dispensable in Hanau's eyes and pressure him to give up on this special domain within the town governments.

Comparisons of Governance

Hanau refused to agree to the desired expulsion. All involved parties knew that authority over the Jews was not merely about wealth, but was also, and perhaps mainly, at least in this instance, about prestige as well. To renounce this imperial right would have meant giving up on a substantial part of Hanau's influence within Münzenberg and Assenheim. Jewish diplomats made clever use of comparisons between the rulers in order to persuade their patron to intervene against the harassment. They emphasized, several times, that they "must give them [the condominial lords] annually much more than [they] give to Your Grace, and yet [they] are not safeguarded in body and property."[47] This was a humiliation for the owner of the Judenregal and thus of the right of taxation. His competitors were demanding a submissive gesture from the Jews that Hanau considered due only to himself. The lords of Solms and Isenburg meanwhile also used the complex situation to strengthen their own positions. Count Reinhard of Isenburg, for example, claimed that he could not give up on the Trinkgeld because Solms, his coruler, was not prepared to do the same.[48] The insistence on certain services and political gestures was intended to exercise and display lordship. It was not the lack of income that troubled the counts of Hanau, but the fact that they were lagging behind other condominial lords in this respect.

Furthermore, the seizures were connected to the violation of the *Burgfrieden*, a multilateral agreement constituting the government of a condominium as a joint entity of all involved parties. Solms, Isenburg, Eppstein, and Hanau agreed in these treaties on guidelines for their rule, such as how to appoint a so-called *Baumeister* as a shared common administrator, how to prevent and resolve conflicts among themselves,

---

46. Löwenstein, *Quellen zur Geschichte der Juden* 3, no. N 52 (December 2, 1507);
47. HStAM 86, no. 6000, fol. 30r-v (May 1502).
48. Löwenstein, *Quellen zur Geschichte der Juden* 1, no. 1420 (May 21, 1554).

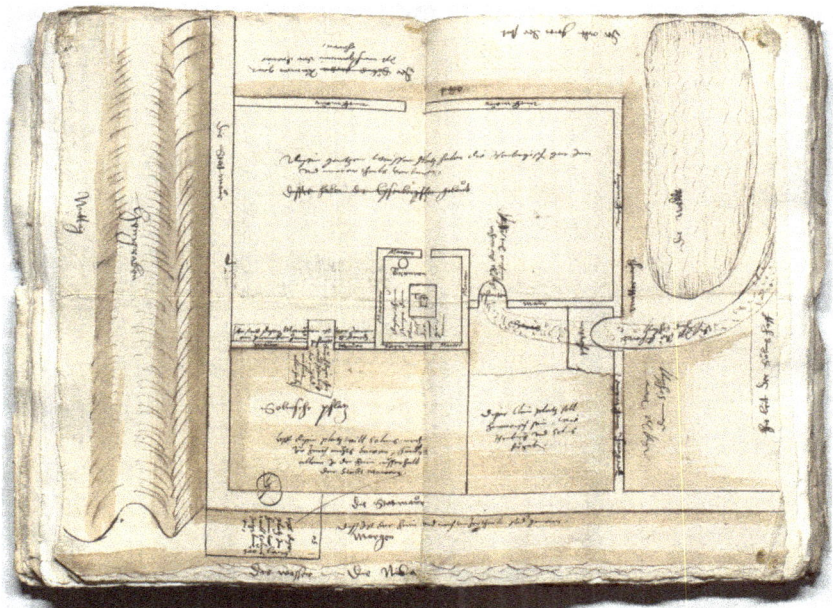

FIGURE 3.1. Historical map of Assenheim Castle, detailing the distinct domains of the lords of Solms, Isenburg, and Hanau. Hessian State Archives Marburg (HStAM). *Teilung des Schlosses zu Assenheim und der von der Herrschaft Solms dort geplante Bau.* 86, no. 20231, fol. 26v–27r (February 22, 1570).

how to deal with feuds and the financing of the defense of the territory, possibilities of redistribution and sale of shares of the estate, and more. These agreements were applied to a precisely defined area, a castle precinct, which was legally distinct from the territories of each participating lord. Within the castle precinct all manifestations of government, such as politics, economic regulation, and jurisdiction, were subject to the agreement of all the rulers.[49]

The Burgfrieden of Münzenberg, which was agreed on in 1448 and reestablished multiple times in the period that followed, included both the castle itself and the town at its feet.[50] The contract attempts to describe the legal area as precisely as possible, naming specific landmarks and streets. In doing so it exceeds the treaty, signed thirty-six years earlier, between Reinhard of Hanau and Werner, archbishop of

---

49. For more details about the practice of shared government under a Burgfrieden see Schneider, "*Ganerbschaften* und Burgfrieden"; Jendorff, "Gemeinsam herrschen."

50. HStAM, Urk. 100, no. 4764 ([1448] 1651).

Trier, about the previously joined estates of Münzenberg, Assenheim, and Hain. This treaty states its applicability, in all three cases, to the "castle and town," without further description.[51] Within the castle precinct every lord had a particular parcel of land for their use, in which to establish their office, presided over by their chosen official, who represented his rule before that of the other lords and the town population. A schematic drawing of the building of a new castle residence for the lords of Solms within the castle of Assenheim in the 1570s shows this distribution.[52]

The premises of the lords of Isenburg are depicted in the upper half of the drawing, while the areas belonging to the lords of Solms appear in both corners of the lower half of the map. Only the small rectangle between these two parcels was designated for the offices of the Count of Hanau. As castles were an expression of lordship, even in cases in which they did not effectively serve a defensive purpose, it was important for sovereigns to maintain and display authority.[53] In the cases of Münzenberg and Assenheim, the counts of Hanau refrained from manifesting their rights through architectural rebuilding.[54] While none of the ruling Ganerben had his permanent residence within the two castles, Isenburg and Solms dominated the physical space through bigger parcels of land and more recently expanded and refurbished seats of office. Considering the necessity of remote governance, Hanau could not tolerate breaches of the castle precincts, which could create the impression that they had abandoned their claims to power.

The contracting partners not only felt the need to establish exact borders, but also put in place a procedure in case of repeated violations of the treaty. The party who did not act in accordance with the Burgfrieden and did not correct their malfeasance after an official warning by the Baumeister "shall not be our *Ganerbe* anymore and everyone who did homage to him based on the castle shall be released from his oath and vow."[55] Peacekeeping was not taken lightly, as this radical punishment shows. Some contracts of this type mention Jews explicitly, as

---

51. HStAM, Urk. 61, no. 185 (January 1, 1412).
52. HStAM 86, no. 20231, fol. 26v–27r (February 22, 1570).
53. Ottersbach, *Burgen der Herren und Grafen von Hanau*, 65–66.
54. Ottersbach, *Burgen der Herren und Grafen von Hanau*, 78; Battenberg, "Assenheimer Judenpogrome," 126, 135–37.
55. HStAM, Urk. 100, no. 4764, fol. 4r.

they were a potential point of contention between the partners.[56] For example, in 1530 Josel of Rosheim explicitly reminded the Count of Hanau of the importance of the castle precincts, urging him to intercede in the kidnapping of a Jewess from his town Münzenberg into the castle of Friedberg.[57] The contract relating to the castle of Münzenberg did not explicitly mention dealings with the Jews. From Hanau's perspective, this might not have seemed necessary since the Jewish population was exempt from the general town government as a result of their imperial status. On the other hand, this enabled Solms and Isenburg to refrain from any formal agreement regarding their terms of conduct with regards to this population.

As a result of the cautious adherence to this mutual agreement, the storage of seized goods often played a role in the conflict between Hanau and his contestants. A letter from the local official of the Count of Solms in Münzenberg illustrates this issue. On July 7, 1502, in response to a demand from the Count of Hanau that goods falsely seized from the Jews be returned, the official wrote that he did not initiate seizures of the Jewish residents.[58] However, other servants of the count might have brought the items to his office without his knowledge and took them out of the castle precincts afterward. He therefore requested that he be considered innocent in the matter.[59] While the interim transfer of the goods to the seat of office seemed to prove that the seizures were directly ordered by the lord of Solms, the official in charge denied any complicity and refused to take responsibility on behalf of his ruler. The institution, which was supposed to serve the shared governance of different rulers, became an instrument of undermining condominial structures. In May 1502 the Jews who had been robbed explicitly mention the removal of their seized property from the divided jurisdiction of the town lords, thus preventing their restitution and the punishment of the intruders by the Count of Hanau: "Under the authority of the bailiff is dealt with us with such violence and iniquity within the free castle and its peace, by which your right of safe-conduct and

---

56. For example in Butzbach, see Battenberg, "Ganerbschaft Buseckertal," 149; Friedrich Battenberg, ed., *Quellen zur Geschichte der Juden im Hessischen Staatsarchiv Darmstadt 1080-1650* (Wiesbaden: Kommission für die Geschichte der Juden in Hessen, 1995), 815.

57. Avi Siluk, *Die Juden im politischen System des Alten Reichs* (Berlin: De Gruyter, 2021), 182-84, also 301.

58. HStAM 86, no. 6000, fol. 33r (July 5, 1502).

59. HStAM 86, no. 6000, fol. 34r (July 7, 1502).

protection and your guarantee and seal are weakened."⁶⁰ The reproach against both ruling parties is clear: the Lords of Solms-Lich enabled and supported the violation of Hanau's rights; and the Count of Hanau or his guardianship government neglected to protect the Jews under his care. Even in cases where the burglaries were not directly attributed to the servants of the town lords, no legal action was taken. In 1502, the Jewish community complained that attackers had "committed great violence and to a good extent everyone knows who they are."⁶¹ The visibility of the crimes and the simultaneous denial of justice was a clear sign of Hanau's lack of authority within the condominium.

Emigration?

In an effort to persuade him to intervene, the Jews drew their patrons' attention to their own problems within the condominium, pointing to financial losses and undermined authority. Their active room for maneuver was, however, limited. Since they lived on territory governed by Isenburg and Solms and their livelihood depended on transactions with the subjects of these lords, a further escalation of the conflict would have been unwise. Negotiations with the aggressors, despite their increasing number of concessions, did not lead to the end of the home invasions and seizures.⁶² Their last resort was therefore to leave the towns in order to completely escape the grasp of the opposing authorities. Thus, as the Münzenberg Jews wrote in May 1502: "But if we cannot find relief and mitigation, we poor must necessarily live in misery with our small children and vacate the town."⁶³

Giving up their real estate and markets was not a decision to be taken lightly. In rural areas, where their economic power was more limited than in larger cities, houses were the Jews' main assets. When in the middle of the sixteenth century, Jews were not allowed to own real

---

60. HStAM 86, no. 6000, fol. 30r (May 1502).
61. HStAM 86, no. 6000, fol. 30r (May 1502).
62. For example, the commitment of the Jews to pay the Trinkgeld, as discussed earlier in this chapter. For discussions between town officials, lords, and Jews about the resulting issues, see Löwenstein, *Quellen zur Geschichte der Juden* 1, no. 1407, 419–20 (September 22, 1551–May 5, 1552).
63. HStAM 86, no. 6000, fol. 30r-v (May 1502). The official of Hanau in Münzenberg reported to his count about the same warning of his Jews multiple times, for example: Löwenstein, *Quellen zur Geschichte der Juden* 3, no. 108 (July 11, 1540); HStAM 86, no. 5925, fol. 7r-v (February 1, 1542); similar: Löwenstein, *Quellen zur Geschichte der Juden* 1, no. 1407 (October 8, 1551; February 3, 1553).

estate in Münzenberg, they complained that "in [their] houses [their] poverty is hewn and built in" and that after the loss of their homes, they had no choice but to move away.[64] Even beyond the financial burden of having to pay rents, the lords refused to allow their subjects to rent houses to Jews in the first place.[65] Weber identified emigration in fourteenth-century Nürnberg and Augsburg as a strategy of mainly low-income families, as they were less likely to recover from liquidation of debt than wealthier businessmen and women.[66] In the small communities of Münzenberg and Assenheim, none of the Jewish settlers had sufficient wealth to recover from repeated seizures.

At the same time, the Jews were contractually bound to their residences for a certain period due to their writs of escort and could not easily cancel their tax obligations and move away.[67] Salman of Assenheim asked to be released from his obligations in 1509, and this was only granted on condition that he continue to pay taxes for a specified amount of time. He justified his emigration by his old age, stating he could no longer withstand the constant threat of violence.[68] Only after the expiration of their letters of protection could the Jews leave without legal consequences. Despite the high price of emigration, the oppression by servants of Solms and Isenburg seems to have had a significant impact on the Jewish population. For example, a drastic reduction in the number of Jewish inhabitants of Münzenberg took place at the beginning of the sixteenth century, following the initiative of Anschel (mentioned above), who hoped to ease his struggles with the authorities by reducing the size of his own community.[69]

---

64. Löwenstein, *Quellen zur Geschichte der Juden* 3, no. 115: "armut nhunmehr [. . .] verpflacket und verbawt"; also Fritz H. Herrmann, "Zur Geschichte der Juden in Münzenberg." *Wetterauer Geschichtsblätter* 23 (1974): 23–30, 24.

65. HStAM 86, no. 6000, fol. 30r (May 1502). Treue, "Diener dreier Herren," 569–70.

66. Andreas Weber, *Die Nürnberger Judengemeinde 1349–1499: Politische Handlungsspielräume jüdischer Akteure im Spätmittelalter* (Nuremberg: Gutenberg Druck, 2022), 130–34; Andreas Weber, "Life and Livelihood at Risk: Strategies of Ashkenazi Jews Facing the Threats of the 1380s and 1390s," in *The Jews of Europe around 1400: Disruption, Crisis, and Resilience*, ed. Lukas Clemens and Christoph Cluse (Wiesbaden: Harrassowitz Verlag, 2018), 55–72, 69–70.

67. Wenninger, *Geleit*, 58.

68. Löwenstein, *Quellen zur Geschichte der Juden* 1, no. 711; HStAM 86, no. 19989, fol. 2v, 3v (June 1509); Treue, "Diener dreier Herren," 566.

69. Treue, "Diener dreier Herren," 567; Löwenstein, "Münzenberg," 915. The expulsion of most of the Münzenberg Jews was surprisingly based on the initiative of the mentioned Jew Anschel, who hoped to ease his struggles with the authorities and his neighbors by getting rid of his own peers, see Annika Funke, "Settlement Policy and Competition in Towns: The Case of Anschel of Münzenberg," *Medieval History Journal* 27, no. 2: 382–410. https://doi.org/10.1177/09719458241263464.

However, it was not only the Jews themselves who suffered from their departure, but also their patron. In a situation where the counts of Hanau held only one-sixth of the dominion, the loss of further rights was a defeat at the hands of his co-lords and was recognized as such by them as well as by their subjects. Aware of their political influence, the Münzenberg Jews therefore added in 1502 that they "do not like to harm Your Grace, but the great hardship forces us in the abovementioned matter."[70] The emigration was thus not necessarily a forced withdrawal but was initially conceived of as a threat against the government. If Reinhard continued to fail to meet his obligations of protection, his subjects threatened to undermine his imperial privileges, which were already on shaky ground. Losing the guardianship over the Jews meant in fact losing not only the prestige attached to it but also his political influence in the territory.

Lacking an inherent interest in the preservation of the Jewish community in their territory, the condominial lords of Solms and Isenburg used the Jews of Münzenberg and Assenheim as leverage and as a catalyst in their efforts to expand their power at the expense of the counts of Hanau. Although, in this instance, the coexistence of different claims to authority often led to systematic violence against the Jews, the latter were also able to employ a political lobby to counter the threat as well as to carry out a series of diplomatic efforts and strategies to help withstand it by negotiating with both sides throughout the sixteenth century.

As shown, the Jews used a variety of argumentative strategies, engaging with and appealing to their rulers in the hopes of projecting themselves and their livelihood. Primarily, they reinforced the interest of the holder of the Judenregal in maintaining and displaying its holder's imperial right and delegitimized the differing legal conception of Solms and Isenburg. Playing one side against the other, they sought to pressure their favored political partner by making their own needs appear to be a crucial part of the preservation of his authority. They drew attention to his financial interests, to the undermining of his power and loss of prestige and, when those arguments failed to provoke him to action, threatened his imperial rights with their emigration. Parallel

---

70. HStAM 86, no. 6000, fol. 30r (May 1502): "We do not wish to harm your Grace, but the great need compels us in the aforementioned matters"; see Treue, "Komplexität auf kleinem Raum," 77–78.

agreements and concessions toward the oppressors supplemented their efforts but did not ease their hardship and contributed to the establishment of undesirable long-term precedents and customary law.

In all of the existing letters written by Jewish representatives to the counts of Hanau we find this same set of arguments, varying in order and emphasis. Bearing this in mind, it was not an innocent mistake on their part when the Jewry of Münzenberg signed a letter with *"Judenschaft zu Windecken,"* another town nearby, and subsequently needed to correct the name of the settlement.[71] The uniformity of diplomatic action points to a developed body of translocal Jewish politics. The small communities in this rural area were interconnected and not only dealt with similar issues, but worked in alliance with each other, helping each other adapt to the territorialization of governance.

By the sixteenth century, most Jews had been expelled from the major urban communities, and forced to move to more rural areas. Although this meant the loss of the numerous well-established political networks of the cities, able to support their interests before the city council and the emperor, further investigation reveals that this change resulted not in the loss of political agency so much as its reorganization. In adapting to their new realities, the Jews embarked on a process that ultimately led to the development of institutionalized territorial bodies, the early modern *Landjudenschaften*, which represented their needs before a variety of rulers. The case of Münzenberg and Assenheim is indicative of an intermediate stage in this process, during which the Jews continued to pursue strategies in accordance with the older form of their protection as direct servants of the emperor but soon found themselves increasingly involved in territorial power struggles that required novel and innovative approaches.

Further Readings

Barzen, Rainer Josef. "Jewish Regional Organization in the Rhineland—the Kehillot Shum around 1300." In *The Jews of Europe in the Middle Ages,* ed. Christoph Cluse, 235–37. Turnhout: Brepols, 2004.

Barzen, Rainer. "West and East in Ashkenaz in the Time of Judah he-Ḥasid." *Jewish History* 34 (2021): 53–81, 68–73. doi: 10.1007/s10835-021-09375-6.

Baskin, Judith. "Mobility and Marriage in Two Medieval Jewish Societies." *Jewish History* 22 (2008): 223–43. doi: 10.1007/s 10835-007-9054-3

---

71. HStAM 86, no. 5925, fol. 8r-9v (October 6, 1557).

Benjamin of Tudela. *The Itinerary of Benjamin of Tudela*, edited by Marcus N. Adler. London: Oxford University Press, 1907.

Breuer, Mordechai. "The Wanderings of Students and Scholars: A Prolegomenon to a Chapter in the History of Yeshivot." In *Culture and Society in Medieval Jewry: Studies Dedicated to the Memory of Haim Hillel Ben-Sasson*, edited by Menachem Ben-Sasson, Robert Bonfil, and Joseph R. Hacker, 450–57. Jerusalem: Merkaz Shazar, 1989 (Hebrew).

Eckoldt, Martin. "Navigation on Small Rivers in Central Europe in Roman and Medieval Times." *International Journal of Nautical Archaeology and Underwater Exploration* 13 (1984): 3–10. doi: 10.1111/j.1095-9270.1984.tb01172.x.

Fütterer, Pierre. "Wasserstraße oder Landweg? Neue Befunde zu einer alten Streitfrage." In *Flusstäler, Flussschifffahrt, Flusshäfen: Befunde aus Antike und Mittelalter*, edited by Peter Ettel and Achim Thomas Hack, 61–78. Mainz: Verlag des Römisch-Germanischen Zentralmuseums, 2019.

Irsigler, Franz. "Rhein, Maas und Mosel als Handels- und Verkehrsachsen im Mittelalter." In *Flüsse und Flusstäler als Wirtschafts- und Kommunikationswege*, edited by Stephan Freund, Matthias Hardt, and Petra Weigel, 9–32. Bonn: Arkum, 2007.

Leighton, Albert. *Transport and Communication in Early Medieval Europe, 500–1100*. Newton Abbot: David and Charles, 1972.

Pfeiffer, Friedrich. *Rheinische Transitzölle im Mittelalter*. Berlin: Akademie Verlag, 1997.

Pranke, Piotr, and Miloš Zečević. *Medieval Trade in Central Europe, Scandinavia, and the Balkans (10th–12th Centuries): A Comparative Study*, trans. Michał Romanek. Leiden: Brill, 2020.

P'tahiah of Regensburg. *Travels of R. P'tahiah of Regensburg*, edited by Elazar ha-Levi Grünhut. Frankfurt: Kauffmann, 1905.

Romain, Jonathan. "River Jews: Medieval Jews along the Thames as a Microcosm of Anglo-Jewry." *Jewish Historical Studies* 43 (2011): 21–25. jstor.org/stable/29780143.

Runde, Ingo. "Der Rhine als Wirtschafts- und Verkehrsachse." In *Die Wittelsbacher und die Kurpfalz im Mittelalter. Eine Erfolgsgeschichte?* edited by Jörg Peltzer, 53–65. Regensburg: Schnell & Steiner, 2013.

Shoham-Steiner, Ephraim. "From Speyer to Regensburg: Reexamining the Migration of the Pietistic Kalonymides from the Rhineland to the Danube." *Zion* 81 (2016): 149–76 (Hebrew). www.jstor.org/stable/24746072.

Toch, Michael. *The Economic History of European Jews: Late Antiquity and Early Middle Ages*. Leiden: Brill, 2013.

Verdon, Jean. *Travel in the Middle Ages*, trans. George Holoch. South Bend: University of Notre Dame Press, 2003.

Werther, Lukas, and Lars Kröger. "Medieval Inland Navigation and the Shifting Fluvial Landscape between Rhine and Danube." *PCA (European Journal of Postclassical Archaeologies)* 7 (2017): 65–96.

Yuval, Israel J. "A German-Jewish Autobiography from the 14th Century." *Tarbiz* 55 (1986): 541–66 (Hebrew). jstor.org/stable/23597644.

Part II

Spaces

Tzafrir Barzilay, Nureet Dermer, and Albert Evan Kohn

Everything happens somewhere. While this point may seem overly trivial as a hinge for historical inquiry, historians have shown that a detailed analysis of the immediate as well as relative location of that "somewhere" is crucial for a complete understanding of historical phenomena. Although research into human societies of the past has always required a consideration of space, interest in this aspect has grown in recent decades, and space has become a central category in historical and sociological research.[1] This stems from the recognition that social dynamics of different kinds are more or less likely in certain spaces. For example, between 1315 and 1317, Europe was

---

1. See, for example, Didier Boisseuil et al., eds., *Écritures de l'espace social: Mélanges d'histoire médiévale offerts à Monique Bourin, Histoire ancienne et médiévale* (Paris: Éditions de la Sorbonne, 2019); Marc Boone and Martha C. Howell, eds., *The Power of Space in Late Medieval and Early Modern Europe: The Cities of Italy, Northern France, and the Low Countries*, Studies in European Urban History 30 (Turnhout: Brepols, 2013); Caroline Goodson, Anne Elisabeth Lester, and Carol Symes, eds., *Cities, Texts, and Social Networks, 400–1500: Experiences and Perceptions of Medieval Urban Space* (Farnham, Surrey, UK: Ashgate, 2010); Albrecht Classen, ed., *Urban Space in the Middle Ages and the Early Modern Age* (Berlin: De Gruyter, 2009); Mike Crang, ed., *Thinking Space* (London: Routledge, 2002); Barbara H. Rosenwein, *Negotiating Space: Power, Restraint, and Privileges of Immunity in Early Medieval Europe* (Ithaca, NY: Cornell University Press, 1999); Wendy Davies, Guy Halsall, and Andrew J. Reynolds, eds., *People and Space in the Middle Ages, 300–1300* (Turnhout: Brepols, 2006).

afflicted with what is known as the Great Famine. Weather patterns in the Atlantic Ocean, however, resulted in more severe famine conditions in the northern plains of Europe than in the south of the continent. The social and economic upheaval ensuing from this environmental crisis thus shaped the experience of Northerners much more than those living in southern Europe. Location thus dictates not only the likelihood of certain historical events, but also determines their scale of impact, both spatially and over time. Natural topography, built architecture, demographics, and even weather patterns are just some of the many features of space that influence historical dynamics.

Space has become particularly important for historians of daily life, who focus on the recurring activities and underlying conditions that constituted life in past societies, specifically, in our case, medieval Jews.[2] Barbara Hanawalt and Michal Kobialka point out that "not only did people create uses for space but having done so, that space could influence the behavior of those who occupied it; defining space tended to proscribe the behavior within it."[3] With this in mind, historians of everyday life pose basic questions about the material circumstances dictated by the places in which people lived: What were the physical features of the places in which they made their homes? How far did they live from the resources they needed to survive? Who were the people they met as they navigated their surroundings? Different questions can be asked about how space shaped the movement of people, objects, and ideas: How easy or difficult, expensive or inexpensive, fast or slow would it have been to move from one particular point to another? What roles did geographical, technological, political, and economic barriers play in determining the kinds of movements and interactions that occurred? Another set of questions relates to the perceptions that determined the social significance of a particular space: How did its features

---

2. For space as a factor in Jewish daily life in medieval northern Europe, see a dedicated special issue by the Beyond the Elite group in *Jewish Studies Quarterly* 28, 3-4 (2021): 245–447 and esp. Elisheva Baumgarten, "Space and Place in Medieval Ashkenaz," 245–58, doi:10.1628/jsq-2021-0013. For other examples see Alfred Haverkamp, "Jews and Urban Life: Bonds and Relationships," in *The Jews of Europe in the Middle Ages (Tenth to Fifteenth Centuries)*, ed. Christoph Cluse (Turnhout: Brepols, 2004), 55–69; Lucia Raspe, "Between Judengasse and the City: Jews, Urban Space and Local Tradition in Early Modern Worms," *Journal of Jewish Studies* 67 (2016): 225–48, doi: 10.18647/3277/JJS-2016; Micha J. Perry, "Imaginary Space Meets Actual Space in 13th-Century Cologne: Eliezer Ben Joel and the Eruv," *Images* 5 (2011): 26–36, doi:10.1163/187180011X604625; Charlotte Fonrobert and Vered Shemtov, "Jewish Conceptions and Practice of Space," *Jewish Social Studies* 11 (2005): 1–8, doi: 10.1353/jss.2005.0022.

3. Barbara Hanawalt and Michal Kobialka, eds., *Medieval Practices of Space*, Medieval Cultures 23 (Minneapolis: University of Minnesota Press, 2000), x (introduction).

determine how it was perceived by those inside and outside its borders? How did spatial environments reflect social and political hierarchies? These questions stand at the heart of the three chapters included in this section, as well as of others in this volume and of the field of quotidian history in general.[4]

How historians approach these questions depends on the scale of their analyses. The scale of spatial analysis can refer to the small, immediate environment that a person frequented: his or her room or house, the local streets, workshops, or communal buildings.[5] Scale can also refer to larger spaces, like cities, counties, kingdoms, or even river basins, which played an important part in shaping social phenomena, as well as the perception of the people who occupied them. Each of these spatial units calls for different research questions and methodological tools, as the chapters in this volume demonstrate. If, for example, we focus on political history, the borders of kingdoms or counties (to the extent that these were clearly demarcated during the Middle Ages) would probably be the most useful. When it comes to issues of daily life, however, spatial elements like houses and their internal layout, cities with their streets and markets, and even the fields of the surrounding countryside might be more pertinent. While the medieval world did not have the firm borders that we have come to expect in modernity, numerous other types of boundaries can be used to define the scale of historical analysis. Some of these were the natural, physical borders of the topography, such as mountain ranges and large rivers. Others were human made, such as the enormous walls built to separate and defend cities from outsiders. Most borders that historians consider, though, had practically no physical presence and were either administrative or of the mind. Political principalities were established by writ and charter. The medieval church divided regions into bishoprics and, more locally, into parishes. Local traditions, such as the kinds of crops planted or the animals raised, differentiated rural areas no less than weather patterns and land conditions. Differing languages resulted in

---

[4]. For a review of the relevant literature, see Baumgarten, "Space and Place," 249–50.

[5]. On domestic space, see Diana Webb, "Domestic Space and Devotion in the Middle Ages," in *Defining the Holy: Sacred Space in Medieval and Early Modern Europe*, eds. Andrew Spicer and Sarah Hamilton (New York: Routledge, 2006), 27–48; Felicity Riddy, "Looking Closely: Authority and Intimacy in the Late Medieval Urban Home," in *Gendering the Master Narrative: Women and Power in the Middle Ages*, ed. Mary Carpenter Erler and Maryanne Kowaleski (Ithaca, NY: Cornell University Press, 2003), 212–28; Katherine L. French, ed., *A Cultural History of the Home in the Medieval Age* (London: Bloomsbury Academic, 2020).

invisible borders limiting the places where individuals felt comfortable settling, visiting, or conducting business. While these borders are not easy to map, they determined the experience of medieval people and are critical to spatial analysis.[6]

An essential feature of the spaces within these borders was the diverse range of people who lived there. Different kinds of people lived in certain regions, specific towns, and even particular neighborhoods. Practitioners of various professions, foreigners, and marginalized groups congregated in distinct areas that consequentially took on particular social characteristics. Among these were Jews, who generally dwelled in towns and tended to inhabit specific urban areas. In some regions, for example, Jewish communities were frequently established in the vicinity of cathedrals, markets, or the city walls. Although not all Jews lived in the same area, and there were no ghettos for Jews in medieval Europe, Jewish areas of settlement were identifiable by their Jewish inhabitants, synagogues, mikvehs, and other communal buildings. The fact that they were occupied by Jews often shaped how these places were perceived in the eyes of other inhabitants.

In the chapters included in this section, the term *space* extends beyond geographical characteristics to elucidate the various social meanings of space to the everyday lives of medieval Jews. The chapters focus on physical urban spaces, that is, those areas where Jews and Christians lived, conducted business, encountered their next-door neighbors, and experienced incidents and occurrences in the public areas and streets of the city. We also explore how the medieval city was a space in which power structures were made manifest; how and why people moved through space; and the social implications of such movement. These different approaches to space as a category of social history (among other possible approaches) enable a diverse and complex perspective on Jewish daily life.

Each angle considers different features of "space" within its analysis. Consideration of topographical features can reveal the extent to which different regions were connected to one another. Like distance, the presence of mountain ranges and large rivers between settlements could have disrupted communication and caused greater cultural and

---

6. For instance: Alfred Hiatt, *Dislocations: Maps, Classical Tradition, and Spatial Play in the European Middle Ages* (Toronto: Pontifical Institute of Mediaeval Studies, 2020); Albrecht Classen, *Rural Space in the Middle Ages and Early Modern Age: The Spatial Turn in Premodern Studies* (Berlin: De Gruyter, 2012).

economic isolation. Yet, as Tzafrir Barzilay suggests in his chapter on river travel, waterways were also connectors. This was particularly the case for the Jewish communities in the Rhineland, which, although many hundreds of miles distant from one another, were connected by a system of rivers that made travel between them relatively easy. What, though, would this have meant for Jewish life and communities in areas far from major waterways?

    Historians are also interested in studying administrative and built environments through smaller-scale spatial analysis, for example, of cities and towns. Studies of this type look at the particular neighborhoods in which certain communities settled, or narrowing the gaze even further, examine specific urban buildings and institutions. Taverns, churches, markets, and courts, for example, were all populated by various types of people who shaped a visitor's experience of these places. The other two chapters in this section pursue these lines of inquiry. Nureet Dermer's contribution focuses on the social significance of specific neighborhoods in medieval Paris. Then, as today, neighborhoods were inhabited by different kinds of people and buildings that fashioned the conditions of local life. Dermer traces shifts in Jewish patterns of settlement in Paris to extrapolate the place of Jews within the urban ecosystem. Albert Kohn, for his part, focuses on the specific locations in which Jewish visitors to medieval cities found accommodations. He shows how the amenities available at inns, hospices, and private homes would have influenced the traveler's decision on where he or she should spend his or her time. These diverse examples of spatial analysis shed new light on the geography of Jewish settlement and the political, economic, and environmental factors behind it. They also reveal how space shaped and exposed intracommunal Jewish practices and hierarchies, local social distinctions, and changes in the policies and perceptions of sovereigns. They illustrate the conclusive value of space as a unique and compelling prism for the study of the everyday life of medieval Jews.

CHAPTER 4

Rivers, Tolls, and Ships
The Movement and Communication of Medieval German Jews

Tzafrir Barzilay

The Nuremberg *Memorbuch*, composed by Isaac of Meiningen in 1296, includes a short list of exemplary leaders of German Jewish communities, whose names are to be commemorated every Sabbath. On this list of famous rabbis and people who successfully prevented violence against Jews, appears the names of "Mr. Isaac and Mrs. Bella, who had cancelled the Koblenz toll."[1] What did these individuals do to deserve being included in such a distinguished list of people honored by Jewish communities throughout the German territories? When did they act? What was the Koblenz toll, and why was

---

This chapter was written with the support of the Haifa Center for Mediterranean History at Haifa University. It was written under the auspices of the Beyond the Elite: Jewish Daily Life in Medieval Europe Project, PI Elisheva Baumgarten, from the European Research Council (ERC) under the European Union's Horizon 2020 research and innovation program, grant agreement No. 681507, and prepared for publication with funding from the Israel Science Foundation Grant 2850/22, Contending with Crises: The Jews of XIVth Century Europe, PI Elisheva Baumgarten. I thank Miri Rubin, Elisheva Carlebach, and Gadi Algazi for their valuable feedback, and also Jörg Müller for sharing his ideas and unpublished work with me. Members of the Beyond the Elite research group, in particular Aviya Doron and Albert Kohn, have assisted me in gaining access to sources and in polishing my arguments, for which I am grateful.

1. "Mar Itzḥak ve-marat Bella she-bitlu mekhes me-Koplintz"—Siegmund Salfeld, *Das Martyrologium des Nürnberger Memorbuches* (Berlin: Leonhard Simion, 1898), 86.

its cancellation so important?[2] This chapter explores these questions as a gateway into the study of the Jewish reliance on river travel in the eleventh to the thirteenth centuries. It discusses toll stations and river travel, the political struggles that evolved around them in the thirteenth century, and its influence on the cost of movement. It then turns to the Jews, their experience of river travel, and the important role it played in their lives. It concludes by suggesting that the incorporation of geographical considerations into the analysis of Jewish social history can open valuable avenues for future research. Overall, it shows that river travel was central for the everyday life of medieval Jews, especially in the German Empire, and that protecting their ability to travel quickly and cheaply was indeed a high priority.

River Tolls and German Jews

Toll stations were commonly used as sources of income across Europe, including in the German-speaking lands, from the early Middle Ages. They were established along major trade routes, and charged passengers for merchandise that passed through the station. These tolls existed in addition to other taxes, adding to the expense of travel. During this period, transportation and trade were largely dependent on river travel. Traveling by ship was faster and cheaper than by land, especially with regards to the transportation of bulk goods over long distances; a situation reinforced by the general inadequacy of the roads, particularly before the thirteenth century.[3] Of course, not all rivers were navigable, especially for larger vessels, and sailing upstream was slow. Obstructions could likewise delay movement, and traveling from one river basin to another still required the portage of goods over land.[4] Generally

---

2. Historians have noted the peculiarity of this phrase. See Salfeld, *Martyrologium*, 290n3; Julius Aronius, Albert Dresdner, and Ludwig Lewinski, *Regesten zur Geschichte der Juden im fränkischen und deutschen Reiche bis zum Jahre 1273* (Berlin: L. Simion, 1902), 96n208.

3. This is a common assumption. See, e.g., Albert Leighton, *Transport and Communication in Early Medieval Europe, 500–1100* (Newton Abbot, UK: David and Charles, 1972), 125–33; Jean Verdon, *Travel in the Middle Ages*, trans. George Holoch (South Bend, IN: University of Notre Dame Press, 2003), 28–30; Lukas Werther and Lars Kröger, "Medieval Inland Navigation and the Shifting Fluvial Landscape between Rhine and Danube," *PCA* 7 (2017): 67, 71–73.

4. Detlev Ellmers, "Techniken und Organisationsformen zur Nutzung der Binnenwasserstraßen im hohen und späten Mittelalter," in *Straßen- und Verkehrswesen im hohen und späten Mittelalter*, ed. Rainer Christoph Schwinges (Ostfildern: Jan Thorbecke, 2007), 161–83; Pierre Fütterer, "Wasserstraße oder Landweg? Neue Befunde zu einer alten Streitfrage," in *Flusstäler, Flussschifffahrt, Flusshäfen: Befunde aus Antike und Mittelalter*, ed. Peter Ettel and Achim Thomas Hack (Mainz: Verlag des Römisch-Germanischen Zentralmuseums, 2019), 61–78; Martin

speaking, however, high medieval travel and trade ran along the major river systems of central Europe.[5]

One of the most important of these was the Rhine, which served as the primary trade route of the western Empire, and had numerous toll stations along its banks. People from different places were charged different tariffs for passing through these stations, and special kinds of merchandise were likewise subjected to various levies. The right to collect tolls was granted to local institutions or rulers by the archbishop or, more often, the emperor.[6] The stations often included fortified buildings with river chains, where ships were halted and their owners forced to comply with inspection and toll collection.[7] These procedures and costs were an inseparable part of long-distance travel, especially by river.

Positioned strategically at the point where the Mosel River flows into the Rhine, the Koblenz toll station was of special importance (see map),[8] controlling not only the flow of goods from the upper to the lower Rhine (as other stations did), but also the trade from the Mosel Valley northwards.[9] The station is first documented in 1018, when Emperor Heinrich II awarded the archbishop of Trier, who controlled Koblenz, the rights to its income, which the archbishop later

---

Eckoldt, "Navigation on Small Rivers in Central Europe in Roman and Medieval Times," *International Journal of Nautical Archaeology and Underwater Exploration* 13 (1984): 3–10, doi: 10.1111/j.1095-9270.1984.tb01172.x; Werther and Kröger, "Medieval Inland Navigation," 71–74.

5. Friedrich Pfeiffer, *Rheinische Transitzölle im Mittelalter* (Berlin: Akademie Verlag, 1997), esp. 98–108, 122–25; Fütterer, "Wasserstraße oder Landweg?" 70–73; Franz Irsigler, "Rhein, Maas und Mosel als Handels- und Verkehrsachsen im Mittelalter," in *Flüsse und Flusstäler als Wirtschafts- und Kommunikationswege*, ed. Stephan Freund, Matthias Hardt, and Petra Weigel (Bonn: Arkum, 2007), 13–27; Piotr Pranke and Miloš Zečević, *Medieval Trade in Central Europe, Scandinavia, and the Balkans (10th–12th Centuries): A Comparative Study*, trans. Michał Romanek (Leiden: Brill, 2020), 48n58, 51, 66–69; Ingo Runde, "Der Rhine als Wirtschafts- und Verkehrsachse," in *Die Wittelsbacher und die Kurpfalz im Mittelalter. Eine Erfolgsgeschichte?* ed. Jörg Peltzer (Regensburg: Schnell & Steiner, 2013), 53–58.

6. Pfeiffer, *Rheinische Transitzölle*; Irsigler, "Rhein," 13–30; Werther and Kröger, "Medieval Inland Navigation," 74–83; Pierre Monnet, "Ports maritimes et fluviaux dans les pays d'Empire," in *Ports maritimes et ports fluviaux au Moyen Âge*, ed. Régine Le Jan (Paris: Éditions de la Sorbonne, 2005), 34–37, 52–55; Pranke and Zečević, *Medieval Trade*, 65–70; Runde, "Der Rhine," 65.

7. Günther Stanzl, "Castles in the Middle Rhine Valley, and the Particular Case of Fürstenberg," in *Mainz and the Middle Rhine Valley: Medieval Art, Architecture and Archaeology*, ed. Ute Engel and Alexandra Gajewski (Leeds: Maney, 2007), 204–20; Runde, "Der Rhine," 65.

8. Koblenz's Latin name, *Confluentia*, is derived from "confluentes," "the meeting place of rivers."

9. Pfeiffer, *Rheinische Transitzölle*, esp. 98–108, 122–25; Irsigler, "Rhein," 13–27; Runde, "Der Rhine," 53–58.

granted to the Saint Simeon collegiate church in Trier.[10] A regulation document from this toll has survived from the mid-eleventh century, which lists tariffs for travelers arriving from various distant locations, including Swabia, the Danube, and the Low Countries. Evidently, even at this early period Koblenz stood at the center of wide-ranging trade networks. This earliest document so far discovered from the Koblenz toll station is also the first to mention Jews, stating that: "Jews have to give four dinars for every slave who was bought, as well as for a pack animal."[11] Although Michael Toch claims that this is referring to slaves who were personal servants of Jews and should not be read as evidence for Jewish involvement in the slave trade, the wording here strongly suggests otherwise.[12] Moreover, the slaves are mentioned immediately after references to travelers from the Danube, Main, and Mosel valleys, which suggests a context of long-distance (slave) trade. In any case, what is of import here is that despite the limited scale of Jewish settlement in the empire during this period, a sufficient number of Jews passed through the Koblenz toll station to merit particular legislation.[13]

The next surviving regulatory document for the Koblenz toll, purportedly issued in 1104, does not mention Jews, and neither does any other twelfth-century German toll regulation. This can perhaps be explained by a decline in Jewish slave trading, or by a general decline in Jewish movement following the persecutions of 1096.[14] It is also possible,

---

10. Monumenta Germaniae Historica (hereafter: MGH), Diplomata, Heinrich II (DD H II), 509-10, no. 397. Theo Kölzer, "Der Koblenzer Zoll im 11 und 12 Jahrhundert: Eine diplomatisch-paläographische Nachlese," *Rheinische Vierteljahrsblätter* 66 (2002): 39-43; Pfeiffer, *Rheinische Transitzölle*, 83-85.

11. Bernhard Diestelkamp, M. A. Martens, C. van de Kieft, and B. A. Fritz, eds., *Elenchus Fontium Historiae Urbanae*, vol. 1 (Leiden: Brill, 1967), 66.

12. Michael Toch, "The European Jews of the Early Middle Ages: Slave-Traders?" *Zion* 64 (1999) 39-63, http://www.jstor.org/stable/23563572; Toch, *The Economic History of European Jews: Late Antiquity and Early Middle Ages* (Leiden: Brill, 2013), 186. Medieval terminology describing unfreedom is obscure, yet "unoquoque sclavo empticio" likely refers to slaves recently purchased rather than household servants (*mancipia* or *servi*, often): Alice Rio, *Slavery After Rome, 500–1100* (Oxford: Oxford University Press, 2017), 6, 15, 156-67. See also Pfeiffer, *Rheinische Transitzölle*, 94-96, 107-8, 126-27.

13. For settlement patterns see: Alfred Haverkamp and Thomas Bardelle, eds. *Geschichte der Juden im Mittelalter von der Nordsee bis zu den Südalpen*, vol. 3 (Hannover: Hahn, 2002), maps A1.1, A2.1, A3.1, A4.1, A5.1, C1.1, C2.1, C3.1, C4.1, C5.1; Michael Toch, "The Formation of a Diaspora: The Settlement of Jews in the Medieval German Reich," *Aschkenas* 7 (1997): 57 (map 1), doi: 10.1515/asch.1997.7.1.55. For medieval long-distance Jewish trade, see Irving Agus, *The Heroic Age of Franco-German Jewry* (New York: Yeshiva University, 1969), 23-51.

14. Heinrich Beyer, Leopold Eltester, and Adam Goerz, eds., *Urkundenbuch zur Geschichte der jetzt die Preussischen Regierungsbezirke Coblenz und Trier bildenden mittelrheinischen Territorien*, 3 vols. (Koblenz: Hölscher, 1860-1874), 1:467-69; Pfeiffer, *Rheinische Transitzölle*, 107-8; Toch,

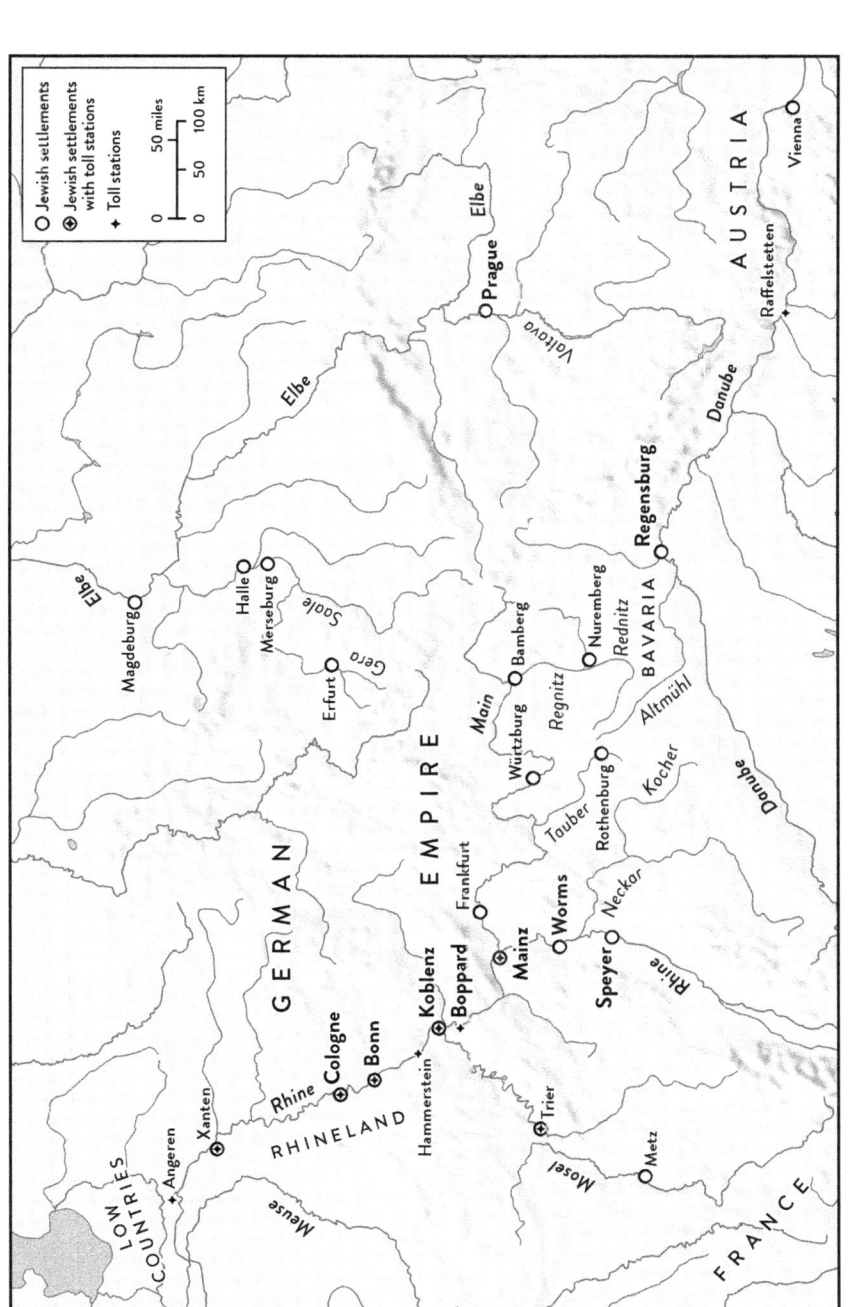

FIGURE 4.1. Map of major rivers and toll stations.

however, that this absence is related to the idea, which took shape in the late eleventh century, that the Jews should adhere to a system of particular laws and enjoy special imperial protection. So, for example, two privileges awarded by Emperor Heinrich IV to the Jews of Worms and Speyer in 1090 (and that likely served as the basis for further acts of legislation) forbade any restrictions on long-distance travel for Jews and exempted them from any tolls (*theloneum*).[15] If indeed, as a result of these privileges, Jewish travelers were not required to pay at toll stations, there would have been less reason to set a tariff for them or otherwise discuss them in toll regulations. Thus, the Koblenz toll, and German river tolls more generally, do not appear to have posed a major problem for Jews in the eleventh and twelfth centuries.[16]

This was not the situation by the time new regulations for the Koblenz toll were issued in 1209, which proclaim that

> those coming from any location beyond the Meuse [river], and all those [coming] from Regensburg, and all those who do not stay within the confines of their area, whether Jews or Christians, have to give a *ferto* [a certain coin] and one dinar. A Jewish woman, if she carries an infant in her belly, has to pay the toll on his behalf. A Jew of that area [beyond the Meuse or Regensburg] has to give nine free dinars or six dinars of Cologne.[17]

There seem to have been two kinds of tariffs at work: First, a small personal tax to be paid by anyone traveling beyond their territory of residence, regardless of whether he or she was a merchant (as the reference

---

Economic History, 188–90; Aronius et al., *Regesten*, 96, no. 208. For additional documents: Kölzer, "Der Koblenzer Zoll," 40–41.

15. MGH, Diplomata, Heinrich IV (DD H IV), 2:543–49, nos. 411–12; Amnon Linder, *The Jews in the Legal Sources of the Early Middle Ages* (Detroit: Wayne State University Press, 1997), 353–58, 391–400. For the scope of these privileges, see Friedrich Lotter, "The Scope and Effectiveness of Imperial Jewry Law in the High Middle Ages," *Jewish History* 4 (1989): 31–34.

16. Emperor Friedrich I ratified Jewish freedom of tolls in a privilege awarded to Worms' Jews in 1157: MGH, Diplomata, Friedrich I (DD F I), 1:284–86, no. 166; Linder, *Legal Sources*, 396–400. Markus Wenninger, "Geleit, Geleitsrecht und Juden im Mittelalter," *Aschkenas* 31 (2021): 47–48; Gerold Bönnen, "Worms: The Jews between the City, the Bishops, and the Crown," in *The Jews of Europe in the Middle Ages (Tenth to Fifteenth Centuries): Proceedings of the International Symposium Held at Speyer, 20–25 October 2002*, ed. Christoph Cluse (Turnhout: Brepols, 2004), 452.

17. Beyer, Eltester, and Goerz, *Urkundenbuch*, 2:280–82, no. 242, here 281; Aronius et al., *Regesten*, 167, no. 378. For the currency involved, see Rory Naismith, *Money and Coinage in the Middle Ages* (Leiden: Brill, 2018), 125–27.

to pregnant women suggests).¹⁸ Second, a larger additional toll to be paid by Jewish merchants of the areas specified. A toll for Christian merchants coming from these areas is not mentioned, either because they paid the same, or because Jews comprised many of those arriving.

Combining these regulations with the evidence from the Nuremberg Memorbuch narrows down the period when Isaac and Bella were likely to have acted. As the problem of a toll for Jewish travelers only became significant in 1209 and the Memorbuch was composed in 1296, it is probable that the pair operated at some point between these dates. Analysis of the Memorbuch list of the great men and women of Ashkenazic communities supports this idea. The list is organized chronologically, and Isaac and Bella appear between R. Samuel b. Meir (Rashbam) and R. Jacob b. Meir (Rabbenu Tam) who lived in the mid-twelfth century, and R. Meir b. Barukh of Rothenburg (Maharam), active in the second half of the thirteenth.¹⁹ So, Isaac and Bella's effort to eliminate river tolls for Jews probably took place around the mid-thirteenth century. Indeed, documents of the Koblenz toll are again silent about the Jews after this time.²⁰ Basing an argument on silence is always dangerous, but other sources serve as clues regarding changes in Jewish-related toll policies during this period. A privilege granted in 1266 by Archbishop Engelbert II of Cologne to local Jews, still preserved as a stone tablet in the Cologne cathedral, deals with their toll obligations. One clause reads: "And all the Jews who would be present or would come from any place to the district of the archbishop of Cologne will owe tolls and fees for themselves and their property, equal to those [owed] by Christians and for their property; they will not be held accountable for any other [payments]."²¹ The privilege also cancels the toll paid for

---

18. Probably the duchies of the German Empire, whose boundaries were familiar to Jews: Rainer Josef Barzen, "West and East in Ashkenaz in the Time of Judah he-Ḥasid," *Jewish History* 34 (2021): 53–81, doi: 10.1007/s10835-021-09375-6. In Bohemia, tolls were also applied to travelers who left their territory: Aronius et al., *Regesten*, 186, no. 415. See also Wenninger, "Geleit, Geleitsrecht," 50.

19. Salfeld, *Das Martyrologium*, 85–86, 289–90. The list was apparently copied by Isaac of Meiningen himself. I reviewed a photostat made for the National Literary of Israel in Jerusalem (PH 2828 / microfilm F 73457). For a similar list: Oxford, Bodleian library, Ms. Michael 328/537 (Neubauer 1108), 197b. See also Lucia Raspe, "Payyeṭanim as Heroes of Medieval Folk Narrative," in *Jewish Studies Between the Disciplines: Papers in Honor of Peter Schäfer on the Occasion of his Sixtieth Birthday*, ed. Klaus Herrmann et al. (Leiden: Brill, 2003), 368–69n50.

20. For the sources: Pfeiffer, *Rheinische Transitzölle*, 143–56.

21. Aronius et al., *Regesten*, 299, no. 718: Joachim Oepen, "Das Judenprivileg im Kölner Dom," in *Kölner Domblatt: Jahrbuch des Zentral-Dombau-Vereins 2008*, eds. Bernd Waker and Rolf Lauer (Cologne: Kölner Dom, 2009), 59–92.

bodies brought by Jews from afar to be buried at the Jewish cemetery of Cologne. These exemptions, significant enough to be among the few rights commemorated on the cathedral's stones, were once standard, but by 1266 they were apparently ignored and had to be reissued. Similar clauses appear in a privilege awarded in 1244 by Duke Fredrich II of Austria to local Jews. Members of the newly established Jewish settlements in the area probably traveled often along the Danube and Rhine to keep their connections with their coreligionists in the Rhineland, and were burdened by the tolls.[22] This is another indication that in the first half of the thirteenth century Jewish travel along German rivers was restricted by high tariffs, in Koblenz and beyond.[23]

Although Jews were particularly burdened by river tolls during this period, Christians were also struggling with new stations established along the Rhine, raising travel costs.[24] Some of these stations were unauthorized, especially those formed during times of political instability, when kings were unable or unwilling to supervise the issue. The period following the death of Emperor Heinrich VI in 1197 precipitated a long dynastic struggle and lingering unrest. The large number of new stations established along the Rhine between 1198 and 1215 is a clear indication of this, as is the more overbearing, and lucrative, operation policies adopted by established toll stations, including Koblenz, during this period. In the Land Peace (*Landfrieden*—an imperial constitutional decree) of 1235, Emperor Fredrich II tried to remedy the issue by emphasizing the illegality of the new toll collection operations and cancelling any stations established without imperial consent since 1197.[25] Despite Fredrich II's efforts, the problem endured, and even worsened during another long period of political instability starting in 1239. Exasperated by this situation, in 1254 many cities and lords of the Upper Rhine came together in an agreement of political and

---

22. Eveline Brugger and Birgit Wiedl, eds., *Regesten zur Geschichte der Juden in Österreich im Mittelalter*, vol. 1 (Innsbruck: Studienverlag, 2005), 35–38, no. 25, clauses 12–13. The earliest evidence of Jewish settlement in Vienna dates to 1204: Brugger and Wiedl, *Regesten*, 18–19, no. 5.

23. Official payment for safe conduct was also established then, contributing to the rising costs of travel: Wenninger, "Geleit, Geleitsrecht," 48–50.

24. Pfeiffer, *Rheinische Transitzölle*, 346–49, 331–32, compare maps 3 and 4; Runde, "Der Rhine," 63–65.

25. MGH, Constitutiones 2:243–44, no. 196, clauses 7–9; Pfeiffer, *Rheinische Transitzölle*, 360–75; Wenninger, "Geleit, Geleitsrecht," 48. Pranke and Zečević, *Medieval Trade*, 70, read fluctuations in toll privileges issued as an indicator of economic rise and decline, but imperial policies were likely more significant.

military cooperation. One of the main issues they addressed was again the unjust tolls (*thelonea injusta*), which the new coalition agreed to cancel, granting equal protection to all travelers, including Jews.[26] Whether Isaac and Bella were involved in these developments is unclear, but they likely acted in the context of this renegotiation of river tolls.[27] Another possibility relates directly to Archbishop Heinrich II of Trier, who in 1264 granted a privilege to the Jews of Koblenz, the content of which is now lost.[28] He extracted an exorbitant sum from the Jews for their protection, perhaps also for their exemption from the Koblenz toll, which was now under his direct rule.[29]

Returning to the larger picture of Jewish travel, the origins of Jewish travelers passing through Koblenz according to the 1209 toll regulation are especially revealing. Jews coming from "beyond the Meuse," namely northern France and the Low Countries, sailed up the Rhine, while from Regensburg in the east, a major center of trade on the Danube, Jews traveled to the Rhine and continued north.[30] There were several routes from the Danube to the Rhine, all involving a segment of land travel, and all passing through the river toll of Koblenz.[31] Any long-distance river journey from Bavaria, the upper Rhine, the Mosel Valley, or the Main Valley to the northern areas of the lower Rhine, the

---

26. Julius Weizsäcker, *Der Rheinische Bund: 1254* (Tübingen: Laupp, 1879), 16. See also Arno Buschmann, "Der Rheinische Bund von 1254–1257: Landfriede, Städte, Fürsten und Reichsverfassung im 13 Jahrhundert," *Vorträge und Forschung* 33 (1987): 167–212, doi: 10.11588/vuf.1987.0.15852; Pfeiffer, *Rheinische Transitzölle*, 376–98.

27. Rainer Barzen, "Jewish Regional Organization in the Rhineland—the *Kehillot Shum* around 1300," in *The Jews of Europe in the Middle Ages*, ed. Christoph Cluse (Turnhout: Brepols, 2004), 235–37; and Barzen, ed., *Taqqanot Qehillot Šum: Die Rechtssatzungen der jüdischen Gemeinden Mainz, Worms und Speyer im hohen und späten Mittelalter*, MGH, 2 vols. (Wiesbaden: Harrassowitz Verlag, 2019), 83–86, suggests that Jews held a political position within the Rhinish "league."

28. Wilhelm A. Günther, ed., *Codex diplomaticus rheno-mosellanus: Urkundensammlung zur geschichte der Rhein- und Mosellande, der Nahe- und Aorgegend, und des Hundsrückens, des Meinfeldes und der Eifel*, vol. 2 (Koblenz: B. Heriot, 1823), 337, no. 212.

29. *Gesta Henrici Archiepiscopi Treverensis*, MGH Scriptores 24, 455; Pfeiffer, *Rheinische Transitzölle*, 145–50. I thank Jörg Müller for bringing this issue to my attention.

30. And had to consider their local tolls: Nureet Dermer, "Between Foreigners, Strangers and Jews: The Changing Perception of Parisian Jews on the Eve of the 1306 Expulsion," *Medieval Encounters* 27 (2021): 309–11, 323–27, doi: 10.1163/15700674-12340110.

31. The main option was sailing up the Danube, traveling by land to the Rednitz around Ingolstadt and then sailing north to the Main, and the Rhine. A second option was traveling by land from Regensburg to Aalen, and then sailing down the Kocher and the Neckar. Another was sailing up the Altmühl and continuing by land from Rothenburg, or by boat down the Tauber: Eva Leitholdt et al., "Fossa Carolina: The First Attempt to Bridge the Central European Watershed—A Review, New Findings, and Geoarchaeological Challenges," *Geoarchaeology* 27 (2012): 91–93; Werther and Kröger, "Inland Navigation," 65–66, 71–74.

Low Countries, northern France, or England had to pass through the Koblenz toll (see map). Thus, the 1209 regulation's emphasis on long-distance travelers is clear. But why single out Jewish travelers and traders in particular? Were they so prominent among those who passed through this hub?

River Travel and Jewish Everyday Life

The answers lie in the major role that river travel played in the everyday life of medieval German Jews. During the early stages of Jewish settlement in the empire in the eleventh century, the communities were few and far between (see map). Three major settlements, Cologne, Mainz, and Worms, were connected by the Rhine, as were the smaller communities of Xanten, Bonn, and Speyer. The communities of Trier and Metz were connected to this group by the Mosel, and that of Bamberg by the Main. The other major settlement, Regensburg, was on the Danube, making its contact with the Rhineland centers more difficult (although Jews, as we will see, still made the trip). A final group of smaller communities: Magdeburg, Halle, Merseburg, Erfurt, and Prague, were connected to the North Sea by the Elbe, or by the Saale and Vltava flowing into it.[32] Of all these settlements, only Erfurt lies on a small tributary (the Gera), and not on a large river navigable throughout the year. While Jews had political reasons for favoring these locations (preferring to settle in cathedral cities), the availability of navigable rivers likely also played a part.[33] They opened important economic possibilities[34] and allowed for regular travel and communications between the different cities and towns.[35] The major Rhineland communities served as centers of administrative and religious authority for other German Jews,

---

32. See note 13 above, and Barzen, "West and East," 68–73.
33. Alfred Haverkamp, "Baptised Jews in German Lands during the Twelfth Century," in *Jews and Christians in Twelfth-Century Europe*, ed. Michael Signer and John Van Engen (Notre Dame: University of Notre Dame Press, 2001), 256–60.
34. Judith Baskin, "Mobility and Marriage in Two Medieval Jewish Societies," *Jewish History* 22 (2008): 232–33; Toch, *Economic History*, 71–72, 94–97; Agus, *Heroic Age*, 26–29.
35. And, less frequently, with Jews throughout Europe, the Mediterranean, and beyond: *Travels of R. P'tahiah of Regensburg*, ed. Elazar Halevi Grünhut (Frankfurt: Kauffmann, 1905); Benjamin of Tudela, *The Itinerary of Benjamin of Tudela*, ed. Marcus N. Adler (London: Oxford University Press, 1907); Baskin, "Mobility," 224–26; Agus, *Heroic Age*, 25–35; Albert Kohn, "To Dwell Away from Home: Lodging Jewish Transients in the Communities of Medieval Ashkenaz (1150–1350)," chapter 6 in this book.

which likely required routine communication.³⁶ The famous traveler Benjamin of Tudela reflected this basic reality when he wrote, around 1173, that "all the communities of Alemania [i.e., Germany] are located on the river Rhine. The largest one is the city of Cologne, the capital of the kingdom. All the way to Regensburg, in the far end of Alemania, is a traveling distance [*mahalkh*] of fifteen days. And it [the land] is called Ashkenaz."³⁷ Here the Rhine is depicted as the backbone of Ashkenaz, allowing quick communication between its two far ends, Cologne and Regensburg (actually on the Danube). Benjamin further lists the major communities of his time, starting with the Mosel Valley, continuing with the Rhineland (surprisingly ignoring Mainz), and finishing with the upper Danube. He notes that the Jews are widely dispersed in these areas, a situation that made rapid travel via rivers essential.

The earliest surviving evidence of Jewish river travel, dated to 903–6, is found in the toll regulations of Raffelstetten, situated on the Danube near Linz, which notes that Jews, as well as other traders passing through the station, must pay for the commodities they transfer with them (slaves or otherwise).³⁸ Jewish trade along the Danube was apparently significant enough during this period to warrant a specific reference. The early toll legislation of Koblenz and the privileges of 1090 suggest that the same was true for the Rhine in the eleventh century.³⁹ Hebrew sources, shedding light on the Jewish perspective, are available starting from the same period. R. Gershom b. Judah of Mainz (Me'or ha-Golah, d. 1028) was asked to rule regarding the property of two Jews who sailed on a river ship together. Their ship had sunk, but some of the property on board was salvaged by Christians. One of them sold

---

36. Haverkamp, "Baptised Jews," 256–60; Barzen, "Regional Organization," 233–37; Elisheva Baumgarten, *Practicing Piety in Medieval Ashkenaz: Men, Women, and Everyday Religious Observance* (Philadelphia: University of Pennsylvania Press, 2014), 3–4. Cologne was an administrative center: Ephraim Shoham-Steiner and Elisabeth Hollander, "Beyond the Rabbinic Paradigm," *Jewish Quarterly Review* 111 (2021): 236–64, doi: 10.1353/jqr.2021.0010. However, *Taqqanot ShUM* indicate that it was the rabbis of the Upper Rhineland who had the most authority: Barzen, *Taqqanot Qehillot Šum*, esp. 41–116.

37. Benjamin of Tudela, *Itinerary*, 71.

38. MGH, Capitularia 2:249–52, no. 253; Linder, *Legal Sources*, 349. Toch challenges this as evidence for Jewish slave trade, but not for Jewish Danube trade in general: Toch, *Economic History*, 184–85; Toch, "European Jews," 47–48, 57–58.

39. Diestelkamp et al., *Elenchus Fontium Historiae Urbanae*, 66; Linder, *Legal Sources*, 354, 392, 396; Pfeiffer, *Rheinische Transitzölle*, 94–96.

CHAPTER 4

this salvaged gold to another Jew, who refused to hand it over to its original owners, but R. Gershom decreed that he must do so.[40]

Another example, from a book of halakhic responsa complied by three German rabbis known as the sons of Makhir,[41] focuses on problems arising when Jews traveled aboard river vessels on the Sabbath: "A ship that arrived on Shabbat from outside of town and also Jews [were on board], and some Jews from the town came and ate on the ship from the food that those who came with the ship brought."[42] The author wondered whether the local Jews were allowed to eat the food arriving from afar on the Sabbath. Evidently, Jews used river vessels to travel between communities, and some journeys were apparently urgent enough to be carried out over Shabbat. Presumably, Christians operated the ship, as the Jews could not work on the Sabbath and were merely travelers.[43] When the ship arrived at its destination, Jews were not permitted, by Jewish law (halakhah) to leave the vessel until the Sabbath had ended, so local coreligionists came on board to keep them company.[44] The response describes a solution designed to allow local Jews to dine with the newcomers, based on the personal experience of the writer, one of the Makhir brothers: "When we travel by ship on Shabbat from Mainz to Worms, we take a piece of wood out of the ship to allow for the carrying [of objects] in and out [of the ship]. And so instructed me our rabbi, the light of the exile, twice as I was traveling with him by ship."[45]

---

40. Gershom b. Judah, *Responsa*, ed. Shlomo Eidelberg (New York: Yeshiva University, 1956), 154–58, §67; Ephraim Shoham-Steiner, *Jews and Crime in Medieval Europe* (Detroit: Wayne State University Press, 2021), 54–58.

41. Abraham Grossman, "The Sons of R. Makhir and Their Collective Work: Ma'ase Ha'Makhiri," *Tarbiz* 46 (1976), 110–32 (Hebrew), https://www.jstor.org/stable/23594303.

42. Jerusalem, The National Library of Israel, Ms. Heb. 8°4199, f. 507a.

43. Jews owning a ship were not even allowed to rent it for Christian use on Sabbath: *Ma'ase Hageonim*, ed. Abraham Epstein and Jacob Freimann (Berlin: Mekitsi Nirdamim, 1910), 31, §47. See also Eleazar of Worms, *Sefer ha-Rokeah ha-Gadol*, 80, §182–83; Isaac b. Moses of Vienna, *Or Zarua*, 4 vols. (Jerusalem: Jerusalem Institute, 2010), 2:78, §146; Jacob b. Moses Moellin, *New Maḥaril Responsa*, ed. Yitzhak Satz (Jerusalem: Jerusalem Institute, 1977), 272–84, §182–83.

44. Halakhic issues involving river ships were different than those pertaining to seafaring vessels: Israel Ta-Shma, *Halakha, Custom and Reality in Ashkenaz, 1100–1350* (Jerusalem: Magnes, 1996), 168–85 (Hebrew). Jews traveling by land had to pause their journey on the Sabbath, giving rivers another important advantage, beyond speed and cost: Eleazar of Worms, *Sefer Harokeah Hagadol* (Jerusalem: Vinefeld, 1960), 81, § 182.

45. Jerusalem, The National Library of Israel, Ms. Heb. 8°4199, f. 507b–508a. The rabbi mentioned was not Gershom b. Judah Me'or ha-Golah, but Isaac b. Judah: Grossman, "Sons of R. Makhir," 132.

The placing of wood between the ship and the surrounding water or the shore symbolically connects it to its environment as a single space, thus (partly) resolving the halakhic issue.[46] Traveling by river from Mainz to Worms, the two major upper Rhineland communities, on the Sabbath (and generally) was a common practice that even rabbis adopted. The wish to immediately dine with local Jews suggests that such voyages were often taken to meet family or friends, and not only to conduct business. The choice to use ships that arrive during the Sabbath, when no business could be conducted, points in the same direction.

The other early large Rhineland community was Cologne, a major port on the lower Rhine.[47] In the late eleventh century, Shlomo b. Shimshon of Worms noted in a halakhic context that a ship traveling from Cologne to Mainz arrived in port on the Sabbath.[48] Eliezer bar Nathan of Mainz commented, in the mid-twelfth century, "And so we are used to doing, to embark on a ship on Shabbat eve [i.e. Friday] before the evening to travel to Worms or Cologne."[49] He also recalled a Jew who traveled by ship from Mainz to Cologne, and arriving in the city on the Sabbath, was forced by the Christian sailors to leave the vessel.[50] Here too, Jewish river travel, even on the Sabbath, is presented as a commonplace activity. While Mainz and Worms, and later Speyer, were the rabbinic centers of Jewish settlement, Cologne was a hub of travel and commerce. Ephraim of Bonn, in the late twelfth century, depicted the killing of one Shimon he-Hasid in Cologne, during the preparations for the Second Crusade in 1147. In describing the incident, Ephraim explains that: "R. Shimon he-Hasid of Trier came back from England, where he spent several days, and arrived at Cologne. And from Cologne he entered a ship to go back to his own town, to Trier."[51]

---

46. BT, Shabbat, 100b. This solution was unnecessary when the ship was anchored within a port: Ta-Shma, *Halakha, Custom and Reality*, 178–82.

47. Monnet, "Ports," 34–35, 52; Irsigler, "Rhein," 13–14; Joseph Huffman, *The Imperial City of Cologne: From Roman Colony to Medieval Metropolis (19 B.C.–1125 A.D.)* (Amsterdam: Amsterdam University Press, 2018), 143–46, 199–200; Benjamin of Tudela, *Itinerary*, 71.

48. Shlomo b. Shimshon, *Siddur Rabbenu Shlomo*, ed. Moshe Hershler (Jerusalem: Ḥemed, 1972), 259–60, §6–10.

49. Eliezer bar Nathan, *Sefer Ra'avan (Even ha-Ezer)*, ed. Shlomo Zalman Ehrenreich, vol. 1 (New York: Grossman, 1958), 47a-b, and also 157b.

50. Eliezer bar Nathan, *Sefer Ra'avan*, 157a.

51. Ephraim of Bonn, *Sefer Zekhirah*, ed. Abraham Habermann (Jerusalem: Mossad Bialik 1970), 18–19.

CHAPTER 4

The unfortunate traveler never returned home, but the story uncovers his planned journey: from Trier via the Mosel and Rhine to Cologne, from there by a seafaring ship to England, and back again—just to spend several days at his destination.[52] Shimon was likely visiting London, or one of the nascent communities of the Thames Valley.[53] London and Trier are more than seven hundred kilometers apart taking the river route, but the efficiency of river transportation was such that this journey was feasible, even for a short stay. The centrality of Cologne as a transportation hub for north-European Jews is also evident—Shimon had to stop there on his way south from England, as likely, did Jews from northern France, where Jewish settlement was better established.[54]

Sources from the late twelfth and thirteenth centuries reveal more about the practice and dangers of river travel. Ephraim of Bonn recalls a ship that traveled from Cologne up the Rhine with Jewish passengers, some of whom went out of the vessel to the shore. Another ship, operated by Christians, happened to follow the first, and its passengers noticed the body of a Christian woman lying on the bank. Assuming that the Jews were responsible for her murder, when both ships stopped at the toll of Boppard they attacked them, injuring some and killing several others.[55] Likely, the Jews originally went to shore for a mundane reason—a bathroom break. Not all passengers felt comfortable defecating from the edge of the vessel into the river,[56] and allowing passengers to occasionally do so on the shore may have been preferable.[57] In any case, river journeys, like any form of long-distance journey, left Jewish

---

52. In Cologne people and merchandise were often transferred from river ships to seafaring vessels and vice versa: Huffman, *Imperial City,* 143. See also Runde, "Der Rhine," 58–62.

53. Jonathan Romain, "River Jews: Medieval Jews along the Thames as a Microcosm of Anglo-Jewry," *Jewish Historical Studies* 43 (2011): 21–25, https://www.jstor.org/stable/29780143.

54. Gérard Nahon, "Ẓarfat: Medieval Jewry in Northern France," in *The Jews of Europe in the Middle Ages,* ed. Christoph Cluse (Turnhout: Brepols, 2004), 205–20; Shoham-Steiner and Hollander, "Rabbinic Paradigm," 238–46; Eva Haverkamp, ed., *Hebräische Berichte über die Judenverfolgungen während des Ersten Kreuzzugs* (Hannover: Hahn, 2005), 401.

55. Ephraim of Bonn, *Sefer Zekhirah,* 34. For the Boppard toll: Pfeiffer, *Rheinische Transitzölle,* 205–10.

56. Judah Wistinetzki, Jacob Freiman, and Abraham Price, eds., *Sefer Ḥasidim,* Parma recension, 3 vols. (Toronto: Torat Ḥaym, 1955–1964), 2:156, §876; Eliezer bar Nathan, *Sefer Ra'avan,* 157a; Eleazar of Worms, *Sefer ha-Rokeah ha-Gadol,* 79, §178; Eliezer b. Joel ha-Levi (Ra'aviah), *Sefer Ra'aviah,* ed. Victor Aptowitzer, 2nd ed. (Jerusalem: Harry Fischel Institute, 1963), 419, §386 (a responsum by Ephraim b. Isaac of Regensburg).

57. Modesty sometimes outweighed other halakhic considerations when allowing Jewish passengers to disembark ships on the Sabbath: Eleazar of Worms, *Sefer ha-Rokeah ha-Gadol,* 79, §178; Eliezer b. Joel, *Sefer Ra'aviah,* 419, §386.

travelers exposed to Christian violence.[58] Moreover, navigable rivers, particularly the Rhine, are deep and of a strong current, as Jews knew well.[59] River ships or boats could sink, resulting in lost goods and even lost lives.[60] Meir of Rothenburg commented that if a person drowns in such a river, the powerful current could slam them into the rocks or under blocks of ice (in the winter), completely dismembering their body.[61] Such dangers did not, however, prevent Jews from relying on this method of transportation.

As for the reasons that drove Jews to travel, the major one was economic. Eliezer b. Joel ha-Levi, active in Bonn and Cologne in the early thirteenth century, stated, with regards to river travel, that "it seems that most people only travel to earn a living."[62] For example, Judah ha-Cohen of Mainz discussed in the eleventh century the case of two Jewish merchants who cooperated to finance the transfer of ships loaded with fish and other commodities from one Rhineland market to another, and could not agree on the proper way to divide their profits.[63] He also ruled in a dispute between three Jewish merchants who partnered to send one of them sailing to Cologne for business.[64] Eliezer bar Nathan mentions that Jews occasionally hired Christians to transport goods on the river for them, and sometimes traveled with them.[65] Another late thirteenth-century response attributed to Meir b. Barukh of Rothenburg discusses economic disputes over the transportation of block goods by river vessels. Two Jews were traveling from Cologne to Worms abroad a ship with Christians, taking with them several packs of goods. Upon arriving, they hired Christian porters to carry the packs to their homes, but the careless porters lost one pack. One of the Jews

---

58. Ephraim of Bonn, *Sefer Zekhirah*, 18–19, 34; Eliezer bar Nathan, *Sefer Ra'avan*, 79a; Jacob b. Moses Moellin, *New Maharil Responsa*, 272–84, §182–83; Baumgarten, *Practicing Piety*, 185–89; Agus, *Heroic Age*, 23–25, 28; Israel J. Yuval, "A German-Jewish Autobiography from the 14th Century," *Tarbiz* 55 (1986): 547, (Hebrew), https://www.jstor.org/stable/23597644.

59. Eliezer b. Joel, *Sefer Ra'aviah*, 421, §386; Eliezer bar Nathan, *Sefer Ra'avan*, 47b–48b.

60. Gershom b. Judah, *Responsa*, 154–58, §67.

61. Meir b. Barukh, *Maharam's Responsa*, 140b, §971.

62. Eliezer b. Joel, *Sefer Ra'aviah*, 416, §385. See also Eleazar of Worms, *Sefer ha-Rokeah ha-Gadol*, 85, § 197; Eliezer bar Nathan, *Sefer Ra'avan*, 48b–49a; Baskin, "Mobility," 232–33; Toch, *Economic History*, 71–72, 94–97; Agus, *Heroic Age*, 26–29.

63. Preserved in Meir b. Barukh of Rothenburg, *Maharam's Responsa* (Prague, 1608), 88b, §898. On Judah Hakohen, see Judah Hakohen, *Sefer Hadinim*, ed. Abraham Grossman (Jerusalem: Shazar Center, 1977).

64. Preserved in Meir b. Barukh, *Maharam's Responsa*, 90a, §910. Shoham-Steiner, *Jews and Crime*, 63–65. Another example discussed above: Gershom b. Judah, *Responsa*, 154–58, §67.

65. Eliezer bar Nathan, *Sefer Ra'avan*, 128b.

claimed that his lost pack ended up in the house of the other, and the dispute was taken to the rabbi.⁶⁶ While some responsa highlight cooperation between Jewish merchants, others indicate the ways in which river travel often required Jews to interact closely with Christian sailors, travelers, and porters.

Some Jews traveled for personal reasons. The custom of transporting dead bodies for burial in central Jewish cemeteries is evident, as we have seen, from charters of the thirteenth century.⁶⁷ Jews sometimes hired ships for this particular purpose, as the body had to be transferred quickly to avoid decay.⁶⁸ Family members of the deceased would occasionally accompany the body and participate in the funeral. When the body of one Eliezer b. Uri was brought to Mainz, his wife, mother, sons, and relatives all traveled aboard the same vessel, although it was both a holiday and a Sabbath.⁶⁹ A late medieval tale suggests that not all Jews would approve. Allegedly, Eliezer bar Nathan was on his death bed in Würzburg, and asked his students to arrange for his burial in his hometown of Mainz. He finally passed away on a Friday, leaving his students unsure how to respect his wish without sailing on the Sabbath (which Eliezer allowed only reluctantly).⁷⁰ Thus, they delivered the body to a sailor asking that he sail it down the Main to Mainz. The negligent sailor fell asleep on his boat, which was carried downstream to Frankfurt, where he woke up. Local Christians alerted him of his location, but he did not trust them. Luckily, the river carried the boat all the way to Mainz, where local Jews postponed the Sabbath to bury the rabbi.⁷¹ While this tale should be read as folklore, its author was clearly familiar with both the practice of transporting bodies by river for burial in remote locations, and with the geographical layout of the Main Valley.

---

66. Meir b. Barukh, *Responsa of Rabbi Meir of Rothenburg and His Colleagues*, ed. Simcha Emanuel, vol. 1 (Jerusalem: World Union of Jewish Studies: 2012), 588, §270.

67. Oepen, "Das Judenprivileg," 91; Brugger and Wiedl, *Regesten*, 35–38, no. 25, clauses 12–13.

68. Eleazar of Worms, *Sefer ha-Rokeah ha-Gadol*, 176, §308.

69. Eliezer b. Joel, *Sefer Ra'aviah*, 428, 436, §391.

70. Eliezer bar Nathan, *Sefer Ra'avan*, 49a. Some later rabbis shared this opinion: Isaac b. Moses, *Or Zarua*, 2:78, §146.

71. Eli Yassif, *Ninety-Nine Tales: The Jerusalem Manuscript Cycle of Legends in Medieval Jewish Folklore* (Tel Aviv: Tel Aviv University Press, 2013), 177 (Hebrew). Yassif, *Ninety-Nine Tales*, 15–22, dates the collection to the thirteenth century, while Rella Kushelevsky argues for late medieval authorship: "Ninety-Nine Tales: Book Review," *Jerusalem Studies in Jewish Folklore* 30 (2016): 265–72 (Hebrew), https://www.jstor.org/stable/24673456. The body of another twelfth-century rabbi was indeed shipped to Mainz for burial: Meir b. Barukh, *Maharam's Responsa*, 58b, §403.

Further personal reasons for travel were family and communal commitments. Jewish teens were occasionally engaged to members of faraway communities, since Jewish settlements were small and many Jews traveled for trade and created ties with peers elsewhere. Such marriages could solidify connections between families of different communities, with the price of having a son, or more often a daughter, move away. Some Jews would even use a proxy to establish engagements (or deliver bills of divorce).[72] Guests from other towns were sometimes invited to wedding ceremonies, especially of people of a high social status,[73] and likely traveled by river to attend.[74] Jews also used river travel to visit the sick, engage in charitable endeavors (*g'milut hasadim*), and participate in funerals.[75] Reasons such as this were probably what compelled Jews who were not merchants or rabbinic scholars to occasionally travel by river, as the reference to pregnant women in the Koblenz toll regulations indicates.[76]

Jews also traveled for scholarly undertakings. The Makhir brothers and Eliezer bar Nathan wrote about river travel as a personal habit.[77] Many rabbinic students in the twelfth and early thirteenth centuries, after studying with a famous rabbi, later settled in a different town, yet kept up correspondence with their former teachers. This movement was key to the establishment of new rabbinic centers during this period.[78]

---

72. Eliezer b. Joel, *Sefer Ra'aviah*, ed. David Deblytski (Beni Brak: Deblytski, 2005), §940; Abraham Grossman, *Pious and Rebellious: Jewish Women in Europe in the Middle Ages* (Jerusalem: Shazar Center, 2003), 104-6 (Hebrew); Baskin, "Mobility," 226, 232-38; Yuval, "Autobiography," 554-55.

73. *Sefer Ḥasidim*, 2:263, §1178; Israel Abrahams, ed., *Hebrew Ethical Wills* (Philadelphia: Jewish Publication Society of America, 1926), 188-89 (Judah b. Asher's will); Václav Hrubý, ed., *Archivum coronae regni Bohemiae*, vol. 2 (Prague: Ministerii Scholarum et Instructionis Publicae, 1935), 237-38, no. 192; Kohn, "Away from Home."

74. Or (traveling from Mainz to Frankfurt) to disrupt a wedding: Jacob b. Moses Moellin, *Maharil Responsa*, ed. Joseph Fischer and Saul Deutscher (Krakow: Beit haSefer, 1881), 48, §96.

75. Eliezer bar Nathan, *Sefer Ra'avan*, 48a-49b. See also Abrahams, *Ethical Wills*, 186-87; Yuval, "Autobiography," 547-48, 564.

76. Beyer, Eltester, and Goerz, *Urkundenbuch*, 2:281; Baumgarten, *Practicing Piety*, esp. 103-28.

77. Jerusalem, The National Library of Israel, Ms. Heb. 8°4199, ff. 507b-508a; Eliezer bar Nathan, *Sefer Ra'avan*, 47a-b.

78. Ephraim Kanarfogel, "From Germany to Northern France and Back Again: A Tale of Two Tosafist Centers," in *Regional Identities and Cultures of Medieval Jews*, ed. Talya Fishman and Ephraim Kanarfogel (Oxford: Littman Library, 2018), 153-57, 160, 163-66; Ephraim Shoham-Steiner, "From Speyer to Regensburg: Reexamining the Migration of the Pietistic Kalonymides from the Rhineland to the Danube," *Zion* 81 (2016): 149-53, 159-60 (Hebrew), https://www.jstor.org/stable/24746072; Mordechai Breuer, "The Wanderings of Students and Scholars: A Prolegomenon to a Chapter in the History of Yeshivot," in *Culture and Society in*

In addition, the extensive culture of sending questions to prominent rabbis must have relied on reliable methods of delivery (even if ad hoc). River transportation likely facilitated these social patterns, but rarely did rabbis report about their modes of travel or communication. However, a tale from the same corpus containing the story about Eliezer bar Nathan's body provides some clues. In the tale, Eliezer is described as conducting a debate pertaining to Passover with other rabbis of Mainz. They cannot agree on a solution, and Eliezer decides to ask the scholars of Bonn (specifically Joel ha-Levi and Ephraim of Bonn), despite the upcoming holiday. He orders a tub to be brought, and sails in it down the Rhine all the way to Bonn. R. Joel, his son in law, prepares to have him for the holiday meal, but to his surprise, Eliezer returns to his little tub and sails back upstream (!) to miraculously arrive in Mainz on time, and provide his peers with the halakhic response.[79] This is a hagiographical tale, but its historical settings are plausible. The scholarly need to travel long distances to consult with prominent rabbis, emanating from the vast distances between the small Jewish communities scattered across northern Europe, was a reality of life. It likely included regular episodes of river travel, though more conventional in nature.

The Larger Context of Jewish River Travel

As shown in the discussion so far, there is copious evidence for the importance of river travel in medieval Jewish daily life. Yet, one wonders whether Jews embarked on long-distance journeys more often than their Christian neighbors. Some Christians traveled quite often, especially merchants, officials, and scholars.[80] However, as Jews lived predominantly in urban communities, more of them, in relative terms, were probably involved in such activities.[81] Moreover, we have noted that due to the dispersed layout of German Jewish settlement, personal

---

Medieval Jewry: Studies Dedicated to the Memory of Haim Hillel Ben-Sasson, ed. Menachem Ben-Sasson, Robert Bonfil, and Joseph R. Hacker (Jerusalem: Shazar, 1989), 450–57 (Hebrew); Yuval, "Autobiography," 550–54; Baumgarten, *Practicing Piety*, 4; Grossman, "Sons of R. Makhir," 132n95.

79. Yassif, *Ninety-Nine Tales*, 205.

80. Verdon, *Travel*, 141–276; Leighton, *Transport*, esp. 13–29; Pranke and Zečević, *Medieval Trade*, 33–65. See also John Block Friedman and Kristen Mossler Figg, eds., *Trade, Travel and Exploration in the Middle Ages: An Encyclopedia* (New York: Routledge, 2000).

81. Baumgarten, *Practicing Piety*, 3–4; Toch, *Economic History*, 92–102. Agus, *Heroic Age*, 29–33, argues that networks of communal support allowed Jews to travel more safely than Christians.

or communal motivations could lead Jews to travel even if they were not traders or rabbinic scholars. Therefore, the disruption of free movement by the cancellation of privileges and the rise in toll collection in the first half of the thirteenth century would have likely had a significant negative impact on Jewish social activities. This context can explain the honorable mention of Isaac and Bella in the Nuremberg Memorbuch. Due to the importance of river travel, they invested much effort, and probably funds, in enabling Jews to pass toll free at Koblenz, and their contemporaries appreciated their endeavors so much that they commemorated them for eternity.

Taking this into consideration, we would expect to see further effects of the rise in the cost and difficulty of movement on thirteenth-century Jews, or a Jewish reaction to these problems. While direct evidence of this exists only for crises of movement later in the medieval period, some clues of this earlier disruption have survived.[82] Scholars of halakhah have noted a sudden decline in the connections between rabbis and students from the Rhineland and from northern France, leading to a gap in German rabbinic leadership in the early to mid-thirteenth century. Ephraim Kanarfogel convincingly points to intellectual reasons that could have caused this break in long-distance communication.[83] That said, the gap also corresponds with the rise in the costs of travel, especially river travel, in the empire, so practical considerations are also a likely cause. A famous document offers another clue to the Jewish response to limitations on movement, a charter awarded by King Heinrich IV to the burghers of Worms in 1074, rewarding their loyalty with exemption from tolls.[84] It lists seven toll stations under royal control that the citizens of Worms may pass freely, three (at least) were river stations—Boppard, Hammerstein, and Angeren.[85] At some point, perhaps in the thirteenth century, someone added after this list the words *iudei et coeteri*, "Jews and others," to modify the next word, *Wormatienses*,

---

82. Jacob b. Moses Moellin, *New Maharil Responsa*, 195-96, §149; Wenninger, "Geleit, Geleitsrecht," 50-73.
83. Kanarfogel, "From Germany to Northern France," esp. 149-50, 153; see also note 78 above, and Simcha Emanuel, *The Crown of the Elders: A New Look at the History of the Sages* (Jerusalem: Magnes, 2021), 85-99, esp. 85-87 (Hebrew).
84. Worms, Stadtarchiv Worms, Abt. 1 A I, no. 3; MGH, Diplomata, Heinrich IV (DD H IV), 1:341-43, no. 267; Linder, *Legal Sources*, 388-91.
85. Pfeiffer, *Rheinische Transitzölle*, 207, 230, 235-36. Pfeiffer identifies "Angere" as Angeren in the Low Countries (see figure and map). Linder's suggestion of Engers, by Koblenz (or Enger, by Bielefeld: Pranke and Zečević, *Medieval Trade*, 66), is less likely, as this toll station was established later: Linder, *Legal Sources*, 391; Pfeiffer, *Rheinische Transitzölle*, 214-16.

CHAPTER 4

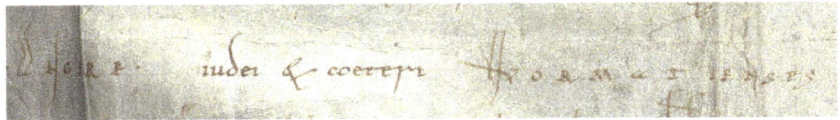

FIGURE 4.2. Worms Charter, 1074. Photo from Worms, Stadtarchiv Worms, Abt. 1 A I, no. 3, a detail.

"citizens of Worms" (see figure 4.2). Thus, he extended the charter explicitly to include local Jews as entitled to exemption from tolls. Whoever did so, must have had access to the city's most valuable documents, and a willingness to protect Jews.[86] The Jews of Worms had enjoyed complete freedom from tolls starting in 1090, and only in the thirteenth century had this privilege likely eroded. The alteration of the 1074 charter, if it indeed occurred in the thirteenth century, was perhaps an attempt to restore old arrangements.[87]

This chapter tells the story of Jewish river travel, the limitations imposed on it in the thirteenth century, and attempts to protect ease of movement. Moreover, it exposes the importance of geographical conditions and limitations in shaping medieval Jewish society. The full effect of social and political factors cannot be understood without considering the geographical layout of Jewish settlement and the rivers that connected communities. Such considerations allow for a clearer analysis of the transfer of information, goods, and people from one community to another, and the costs, limitations, and speed of such transfers. These factors, in turn, could hinder or facilitate social, intellectual, and communal interactions. They could lead a rabbinic student to choose one mentor over another, a young man to marry a particular woman, and of course, a merchant to favor a certain market. But in order to include geographic factors in the study of these phenomena, and analyze Jewish interactions within social networks, we have to better map the changing factors that determined Jewish travel, both by river and by land. This chapter serves as a first step toward this goal, especially in the context of everyday life.

---

86. Linder, *Legal Sources*, 388–89 suggests that the document was modified in the thirteenth century. However, Sara Schiffmann, *Heinrich IV und die Bischöfe in ihrem Verhalten zu den deutschen Juden zur Zeit des ersten Kreuzzuges: Eine Untersuchung nach den hebräischen und lateinischen Quellen* (Berlin: Lichtwitz, 1931), 17–19, claims that this happened shortly after its creation. Paleographical considerations point toward the earlier date, but whoever added the words may have been trying to fit the script to the existing style.

87. Linder, *Legal Sources*, 392. For the Worms context: Bönnen, "Worms," 450–52.

Further Readings

Barzen, Rainer Josef. "Jewish Regional Organization in the Rhineland—the *Kehillot Shum* around 1300." In *The Jews of Europe in the Middle Ages*, edited by Christoph Cluse, 235-37. Turnhout: Brepols, 2004.

Barzen, Rainer. "West and East in Ashkenaz in the Time of Judah he-Ḥasid." *Jewish History* 34 (2021): 53-81, 68-73. doi: 10.1007/s10835-021-09375-6.

Baskin, Judith. "Mobility and Marriage in Two Medieval Jewish Societies." *Jewish History* 22 (2008): 223-43. doi: 10.1007/s 10835-007-9054-3

Benjamin of Tudela. *The Itinerary of Benjamin of Tudela*, ed. Marcus N. Adler. London: Oxford University Press, 1907.

Breuer, Mordechai. "The Wanderings of Students and Scholars: A Prolegomenon to a Chapter in the History of Yeshivot." In *Culture and Society in Medieval Jewry: Studies Dedicated to the Memory of Haim Hillel Ben-Sasson*, edited by Menachem Ben-Sasson, Robert Bonfil, and Joseph R. Hacker, 450-57. Jerusalem: Merkaz Shazar, 1989 (Hebrew).

Eckoldt, Martin. "Navigation on Small Rivers in Central Europe in Roman and Medieval Times." *International Journal of Nautical Archaeology and Underwater Exploration* 13 (1984): 3-10. doi: 10.1111/j.1095-9270.1984.tb01172.x.

Fütterer, Pierre. "Wasserstraße oder Landweg? Neue Befunde zu einer alten Streitfrage." In *Flusstäler, Flussschifffahrt, Flusshäfen: Befunde aus Antike und Mittelalter*, edited by Peter Ettel and Achim Thomas Hack, 61-78. Mainz: Verlag des Römisch-Germanischen Zentralmuseums, 2019.

Irsigler, Franz. "Rhein, Maas und Mosel als Handels- und Verkehrsachsen im Mittelalter." In *Flüsse und Flusstäler als Wirtschafts- und Kommunikationswege*, edited by Stephan Freund, Matthias Hardt, and Petra Weigel, 9-32. Bonn: Arkum, 2007.

Leighton, Albert. *Transport and Communication in Early Medieval Europe, 500-1100*. Newton Abbot: David and Charles, 1972.

Pfeiffer, Friedrich. *Rheinische Transitzölle im Mittelalter*. Berlin: Akademie Verlag, 1997.

Pranke, Piotr, and Miloš Zečević. *Medieval Trade in Central Europe, Scandinavia, and the Balkans (10th-12th Centuries): A Comparative Study*, trans. Michał Romanek. Leiden: Brill, 2020.

P'tahiah of Regensburg. *Travels of R. P'tahiah of Regensburg*, ed. Elazar ha-Levi Grünhut. Frankfurt: Kauffmann, 1905.

Romain, Jonathan. "River Jews: Medieval Jews along the Thames as a Microcosm of Anglo-Jewry." *Jewish Historical Studies* 43 (2011): 21-25. jstor.org/stable/29780143.

Runde, Ingo. "Der Rhine als Wirtschafts- und Verkehrsachse." In *Die Wittelsbacher und die Kurpfalz im Mittelalter. Eine Erfolgsgeschichte?* edited by Jörg Peltzer, 53-65. Regensburg: Schnell & Steiner, 2013.

Shoham-Steiner, Ephraim. "From Speyer to Regensburg: Reexamining the Migration of the Pietistic Kalonymides from the Rhineland to the Danube." *Zion* 81 (2016): 149-76 (Hebrew). www.jstor.org/stable/24746072.

Toch, Michael. *The Economic History of European Jews: Late Antiquity and Early Middle Ages*. Leiden: Brill, 2013.

Verdon, Jean. *Travel in the Middle Ages,* trans. George Holoch. South Bend: University of Notre Dame Press, 2003.

Werther, Lukas, and Lars Kröger. "Medieval Inland Navigation and the Shifting Fluvial Landscape between Rhine and Danube." *PCA* (*European Journal of Postclassical Archaeologies*) 7 (2017): 65–96.

Yuval, Israel J. "A German-Jewish Autobiography from the 14th Century." *Tarbiz* 55 (1986): 541–66 (Hebrew). jstor.org/stable/23597644.

CHAPTER 5

Jews and Lombards in Fourteenth-Century Paris
A Comparative Look

Nureet Dermer

In 1322, the street previously called rue de la Buffeterie in Paris was renamed rue des Lombards. This marks the first time in the history of Paris that a street was named after its Lombard inhabitants.[1] The Lombards were northern Italian merchants who originally traded in products, especially spices, from across the Mediterranean in the fairs of Champagne and the markets of Paris. They soon became known, however, for their extensive moneylending activities as

---

This chapter was written under the auspices of the Beyond the Elite: Jewish Daily Life in Medieval Europe Project, PI Elisheva Baumgarten, from the European Research Council (ERC) under the European Union's Horizon 2020 research and innovation program, grant agreement No. 681507, and prepared for publication with funding from the Israel Science Foundation Grant 2850/22, Contending with Crises: The Jews of 14th Century Europe, PI Elisheva Baumgarten.

1. This street was located in what is now the distinguished first arrondissement of the city, close to the current rue des Lombards. A Lombards' Street also existed in medieval London and in Nijmegen, and in the early modern period there was a Lombards' Square in Amsterdam. See Walter Bagehot, *Lombard Street: A Description of the Money Market* (New York: Scribner, Armstrong & Co., 1873), especially 75–81; Remi Van Shaik, "On the Social Position of Jews and Lombards in the Towns of the Low Countries and Neighbouring German Territories during the Late Middle Ages," in *Core and Periphery in Late Medieval Urban Society: Proceedings of the Colloquium at Ghent*, eds. Myriam Carlier and Anke Greve (Leuven: Garant, 1997), 176; Francesca Trivellato, "Credit, Honor, and the Early Modern French Legend of the Jewish Invention of Bills of Exchange," *Journal of Modern History* 84, no. 2 (2012): 309, https://doi.org/10.1086/664732.

well.² While originally the name *Lombards* designated merchants from Asti, Alba, and Chieri in the Piedmont region of northwestern Italy, by the thirteenth century this was often a name used to designate all Italian merchants and moneylenders in the French kingdom, and the distinction between Lombards and Italians became rather blurred.³ The Lombards' street in Paris was situated on the right bank of the River Seine, between the parish of St. Jacques and that of Saint-Germain-l'Auxerrois. This was the very heart of the city and its thriving economic center. Adjacent to it was the principal area of Jewish residency, until the Jews were expelled from the city in 1306 and 1322.⁴ The proximity of Jews and Lombards in medieval Paris was no coincidence, nor was it the only affinity between the two groups.

Researchers have often associated the economic status of Lombards with that of Jews, perhaps because of their similar moneylending activities and the frequent mention of both groups together in royal and municipal charters.⁵ While previous scholarship pointed out the economic resemblance and the evidence indicating that Lombards

---

2. Robert Henri Bautier, "Le marchand Lombard en France aux XIIIe et XIVe siècles," *Shmes, Actes des congrès de la société des historiens médiévistes de l'enseignement supérieur public- Le marchand au Moyen Âge* 19 (1988): 65–71; Camille Piton, *Les Lombards en France et à Paris* (Paris: Honoré Champion, Libraire, 1892), 14. Gèraud Hercule, *Paris sous Philippe le bel—des documents originaux et notamment d'après un manuscrit, contenant le role de la taille imposèe sur les habitants de Paris en 1292* (Paris: Imprimerie de Crapelet, 1837), 2, note a.

3. Rowan Dorin, *No Return: Jews, Christian Usurers, and the Spread of Mass Expulsion in Medieval Europe*, Histories of Economic Life (Princeton: Princeton University Press, 2023), 10–11; Piton, *Les Lombards en France et à Paris*, 1–3; Pierre Racine, "Les Lombards et le commerce de l'argent au Moyen Âge," *Clio voyages culturels* (2002): 1–2; Pierre Champion, "Juifs et Lombards à Paris au Moyen Âge," *Revue de Paris* 15 (1933): 856; Roger Kohn, "Le statut forain: marchands étrangers, lombards et juifs en France royale et en Bourgogne (seconde moitié du XIVème siècle)," *Revue historique de droit français et étranger (1922-)* 61, no. 1 (1983): 9, http://www.jstor.org/stable/43847920; Kurt Grunwald and Robert Henri Bautier claimed that the designation *Lombard* differed from other Italian merchants, see Kurt Grunwald, "Lombards, Cahorsins, and Jews," *Journal of European Economic History* 4 (1975): 394; Bautier, "Le marchand Lombard en France," 64.

4. The definition of the banishment of 1322 as an expulsion is controversial, see Elizabeth A. R. Brown, "Philip V, Charles IV, and the Jews of France: The Alleged Expulsion of 1322," *Speculum* 2, no. 66 (1991): 294–329, https://doi.org/10.2307/2864146; William Chester Jordan, "Home Again: The Jews in the Kingdom of France, 1315–1322," in *The Stranger in Medieval Society*, ed. F. R. P. Akehurst and Stephanie Cain Van d'Elden (Minneapolis: University of Minnesota Press, 1997), 27–45.

5. Myriam Greilsammer, *L'usurier chrétien, un juif métaphorique: histoire de l'exclusion des prêteurs Lombards (XIIIe-XVIIe siècle)* (Rennes: Presses universitaires de Rennes, 2012); Grunwald, "Lombards, Cahorsins and Jews," 168; Rowan Dorin, "L'expulsion des usuriers hors de France à la fin du xiiie siècle," *Hypotheses* 17, no. 1 (2014): 157–66, https://doi.org/10.3917/hyp.131.0157; Champion, "Juifs et Lombards," 846–47; Dorin, *No Return*, 80–81; for a particular study on the similarities in the social position of Jews and Lombards in the Low Countries

replaced Jews in the money market, this chapter draws attention to the salient differences between these two groups by focusing on Jews and Lombards in fourteenth-century Paris—the capital of the Capetians, one of the largest cities in western Europe, and an international commercial center.[6] The following discussion demonstrates how the calamitous years of that century shaped the perception and attitudes concerning both Jews and Lombards in legal terms as well as in daily life. Using administrative sources and socio-topographical analysis, the chapter points out the differences between the two groups throughout the course of the fourteenth century, underscoring the social and economic developments that ultimately led to the collective expulsion of all the Jews from the French realm in 1394.

Jews and Lombards in Fiscal Policy

The linkage between tax payment, local citizenship, social inspection, and the inclusion and exclusion of inhabitants of medieval cities has long been established in historical and economic research and was also mentioned explicitly in contemporaneous legislation.[7] For example, a royal ordinance from 1287 tied the eligibility of the bourgeois privilege with the fulfillment of municipal tax payments. This ordinance stated that if a citizen of one city wished to leave for a different city and acquire citizenship there, he would not be allowed to do so until he settled all his *taille* tax duties to his former city of residence: "If anyone that is a Bourgeois . . . wishes to leave, or already has left to any place or any community, he must pay the taille he was obliged to [in the former city] before he obtains the citizenship of the other city, where he asks to be a citizen."[8] Similarly, in 1308 a court case of the *parloir*, the

---

during the Middle Ages, see Van Shaik, "On the Social Position of Jews and Lombards," 165–91.

    6. Jörg Oberste, *The Birth of the Metropolis: Urban Spaces and Social Life in Medieval Paris*, vol. 1 (Leiden: Brill, 2001), 56–61; Jean Favier, *Le bourgeois de Paris au Moyen Âge* (Paris: Tallandier, 2012), 55–79; Boris Bove and Claude Gauvard, eds., *Le Paris du Moyen Âge* (Paris: Belin, 2014), 118–21.

    7. See, for example, Osavaldo Cavallar and Julius Kirshner, "Jews as Citizens in Late Medieval and Renaissance Italy: The Case of Isacco Da Pisa," *Jewish History* 25 (2011): 269–318, http://www.jstor.org/stable/41478407; Miri Rubin, *Cities of Strangers: Making Lives in Medieval Europe* (New York: Cambridge University Press, 2020), 58.

    8. "Item, Il est ordonné que aucuns ou aucun reçus à la Bourgeoisie, ou à recevoir en la fourme dessus dite, s'estoit partis, ou partoit de y en avant, d'aucun lieu, ou d'aucune Commune, il payera les tailles, les frez de la ville, de tant come il fut taillez, ou girè fus li, avant ce qu'il fut recuz & avoez comme Bourgeoise a l'autre Ville, dont il aura requis la Bourgeoisie."

municipal judicial authority in charge of economic infractions in Paris, implied that a *bourgeois* was a person who lived in the city and paid the taille and other municipal fees.[9] Furthermore, research on the lists of the city's taille tax from the end of the thirteenth century indicates that these lists included only those considered citizens of Paris—in a formal matter, that is, having bourgeois rights, or even just conceptually considered as a Parisian, despite not being bourgeois.[10]

Although the Paris taille tax was levied and collected annually, only seven lists, from 1292 to 1313, documenting these censuses have survived.[11] The tax was imposed on hearths and was registered geographically by parish and street. According to these lists, those required to pay the taille include wealthy inhabitants (*Les gros gens*), poor yet taxpaying inhabitants (*Les menues gens*), Jews, and Lombards. Among those automatically excluded from this obligation were nobles, clergy, non-residents, students, teachers, foreigners, and the destitute, each group exempted for different reasons. Although both Jews and Lombards were obliged to pay this tax, attention should be given to three essential differences relating to the manner of their inclusion in the registers. First, Jewish taxpayers are consistently positioned in a separate section at the end of the lists in which they appear. In contrast, the inclusion of Lombards in the registers was inconsistent. The 1292 tax list opens with a separate list of 173 taxpaying Lombards in Paris, while 19 other

---

In *Ordonnances des roys de France de la troisième race*, ed. M. de Laurière, Premier volume, 1723, 315; Boris Bove and Claude Gauvard, eds. *Le Paris du Moyen Âge*, 118-21.

9. Le Roux de Lincy, *Histoire de l'Hôtel de ville de Paris*, suivie d'un essai sur l'ancien gouvernement municipal de cette ville (Paris: Librarie de la Société de l'École des chartes, 1846), 171; Caroline Bourlet and Boris Bove, "Religion civique ou affiliation communautaire ? Le témoignage des testaments Parisiens des XIIIe-XVe siècles," *Histoire Urbaine* 60 (2001): 71-96, https://doi.org/10.58079/u507; Nathan Sussman and Al Slivinski, "Tax Administration and Compliance: Evidence from Medieval Paris," CEPR Discussion Paper No. DP13512, Available at SSRN: https://ssrn.com/abstract=3332315, 2019, 9; Favier, *Le bourgeois de Paris au Moyen Âge*, 11-24.

10. Bove and Gauvard, *Le Paris du Moyen Âge*, 121; Pierre Racine, "Paris, rue des Lombards, 1280-1340," in *Comunità forestiere e nationes nell'Europa dei secoli 13-16*, ed. Giovanna Petti Balbi, Europa Mediterranea 19 (Napoli: Liguori, 2001), 96. Sussman and Lincy, "Tax Administration and Compliance," 34.

11. Four of these lists are available in printed editions: Hercule, *Paris sous Philippe le bel*; Karl Michaëlsson, *Le livre de la taille de Paris l'an 1296* (Göteborg: Universitets Årsskrift, 1958); Karl Michaëlsson, *Le livre de la taille de Paris l'an 1297* (Göteborg: Universitets Årsskrift, 1962); J-A Buchon, *Le livre de la taille de Paris l'an 1313* (Paris: Imprimerie de crapelet, 1827). The manuscripts of these municipal tax lists are in the Bibliothèque nationale (Paris) and Archives nationales (Paris): Paris, Bibliothèque nationale de France, Ms. Français 6220 (1292 list); Paris, Archives Nationales, KK//283 (1296-1300 lists), and Paris, Bibliothèque nationale de France, Ms. Français 6736 (1313 list).

Lombards were registered in the same list under the parishes they lived in and among other local taxpayers (figure 5.1).[12] In the five tax lists from 1296 to 1300, all taxpaying Lombards were listed according to their parishes of residency, and in 1313, they were exempt from paying the taille, instead paying a considerable sum to cover the costs of the marriage of King Philip IV's daughter.[13] Second, according to an earlier royal charter from 1282, granted by King Philippe III, the Lombards of Paris were specifically taxed as noncitizens, and the charter gives special permission to the municipal authorities to now include Lombards in the taille tax collections.[14] No similar charter was granted to city authorities concerning the taxation of Jews, pointing to a clear difference between Jews and Lombards in their legal status and their participation in fiscal policy.[15] While Jews shared the taille tax burden with Christian citizens of Paris, supposedly as equals, Lombards were not, a priori, eligible to pay the taille tax, and it was only due to exceptional legal permission, in which their unique status as noncitizen taxpayers was stipulated, that they were included in the municipal tax burden.

Third, Jews appear only in the tax lists of 1292, 1296, and 1297. As of 1298, they were no longer included in the municipal taille, and instead, there are indications of a unique annual tax replacing the taille, collected from Parisian Jews from 1298 until their expulsion in 1306. This tax was called *tallia Judeorum*, or *de finantione Judeorum Parisius*.[16] Concurrently, another development concerning Jews in royal fiscal policy evolved in the years leading to the expulsion of Jews in 1306. In 1288 King Philip IV appointed Danyel le Breton to serve as the royal commissioner in charge of Jewish affairs.[17] Eight years later, in 1296, a

---

12. These taxpayers were included with a specific addition - *le lombart*, or under the title indicating the Lombards residing in St. Germains des Pres. See Hercule, *Paris sous Philippe le bel*, 176.

13. Racine, "Paris, rue des Lombards, 1280–1340," 96.

14. Le Roux de Lincy, *Histoire de l'hôtel de ville de Paris; suivie d'un essai sur l'ancien gouvernement municipal de cette ville*, deuxième partie, 261.

15. This distinction was also made in Racine, "Paris, rue des Lombards, 1280–1340," 96.

16. The taille that was levied on Jews as of 1298 was also registered differently, see Jules Viard, *Les journaux du trésor de Philippe IV le bel* (Paris: Imprimerie Nationale, 1940), xvii, and registers n. 707; n. 1307; n. 1607 there for example.

17. Lucien Léon Lazard, "Les revenus tirés des juifs de France," *Revue des études Juives* 15 (1887): 238–39, https://doi.org/10.3406/rjuiv.1887.3535; William Chester Jordan, *The French Monarchy and the Jews: From Philip Augustus to the Last Capetians* (Philadelphia: University of Pennsylvania Press, 1989), 188. In 1297 Danyel le Breton reinforced the royal obligation for Jews to carry the *rouelle*—a small round piece of cloth that Jews were obligated to wear—on their vestments.

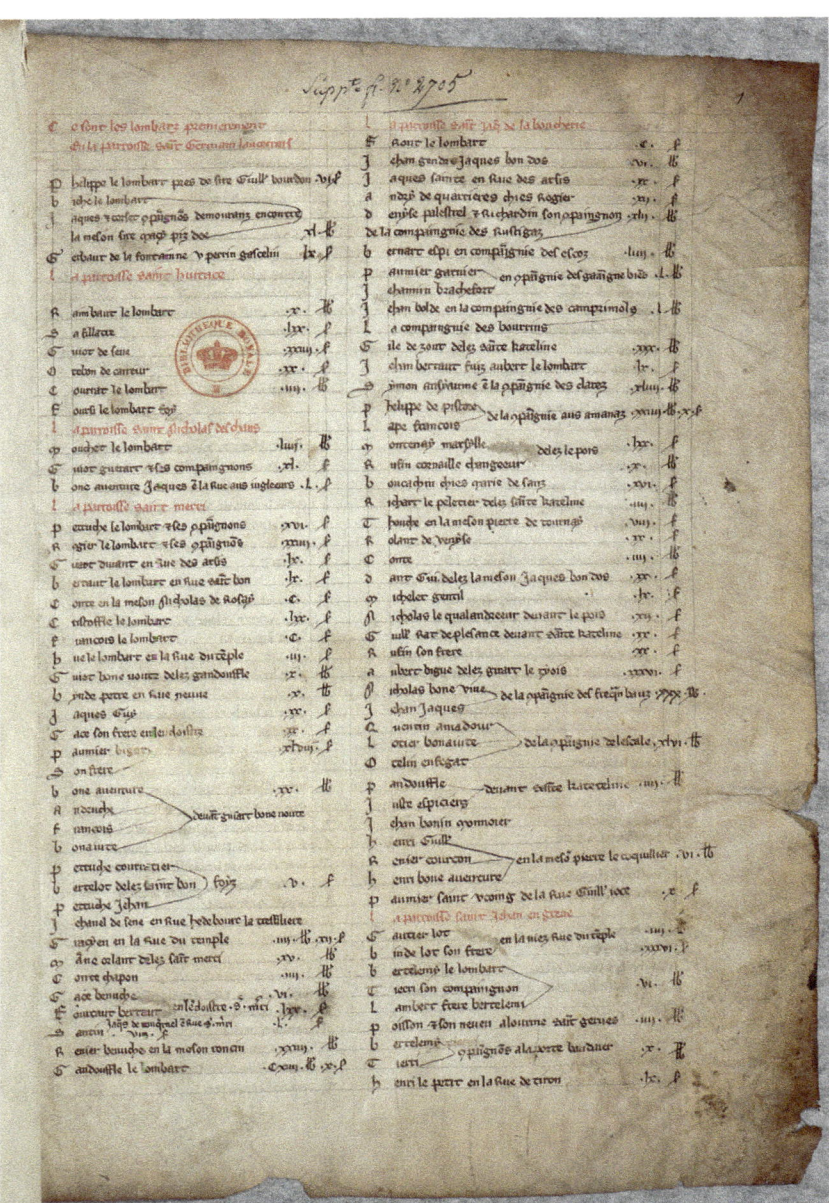

FIGURE 5.1. The opening page of the 1292 Parisian taille tax list stating the names and payments collected from Lombards in Paris. Bnf MS. Francaise 6220 f.1r.

new administrative function was added to the royal bureaucracy when the Jews Kalot de Rouen and Joucet de Pontoise were appointed royal arbitrators in charge of handling financial disputes between the king and the Jews of the realm (*Procureur général des juifs*).[18] As of 1297, two Jews of each *bailliage* were appointed as *Procureurs* in charge of collecting royal taxes from Jews in their respective jurisdictions.[19] Hence, not only did the treasury begin to impose, register, and collect the taille of Jews separately in the years before their expulsion, but the bureaucratic measures taken imply a change in the king's perception of the Jews in his realm. Namely, toward the end of the thirteenth century, the king saw the Jews as a distinct group that required special scrutiny and particular administration.[20] No such special commissioner was officially appointed to handle the affairs relating to Lombards or other Christian moneylenders.

The taille lists from Paris reflect the duality of the Jews' status in the city: on the one hand, their inclusion in fiscal policy and their distinction from Lombards who were taxed as noncitizens suggest that Jews were perceived as Parisian citizens, at least for fiscal purposes. The exclusion of Jews from the lists as of 1298, the separate collection of taille taxes from Jewish inhabitants as of that year, the outstanding levies imposed on Parisian Jews, and the appointing of a royal agent to handle Jewish financial affairs all emphasize the increasing exclusion or particularization of Jews in the eyes of the royal sovereigns and municipal officials during this period. Lombards, on the other hand, despite their legal status as noncitizens during the end of the thirteenth and beginning of the fourteenth century, were not excluded from fiscal policy. On the contrary, despite being identified as Lombards, as the years advanced, they were incorporated into the tax lists according to their domiciles, intertwined with the Parisian bourgeoisie. In addition, at the end of the thirteenth or beginning of the fourteenth century, Lombards were granted bourgeois privileges. This is attested in the revocation of these rights by King Philippe V in 1322: "By our dearest lord . . . [that] to several Lombards, Italians and Genoists [granted] the liberties and

---

18. Lazard, "Les revenus tirés des juifs de France," 238–39.
19. In the accounts dated September 1, 1298, Kalot is mentioned as the representator of the Jews of Paris, and in an account from 1299 as responsible of the collection of the taille tax of the Jews of Normandie. Lazard, "Les revenus tirés des juifs de France," 239–40.
20. The position of the royal commissioner in charge of Jewish affaires was revoked in 1388, six years before the final expulsion of Jews from the French realms in 1394: Paris, Archives Nationales, Y//2, f.98r-98v (*Les livres de couleur*).

bourgeois rights... because of the frauds and malice of those who have had received the said liberties and bourgeois right... [and] from certain knowledge and reasons, we revoke the said liberties and privileges granted... and totally nullify them."[21] This ordinance unequivocally testifies that at some point between 1287 and 1322 Lombards were formally granted bourgeoise privileges. While Jews were expelled from the kingdom in 1306 and again in 1322, the legal, social, and economic status of Lombards was considerably improved.

Another comparative fiscal aspect between Jews and Lombards is the substantial compulsory taxes each group was required to pay to the Royal Treasury. In addition to being obliged to pay the taille tax, Jews were also forced to make numerous "one-time" payments to the royal treasury throughout the thirteenth century and the beginning of the fourteenth century. For example, in 1269, they were required to purchase the *rouelle*—a distinguishing sign in the form of a round piece of cloth meant to be placed on their clothing as identification. They also made similar payments for the same purpose in 1285, 1295, 1296, 1299, 1300, and 1301, when the *Journaux du trésor des chartes*—the records of the royal treasury—reported these payments to have been a significant component of the total revenues derived from the Jews of the realm;[22] in 1285 Philip IV forced a payment of 25,000 livres from the Jews of the realm, donated on the occasion of the king's birthday;[23] and in

---

21. "Cum per carissimos dominos genitorem ey germanos nostros, quondam dictorum regnorum Reges, et per nos metipsos ipsos, pluribus Lombardis, sive Ytalicis, ett Januensibus, concessaee fuerint gratiae, libertates & Burgesiae ... propter fraudes et malitias ipsorum qui dictas gratias libertates et Burgesias habet ... ex certa scientia et ex causa, dictas gratias et libertates sic concessas, ad requisitionem et supplicationem quorumcumque concessae fuerint, et sub quacumque forma verborum, tenore praesentium revocamus et totaliter ad nullamus." de Laurière, *Ordonnances des roys de France de la troisième race. Premier volume*, 749.

22. Lazard, "Les revenus tirés des juifs de France," 237; Viard, "*Les journaux du trésor de Philippe IV le bel.*," xvi, and see for examples registries n.707, 2097, 2448, and 2683 therein. Research has often referred to the *rouelle* as a distinguishing or ignominious sign, overlooking the financial aspect of that obligation. See, e.g., Shalom Sabar, "The Jewish Hat and the Yellow Badge (Hebrew)," *Mishkafayim* 34 (1998): 64-67; Danièle Sansy, "Marquer la différence : l'imposition de la rouelle aux XIIIe et XIVe siècles," *Médiévales* 41 (2001): 15-36, https://doi.org/10.3406/medi.2001.1523; Sara Lipton, *Dark Mirror: The Medieval Origins of Anti-Jewish Iconography* (New York: Metropolitan Books, 2014), 21-24. Robert Ulysse mentioned the payments made by Jews to purchase the *rouelle*, but did not elaborate on this matter: Robert Ulysse, "Étude historique et archeologique sur la roue des juifs depuis le XIIIéme Siècle," *Revue des Études Juives* 6 (1883): 9, https://doi.org/10.3406/rjuiv.1883.3341.

23. Lazard, "Les revenus tirés des juifs de France," 236.

1322 Jews were required to pay the exorbitant amount of 150,000 livres, before being banished from the realms.[24]

Overall, the frequency and extent of payment demanded from the Jews in the final decades of the thirteenth century were much higher and not comparable to those received from the Lombards at the same period.[25] Nonetheless, after the banishments of the Jews from France in 1306 and 1322, the *Journaux du trésor des chartes* attest that similar "onetime" charges were then more frequently levied on Lombards. From the *tallia Judeorum*, the treasury shifted to the *financia Lombardorum*.[26] For example, while already in 1295 Lombards were obliged to pay tax on revenues drawn from the sale of merchandise, this tax was doubled in 1315.[27] Between 1320 and 1322, King Charles IV issued compulsory payments that only Lombard merchants were required to make,[28] and between the years 1323 and 1325, Lombards were obliged to pay a tax called *la taxe sur le chiffre d'affaire*—an added value tax on their transactions.[29] In 1323 Lombards were forced to contribute considerable donations in celebration of the accession of King Charles IV,[30] and in 1330 paid a further 120,000 livres to the king,[31] with an additional 18,000 livres paid to the treasury a year later.[32] The currency crisis in France at the beginning of the fourteenth century, and the expensive wars and expeditions of the Capetians amplified the king's need for an immediate replacement source of finance.[33] The evidence in the *Journaux du trésor des chartes* of mounting charges levied solely on Lombards

---

24. Champion, "Juifs et Lombards," 854.
25. Viard, *Les journaux du trésor de Philippe IV le bel.*, xvii. Lazard, "Les revenus tirés des juifs de France," 236; Simeon Luce, "Catalogue des documents du trésor des chartes relatifs aux juifs sous le reign de Philippe le Bel," *Revue des études Juives* 2 (1881): 15-72, https://doi.org/10.3406/rjuiv.1881.3210; Gérard Nahon, "Condition fiscale et économique des juifs," in *Juifs et judaïsme en Languedoc XIIIe siècle-au début du XIVe siècle*, ed. Marie-Humbert Vicaire and Bernhard Blumenkranz (Toulouse: Privat, 1977), 52-63.
26. Bautier, "Le marchand Lombard en France," 71.
27. de Laurière, *Ordonnances des roys de France de la troisième race. Premier volume*, 326-27, and 582.
28. Bautier, "Le marchand Lombard en France," 78.
29. Bautier, "Le marchand Lombard en France," 78.
30. Racine, "Paris, rue des Lombards, 1280-1340," 106; Viard, *Les journaux du trésor de Charles IV le Bel*, n. 2334.
31. Paris, Archives Nationales Francais, PP//109 f.13v. See also Bautier, "Le marchand Lombard en France," 77-78.
32. Racine, "Paris, rue des Lombards, 1280-1340," 98.
33. Stephane Mechoulan, "The Expulsion of the Jews from France in 1306: A Modern Fiscal Analysis," *Journal of European Economic History* 33, no. 3 (2006): 560-61; Jordan, *The French Monarchy*, 239-40; Joseph R. Strayer, *The Reign of Philip the Fair* (Princeton: Princeton University Press, 1980), 392-97.

throughout the fourteenth century indicates that the royal treasury's reliance on occasional payments was first supported by excessive taxation of Jews of the kingdom, and then, facing a loss of income following their expulsion, the treasury relied more extensively on Lombards to fill the shortfall in their coffers. The replacement of Jews by Lombards might imply a solidification in the perceived role of Jews and Lombards in the third decade of the fourteenth century. Yet we have seen that during this period, the status of Jews and Lombards differed, especially in light of the granting of bourgeoise rights to Lombards. Examining how these legal perceptions shaped Jews' and Lombards' places of residency in Paris over the course of the century further illustrates the distinctions between the two groups.

Jews and Lombards in Paris, Between Expulsions

By the final decades of the thirteenth century, the Jewish community in Paris was one of the largest in western Europe, estimated to be between 1,000 to 1,500 individuals, making up approximately 1 percent of the city's overall population.[34] The Lombards also constituted about 1 percent of the city's overall population during this period.[35] Although there was a "Jewish Street" (*Juiverie* or rue des Juifs) on the Île de la Cité,[36] where Jews had lived before the expulsion of 1182, on their

---

34. Favier, *Le bourgeois de Paris au Moyen Âge*, 11; Jordan, *The French Monarchy*, 183; Michel Roblin, *Les juifs de Paris: démographie, économie, culture* (Paris: A. et J. Picard, 1952), 20. Estimations on the overall population of Paris at the end of the thirteenth century range between 80,000 and 200,000. For different estimations, see Alain Layec and Caroline Bourlet, "Densité de population et socio-topographie: La géolocalisation de rôle de taille de 1300," in *Paris de parcelles en pixels*, edited by Hélène Noizet, Boris Bove, and Laurent Jacques Costa (Saint Denis: Presses universités de Vincennes, 2013), 230-31. John Baldwin, *Paris, 1200* (Stanford: Stanford University Press, 2010), 30-31; Raymond Cazelles, "La population de Paris avant la peste noire," *Comptes rendus des séances de l'Académie des Inscriptions et Belles-Lettres* 110, no. 4 (1966): 539-41, https://doi.org/10.3406/crai.1966.12047; Sharon A. Farmer, *The Silk Industries of Medieval Paris: Artisanal Migration, Technological Innovation, and Gendered Experience* (Philadelphia: University of Pennsylvania Press, 2017), 226; David Herlihy, *Opera Muliebria: Women and Work in Medieval Europe*, New Perspectives on European History (New York: McGraw-Hill, 1990), 128-31; Roblin, *Les juifs de Paris*, 18-19; Rubin, *Cities of Strangers*, 5.

35. Racine, "Paris, rue des Lombards, 1280-1340," 100.

36. Paris had two Roman roads crossing it from north to south. The juiverie de la cité was situated on the eastern Roman road, called "route Saint Martin,' and the rue de la Harpe was situated on the western Roman road, often called Chaussée de Saint Lazar. See map in Philippe Lorentz et al., *Atlas de Paris au Moyen Âge: Espace urbain, habitat, société, religion, lieux de pouvoir* (Paris: Éditions Parigramme, 2006), 17; Roblin, *Les juifs de Paris*, 12; Urban T. Holmes, *Daily Living in the Twelfth Century: Based on the Observations of Alexander Neckam in London and Paris*, reprint (Madison: University of Wisconsin Press, 1982), 57.

return to Paris most Jews settled on the left bank of the Seine River near rue de la Harpe, one of the city's more vibrant trading centers,[37] with another community springing up on the right bank, in rue St. Bon and rue de la Tacherie,[38] as well as along the streets adjacent to the Pont au Change during the early thirteenth century.[39] After the river flooded in midcentury, most Jews moved back to the right bank. Thus, by the beginning of the fourteenth century, the Juiverie of St. Bon and its environs became the central venue of Jewish inhabitants in Paris, although several Jewish families still resided on the Petit Pont.[40] Mapping the different Jewish areas of settlement in Paris highlights a critical element concerning their settlement—until the expulsion of 1306, they were scattered between three different parishes in the city and did not live in a particular or distinct Jewish street, although streets with this name (rue des Juives or Juiverie) existed throughout the thirteenth and fourteenth centuries (figure 5.2). Rather, Jews and Christians lived and shared the same streets and sometimes even the same buildings.[41]

Jewish cemeteries also attest to Jews' mobility throughout the city. According to the sixteenth-century chronicler Henri Sauval, during the thirteenth and fourteenth centuries, there were two Jewish cemeteries

---

37. Roblin, *Les juifs de Paris*, 12; Henri Sauval, *Histoire et recherches des antiquités de la ville de Paris*, vol. 1 (Paris: Charles Moette- libraire et Jacques Chardon Imprimeur-Libraire, 1724), 338. Evidence of Jewish settlement on the petit pont and the street that extended from it on the Île de la Cité (rue de juiverie) exists as early as the seventh century, in the description of Gregorius of Tour: Robert Anchel, "The Early History of the Jewish Quarters in Paris," *Jewish Social Studies* 2, no. 1 (1940): 46–49, http://www.jstor.org/stable/4615125. Anchel also described the Jewish settlement on rue de la Harpe on the left bank in the early thirteenth century; see Anchel, "The Early History of the Jewish Quarters in Paris," 49.

38. Anchel, "The Early History," 51–55; Roblin, *Les juifs de Paris*, 14–15; Juliette Sibon, *Chasser les juifs pour régner: Les expulsions par les rois de France au Moyen Âge* (Paris: Perrin, 2016), 44. Holmes, *Daily Living in the Twelfth Century*, 61. Rue de la tacherie is a modification of the old name "l'attacherie," and it owed this name to the artisans who manufactured and sold attachments or fasteners such as pins, buckles, hooks, and similar small objects for fastening clothing in that location. Anchel, "The Early History," 53.

39. This bridge received its name in the twelfth century, when King Louis VII fixed it as the place for moneylenders, goldsmiths, and moneychangers to handle their business. See Walton William, *The History of Paris from the Earliest Period to the Present Day*, vol. 3 (London: George Barrie and Sons Publishers, 1827), 150–51; Anchel, "The Early History," 49.

40. Sauval, *Histoire et recherches*, tome 1:117; Anchel, "The Early History," 49; Roblin, *Les juifs de Paris*, 14–18; Joseph Morsel, "Comment peut-on être parisien? Contribution à l'histoire de la genèse de la communauté parisienne au XIIIe siècle," in *Religion et société urbaine au Moyen Âge. Mélanges offerts à Jean-Louis Biget*, eds. Patrick Boucheron, Jacques Chiffoleau (Paris: Publications de la Sorbonne, 2000), 11. Michel Félibien, *Histoire de la ville de Paris* (Paris: Guillaume Desprez et Jean Desessartz, 1725), 38 (278).

41. See also Roblin, *Les juifs de Paris*, 13. Jews and Christians often entered one another's homes to work as domestic laborers, receive loans, repay debts, or negotiate business deals.

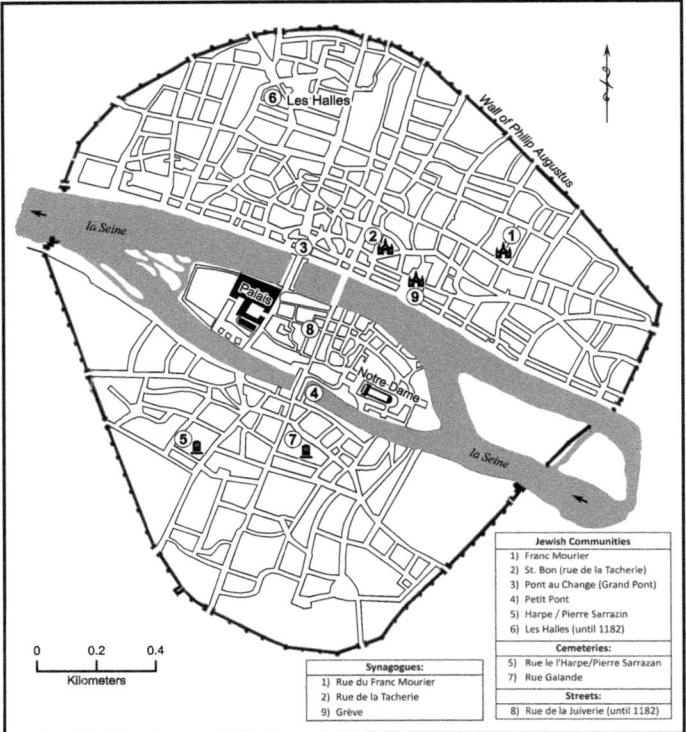

FIGURE 5.2. Jewish communities in Paris before 1306. © Nureet Dermer 2024, Cartography by Gordon Thompson.

in Paris, both on the left bank. One was located on rue Pierre Sarrazin, adjacent to rue de la Harpe, and another, older, cemetery was located on rue Galande.[42] Several archival documents from the thirteenth and fourteenth centuries also mention the Jewish cemetery on rue de la Harpe.[43] Although Jews mainly lived on the right bank of the River

---

42. Sauval, *Histoire et recherches*, vol. 1:145; Anchel, "The Early History," 50–53; Moïse Schwab, *Rapport sur les inscriptions hébraïques de la France* (Paris: Imprimerie nationale, 1904), 237. Eighty Jewish tombstones from the thirteenth and early fourteenth centuries were discovered around the street Pierre Sarrazan, in 1849: Schwab, *Rapport sur les inscriptions hébraïques*, 238–39.

43. This Jewish cemetery was confiscated in 1287 by King Philippe le Bel: Anchel, "The Early History," 52; Another royal charter from the same year contains information about granting a house and a garden to "magistri Gilberri de saana cononici Parisiensi" on the left bank, located 'next to the cemetery of the Jews" (*iuxta cimiterium judeorum*): Paris, Archives Nationales, S//87 n.5; In 1311 Philippe le Bel gave the rights of this cemetery to the religious order of Poissy: Sauval, *Histoire et recherches*, tome 1:21.; and in the second half of the

Seine at the end of the thirteenth and fourteenth centuries, their cemeteries remained on the left bank. The tax lists of 1292, 1296, and 1297 (the only ones that include Jewish inhabitants) indicate that the taxpaying Jews of Paris lived on five main streets: on the street over the Petit Pont that connected Île de la Cité with the left bank, and on the streets la Tacherie, Neuve St. Merri, Franc Mourier, and Cour Robert. Apart from the street Petit Pont that connected the Île de la Cité with the left bank, the other four streets were on the right bank, in the parish of St. Merri, known today as le Marais. This parish constituted the Juiverie de St. Bon, and it was situated in close proximity to the Hôtel de Ville and Place du Grève, which were both central entry points of merchandise into medieval Paris via the Seine and the place of the commercial court. In other words, Jews resided in the city's core, close to the palace and the official economic institutions.

After the expulsion of 1306, Jews were permitted to return in 1315, only to be banished again in 1322. They were then not allowed back into the kingdom until 1360,[44] at which point they were restricted to living on one street, a new rue des Juifs, also known as rue de Rosieres, close to the city's walls (figure 5.3). This street, surrounded by walls and a gate (*clôture*) that separated it from the adjacent streets, is attested to in a royal protocol from 1365.[45] This protocol: (1) forbade Jews to demand from their debtors a weekly interest higher than two deniers for one livre; (2) instructed Jews to establish their homes in a street that would be assigned to them for this purpose, to which Christians were excluded, and which would be closed by a barrier; (3) prohibited any Christian woman from crossing this barrier without the company of a Christian male; (4) allowed Jews to hold a market within the Jewish quarter, which included a Jewish butcher; and (5) forbade any Christian

---

fourteenth century, Philippe the Bold, Count of Burgundy, granted ownership rights of the Jewish cemetery to the Canon of Bayeux: Anchel, "The Early History," 52; Paris, Bnf, Ms. NAF. 7910, f.216.

44. Denis-François Secousse, ed., *Ordonnances des roys de France de la troisième race, troisième volume, contenant les ordonnances du roy Jean depuis le commencement de l'année 1355 jusqu'à sa mort arrivée le 8 Avril 1364* (Paris: Imprimerie royal, 1732), 467–70. There are indications for the return of Jews to the realms already in 1359, as the king appointed *Roberto de ultra aquam* as the judge of the Jews and keeper of their privileges: Secousse, *Ordonnances des roys de France de la troisième race, troisième volume*, 351–52. Roger Kohn notes that most Jews postponed their return for almost ten years. See Roger Kohn, "Les juifs de Paris (1359-1394): Problèmes de topographie urbaine," *Proceedings of the World Congress of Jewish Studies* 7 (1977): 3–4.

45. Bibliothèque nationale de France. Département des Manuscrits. Latin 13868, f. 37r-38r.

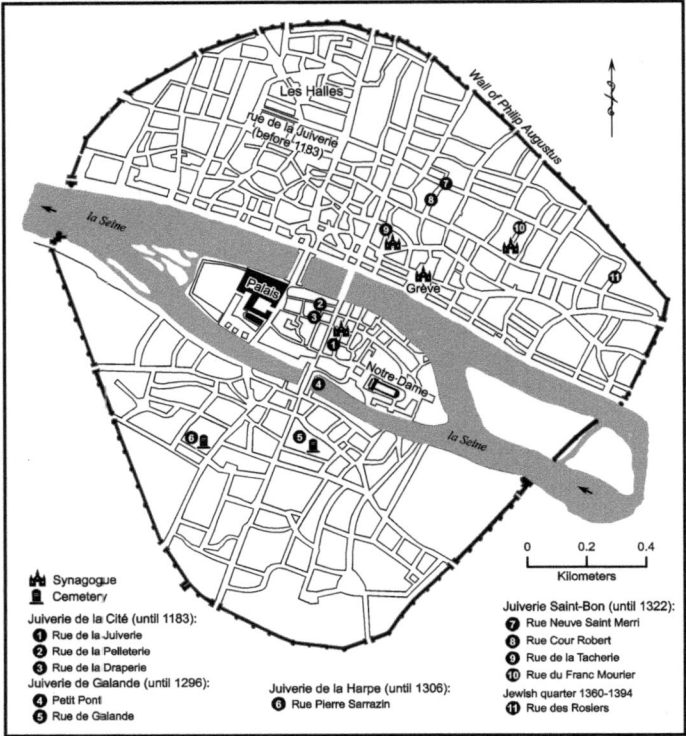

FIGURE 5.3. Jewish residency in Paris until 1394. © Nureet Dermer, 2024, cartography by Gordon Thompson. Adapted from *Atlas de Paris au Moyen Âge*, 2018.

man or woman to be a servant of a Jew.[46] These regulations indicate that the demand to live in this enclosed area was not meant to protect the Jews but to restrict the interaction of Jews and Christians within the Jewish space.

This is confirmed by the anonymous chronicler of the *Chronique du religieux de Saint-Denis* in the second half of the fourteenth century.[47] While describing the riots in Paris in the 1380s, the chronicler recounts, almost anecdotally, how a seditious mob entered the Jewish quarter:

> Enraged with fury, they started to cross the city, opening by force the coffers that contained the proceeds of taxation, throwing money

---

46. Georges Tessier, "L'activité de la chancellerie royale au temps de Charles V," *Moyen Age* 1 (1938): 26.

47. Michel Pintoin, *Chronique du religieux de Saint-Denys: contenant le règne de Charles VI, de 1380 à 1422. tome 1*, ed. M. L. Bellaguet (Paris: Imprimerie de Crapelet, 1839).

all over the streets, seizing the registers of royal contributors, tearing them up to pieces, and ultimately destroying them. Then, still driven by the same spirit of destruction, they furiously entered the quarter, where the Jews had established about forty houses with the King's permission. [There], pursuing their exaggerations, they gave freedom to their instincts and passions derived from their diverse characters, ages, and conditions. Forcing the doors, some searched everywhere, stealing everything that suited them. Others grabbed women's necklaces, rings, and other ornaments that were easy to carry. Others, with greed, looked for silk garments and precious vestments; others threw away silver vessels through the windows so they could later take them home; and others preferred to subtract the obligations written by the nobles and the bourgeois, looking at this price as the most advantageous. Several nobles, who joined the mob, encouraged them in their disorder. Some even gave further liberty to their cruelty and killed every Jew they met.[48]

Consistent with the protocol from 1365 that compelled Jews to reside in one specific street, the chronicler testified that by the 1380s, there were about forty houses in the Jewish Street and that these houses had been established there with the king's permission. Aware of the clear distinction of the Jewish Street, the chronicle pointed out the vulnerability of Jews residing in this specific area, as they were easily recognized and targeted.

The Jews who returned to Paris in 1360 thus were subjected to a new spatial and social reality. Located on the edge of the city, the rue des Juifs was a distinct closed area, occupied mostly or exclusively by Jewish inhabitants, indicating the increasing repudiation of Jews from urban space and society and their highly vulnerable situation. Jean-Pierre Leguay explains that the isolation of Jews into distinct areas in the medieval city is consistent with the treatment of other marginal groups, such as criminals, prostitutes, immigrants, and so on, who were also pushed into unique areas within the city, which were then considered dangerous and often referred to as "the hot streets" (*les rues chaudes*).[49]

---

48. Translated into English by the author. Source in Latin: Pintoin, *Chronique du religieux de Saint-Denys*, 54–55.

49. Jean-Pierre Leguay, *La rue au Moyen Âge, de mémoire d'homme* (Rennes: Ouest France, 1984), 169–70.

140   CHAPTER 5

Where did Lombards live in Paris? Can the same patterns be traced concerning their settlements in the city? According to the municipal taille lists from 1292 to 1300, Lombards were dispersed all over Paris—living on the right bank, the left bank, and on the Île de la Cité. Wherever they settled was close to the economic and political centers of the city—the great market of Les Halles, the Place du Grève, and the palaces and royal institutions on the Île de la Cité.[50] The most significant number of Lombards resided on the right bank, in the parishes of St. Merri (with 25 household registers) and St. Jacque de la Boucherie (with 37 entries), meaning in the same parish as the central Jewish community of St. Bon. Interestingly, the 173 entries of Lombards included 14 names of individual taxpayers under the title "companies" (*compaignies*).[51] These consortia were formed by merchants who were originally from the same Italian cities and worked together to carry out commercial and/or financial transactions.[52] The lists of 1292 thus distinguished between Lombards who arrived in Paris to work for their companies and settled there for the long-term, and singulars (*singuliers*)— Lombards who were not associated with any organization.

Unlike Jews, Lombards were never expelled collectively from the French realm. While several expulsions of Lombards were carried out during the thirteenth and fourteenth centuries, these were distinctively designed to banish only those who practiced usury and often included other Christian moneylenders as well.[53] Accordingly, the royal ordinances that proscribed these expulsions specifically listed the description of moneylenders, meaning that those not engaged in moneylending activities could remain. Since Lombards were not banished collectively, they were not absent from Paris or other cities for continuous periods, and there were no ordinances regulating their return to

---

50. On the right bank in the parishes of St. Germain-l'Auxerrois, St. Eustache, St. Nicolas des Champs, St. Merri, St. Jacque de la Boucherie, St. Jean en Grève, St. Paul. On the ile de la cité: in the parish of St. Barthéléméi. On the left bank in the parish of St. Germain de Pres, and on the Petit Pont. See a detailed map of Paris's parishes in Bourlet, "Densité de population," 234. Hercule, *Paris sous Philippe le Bel*, 1-4; Favier, *Le bourgeois de Paris au Moyen Âge*, 384-85. On the great market of Les Halles, see, for example, Anne Lombard-Jourdan, *Les Halles de Paris et leur quartier dans l'espace urbain: 1137-1969*, Études et rencontres de l'École des chartes 28 (Paris: École nationale des chartes, 2009), 113-32; Favier, *Le bourgeois de Paris au Moyen Âge*, 221-23.

51. In Latin, *Societates*.

52. Bautier, "Le marchand Lombard en France aux XIIIe et XIVe siècles," 65; Racine, "Paris, rue des Lombards, 1280-1340," 99-100; Van Shaik, "On the Social Position of Jews and Lombards," 186.

53. Dorin, *No Return*, 92-101.

the city, nor indications of specific limitations concerning their settlement in Paris. Thus, it is more difficult to trace their intra-immigration across the city throughout the century.

That being said, the *Journaux du trésor* of Charles IV reveals a significant increase in the Lombard population in Paris. In 1322, 39 of 161 Italian companies active in the realm and mentioned in the registers of the *Journaux du trésor* were Parisian companies, signifying that Paris had become a central hub of commercial and financial activities for Lombards and other Italians. This level of activity was only equaled, extrapolating from the number of companies registered, to their extensive activities in the fairs of Champagne.[54] It was also in this year that, as noted in the opening of this chapter, a street, adjacent to the former location of the prominent Jewish community, was inaugurated as the "rue des Lombards," surely indicative of a significant level of settlement. It further demonstrates the need to distinguish Lombards in Paris, revealing yet again how urban space reflected changes in the social perceptions of Lombards within urban society. However, unlike Jews, Lombards were not required to live solely on Lombards Street, nor were other Parisians restricted from living there. In this respect, it can be argued that the designation of a Lombard Street in Paris was reflective of social distinction rather than exclusion.

Abolishing the citizenship privileges of Lombards in 1322 prevented them from obtaining the social and economic opportunities reserved for only the highest strata of society, that is, citizens, bourgeoise. It happened in the same year that Jews were expelled from the kingdom for the second time. Following the expulsion of the Jews, attention seems to have turned to the Lombards, who began to be heavily taxed, much more than other populations, and similarly to the taxation of Jews prior to their banishment. In this sense, Lombards not only replaced Jews in terms of their moneylending activities but also came to fill a similar role in the broader economic and social sense.

---

54. Viard, *Les journaux du trésor de Charles IV le bel*; Racine, "Paris, rue des Lombards, 1280–1340," 106. However, these companies went bankrupt by the mid-fourteenth century after the financial crisis caused by the Black Death, causing a decrease of Lombards in cities throughout the kingdom. See Racine, "Paris, rue des Lombards, 1280–1340," 111. See also a survey of all Lombard companies in Paris throughout the Middle Ages in Piton, *Les Lombards en France et a Paris*, 57–83.

Desirable and Undesirable Foreigners

The calamities of the fourteenth century solidified a Christian local urban identity among inhabitants of French cities and increased the sense of mistrust they felt toward minority groups, newcomers, and other populations at the margins of society.[55] In parallel, the traditional association established in Roman law between city of origin and citizenship had disentangled, leaving the power to grant privileges of citizenships in the hands of the king. In being able to grant privileges to those previously considered foreigners and thus denied the possibility of holding such rights, the king increased his hold over vulnerable populations, who depended on his discretionary power to bestow or revoke privileges. Additionally, he established the criteria for identifying locals and citizens, further delineating the boundaries of belonging.[56] But formal status and legal rights were not the only markers of urban citizenship in Paris. Another decisive factor was the de facto social perception of the inhabitants. In this respect, Jean Favier argues that "the bourgeois was he who was a member of a social corporation, defined by charters, statues, and privileges," yet "the notion of a bourgeois was derived from practice, not from the law."[57] Joseph Morsel undertook the same approach in examining the cohesion of Parisian medieval urban identity between the eleventh and the fourteenth centuries. He argued that the status of a bourgeois in Paris went beyond the formal legal status and included a social conception of urban identity, which crystallized during the thirteenth and fourteenth centuries.[58] The arguments concerning the changing status and perceptions of Jews and Lombards in Paris presented in this chapter strengthen and further demonstrate this observation.

The comparison of the treatment of and attitude toward Jews and Lombards with regards to fiscal policy and in light of their patterns of settlement in Paris reflects the multifaceted and complex perception of

---

55. On the exclusion of different minority groups in France as an essential manifestation or outcome of the evolution of national sentiment and the building of the French state, see for example: Christian Jaouich, *L'exclusion des Templiers de l'Église et du Royaume. Le rôle du procès des Templiers dans la construction de l'État (1307–1314)* (Quebec: Presses de l'Université Laval, 2022).

56. Rubin, *Cities of Strangers*, 17; Bernard D'alteroche, "L'évolution de la notion et du statut juridique de l'étranger a la fin Moyen Âge (XIe-XVe siècle)," *Revue du nord* 2 (2002): 231–35, https://doi.org/10.3917/rdn.345.0227.

57. "Le bourgeois est celui qui est membre du corps social dirigeant que définissent les chartes, les statuts et les privilèges," and "La notion de bourgeois émerge donc en pratique, non en droit." Favier, *Le bourgeois de Paris au Moyen Âge*, 11, 20.

58. Morsel, "Comment peut-on être Parisien," 363–81.

foreignness during this period and illustrates the changes in this conception throughout the century.[59] Although both groups were often perceived as foreign, Jews and Lombards constituted two very different kinds of foreigners. Fiscal evidence from the beginning of the century suggests that both Jews and Lombards were considered and included in the local fiscal regime as distinct foreign groups. However, while Lombard moneylenders and Jews were banished throughout the century, the repeated expulsions of the Jews from the French realms and the revival of the moral justifications for their banishment from Christian society toward the end of the century, provide unequivocal proof that the "othering" of Jews crystallized and solidified during the course of the century. While at the beginning of the century, the attitude toward Jews was rather volatile, perhaps explaining their admittance back to the realm after the expulsions of 1306 and 1322, by the end of the century, their exclusion led to a final and definitive expulsion. The coalescence of the pervasive view of Jews as outsiders—economically, politically, and religiously—was manifested in the new limitations on their physical presence in Paris and other cities in northern France.[60]

During the fourteenth century, Lombards started to take on the economic and social role of Jews. On the one hand, according to the privileges granted to them at the beginning of the century, they were citizens, bourgeois. On the other hand, according to fiscal policy throughout the century, they were viewed as "desirable foreigners" who could be extorted to fill the crown's coffers, a role formerly held by the Jews. Obviously, as Christians, the Lombards did not experience the same level of theological or spiritual antagonism as the Jews.[61] This crucial distinction between the two groups emphasizes the different xenophobic and theological notions of foreignness that evolved during the century. Indeed, in this respect, the perceptions regarding Jews and their place in French society became increasingly negative throughout the century until their final expulsion from the French realms in 1394.

---

59. Van Shaik, "On the Social Position of Jews and Lombards," 168.

60. The medieval revival of the use of spatial segregation as a form of "othering" specific populations was the first step of what later developed into the complete segregation of Jews in cities, specifically in fifteenth- and sixteenth-century Italy. See Michaël Gasperoni and Giacomo Todeschini, "Le Ghetto : 'Une technique de gouvernement,'" *Presses Universitaires de France, Dix-septième siècle—le siècle des ghettos: la marginalisation sociale et spatiale des juifs en Italie au xviie siècle* 282 (2019): 21-24, 31; Atilio Milano, *Il Ghetto Di Roma: Illustrazioni Storiche* (Hebrew), trans. Dina Milano (Jerusalem: Keter Press, 1992), 37.

61. Laurence Fontaine, *The Moral Economy: Poverty, Credit, and Trust in Early Modern Europe* (New York: Cambridge University Press, 2014), 43; Piton, *Les Lombards en France et a Paris*; Kohn, "Le statut forain," 7; Grunwald, "Lombards, Cahorsins and Jews," 397-98.

Further Readings

Anchel, Robert. "The Early History of the Jewish Quarters in Paris." *Jewish Social Studies* 2 (1940): 45–60. jstor.org/stable/4615125.

Baldwin, John. *Paris, 1200*. Stanford: Stanford University Press, 2010.

Bourlet, Caroline, and Boris Bove. "Religion civique ou affiliation communautaire ? Le témoignage des testaments Parisiens des XIIIe-XVe siècle." *Histoire Urbaine* 60 (2001): 71–96. doi.org/10.58079/u507.

Bove, Boris, and Claude Gauvard, eds. *Le Paris du Moyen Âge*. Paris: Belin, 2014.

Cazelles, Raymond. "La population de Paris avant la peste noire." *Comptes rendus des séances de l'Académie des Inscriptions et Belles-Lettres* 110 (1966): 539–41. doi.org/10.3406/crai.1966.12047.

Dorin, Rowan. *No Return: Jews, Christian Usurers, and the Spread of Mass Expulsion in Medieval Europe*. Princeton: Princeton University Press, 2023.

Farmer, Sharon A. *The Silk Industries of Medieval Paris: Artisanal Migration, Technological Innovation, and Gendered Experience*. Philadelphia: University of Pennsylvania Press, 2017.

Favier, Jean. *Le bourgeois de Paris au Moyen Âge*. Paris: Tallandier, 2012.

Greilsammer, Myriam. *L'usurier chrétien, un juif métaphorique: Histoire de l'exclusion des prêteurs Lombards (XIIIe-XVIIe siècle)*. Rennes: Presses universitaires de Rennes, 2012.

Grunwald, Kurt. "Lombards, Cahorsins, and Jews." *Journal of European Economic History* 4 (1975): 393–98.

Jordan, William Chester. "Home Again: The Jews in the Kingdom of France, 1315–1322." In *The Stranger in Medieval Society*, edited by F. R. P. Akehurst and Stephanie Cain Van d'Elden, 27–45. Minneapolis: University of Minnesota Press, 1997.

Kohn, Roger. "Les juifs de Paris (1359–1394): Problèmes de topographie urbaine." *Proceedings of the World Congress of Jewish Studies* 7 (1977): 1–8.

Layec, Alain, and Caroline Bourlet. "Densité de population et socio-topographie: La géolocalisation de rôle de taille de 1300." In *Paris de parcelles en pixels*, edited by Hélène Noizet, Boris Bove, and Laurent Jacques Costa, 223–45. Saint Denis: Presses universités de Vincennes, 2013.

Lorentz, Philippe, et al. *Atlas de Paris au Moyen Âge: Espace urbain, habitat, société, religion, lieux de pouvoir*. Paris: Éditions Parigramme, 2006.

Nahon, Gérard. "Condition fiscale et économique des juifs." In *Juifs et judaïsme en Languedoc XIIIe siècle-au début du XIVe siècle*, edited by Marie-Humbert Vicaire and Bernhard Blumenkranz, 52–63. Toulouse: Privat, 1977.

Oberste, Jörg. *The Birth of the Metropolis: Urban Spaces and Social Life in Medieval Paris*. Leiden: Brill, 2001.

Rubin, Miri. *Cities of Strangers: Making Lives in Medieval Europe*. Cambridge: Cambridge University Press, 2020.

Sibon, Juliette. *Chasser les juifs pour régner: Les expulsions par les rois de France au Moyen Âge*. Paris: Perrin, 2016.

Strayer, Joseph R. *The Reign of Philip the Fair*. Princeton: Princeton University Press, 1980.

CHAPTER 6

Between Inns, Hospices, and Homes
Jewish Travel and Communal Hospitality in Medieval Ashkenaz

Albert Evan Kohn

Around the turn of the thirteenth century, R. Eliezer ben Yoel ha-Levi (ca. 1140–1220) responded to a quandary from central Europe about the composition of a *get*, the legal writ used to effect a Jewish divorce. The questioner asked how to identify a man without a clearly defined place of residence in this important document whose validity depended on the clear specification of the parties involved. In his response, R. Eliezer wrote:

> When a person leaves his place of residence, either for business or for study, his destination is not considered his residence. Even if his purpose keeps him there for a long time, his intention is to return [to his place of origin]. . . . And this applies to the man under discussion. Witnesses testified before us that he was born in Krakow, but he went several times to Magdeburg, where his brothers had married women and settled. He remained there as a lodger for a while before going here or there either to study or to hire himself out. Along the way, he never established a permanent residence.

Eliezer concluded that the itinerant individual ought to be identified by his birthplace "since he does not have a place of dwelling."[1]

This man, who repeatedly made the more than six-hundred-kilometer journey between his birthplace of Krakow and his brothers' homes in Magdeburg, was not alone in his peripatetic lifestyle.[2] Many medieval men, women, and children—both Jewish and Christian—took to the roads, rivers, and seas to visit or to settle distant places.[3] Focusing on northern French- and German-speaking lands from the twelfth through the fourteenth centuries, this study uses Hebrew and Latin sources to examine how Jews responded to one of the most pressing practical concerns faced by travelers: lodging. Having braved the perils of travel and passed through the city gates, housing became the most immediate challenge facing new arrivals.[4] A tenth-century traveler's phrase book addressed this need in its very first entry when it instructed

---

This work was made possible by the two enriching years I spent in Jerusalem as part of the Beyond the Elite research team. Amid global pandemic, I found a vibrant and creative community of scholars who continue to inform my intellectual commitments. I would like to thank Elisheva Baumgarten for her initial invitation as well as each and every member of the group for their warm welcome and continued friendship. I would also like to acknowledge William Chester Jordan, Elisheva Baumgarten, Andreas Lehnertz, Tzafrir Barzilay, Eyal Levinson, and Hannah Teddy Schachter for their helpful feedback on earlier drafts. This chapter was written under the auspices of the Beyond the Elite: Jewish Daily Life in Medieval Europe Project, PI Elisheva Baumgarten, from the European Research Council (ERC) under the European Union's Horizon 2020 research and innovation program, grant agreement No. 681507, and prepared for publication with funding from the Israel Science Foundation Grant 2850/22, Contending with Crises: The Jews of 14th Century Europe, PI Elisheva Baumgarten.

1. Eliezer b. Joel ha-Levi, *Sefer Ra'aviah*, vol. 3, ed. David Deblytski (Bnei Brak: n.p., 2005), 146.

2. For an example of a Jew who was regularly on the move, see a short fourteenth-century autobiography in which the anonymous author claimed to have resided in several towns for anywhere from a few months to a few years without permanently settling down in Israel Jacob Yuval, "A German-Jewish Autobiography of the Fourteenth Century," *Tarbiz* 55 (1986): 564-66 (Hebrew). English translation: Yuval, "A German-Jewish Autobiography, trans. Zippora Brody, *Binah* 3 (1994): 97-98.

3. René Germain, "Déplacements temporaires et déplacements définitifs dans le centre de la France aux XIVe et XVe siècles," in *Voyages et voyageurs au Moyen Age* (Paris: Publications de la Sorbonne, 1996), 53-61. Michael Toch, "Jewish Migrations to, within and from Medieval Germany," in *Le migrazioni in Europa: secc. XIII-XVIII: atti della "Venticinquesima settimana di studi," 3-8 maggio 1993*, ed. Simonetta Cavaciocchi (Firenze: Le Monnier, 1994), 639-52. For an overview of Jewish migration, see Robert Chazan, *Reassessing Jewish Life in Medieval Europe* (Cambridge: Cambridge University Press, 2010), 85-106.

4. On housing migratory populations, see Jean Verdon, *Voyager au Moyen Âge* (Paris: Perrin, 1998), 121-53; Norbert Ohler, *The Medieval Traveller*, trans. Caroline Hillier (Woodbridge, Suffolk, UK: Boydell Press, 1989), 79-101; Florence Berland, "Arriver, s'établir, repartir: Les gens de la cour de Bourgogne à Paris (1363-1422)," in *Arriver en Ville: Les migrants en milieu urbain au Moyen Âge*, ed. Cédric Quertier, Roxane Chilà, and Nicolas Pluchot (Paris: Publications de la Sorbonne, 2019), 131-43.

its German user how to ask in French "Where have you found lodging this evening, companion [or buddy]?"[5]

Sources testify to the sheer number of Jews who found themselves in distant places and in need of accommodation. The Nuremburg Memorbuch, which collated by city the names of Jews martyred during the thirteenth and fourteenth centuries, specified those who met their fate while living as guests in various communities.[6] The count of martyrs included "four guests" in Rothenburg ob der Tauber, one guest as well as two students in Konstanz, and "three Frenchmen" in the Germanic town of Bamberg. In contrast to these small populations of visitors, the record from Würzburg memorialized "100 souls of those guests, both poor and rich, who were killed and burned with the holy community."[7] These and other Hebrew sources refer to temporary residents interchangeably as *Orhim* (guests), *Akhsaniim* (lodgers), and less frequently, *Nokhrim* (foreigners).[8] So ubiquitous was their presence that rabbinic decisors felt compelled to clarify how temporary lodgers fit into the social and religious life of the communities hosting them. For example, R. Isaac b. Moses (1200–1270) outlined the extent to which visitors should contribute to local poor relief given that they were not permanent members of the community.[9] Rabbinic sources like these furnish a recent study by Vadislav Zeev Slepoy about the integration of guests into the cultural and liturgical life of the synagogue of German-speaking Jewish communities during the high and later Middle Ages.[10]

---

5. Wilhelm Braune, ed., *Althochdeutsches Lesebuch: Zusammengestellt und mit Wörterbuch versehen* (Tübingen: Max Niemeyer Verlag, 1994), 9. Translated in John Romano, ed., *Medieval Travel and Travelers: A Reader* (Toronto: University of Toronto Press, 2020), 36.

6. Israel Yuval suggests that most of those referred to as anonymous "guests" in the Memorbuch were poor residents of the community. Even according to Yuval, however, this was not always the case. Many of the lists use the term *guest* to refer to visitors reliant on hospitality, not charity. In the years before the Black Death, the word *orhim* should not be taken as a technical term for the residential poor. See Israel Jacob Yuval, "Hospices and Their Guests in Jewish Medieval Germany," *Proceedings of the Tenth World Congress of Jewish Studies* (1990): 129 (Hebrew); Rainer Josef Barzen, "'Was der Arme benötigt, bist Du verpflichtet zu geben': Forschungsansätze zur Armenfürsorge in Aschkenas im hohen und späten Mittelalter," in *Wirtschaftsgeschichte der mittelalterlichen Juden*, ed. Michael Toch (Berlin: De Gruyter, 2008), 150–52.

7. *Das Martyrologium des Nürnberger Memorbuches*, ed. Siegmund Salfeld (Berlin: Leonhard Simion, 1898), 40, 60, 50, 48.

8. On the late medieval use of the word *Nokhri*, see Zeev Vladislav Slepoy, "Die Stellung von Gästen, Fremden und Armen in einer mittelalterlichen jüdischen Gemeinde," *Chilufim* 27 (2020): 2–5. On *Orhim*, see Yuval, "Hospices and Their Guests in Jewish Medieval Germany," 126.

9. See Rainer Josef Barzen, "The Meaning of 'Tzedakah' for Jewish Self-Organization within a Non-Jewish Environment," *Iggud: Selected Essays in Jewish Studies* (2005): 10.

10. Slepoy, "Die Stellung von Gästen," 1–26.

An awareness of and concern with visiting Jews also took shape outside of the Jewish community.[11] Christian municipal documents refer explicitly to Jewish visitors in their towns. Bishop Rudiger of Speyer's well-known charter granted to the Jewish community in 1084 exempted "any Jew from another place who will be lodged in the city" from paying an unspecified toll, likely either for remaining overnight or for selling wares in the marketplace.[12] A 1331 charter from Cologne similarly discussed the rights and obligations assigned to a Jew who "resides in the city for 15 consecutive days, whether he intends to make a home for himself there or not."[13]

Thus, whether stopping by for a few days or lingering for an extended period with no intention to settle, visitors were a common part of Jewish communal life—and they all needed housing. Before looking at how Jews and Jewish communities addressed this challenge, however, we must first consider the variety of medieval travelers and their lodging options.

Medieval Travelers and Their Lodgings

Medieval people took to the roads for any number of reasons. Those who did so in pursuit of economic opportunities have been well documented.[14] R. Eliezer specified business and labor as reasons the subject of the above responsum adopted a peripatetic lifestyle. Particularly during the High Middle Ages, the constant need for hired labor scattered migratory workers across towns and the countryside alike.[15] These workers lodged near to where they worked, typically in encampments outside of town.[16] More familiar are the merchants and traders who

---

11. For examples, Slepoy, "Die Stellung von Gästen," 4n20.
12. "Illud quoque addidi, ut si quis Iudeus aliunde apud eos hospitatus fuerit, nullum ibi solvat thelonium," *Regesten zur Geschichte der Juden im fränkischen und deutschen Reiche bis zum Jahre 1273*, ed. Julius Aronius (Berlin: Leonhard Simion, 1902), 70n168.
13. *Urkundenbuch für die Geschichte des Niederrheins*, vol. 3, ed. Theodor Joseph Lacomblet (Düsseldorf: H. Voss, 1853), 210. "Item volumus, quod quilibet judeus ad ciuitatem Coloniensem veniens per quindecim dies continuos sub nostra firma protection moram trahat ibidem ad deliberandum, utrum mansionem in ea facere voluerit, an non."
14. See Sharon Farmer, *Surviving Poverty in Medieval Paris: Gender, Ideology and the Daily Lives of the Poor* (Ithaca: Cornell University Press, 2002), 11–32; Toch, "The Economic Activities of German Jews," 181–210.
15. On medieval artisans as a mobile segment of society, see Bronisław Geremek, *The Margins of Society in Late Medieval Paris*, trans. Jean Birrell (Cambridge: Cambridge University Press, 1987), 256–62.
16. See William Chester Jordan's forthcoming study of migrant labor in medieval Europe.

peddled goods while traveling between cities, ports, and seasonal fairs. Among the traveling merchants were Jews, for whom, according to Michael Toch, "to be on the road was the normal condition."[17] Such travel for business was a defining feature of Jewish economic and social life during this period.[18] These economic migrants usually relied on inns that provided services integral to the trader's success, such as storage and access to local networks.[19]

Other travelers ventured out to accrue knowledge. The willingness to cover great distances was seen as a necessary and praiseworthy indication of dedication to one's education.[20] Students—Jewish and Christian—journeyed to unknown places hoping to leave them one day with greater knowledge and/or professional opportunities.[21] Christian men set out for the educational centers in Paris, Oxford, and Bologna; Jewish students traveled hundreds of miles in pursuit of the mentorship of well-known rabbis in northern France and the Rhineland. These young men, especially those without guaranteed financial support, struggled to get by as foreigners in their places of learning.[22] During their studies, Christian students could find hospitality in charitable houses and colleges established by pious benefactors in university towns.[23] Jewish students, as we will see, looked elsewhere.

---

17. Toch, "The Economic Activities of German Jews," 183. For Hebrew sources in German translation about traveling merchants, see Moses Hoffmann, *Der Geldhandel der deutschen Juden während des Mittelalters bis zum Jahre 1350* (Berlin: Duncker & Humblot, 1910), passim.

18. *Taqqanot Qehillot Šum: Die Rechtssatzungen der jüdischen Gemeinden von Mainz, Worms und Speyer im hohen und späten Mittelalter*, vol. 2, ed. Rainer Josef Barzen (Wiesbaden: Harrassowitz Verlag, 2019), 705, 713, 771. Grossman argues that various communal ordinances from this period stemmed from the commonality of Ashkenazic Jewish men spending extensive time away from home. See Avraham Grossman, *Pious and Rebellious: Jewish Women in Medieval Europe*, trans. Jonathan Chipman (Waltham: Brandeis University Press, 2004), 74–75.

19. Peter Spufford, *Power and Profit: The Merchant in Medieval Europe* (New York: Thames & Hudson, 2002), 203–15.

20. Mordechai Breuer, "The Wanderings of Students and Scholars: A Prolegomenon to a Chapter in the History of Yeshivot," in *Culture and Society in Medieval Jewry: Studies Dedicated to the Memory of Haim Hillel Ben-Sasson*, eds. Menahem Ben-Sasson, Robert Bonfil, and Joseph R. Hacker (Jerusalem: Shazar, 1989), 445–68 (Hebrew).

21. For one of many examples, see Olle Ferm and Élisabeth Mornet, eds., *Swedish Students at the University of Paris in the Middle Ages I: Origin, Studies, Carriers, Achievements* (Stockholm: Sällskapet Runica et Mediævalia, 2021).

22. John W. Baldwin, *Masters, Princes, and Merchants: The Social Views of Peter the Chanter & His Circle* (Princeton: Princeton University Press, 1970), vol. 1, 128–30.

23. J. M. Reitzel, "The Medieval Houses of 'Bons-Enfants,'" *Viator* 11 (1980): 179–207, https://doi.org/10.1484/j.viator.2.301505; Alan B. Cobban, "The Role of Colleges in the Medieval Universities of Northern Europe, with Special Reference to England and France," *Bulletin of the John Rylands Library* 71:1 (1989): 49–70, https://doi.org/10.7227/bjrl.71.1.4.

Pilgrims also traveled prolifically during this period, crisscrossing Europe in search of grace and miracles at the tombs of venerated saints.[24] While Christian pilgrims technically had a right to lodge in religious institutions and hospices, their ability to access such hospitality depended on local resources and norms.[25] Some were forced to pay for beds or to build camps. Jews and Christians who traveled between settlements to visit relatives or to participate in celebrations were left with the same options, assuming they did not find hospitality in the homes of well-meaning hosts.[26] Worse off were the so-called 'wandering poor' who roamed between towns in search of temporary employment or charity. Hebrew sources confirm that destitute Jews, especially in the wake of the Black Death and its wave of expulsions, adopted the same methods.[27] *Sefer Hasidim*, already at the turn of the thirteenth century, describes "moving from city to city collecting money" as a viable option for someone in financial distress.[28] Such individuals with limited financial and social resources were forced to rely on charity for their lodging.

Regardless of socioeconomic status or reason for entering the city, every new arrival needed a place to reside during their stay. During the High Middle Ages, a range of charitable hospitality institutions emerged in medieval Europe. These religious foundations assisted needy people, including travelers, pilgrims, and the poor.[29] Staffed by men and women of the religious life and funded by pious donations, such hospitals, hospices, and monasteries were not intended to serve non-Christians. Such inhospitality constituted an added hurdle

---

24. Diana Webb, *Medieval European Pilgrimage* (London: Bloomsbury, 2017), 114–53.

25. Adrian R. Bell and Richard S. Dale, "The Medieval Pilgrimage Business," *Enterprise & Society* 12, no. 3 (2011): 617–20. https://doi.org/10.1093/es/khr014.

26. See below and Eyal Levinson, "There Was a Wedding . . ." in *In and Out, Between and Beyond: Jewish Daily Life in Medieval Europe*, eds. Elisheva Baumgarten and Ido Noy (Jerusalem: The Hebrew University of Jerusalem, 2021), 35–38.

27. Yacov Guggenheim, "Meeting on the Road: Encounters between German Jews and Christians on the Margins of Society," in *In and Out of the Ghetto: Jewish-Gentile Relations in Late Medieval and Early Modern Germany*, ed. Hartmut Lehmann and R. Po-Chia Hsia (Cambridge: Cambridge University Press, 1995), 125–36.

28. Israel Yuval, "Hospices," 125–26. Barzen, "The Meaning of 'Tzedakah,'" 14–17. Yacov Gugenheim, "Von den Schalantjuden zu den Betteljuden: Jüdische Armut in Mitteleuropa in der Frühen Neuzeit," in *Juden und Armut in Mittel- und Osteuropa*, ed. Stefi Jersch-Wenzel (Köln: Böhlau, 2000), 55–69. *Sefer Hasidim*, Parma, ed. Jacob Freimann (Berlin: Wahrmann, 1924), §1248. See a similar story in Eli Yassif, ed., *Ninety-Nine Tales: The Jewish Manuscript Cycle of Legends in Medieval Jewish Folklore* (Tel Aviv: Tel Aviv University Press, 2013), 243–44.

29. Julie Kerr, *Monastic Hospitality: The Benedictines in England, C.1070–c.1250* (Woodbridge: Boydell Press, 2007); Adam Davis, *The Medieval Economy of Salvation: Charity, Commerce, and the Rise of the Hospital* (Ithaca: Cornell University Press, 2019), 7.

for Jewish travelers that distinguished them from the Christians with whom they shared the roads.[30] Without access to Christian charitable hospitality, some Jewish travelers paid for temporary quarters at inns or in the homes of locals. Most, though, sought hospitality among their coreligionists. We can now look more closely at three spaces of lodging and how they shaped Jewish travel.

Inns, Taverns, and the Medieval Hospitality Industry

New arrivals to the city with money to spend could expect to find room and board for themselves and their animals at inns, taverns, and other manifestations of the for-profit hospitality industry. Popular in Antiquity, these businesses reemerged as central to European travel in the wake of urban and economic growth during the twelfth and thirteenth centuries.[31] By the High Middle Ages, they had become integral to social and economic life.[32] While humble hospices dotted well-traversed roads, inns offering more sophisticated services clustered around entranceways to towns and cities where they could lure new arrivals. Inns ranged in size from normal houses retrofitted with a few beds to large buildings with ample living and storage space.[33] Kathryn Reyerson has demonstrated that innkeepers and the businesses they operated were among "the most important players of the trade

---

30. Although these is no prescriptive rule against Jews seeking shelter in religious institutions, the current author has not identified any source suggesting that medieval European Jews did so. Benjamin Kedar has observed, with some surprise, that during the twelfth century sick Jews (as well as Muslims) were invited to seek care in the Hospitaler's hospital in Jerusalem. This is likely the exception that proves the rule. See Benjamin Kedar, "A Twelfth-Century Description of the Jerusalem Hospital," in *The Military Orders*, ed. Helen Nicholson (Aldershot, UK: Ashgate, 1998), vol. 2, 67. In general, Jews saw travel as especially dangerous because of their vulnerability to religiously motivated violence. Various texts recommend that Jews dress up as Christians to protect themselves on their journeys. See the discussion and cited sources in Elisheva Baumgarten, *Practicing Piety in Medieval Ashkenaz: Men, Women, and Everyday Religious Observance* (Philadelphia: University of Pennsylvania Press, 2014), 184-87. Whether some Jews masquerading as Christians were able to access religious hospitality remains unknown.

31. On the history of inns and taverns, see Hans Conrad Peyer, *Von der Gastfreundschaft zum Gasthaus: Studien zur Gastlickeit im Mittelalter* (Hannover: Hahnsche Buchhandlung, 1987), 77-116; Noel Coulet, "Inns and Taverns," in *The Dictionary of the Middle Ages*, ed. Joseph R. Strayer (New York: Scribner, 1985), vol. 6, 468-77; David Nicholas, *The Later Medieval City, 1300–1500* (New York: Routledge, 2014), 341-42.

32. Noël Coulet, "Les hôtelleries en France et en Italie au Bas Moyen Âge," in *L'homme et la route : En Europe occidentale, au Moyen Âge et aux Temps modernes*, ed. Charles Higounet (Toulouse: Presses universitaires du Midi, 1982), 181-205.

33. Noel Coulet, "Inns and Taverns," 470.

infrastructure in the medieval European marketplace."³⁴ They provided the loans, storage services, and introductions that made business possible for visiting and local traders alike.³⁵

Scholars have shown that medieval Jews in southern Europe engaged with the economics and culture of the hospitality industry. Juliette Sibon, for example, identified a Jewish-owned tavern in the Jewish quarter of Marseille that operated at the end of the fourteenth century.³⁶ Jewish taverns were at the same time common in Umbria, according to the work of Ariel Toaff.³⁷ Jessica Elliot has recently argued that Jews' participation in tavern culture grew naturally out of their work in the production and sale of wine. As evidence of this trend, she points to the Jewish converts to Christianity who worked in this industry after their conversion, some of whom lived in thirteenth-century Paris.³⁸

Leaving aside converts to Christianity, sources about Jewish participation in the hospitality industry of northern France and German-speaking lands are scarce. We know from the Parisian tax lists that many Jews lived on the same streets as taverns, but to what extent did they rely on them for food, drink, and/or lodging?³⁹ Hebrew sources from high medieval Ashkenaz describe Jews frequenting local hospitality businesses. They mention, for example, Jews spending time in a

---

34. Kathryn Reyerson, *The Art of the Deal: Intermediaries of Trade in Medieval Montpellier* (Leiden: Brill, 2002), 79; see also, 84–91.

35. For the importance of inns for business dealings, Kathryn Reyerson, "Medieval Hospitality: Innkeepers and the Infrastructure of Trade in Montpellier during the Middle Ages," *Proceedings of the Western Society for French History* 24 (1997): 38–51. Spufford, *Power and Profit*, 203–8.

36. Juliette Sibon, "Vin cacher et non cacher à Marseille et en Provence au bas Moyen Âge et 'professionnalisation' des acteurs économiques juifs et chrétiens," *Rives méditerranéennes* 55 (2017): 70, https://doi.org/10.4000/rives.5286.

37. Ariel Toaff, *Love, Work, and Death: Jewish Life in Medieval Umbria* (Liverpool: Liverpool University Press, 1996), 81–2.

38. Jessica Marin Elliot, "From Vine to Tavern: Jews, Christians, and Wine in Medieval France and Italy," in *Medieval Work, Worship, and Power: Persuasive and Silenced Voices*, ed. Abigail P. Dowling, Nancy Ann McLoughlin, and Tanya Stabler Miller (New York: Routledge, 2024). I am grateful to Dr. Elliot for sharing her work ahead of publication.

39. See Gèraud Hercule, *Paris sous Philippe le bel—des documents originaux et notamment a'après un manuscrit, contenant le role de la taille imposèe sur les habitants de Paris en 1292* (Paris: Imprimerie de Crapelet, 1837); Karl Michaëlsson, *Le livre de la taille de Paris l'an 1296* (Göteborg: Universitets Årsskrift, 1958); Karl Michaëlsson, ed., *Le livre de la taille de Paris l'an 1297* (Göteborg: Universitets Årsskrift, 1962). Nureet Dermer, "Jews in the Tax Lists of Paris at the End of the 13th Century: Social, Gender and Interreligious Features" (MA thesis, Hebrew University of Jerusalem, 2017), 93–106 (Hebrew). For background, see Nureet Dermer's chapter in this collection.

"house of drinking," probably a tavern.[40] Some explicitly refer to Jews lodging there. Isaac b. Moses, author of *Sefer Or Zaru'a*, mentions Jews "traveling on the roads and hosted in the house of a gentile."[41] This referred to an inn, as Isaac specified that the Jews under discussion resided there briefly without becoming a fixture in the house. R. Tzedkiah b. Abraham (thirteenth century), who worked in Rome but studied in the Rhineland, similarly referred to Jews "who lodge in the house of a gentile when they go on business to the towns and the villages."[42] Clearer indications of Jews frequenting these businesses come from Christian legal sources. Following the Fourth Lateran Council's call to limit familiarity and fraternization between religious others, thirteenth-century codes attempted to curtail Jews' use of "the taverns of Christians."[43] Taverns were, of course, hotbeds for the drunken and sexualized interreligious socializing that medieval churchmen sought to prevent.[44] One formulation, recorded in Normandy in 1235, dictated that Jews "should not be received in taverns," yet stipulated that this would not apply if "they are travelers."[45] Although part of a wider attempt to limit Jewish use of the hospitality industry, this addendum reveals Jews' reliance on it.

Given the hazards of premodern road faring and Jews' deep involvement in peripatetic trade, Jewish travelers could not have avoided the inns, hospices, and other hospitality businesses along their routes. Even inside the walls of populated towns and cities, Jewish traders arriving

---

40. Isaac b. Moses, *Sefer Teshuvot Maharah Or Zaru'a: Derashot u-fiske halakhot*, ed. Menahem Avitan (Jerusalem: 2002), New Responsa §4.

41. *Sefer Or Zaru'a*, vol. 3, ed. Yacov Farbstein (Jerusalem: Mekhon Yerushalyim, 2009), 612 (§163)

42. *Sefer Shibolei ha-Leket ha-Shalem*, vol. 1, ed. Solomon Buber (Vilna: Romm, 1886), 70 (Shabbat §99).

43. For some examples, see Solomon Grayzel and Kenneth R. Stow, eds., *The Church and the Jews in the XIIIth Century* (Detroit: Wayne State University Press, 1989), vol. 2, 246 (Breslau, 1266); 247 (Vienna, 1267). Guido Kisch, *The Jews in Medieval Germany: A Study of Their Legal and Social Status* (New York: KTAV, 1970), 555. Guido Kisch, *Jewry-Law in Medieval Germany: Laws and Court Decisions Concerning Jews* (Ann Arbor, MI: American Academy for Jewish Research, 1949), 115.

44. On the culture of the tavern, see Hannah Skoda, *Medieval Violence: Physical Brutality in Northern France, 1270–1330* (New York: Oxford University Press, 2013), 88–118. On the attempt to separate and distinguish Jews from Christians, see Irven Resnick, "The Jews' Badge," in *Jews and Muslims under the Fourth Lateran Council*, eds. Irven Resnick and Marie-Thérèse Champagne (Turnhout: Brepols, 2019), 65–79.

45. "quod in tabernis non recipiantur nisi transeuntes." Léopold Delisle, ed., *Recueil des jugements de l'Echiquier de Normandie* (Paris: Imprimerie impériale, 1864), 133 (§581). See the brief discussion in William Chester Jordan, *The French Monarchy and the Jews* (Philadelphia: University of Pennsylvania Press, 1989), 135, 296n39.

with carts laden with wares would have had to turn to inns and their staff for assistance. This was far from a perfect solution, however. The restrictions on Jewish-Christian fraternization along with the rowdiness of medieval tavern culture would have disquieted Jews, especially those who had just arrived in an unfamiliar locale. Any Jew concerned with rabbinic dietary restrictions would have encountered further complication when relying on these Christian enterprises.[46] The sheer expense was also a deterrent. Many late medieval contracts include an *Einlager* clause that required debtors to incur the added burden of paying for the lender or his representatives to lodge at an inn for each day that a contracted payment was late.[47] While not an astronomical sum, that this was an effective means of enforcing payment reminds us that residing in an inn could quickly add up. Although the hospitality industry remained unavoidable, social, religious, and economic concerns would have driven most Jewish travelers to seek alternative accommodations whenever possible.

Jewish Hospitality Institutions

Most Jewish travelers looked to local coreligionists for lodging. This was not unusual. Newcomers to the city tend to gravitate toward residents with whom they share an affinity, as, for example, Sharon Farmer has demonstrated about poor immigrants to Paris in the thirteenth century.[48] Local contacts with a shared cultural and linguistic background helped new arrivals find jobs and housing. The Jewish community filled a similar role. With limited housing options available, they took it on themselves to house their coreligionists.[49]

Benjamin of Tudela (1130–1173), the famed Jewish traveler, referred to this when he praised the Jews of Paris as "charitable and hospitable to all travelers, and are as brothers and friends unto all their brethren

---

46. On the challenge of finding kosher food while traveling, *Sefer Hasidim*, Parma §176.
47. On the Einlager, see Guido Kisch, *The Jews in Medieval Germany*, 238
48. Farmer, *Surviving Poverty*, 36-37. Farmer argues that arriving in the city without any local contacts made one's life substantially more difficult so new arrivals would seek out those with whom they shared any background. Kathryn Reyerson suggests that this brought visitors to innkeepers with whom they shared a place of origin. Reyerson, "Medieval Hospitality," 44.
49. On this trend in the early modern period, see Debra Kaplan and Verena Kasper-Marienberg, "Nourishing a Community: Food, Hospitality, and Jewish Communal Spaces in Early Modern Frankfurt," *AJS Review* 45, no. 2 (2021): 302-33. https://doi.org/10.1017/s0364009421000027.

the Jews."⁵⁰ Benjamin, who had visited Jewish communities throughout the world, was sensitive to the importance of hospitality. Joseph Shatzmiller has argued that one purpose of his travelogue was to help Jewish travelers locate communities who would host them.⁵¹ Whether Benjamin had experienced the hospitality of Parisian Jews or only heard of their generosity, his emphasis highlights the role communities played in housing visitors. Even Christians noted Jews' commitment to support new arrivals. Richer of Sennones (1190–1266), in a polemical tale, recounted how "a certain Jew from foreign lands arrived to live in Cologne. When he arrived, he asked among the Jews if it was possible for him to find a house in which to dwell. Various Jews, delighted by this, showed him a house [he could rent].... Then with a multitude of Jews congregating, he took over the house with great joy."⁵² According to this tale, the local Jewish community helped their coreligionist find a house—just as Farmer argues affinity communities did for new arrivals in medieval Prais.⁵³

Jewish communities helped lodge newcomers by supporting formal hospitality institutions and by opening their private homes to guests. Communally funded Jewish hospices (*hospitales Iudeorum*) existed in large Jewish communities. Their growth reflected the investment in hospitality and support for the poor extant in the surrounding Christian culture. Already during the twelfth century, Christian benefactors contributed to hospices along major trade and pilgrimage routes to support needy travelers and pilgrims.⁵⁴ Christian hospitals sprang up during the thirteenth century mainly to care for the ill, but also to

---

50. *The Itinerary of Benjamin of Tudela: Critical Text, Translation and Commentary*, ed. Marcus Nathan Adler (London: Oxford University Press, 1907), 81, 73*.

51. Joseph Shatzmiller, "Jews, Pilgrimage, and the Christian Cult of Saints: Benjamin of Tudela and His Contemporaries," in *After Rome's Fall: Narrators and Sources of Early Medieval History: Essays Presented to Walter Goffart*, ed. Alexander C. Murray (Toronto: University of Toronto Press, 1998), 347.

52. Richerus Senoniensis, *Gesta Senoniensis Ecclesiae*, ed. G. Waitz (MGH, 1880), 322. "Quendam Iudeum de extraneis partibus ad habitandum Coloniam devenisse. Et cum inter Iudeos venisset, inquirebat, si domum ad habitandum invenire posset. Alii vero Iudei leti effecti monstraverunt ei domum, in qua ill christianus habitaverat. Ille vero ad civem illum accedens, convenit eum eo, ut ibi habitaret; et congregate multudine Iudeorum, introivit in domum illam et cum m eis cum magno tripudio epulatas est." See also a story from the Decameron in which a Jew from Paris is warmly received by his coreligionists in Rome. Giovanni Boccaccio, *Decameron*, trans. J. G. Nichols (London: Everyman's Library, 2009), 45–49.

53. Farmer, *Surviving Poverty*, 36–37.

54. Spufford, *Power and Profit*, 208–15.

provide for needy travelers.⁵⁵ Similarly, according to Rainer Barzen, already by the end of thirteenth century, most large Jewish communities were supporting a hospice.⁵⁶ The earliest mention of such an institution was in Regensburg in 1210, but others followed in Cologne (1247–53), Augsburg (1290), Nuremberg (1298), Würzburg (1322), and others.⁵⁷ The original purpose of these institutions was to shelter and support impoverished Jews passing through. Later in the Middle Ages, they housed poor Jews who were permanent members of the community yet could not support themselves on their own.⁵⁸ As centralized institutions, hospices allowed community members to distribute the burden of care more evenly.⁵⁹ A fourteenth-century autobiographical account indicates that the community of Koblenz even maintained a hospice keeper as a formal communal position.⁶⁰

A reference to these hospices in an ethical will from the middle of the fourteenth century helps clarify their role: "Do not turn away the poor man empty handed, rather give to him whether it be a lot or a little. If he requests lodging and you do not know him, appease him with a Heller or two that he might give to the hospice-keeper."⁶¹ Hospices, then, appear to have served destitute Jews without local connections. *Sefer Hasidim*, revealingly, refers to the institution as the "house of the poor."⁶² Their role was not to welcome middling travelers, who, one assumes, constituted the majority of Jews who took to the road. Peter Spufford, writing about Christian traders, notes that traveling merchants would have deigned to stay in hospices only as a last resort.⁶³ In any case, even if some travelers sought lodging at hospices, they would have found them only in the largest Jewish communities. Many

---

55. Lucy C. Barnhouse, *Hospitals in Communities of the Late Medieval Rhineland: Houses of God, Places for the Sick* (Amsterdam: Amsterdam University Press, 2023), 86 and sources cited there.

56. Barzen, "'Was der Arme benötigt," 149.

57. Ahuva Liberles, "Home and Away: The Opposition to Travel in *Sefer Hasidim*," *Jewish History* 34, no. 1 (2021): 111. https://doi.org/10.1007/s10835-021-09376-5. Israel Yuval, "Hospices," 125. For a list of references to Jewish hospices, see Barzen, "The Meaning of 'Tzedakah,'" 15–16.

58. Yuval argues that those in this latter category continued to be described as guests, even though they lived permanently in the hospice at the expense of the community. Yuval, "Hospices," 126.

59. Yuval, "Hospices," 125–29.

60. Yuval, "A German-Jewish Autobiography," 565.

61. Israel Abrahams, ed., *Hebrew Ethical Wills* (New York: Jewish Publication Society, 1926), 209. My translation of the term *Akhsanai* follows Yuval, "A German-Jewish Autobiography," 565.

62. *Sefer Hasidim*, Parma §1529.

63. Spufford, *Power and Profit*, 208.

Jews traveling through the small- and moderate-sized communities in northern France, England, and German-speaking lands would never have encountered a Jewish hospice.

Private Homes

Much more appropriate for most Jewish visitors in need of room and board were the private homes of their local coreligionists. Travelers who intended to stay in town for an extended period could lease space in local houses.[64] The ease of moving into a previously established domestic unit would have made such rentals ideal. Florence Berland showed that members of the Burgundian court did just this when they rented rooms from Parisians during their stays in the city.[65] This practice became so common and troubling that some municipalities outlawed citizens from lodging visitors in their homes.[66] Jews too, as administrative records and responsa reveal, were active participants in this market. Ottokar II of Bohemia (ca. 1233–1278), for example, tried in 1254 to uproot the common practice by decreeing that "no one may be hosted in the house of a Jew."[67] Jews across western Europe were leasing sections of their homes for short and long periods to fellow Jews and possibly even to Christians as well. For Jewish visitors, renting rooms from Jews was an ideal solution because it brought them into households operating according to their specific religious needs.

Various Hebrew sources describe single houses shared by Jewish landlords and their paying tenants. Because rabbinic texts generally expunge details ancillary to the legal question at hand, these sources rarely specify whether the tenant was a temporary visitor or a long-term resident. Regardless, sources about shared homes shed light on the visitor's experience. One responsum describes a situation in which "someone leased to his friend a room" in his house for half the market rate.[68] While not specified, it is possible that this tenant came to town

---

64. On the subdivision of houses and the resulting market, see Nicholas, *The Later Medieval City*, 322–25; Geremek, *The Margins of Society*, 78–81.
65. Berland, "Arriver, s'établir, repartir," 131–43. Par. 13.
66. Rubin, *Cities of Strangers*, 36.
67. "Item nullum in domo Judei volumus hospitari." Gottleb Bondy and Franz Dworsky, eds., *Zur Geschichte der Juden in Böhmen, Mähren und Schlesien von 906 bis 1620*, vol. 1 (Prague: Gottlieb Bundy, 1906), 21. Christians also invited travelers and guests into their homes. Kerr, *Monastic Hospitality*, 6.
68. *Responsa of Rabbi Meir of Rothenburg and his Colleagues*, vol. 1, ed. Simcha Emanuel (Jerusalem: World Union of Jewish Studies, 2012), 577, (§263).

with the express intention of living in his friend's home for an extended period. The stigmatization of outsiders in medieval towns meant it was a major boon for him to know someone in the city who could vouch for his decency while providing a helping hand and a discounted bed.[69] Personal bonds like these would have been the starting point for most travelers in search of lodging. Even if their own contact had no space to offer, they could introduce them to others who did.

Leasing sections of one's home was common specifically among widows. By letting rooms, widows generated income from property bequeathed to them. While allowing strangers into their homes put these women at risk of gendered violence, the financial security it provided made it a worthwhile venture for some.[70] A responsum from northern France describes how "Reuven rented a portion of the house of a woman and her sons and agreed to lend to them clothing, pillows, and sheets."[71] In this specific case, two familial groups shared the house: a widowed landlord with her children and Reuven with his wife. As usual, the responsum is laconic. We do not know why Reuven and his wife chose to stay with this widow. The author also does not explain why the widow later sought to evict her tenant. The fact that it followed Reuven's wife abandoning him suggests there may have been concerns about safety. Several other responsa describe similar arrangements in which widows opened their homes by renting space to men, women, and families.[72]

Jewish visitors who intended to stay for an extended period likely found comfort in paying for a formal lease that guaranteed them lodging for the duration of their visit. Travelers who were only briefly passing through town relied more on the charitable hospitality of their fellow Jews. R. Isaac of Corbeil (d. 1280) referenced this norm when he promised support to those who traveled to copy his newly completed

---

69. For an interesting discussion of the challenges faced by a new arrival without any family ties, see Anna Paulina Orłowska, "How to Develop a Trade Network as a Newcomer without Getting Married? Examples from the Account Book of Danzig Merchant Johan Pyre," in *Networking in Late Medieval Central Europe*, eds. Beata Możejko, Anna Paulina Orłowska, and Leslie Carr-Riegel (New York: Routledge, 2023), 38–50.

70. For discussion, see Etelle Kalaora, "Jewish Widows' Homes in Ashkenaz in the 12th and 13th Centuries," *Jewish Studies Quarterly* 28, no. 3 (2021): 322–29, https://doi.org/10.1628/jsq-2021-0017.

71. *Responsa of Rabbi Isaac ben Samuel of Dampierre*, eds. Avraham (Rami) Reiner and Pinchas Roth (Jerusalem: Mekitze Nirdamim, 2019), 197–98.

72. *Responsa of Maharam of Rothenburg*, vol. 1, Prague, ed. Yacov Farbstein (Jerusalem: Mekhon Yerushalayim, 2015), 353–5 (§680).

religious compendium: "If the messenger should need to wait in the city to copy the text, they will provide him his payment . . . [as well as] meals and lodging among the community members, as is the standard for other guests."⁷³ While he wrote about special circumstances, Isaac understood it to be a communal norm for Jews to welcome traveling coreligionists into their homes.⁷⁴

Jews of all stations found hospitality among everyday community members. A charming story was told, for example, about the prominent rabbi, Moses of Évreux (thirteenth century), who

> was hosted on several occasions by people who would mispronounce God's name or the declaration of His kingship when reciting the blessing over the bread, in the manner of those who swallow their letters. When this happened, R. Moses would quietly make his own blessing on the piece of bread handed to him.⁷⁵

R. Moses distinguished himself by fulfilling the obligation to recite the blessing properly without embarrassing his host. What emerges from this source and others like it is that visiting Jews, included distinguished rabbis, found hospitality among local community members, staying in their homes and eating at their tables. This explains the frequent repetition of Mordekhai ben Hillel's (ca. 1250-1298) legal decision that unless there is reason to believe otherwise, a guest may assume that the food being served is kosher "even though one does not know the host, besides that he is a Jew."⁷⁶ While seemingly an abstract ruling, this had serious relevance for traveling Jews who relied on unfamiliar coreligionists for their food and lodging.

Students who traveled from distant locations to study in small groups under distinguished rabbis were generally housed in the home of their teacher or nearby community members.⁷⁷ Benjamin of Tudela saw this practiced in the Jewish community of Lunel, where "the students

---

73. Isaac of Corbeil, *Sefer Amudei Golah* (Tel Aviv: Mefitse Or, 1968), 3 (Introduction).
74. This is also identified as a Jewish communal norm by Joseph Kimhi, *The Book of the Covenant of Joseph Kimhi*, trans. Frank Talmage (Toronto: Pontifical Institute of Mediaeval Studies, 1972), 33. For the original: Joseph Kimhi, *The Book of the Covenant and Other Writings*, ed. Frank Talmage (Jerusalem: Mosad Bialik, 1974), 26.
75. *Sefer 'al ha-Kol: Kolel piske dinim ya-halakhot u-minhagim*, ed. Max Weisz (Berdychiv: n.p., 1908), 13. A similar exemplum about a pious man staying in the home of a wealthy Jew is described in *Sefer Hasidim*, Parma §236.
76. Mordekhai ben Hillel, *Avodah Zarah* 51a, §848. This ruling is repeated in various codes.
77. On this phenomenon, Breuer, "The Wanderings of Students and Scholars," 445-68.

who come from distant lands to learn the Law are taught, boarded, lodged and clothed by the congregation, so long as they attend the house of study."[78] Echoes of this practice in Ashkenaz appear scattered throughout the writings of scholars who experienced this hospitality during their own rabbinic training.[79] An exemplum from *Sefer Hasidim* described how "in one house several students were hosted" and then recorded what happened after one of them stole wine from their benefactor.[80] The famed R. Meir of Rothenburg housed numerous students in his own home. In a responsum, he claimed to have affixed twenty-four *mezuzot* to the doorposts of each room in his house, including "each room of every single student."[81] Based on Meir's description, his house had over twelve such rooms. Meir of Rothenburg's wealth and prestige enabled him to host such a large group of students; in most other towns, even a smaller group would have been distributed among several community members.

More sparsely documented are the Jewish merchants who trekked between commercial hubs and stayed with their coreligionists along the way. A responsum attributed to Eliezer ben Nathan of Mainz (1090–1170) describes a dispute that broke out because of this norm: "Reuven was hosting merchants, yet Shimon pursued them to purchase their wares. Reuven said to Shimon, 'I want to benefit from this deal by buying this merchandise myself. Since [they are staying] in my house, I deserve it.' Shimon did not heed him and bought the merchandise when Reuven was not at home."[82] The responsum emphasizes it was customary for medieval Jews to welcome traveling merchants into their homes. While in this case the traders were a boon for their host, merchants would have been the primary beneficiaries of the norm of hospitality. They profited from their hosts' food, lodging, and knowledge

---

78. *The Itinerary of Benjamin of Tudela*, 3, 3*.

79. Mordechai Breuer, "Toward the Investigation of the Typology of Western Yeshivot in the Middle Ages," in *Studies in Jewish Society in the Medieval and Early Modern Periods*, eds. Immanuel Etkes and Yosef Salmon (Jerusalem: Magnes Press, 1980), 49–51 (Hebrew); Ephraim Kanarfogel, *Jewish Education and Society* (Detroit: Wayne State University Press, 1992), 66–67, 165n7-12.

80. *Sefer Hasidim*, Parma §1416. For other exempla about foreign students hosted in their teachers' houses, see *Sefer Hasidim*, Parma §1479

81. *Responsa of Maharam of Rothenburg*, vol. 2: Cremona, ed. Yakov Farbstein (Jerusalem: Mekhon Yerushalyim, 2015), 86 (§108).

82. Eliezer ben Nathan, *Sefer Ra'avan, Hu Sefer Ever ha-Ezer*, vol. 3, ed. David Deblytski (Bnei Brak: n.p., 1984), §104:11. It was decided that Reuven, who hosted the merchants, was entitled to profit from his guests' wares.

about the city. A communal ordinance reveals the importance of such services for Jewish traders. It dictated that traveling merchants who spent too long away from their wives "should not be received or hosted by anyone."[83] That a loss of access to communal hospitality was a deterrent demonstrates Jewish traders' reliance on their coreligionists during their travels.

An understudied group of Jewish visitors dependent on the hospitality of their coreligionists were wedding guests. Several Hebrew sources relate how Jews traveled great distances to attend weddings, occasionally even in large numbers.[84] In 1351, a royal decree gave special permission for the Jews of neighboring lands and cities to stay in Prague for two weeks for the celebration of a wealthy Jewish citizen's wedding.[85] Whether individuals, large groups, or entire communities, these traveling wedding guests needed somewhere to stay. A teaching from *Sefer Hasidim* reveals that local community members bore the burden of housing them:

> One should not be honored on another's dime. An example of this is one who arranges a wedding for his son or daughter and invites people from a distant place to come to the wedding. These guests will be hosted in the houses of others. Three or four times they will eat from the wedding feasts, but the rest from their hosts' meals.[86]

While warning against abuse, the teaching assumes that community members provided wedding guests with places to sleep and food to eat. A responsum composed by R. Eliezer ben Nathan offers a look at an interaction born from this communal norm: "Reuven sued Shimon saying 'My wife and I were hosted in your house. Because there was a wedding in the city, you pleaded with my wife to lend her golden

---

83. This threat is recorded in a sixteenth-century copy of the communal ordinance attributed to Jacob b. Meir Tam (1100–1171), which restricted Jewish merchants from spending too much time away from their families. Louis Finkelstein, *Jewish Self Government in the Middle Ages* (New York: Jewish Theological Seminary, 1924), 169. On this ordinance, see Avraham Grossman, *Pious and Rebellious: Jewish Women in Medieval Europe*, trans. Jonathan Chipman (Waltham: Brandeis University Press, 2004), 74–75; *Taqqanot Qehillot Šum*, vol. 2, 705, 713, 771.

84. Judah ben Asher reported that there were about five hundred of his extended relatives, both men and women, at the wedding celebration of his uncle in Germany at the end of the thirteenth century. *Hebrew Ethical Wills*, 189.

85. Tzvi Avneri, ed., *Germania Judaica*, vol. 2 (Tübingen: Mohr Siebeck, 1968), 660.

86. *Sefer Hasidim*, Parma §1178.

earrings to your unmarried daughter so that she could adorn herself at the wedding.'"[87] Guests, who seem to have been in town for a wedding celebration, slept in the homes of locals with whom they had friendly (at least for a time) interactions.[88]

Whatever the circumstances, hosting guests was a drain on resources, both financial and emotional. We already saw how *Sefer Hasidim* warned about the cost of feeding wedding guests borne by the community. In several responsa, homeowners lamented the emotional costs of having welcomed in even a paid tenant. One such householder tried to evict his tenant because the man's wife did not get along with the other women in the house.[89] Another pleaded, "I cannot tolerate [the tenant] in my house" and offered to return the remaining rent if his boarder would only leave.[90] In tightly packed urban homes, additional residents, along with the financial burden and disruption to family life they brought, could be acutely taxing.[91] In recognition of this, *Sefer Hasidim* in a passage praising hospitality warned guests "not to burden their host."[92]

It is unclear whether community members saw their hospitality as pious charity or expected remuneration, either in money or in kind, from the visitors or the wider community. Not everyone lodged by the community did so out of financial need. Some arrived with golden earrings that they could lend out! Did these middling to elite visitors pay for their stays as they would have at an inn? Or did Jewish communities graciously accept all guests—as Joseph Kimhi claimed in the middle of the twelfth century—regardless of the expense?[93] Further research on these questions could shed light on relations within and between Jewish communities.

Regardless of financial arrangements, women were expected to bear the burden of caring for domestic guests. This aligns with Adam Davis's observation that women performed most of the actual physical labor in Christian hospitals serving the needs of the ill, the poor, and travelers.[94] Jewish women did the same in their own homes. Eleazar of Worms

---

87. Eliezer ben Nathan, *Sefer Ra'avan*, 171:56.
88. For discussion of this responsum, Levinson, "There Was a Wedding . . ." 35–38.
89. *Responsa of Rabbi Meir of Rothenburg and his Colleagues*, vol. 2, 850 (§443).
90. *Responsa of Rabbi Meir of Rothenburg and his Colleagues*, vol. 1, 577 (§263).
91. One finds opposition to the constant intrusion of guests on one's family in *Sefer Hasidim* in particular. Liberles, "Home and Away," 111.
92. *Sefer Hasidim*, Bologna 1538, §1019.
93. Joseph Kimhi, *The Book of the Covenant*, 33.
94. Davis, *The Medieval Economy of Salvation*, 21, 48–52.

sprinkled his elegy for his martyred wife, Dulcea, with descriptions of how she cared for his students, many of whom were their guests:

> She supplied provisions for her household and bread to the boys ... she was as swift as a deer to cook for the young men and to fulfill the needs of the students. ... Her hands stitched the students' garments and torn books. ... She honored the Sabbaths and festivals for those who devoted themselves to the study of Torah. ... She purchased milk for the students and hired teachers from her exertions.[95]

Dulcea was not the only woman known for being hospitable. Two women buried in Worms, one in 1143 and the other in 1307, were praised on their tombstones for their commitment to welcoming guests.[96] No tombstone from this period honored a man for this characteristic.[97] The expectation that women were responsible for guests was made explicit in a rabbinic deliberation about how long a man had to wait after the death of his wife before remarrying.[98] The early thirteenth-century discussants debated the applicability of various Talmudic reasonings to the situation of the recently widowed R. Haim Cohen, a prominent scholar in Mainz, who was eager to remarry.[99] One potential reason for shortening the waiting period focused on Haim's need to have a woman in the house to perform certain tasks "that are not usually carried out by men." Included in this category was taking care of guests, since it was

---

95. Avraham Habermann, ed., *Gezerot Ashkenaz ve-Tsarfat* (Jerusalem: Tarshish, 1945), 165-66. Translation from Judith R. Baskin, "Dolce of Worms: The Lives and Deaths of an Exemplary Medieval Jewish Woman and her Daughters," in *Judaism in Practice: From the Middle Ages through the Early Modern Period*, ed. L. Fine (Princeton: Princeton University Press, 2001), 435-36.

96. Epidat - Epigraphische Datenbank, Jüdischer Friedhof Worms, wrm-8 (1143) & wrm-445 (1307).

97. On these tombstones and their gendered language, Elisheva Baumgarten, "Reflections of Everyday Jewish Life: Evidence from Medieval Cemeteries," in *Les vivants et les morts dans les sociétés médiévales: XLVIIIe Congrès de La SHMESP* (Paris: Éditions de la Sorbonne, 2018), 95-104.

98. See the issues at hand in BT Moed Katan 23a and PT Yavamot 4:11.

99. It was long presumed that R. Haim lived in Paris after completing his studies with Jacob Tam in Ramerupt. Rami Reiner has recently argued that R. Haim instead returned to Mainz in Germany. See Avraham (Rami) Reiner, "Between Ashkenaz and France in the Tosafist Period: Rabbi Haim Cohen as a Test Case," in *The Blessings of Avraham: A Conference in Honour of Avraham Grossman on the Occasion of his Eightieth Birthday*, ed. Yosef Kaplan (Jerusalem: Israel Academy of Sciences & Humanities, 2018), 46-51.

"known that the poor are regularly hosted in the house" of R. Haim.[100] The expectation that women would perform the labors associated with hospitality served as a potential reason to shorten the waiting period before a hospitable widower could remarry.

Domestic Hospitality and Communal Networks

For Jews in medieval northern Europe, hospitality took place in the home. The inhospitableness of inns and religious institutions made homes the primary space for transient Jews to find temporary accommodations, especially in communities that did not have a well-endowed hospice.[101] Lodging in the homes of coreligionists satisfied the specific needs of Jewish travelers and oriented them to their new environments. Because hosting needy travelers in one's home was a burden, both financial and emotional, hospitality was championed as a communal value worthy of respect and reward. *Sefer Hasidim*, for example, promised financial success to all those who would push aside miserliness and "accept guests with a pleasant demeanor."[102]

Hospitality, however, was not just about piety. Traveling connected people and facilitated the spread of ideas and practices.[103] Each new arrival brought with them knowledge about other communities and their customs. Scholars have argued that places of hospitality functioned as sealed, yet accessible spaces in which economic, political, and religious knowledge spread among diverse groups.[104] As gathering places for traders and tourists, inns, hospices, and hospitals were central to the exchange of information in the premodern world. The tendency of Jewish travelers to lodge with their coreligionists thus transformed private homes into hubs for Jewish cultural exchange.

As visitors and hosts shared knowledge and customs with one another, hospitality facilitated the spread of Jewish cultural content

---

100. *Teshuvot Maimuniyyot, Shoftim* §20 in *Mishneh Torah - Shoftim* (Warsaw: Mordechai Kleinberg, 1881), 212.
101. Rainer Barzen notes hospitality institutions like hospices may have separated poor and visiting Jews from the community members who financed their stay. Barzen, "'Was der Arme benötigt,'" 152.
102. *Sefer Hasidim*, Parma §1233.
103. Harald Kleinschmidt, *People on the Move: Attitudes Toward and Perceptions of Migration in Medieval and Modern Europe* (Westport, CN: Praeger, 2003), 51–126.
104. Sabrina Corbellini and Margriet Hoogvliet. "Indoor Public Spaces and the Mobility of Religious Knowledge in Late Medieval Deventer and Amiens," *Urban History: First View* (2023): 13–16. https://doi.org/10.1017/S0963926823000524.

in every stratum of the community. Jewish scholars, who dwelled and studied in the homes of their masters, learned from their teacher's domestic conduct.[105] When scholars traveled, the homes of their hosts became places for formal and informal religious instruction. Samson b. Abraham of Sens (d. ca. 1230) recalled a lesson he learned when his teacher, Isaac b. Samuel (d. 1184), stayed in the home of his father.[106] Hospitality could also fuel religious exchange outside of the scholarly sphere. Exempla from *Sefer Hasidim* describe how guests and hosts shared knowledge about religious praxis with one another. In one, disregard of a pious guest's religious instruction explains a host's bout of misfortune.[107] Another advises how to discuss religious teachings with one's unknown guest: "If a guest comes to your house, do not ask him about matters of religion unless you are certain he can respond. If you are unsure, ask him privately so he will not be embarrassed."[108] In both cases, domestic hospitality serves as the background for the exchange of religious knowledge between hosts and guests.

This could help explain the movement of devotional ideas and pious customs between Jewish communities. Instead of textual transmission or the migration of scholars, the regular contact between traveling Jews and their hosts can account for the spread of certain customs. Domestic pieties, which were performed in the home and with guests, would have been the most easily transmitted.[109] For example, the practice of singing specific table songs on the Sabbath emerged in northern France at the end of the twelfth century and then spread across German-speaking lands over the following decades.[110] The songs appear rarely in scholarly texts, but manuscript evidence shows that a consistent repertoire of songs migrated around the continent with new additions being introduced sporadically. Guests—whether students, traders, or travelers—would have encountered new compositions while spending

---

105. Breuer, "Typology of Western Yeshivot," 49–51.
106. *Sefer Or Zaru'a*, vol. 2, ed. Yacov Farbstein (Jerusalem: Mekhon Yerushalyim, 2009), 9 (§3). See Ephraim E. Urbach, *Baalei ha-Tosafot*, 4th ed. (Jerusalem: Mossad Bialik, 1980), 273.
107. *Sefer Hasidim*, Bologna (1538), §215.
108. *Sefer Hasidim*, Parma §834.
109. Katherine L. French and Elisheva Baumgarten, "Religion and the Home: Jewish and Christian Experiences," in *A Cultural History of the Home in the Medieval Age*, ed. Katherine L. French (New York: Bloomsbury Academic, 2020), 163–83.
110. Albert Evan Kohn, "'To Sing on Shabbat Evening and Day, Each Person at Their Table': On the Medieval Development of the Custom to Sing Shabbat Zemirot," *AJS Review* 47, no. 2 (2023): 243–84, https://doi.org/10.1353/ajs.2023.a911523.

the Sabbath around their hosts' tables. As they continued their journey, they brought these songs and their tunes with them.

Travel and hospitality forged links between medieval people in distant places. Wherever they lodged, visitors—both Jewish and Christian—brought news about surrounding communities and accounts of their lifestyles. Even visiting Jews who boarded in community hospices or for-profit inns could still encounter local liturgical customs and share observations gleaned during their travels.[111] The primarily domestic context of Jewish hospitality ensured the spread of quotidian ideas and practices between Jews of different communities and regions. Christian voyagers congregated in spaces meant for and occupied by travelers and traders, such as inns and hospices. There they exchanged information relevant to their shared pursuits, such as updates about foreign markets and warnings about travel conditions. Jewish visitors found hospitality in the homes of local coreligionists. Along with beds and food, these travelers and hosts exchanged religious ideas and personal pieties. This regular interchange made hospitality a central node in the dissemination of Jewish knowledge and practice across medieval Europe.

Further Readings

Barnhouse, Lucy C. *Hospitals in Communities of the Late Medieval Rhineland: Houses of God, Places for the Sick*. Amsterdam: Amsterdam University Press, 2023.

Barzen, Rainer Josef. "The Meaning of 'Tzedakah' for Jewish Self-Organization within a Non-Jewish Environment." *Iggud: Selected Essays in Jewish Studies* (2005): 7–17.

Bell, Adrian R., and Richard S. Dale. "The Medieval Pilgrimage Business." *Enterprise & Society* 12, no. 3 (2011): 601–27. doi.org/10.1093/es/khr014.

Berland, Florence. "Arriver, s'établir, repartir: Les gens de la cour de Bourgogne à Paris (1363–1422)." In *Arriver en Ville: Les migrants en milieu urbain au Moyen Âge*, edited by Quertier, Cédric, Roxane Chilà, and Nicolas Pluchot, 131–44. Paris: Publications de la Sorbonne, 2019.

Breuer, Mordechai. "The Wanderings of Students and Scholars: A Prolegomenon to a Chapter in the History of Yeshivot." In *Culture and Society in Medieval Jewry: Studies Dedicated to the Memory of Haim Hillel Ben-Sasson*, edited by Menachem Ben-Sasson, Robert Bonfil, and Joseph R. Hacker, 445–68. Jerusalem: Shazar, 1989 (Hebrew).

Cobban, Alan B. "The Role of Colleges in the Medieval Universities of Northern Europe, with Special Reference to England and France." *Bulletin of the John Rylands Library* 71:1 (1989): 49–70. doi.org/10.7227/bjrl.71.1.4.

---

111. Slepoy, "Die Stellung von Gästen," 13–26.

Corbellini, Sabrina, and Margriet Hoogvliet. "Indoor Public Spaces and the Mobility of Religious Knowledge in Late Medieval Deventer and Amiens." *Urban History* (2023): 1–24. doi.org/10.1017/S0963926823000524.

Coulet, Noël. "Les hôtelleries en France et en Italie au Bas Moyen Âge." In *L'homme et la route : En Europe occidentale, au Moyen Âge et aux Temps modernes*, edited by Charles Higounet, 181–205. Toulouse: Presses universitaires du Midi, 1982.

Elliot, Jessica Marin. "From Vine to Tavern: Jews, Christians, and Wine in Medieval France and Italy." In *Medieval Work, Worship, and Power: Persuasive and Silenced Voices*, edited by Abigail P. Dowling, Nancy Ann McLoughlin, and Tanya Stabler Miller, 267–79. New York: Routledge, 2024.

French, Katherine L., and Elisheva Baumgarten. "Religion and the Home: Jewish and Christian Experiences." In *A Cultural History of the Home in the Medieval Age*, edited by Katherine L. French, 163–83. New York: Bloomsbury Academic, 2020.

Germain, René. "Déplacements temporaires et déplacements définitifs dans le centre de la France aux XIVe et XVe siècles." In *Voyages et voyageurs au Moyen Age*, 53–61. Paris: Publications de la Sorbonne, 1996.

Kaplan, Debra, and Verena Kasper-Marienberg. "Nourishing a Community: Food, Hospitality, and Jewish Communal Spaces in Early Modern Frankfurt." *AJS Review* 45 (2021): 302–33. doi.org/10.1017/s0364009421000027.

Kerr, Julie. *Monastic Hospitality: The Benedictines in England, C.1070–c.1250*. Woodbridge: Boydell Press, 2007.

Liberles, Ahuva. "Home and Away: The Opposition to Travel in *Sefer Hasidim*." *Jewish History* 34 (2021): 107–23. doi.org/10.1007/s10835-021-09376-5.

Ohler, Norbert. *The Medieval Traveller*, trans. Caroline Hillier. Woodbridge, Suffolk: Boydell Press, 1989.

Peyer, Hans Conrad. *Von der Gastfreundschaft zum Gasthaus: Studien zur Gastlichkeit im Mittelalter*. Hannover: Hahnsche Buchhandlung, 1987.

Reitzel, J. M. "The Medieval Houses of 'Bons-Enfants.'" *Viator* 11 (1980): 179–207. doi.org/10.1484/j.viator.2.301505.

Reyerson, Kathryn. "Medieval Hospitality: Innkeepers and the Infrastructure of Trade in Montpellier during the Middle Ages." *Proceedings of the Western Society for French History* 24 (1997): 38–51.

Romano, John, ed. *Medieval Travel and Travelers: A Reader*. Toronto: University of Toronto Press, 2020.

Part III

Objects

Neta Bodner, Ariella Lehmann, Aviya Doron, and Ido Noy

In the late twentieth century, scholars from different disciplines established that material objects from the past have as much to say about the cultures from which they came as the written word, complementing and enhancing the latter and refining historical, sociological, religious, and subjective perspectives on individuals and societies.[1] The importance of material culture has been demonstrated extensively in recent years, whether based on actual material finds or on written descriptions of these now lost materials. Home settings, for example, have been described and reconstructed using information on furnishing and smaller items in inventory lists.[2] Treasure troves hidden for safekeeping

---

1. On the "Material Turn," or the more recent "Thing Theory," see, for example, Bill Brown, "Thing Theory," *Critical Inquiry* 28 (2001): 1-22, https://www.jstor.org/stable/1344258; Lorraine Daston, ed., *Things That Talk: Object Lessons from Art and Science* (New York: Zone Books, 2004); Daniel Miller, ed., *Materiality* (Duke University Press, 2005); David Morgan, ed., *Religion and Material Culture: The Matter of Belief* (New York: Routledge, 2010); Martha Rosler et al., "Notes from the Field: Materiality," *Art Bulletin* 95 (2013): 11-37, http://www.jstor.org/stable/43188793; Ivan Gaskell and Sarah Ann Carter, eds., *The Oxford Handbook of History and Material Culture* (New York: Oxford University Press, 2020).

2. Katherine L. French, ed., *A Cultural History of the Home* (London: Bloomsbury Academic, 2020), and Katherine L. French, *Household Goods and Good Households in Late Medieval London: Consumption and Domesticity after the Plague* (Philadelphia: University of Pennsylvania Press, 2021).

by Jewish pawnbrokers or merchants in the Middle Ages contain objects with a mix of identifiably Jewish and Christian artifacts, shedding light on craftsmanship, aesthetic preferences, the appearance and character of luxury goods, and more.³ Literary descriptions of cloths or cleaning materials have helped enliven the reconstruction of daily life in the Middle Ages, even when this was not the explicit aim of the stories in which they are found.⁴ While there are few surviving Jewish artifacts that can be dated to the Middle Ages, the rich illuminations in Hebrew manuscripts of the period, with their depictions of figures in contemporary styles of dress, using identifiable objects, and situated in local architectural settings, serve as partial windows into medieval lives.⁵

All objects, by their very nature, provide information beyond their primary use: embodying "values, assumptions, and thought structures" that were likely transparent to their makers, owners, and users, and which can be described and reconstructed using complementary written sources.⁶ Their combined material, practical, and symbolic characteristics makes objects especially relevant when seeking to build a picture of the quotidian experiences of past communities. Building on this approach, the contributions in this section express two complementary points.

The first point is that objects serve multiple functions and are imbued with a myriad of meanings from the symbolic to the practical. They store financial value, convey social and economic status, political hierarchy, and power, and signify particular religious and cultural identities. They can also be embedded with memories (private and communal) that add sentimental and intellectual worth to their economic, cultural, and social roles. Even the very materials of which the objects

---

3. Ido Noy, "Treasure Hunt: Jews, Property, Catastrophe," in *In and Out, Between and Beyond: Jewish Daily Life in Medieval Europe*, eds. Elisheva Baumgarten and Ido Noy (Jerusalem, The Hebrew University of Jerusalem, 2021), 23–7.

4. See, for example, the story of a holy robe and its cleaning with vinegar, which reveal general assumptions about materiality: Elisheva Baumgarten, "Local Knowledge: The Story of a Holy Robe," in *Medieval Ashkenaz: Papers in Honour of Alfred Haverkamp Presented at the 17th World Congress of Jewish Studies, Jerusalem 2017* (Wiesbaden: Harrassowitz Verlag, 2021), 182–96.

5. Shalom Sabar, "See and Sanctify: Ceremonies and Ceremonial Art in Medieval Ashkenaz and Italy," in *Routledge Handbook of Jewish Ritual and Practice*, ed. Oliver Leaman (New York: Routledge, 2022), 72.

6. Sara Lipton, "Images and Objects as Sources for Medieval History," in *Understanding Medieval Primary Sources*, ed. Joel T. Rosenthal (Routledge, 2012) 227.

were made cannot be separated from religious assumptions concerning those materials.[7]

Due to their multiplicity of meaning, the context in which the objects were used and placed is crucial to determining what they meant to medieval people in specific circumstances. Quotidian commodities such as bread, candles, and clothes become carriers of ritual meaning in specific circumstances.[8] So, for example, preparing candles and food for the Sabbath and Jewish holidays demonstrates the porous boundaries between the synagogue and the home and are the material means by which a sanctified domestic space is delineated at set times.[9]

The specific framing of contexts meant that similar objects could be imbued with different meanings in Jewish and Christian settings, a vestment used in church could convey financial value when found in the house of a pawnbroker, while still maintaining ecclesiastical associations.[10] However, sometimes long-enduring ideas regarding materials were connected to their inherent natural characteristics, such as the perception of water as purifying or stone as able to hold a lasting and eternal memory.[11] The association of meaning arising from the natural qualities of these objects often led to a similarity in their culturally assigned symbolic significance, even across the religious divide. Thus, putting the spotlight specifically on the materials out of which the objects were made, understanding the significance imbued in these materials, and the efforts involved in their production and use, opens a window to the conceptions and ideologies of the people who were

---

7. Caroline Walker Bynum, *Christian Materiality: An Essay on Religion in Late Medieval Europe* (New York: Zone Books, 2011). Neta Bodner, "Earth from Jerusalem in the Pisa Camposanto," in *Between Jerusalem and Europe: Essays in Honour of Bianca Kühnel*, ed. Renana Bartal and Hanna Vorholt (Leiden: Brill, 2015), 74–93; Sible de Blaauw, "Jerusalem in Rome and the Cult of the Cross," in *Pratum Romanum: Richard Krautheimer zum 100: Geburtstag*, ed. Renate L. Colella, Meredith J. Gill, Lawrence A. Jenkens, and Petra Lamers (Wiesbaden: Dr. Ludwig Reichert Verlag, 1997), 55–74.

8. Elisheva Baumgarten, "Daily Commodities and Religious Identity in the Medieval Jewish Communities of Northern Europe," in *Religion and the Household*, ed. John Doran, Charlotte Methuen. and Alexandra Walsham (Suffolk, UK: Boydell Press, 2014), 97–121.

9. Ariella Lehmann, "Between Domestic and Urban Spaces: Preparing for Shabbat in Ashkenazic Communities, 13th-15th Centuries," *Jewish Studies Quarterly* 28, no. 3 (2021): 259–77, https://doi.org/10.1628/jsq-2021-0014.

10. See the discussion by Aviya Doron in chapter 8 of this book.

11. For the idea that stones and epigraphy on them could maintain a lasting memory, see the contribution by Bodner and Lehmann in chapter 7 of this book. On the symbolism of water in the Middle Ages, see Carolyn Twomey and Daniel Anlezark, eds., *Meanings of Water in Early Medieval England* (Turnhout: Brepols, 2021).

shaped by the materials surrounding them, even if they did not directly own, produce, or use the objects in question.

The second point is that objects serve as bridges between different classes and social groups within societies. The processes involved in turning raw material into objects, whether intended for everyday use or for elite goods, necessarily involved a wide spectrum of actors: those who produced the raw materials, such as miners and farmers; the laborers who converted these into commodities, such as wool, linen, and parchment; the artisans who transformed these commodities into material objects, such as jewelry, manuscripts, clothes; the merchants who sold these goods; and the different types of people who bought and used them. The production of objects thus provides a window into the practices of a wide variety of people across all facets and classes that made up medieval daily life. In addition, the tendency of objects to outlive their makers and original owners weaves further connections between those inhabiting the same place over different periods. This path from raw material to object was also traversed by people from different religious backgrounds, making the study of objects an important prism for assessing Jewish-Christian relations or indeed any of the "entangled histories" of minority and majority groups, as no social group can stay insular in terms of material culture.[12]

The three chapters in this section demonstrate both points. The stones in the chapter by Lehmann and Bodner were both practical construction materials and the locus of poetic reflection. By highlighting the building materials and the inscriptions describing the construction process, the authors demonstrate Jewish participation in the general shift to stone construction in the eleventh and twelfth centuries, as well as the particular significance Jewish communities afforded to stone as a witness of communal memory. In Aviya Doron's chapter, objects used as pawns had an economic value that changed according to the person who possessed them and were used as part of an intricate system of financial exchange that served as a junction of interreligious and intercultural interactions and communications. In the case of the *kiddushin* (betrothal) rings discussed in Ido Noy's chapter, the meaning and importance of the rings expanded far beyond its halakhic significance

---

12. Elisheva Baumgarten, Ruth Mazo Karras, and Katelyn Mesler, eds., *Entangled Histories: Knowledge, Authority, and Jewish Culture in the Thirteenth Century* (Philadelphia: University of Pennsylvania Press, 2017). For theorization of the idea of "entangled histories," see especially the editors' introduction, 1–22.

and ceremonial function to become one of the most important objects owned by a married woman.

Alternating the analytical gaze between people, spaces, rituals, and objects enables a multidimensional investigation into societies. Objects that were in the possession of people, made by and for them, stood at the base of their activities—religious or otherwise—and are therefore an important prism through which to paint the historical picture of the fabric of daily life.

CHAPTER 7

The Medieval Stone Revolution Reflected in Hebrew Inscriptions from Worms and Mainz

Neta Bodner and Ariella Lehmann

In medieval Europe, erecting a religious building made of stone was about more than walling off a space for prayer and ritual. The efforts involved in quarrying, carrying, and constructing with stone, particularly finely cut (ashlar) stone, were extensive.[1] Yet despite the enormous expenditure of effort and resources it demanded, by the eleventh century stone architecture for religious buildings had become the norm. The French monk and chronicler Ralf (Rodulf) Glaber succinctly described in real time what historians later noted regarding the High Middle Ages—a surge in building that seemed

---

We wish to thank Miri Rubin, Gadi Algazi, and Elisheva Carlebach for their helpful comments and suggestions on an earlier draft of this chapter. This research was supported by the Open University of Israel's Research Fund (grant no. 513255) and the Israel Science Foundation, Project: Digging Deep: An Interdisciplinary Study of the Medieval Mikveh (Jewish Ritual Bath) in Cologne, grant no. 102725 and was written under the auspices of the Beyond the Elite: Jewish Daily Life in Medieval Europe Project, PI Elisheva Baumgarten, from the European Research Council (ERC) under the European Union's Horizon 2020 research and innovation program, grant agreement No. 681507, and prepared for publication with funding from the Israel Science Foundation Grant 2850/22, Contending with Crises: The Jews of XIVth Century Europe, PI Elisheva Baumgarten.

1. Ashlar blocks are the result of stone masonry comprising blocks with carefully worked beds and joints, finely jointed (generally under 6mm) and set in horizontal courses. "Ashlar" is often wrongly used as a synonym for facing stone.

to be disconnected from practical necessity.² St. Odilo, the senior abbot of Cluny, concisely phrased the spirit of the day when recording his own architectural patronage by declaring: "I found an abbey of wood and I leave one of stone."³ The most significant transition was from interior roofing out of timber to stone vaulting. The latter was a marked characteristic of the new and innovative style of building prominent in the eleventh and twelfth centuries,⁴ which has come to be broadly defined as Romanesque.⁵ Churches and other public monuments built in stone became taller and more sophisticated throughout the twelfth century, and with the advent of Gothic architecture (essentially a development of Romanesque architecture) in the thirteenth century, buildings rose to even greater heights; decorative stone elements became more varied and complicated to produce; and novel types of arches and stone vaulting enabled creative, new spatial organizations.⁶ From the eleventh century, the increasing use of ashlar stone led to the rapid growth and renewal of stone industries such as quarrying, transportation, and masonry.⁷ Along with the new architectural styles, and likely inspired by classical practices, public epigraphy and monumental writing also flourished.⁸

While this revolutionary shift in building practices and the politics behind it are well attested to with regards to Christian architecture in German lands, they have not yet received the same attention in the study of Jewish medieval architecture.⁹ We wish to argue, however, that

---

2. Ralph Glaber, *Historiarum libri quinque: The Five Books of the Histories*, ed. and trans. John France (Oxford: Clarendon Press, 1989), 115.

3. Jean Gimpel, *The Cathedral Builders*, trans. Teresa Waugh (New York: Harper & Row, 1984), 8.

4. On the proliferation of stone in church buildings and furnishings during the eleventh and twelfth century see Aleksandra N. McClain and Carolyn I. Twomey, "Baptism and Burial in Stone: Materializing Pastoral Care in Anglo-Norman England," *Fragments: Interdisciplinary Approaches to the Study of Ancient and Medieval Pasts* 7 (2018): 4–36, http://hdl.handle.net/2027/spo.9772151.0007.006.

5. Gimpel, *Cathedral Builders*, 59–77.

6. Gimpel, *Cathedral Builders*, 7–8. The period associated with the Gothic style continued until the Hundred Years War in 1337. See Gimpel, *Cathedral Builders*, 87.

7. Jean Gimpel, *The Medieval Machine: The Industrial Revolution of the Middle Ages* (London: Wildwood House, 1988), 59–62 and 113.

8. Armando Petrucci argues that epigraphy, very common in Roman architecture, was less prominent in early medieval architecture, and returned extensively with the dawn of Romanesque. See Armando Petrucci, *Public Lettering: Script, Power, and Culture*, trans. Linda Lappin (Chicago: University of Chicago Press, 1993), 3–4.

9. Rolf Toman, "Introduction," in *Romanesque: Architecture, Sculpture, Painting*, ed. R. Toman (Köln: Könemann, 1997), 48 and 58. Eric Fernie, "Romanesque Architecture," in *A Companion to Medieval Art: Romanesque and Gothic in Northern Europe*, ed. C. Rudolph (Lynchburg, VA:

these winds of architectural change did not pass unnoticed by the Jewish communities living in German-speaking lands, and that the stone revolution is critical to understanding Jewish architecture during this period. Jews renewed their synagogues, constructed ritual baths of unparalleled size and monumentality, and wrote inscriptions to convey the meanings which the buildings, their construction, and their specific materials bore for the Jewish community. This chapter focuses on five inscriptions from the Rhineland cities of Worms and Mainz, all of which mention the technical efforts needed to work with stone while referencing biblical stories and metaphors connected with this material. Our study of the inscriptions highlights how, although employing a distinctively Jewish interpretation of stone, Jews still sought to participate in a dominant cultural, aesthetic, and economic phenomenon of their time. These inscriptions evidence an awareness of and engagement with stone as unique, durable, and laden with symbolism.

The inscriptions discussed in this chapter, and the construction and renovations they record, date from the eleventh to the thirteenth centuries. Four are from the synagogue complex in Worms and are part of the largest surviving Jewish medieval corpus of inscriptions from Ashkenaz.[10] Dating from 1034, 1174/5, 1185/6, and 1212/3, they were composed to mark either preliminary construction or renovations large enough in scale to be worthy of commemoration. We will demonstrate that they all include a literary reference to the materiality of the stone into which they were cut, a reference to the process of building the monument whose foundation they commemorate, and a reference to the process of inscribing the words themselves into the stone surface. The last inscription is a thirteenth-century inscription from Mainz that echoes all the same themes, indicating that these attitudes may have been more widespread than the surviving epigraphy from Worms.

Blackwell, 2006), 302–4. On innovation in Rhenish Romanesque architecture, see Wolfgang Kaiser, "Romanesque Architecture in Germany," in *Romanesque: Architecture, Sculpture, Painting*, ed. R. Toman (Köln: Ullmann & Könemann, 2007), 46–53.

10. All translations in this chapter were done by Ariella Lehmann from the Hebrew, mostly in line with the original biblical contexts. Any words placed within quotation marks indicate that the biblical Hebrew and the Hebrew of the inscription are identical. For a comprehensive presentation of the inscriptions, see Otto Böcher, *Die alte Synagoge zu Worms: Festschrift zur Wiedereinweihung der Alten Synagoge zu Worms* (Frankfurt am Main: Verlag Stadtbibliotek, 1961); and Rainer J. Barzen, "Materialization of Memoria: Memory and Remembrance of Benefactors in Building Inscriptions in Medieval Ashkenaz," in *Perception and Awareness: Artefacts and Imageries in Medieval European Jewish Cultures*, ed. Katrin Kogman-Appel, Elisheva Baumgarten, Elisabeth Hollender, and Ephraim Shoham-Steiner (Turnhout: Brepols, 2023), 77–116.

The Mainz inscription not only mentions the stone and the process of inscribing the words on it, but also the effort to mine and carry it from its quarry to the synagogue site where it was mounted onto the wall for posterity. Such literary fragments tell a story of the efforts involved in constructing public stone buildings and of the craftspeople who dug, cut, chiseled, mounted, heaved, carried, transported, raised, set, and finally, inscribed the process.

Analysis of some of the assumptions and metaphors in these inscriptions is rich ground for thinking about the daily lives of Jews in the Middle Ages who founded and renovated their community's centers of worship, and then used a metal stylus to record the meanings the stones held for them. It shows participation in the technological innovations characteristic of the time and is a way of gauging the significance attributed to physical materials in Jewish, as well as in Christian, medieval society.[11]

The Worms Synagogue Complex and its Medieval Epigraphy

The earliest evidence of Jewish settlement in Worms dates to the beginning of the eleventh century.[12] The Jews settled in the northern part of the city, immediately to the south of the city walls, where remains of the medieval *Judengasse* can still be seen.[13] During the eleventh and, more so, the twelfth century, the community evolved into one of the most significant centers of Jewish learning in western Europe.[14]

---

11. On the significance of materials in Christian piety in the Middle Ages, see Caroline W. Bynum, *Christian Materiality: An Essay on Religion in Late Medieval Europe* (Cambridge, MA: Zone Books, 2015).

12. Katrin Kogman-Appel, *A Mahzor from Worms: Art and Religion in a Medieval Jewish Community* (Cambridge, MA: Harvard University Press, 2012), 41. An early mention of Jews in Worms is from the privilege of Heinrich IV from 1074 and a second privilege from 1090 that granted them legal autonomy and freedom of movement for the purposes of commerce. Böcher, *Die alte Synagoge*, 24; Julius Aronius, *Regesten zur Geschichte der Juden im Fränkischen und Deutschen Reiche bis zum Jahre 1273* (Berlin: L. Simion, 1887), #162, #171, 67-68 and 74-75. Fritz Reuter, *Warmaisa: 1000 Jahre Juden in Worms* (Worms: Stadtarchiv Worms, 1984), 22-26. From 1157, the Jews belonged to the imperial court. Richard Krautheimer, *Medieval Synagogues* (Jerusalem: Mossad Bialik, 1993), 50 (Hebrew).

13. Gerold Bönnen, "Worms: The Jews between the City, the Bishops, and the Crown," in *The Jews of Europe in the Middle Ages (Tenth to Fifteenth Centuries)*, ed. Christoph Cluse (Turnhout: Brepols, 2004), 449; Alfred Haverkamp, *Jews in the Medieval German Kingdom*, trans. Christoph Cluse (Trier: Trier University, 2015), 14-15, https://ubt.opus.hbz-nrw.de/opus45-ubtr/frontdoor/deliver/index/docId/671/file/Jews_German_Kingdom.pdf.

14. Bönnen, "Worms," 449-50; Kogman-Appel, *A Mahzor from Worms*, 41.

The oldest surviving Hebrew inscription from all of medieval Ashkenaz was found in Worms. Dating to 1034, it commemorates the construction of the earliest known phase of the Worms synagogue.[15] Nothing remains of this phase of the synagogue save a section of what might have been one of its foundation walls.[16] Whether partly damaged or even destroyed in attacks on the Jews in 1096 as part of the First Crusade,[17] or in a fire that broke out in 1146 during the Second Crusade, the synagogue was extensively renovated, or perhaps entirely rebuilt, in 1174/5, as recorded in three different inscriptions.[18] This second iteration of the synagogue was built out of sandstone blocks, originally plastered to look like larger, ashlar blocks.[19] It was of an essentially rectangular form (not all the walls are of equal length) with windows in all four walls, divided into a double-nave space by two internal columns on red, sandstone plinths that supported a central stone vault.[20] A small niche for the Torah scroll was situated in the eastern end and a platform for reading the Torah and leading the prayer (a *bimah*) stood in the center of the space between the columns. It is the form of this twelfth-century synagogue—with fourteenth- and seventeenth-century changes to the upper levels—that the current restored building on the site records.[21] Despite being periodically damaged, the synagogue remained in almost continuous use until it suffered extensive damage in 1938 and was subsequently completely destroyed during the Second World War. It was rebuilt between 1957 and 1961 using photographs,

---

15. Barzen, "Materialization of Memoria," 79; Christoph Cluse, "The Jews of Medieval Ashkenaz: Topographies of Memory," *Rostros judíos del Occidente medieval* 45, Semana Internacional de Estudios Medievales Estella-Lizarra (2018): 158, https://www.medieval-ashkenaz.org/fileadmin/user_upload/online-publikationen/Cluse__Topographies.pdf.

16. Simon Paulus, *Die Architektur der Synagoge im Mittelalter: Überlieferung und Bestand* (Petersberg: Imhof, 2007), 98. For a full survey of architecture and inscriptions, see Ole Harck, *Archäologische Studien zum Judentum in der europäischen Antike und dem zentraleuropäischen Mittelalter* (Petersberg: Imhof, 2014), 290.

17. The violent attacks of 1096 hit the Jews of Worms hard and perhaps also led to damage to its public Jewish buildings, though this is not recorded. Nils Roemer, *German City, Jewish Memory: The Story of Worms* (Waltham, MA: Brandeis University Press, 2010), 13–15. See also Reuter, *Warmaisa*, 31.

18. Paulus, *Die Architektur*, 99.

19. Paulus, *Die Architektur*, 100.

20. The windows were later slightly changed in shape during the fourteenth and the seventeenth centuries, when the exterior roofing was altered to accommodate a change to the shape of the building. Krautheimer, *Medieval Synagogues*, 103.

21. Christoph Cluse, Florence Fischer, Stefanie Hahn et al., *ShUM Sites of Speyer, Worms and Mainz: Nomination for the UNESCO World Heritage List: Nomination Dossier* (State of Rhineland-Palatinate, 2020), 91.

drawings, and some stone structural elements restored from original parts.[22] Some of the medieval inscription stones survived through reuse or were found in the rubble and remounted in the reconstructed building.

We know of at least eight inscriptions from the Worms synagogue that date to between the eleventh and thirteenth centuries.[23] The whole inscription ensemble was preserved through the writings of a Jewish traveler named Eliezer ben Shmuel, who recorded them in 1559.[24] Today, many of the inscriptions in situ are reconstructions based on both the stone fragments and these transcriptions, resituated for the most part in the same places they occupied before the building was destroyed.[25]

Stones and Commemoration

Writing filled the Roman world, with multiple inscriptions strategically placed for maximum legibility and impact on public buildings. This disappeared from European cities during the early medieval period. It was not until the eleventh century that writing reemerged as a public feature, with the names of donors, architects, and artisans inscribed on church facades. The following two centuries saw the spread of monumental inscriptions, primarily in religious architecture, which commemorated the construction of public buildings, celebrated memorable events, and immortalized new statutes and laws.[26] The Hebrew inscriptions from the synagogue complexes at Worms and Mainz were part of this trend. They commemorated the construction of public buildings and supplied technical information about the founders, dates, and sums contributed. They also used biblical examples of memorable events and buildings to frame the significance of the act of construction and to highlight meanings that could be read in the physical building. While the Hebrew inscriptions contain no new laws

---

22. Cluse, Fischer, Hahn et al., *ShUM Sites*, 91. The major structural elements were preserved, enabling a faithful reconstruction. Barzen, "Materialization of Memoria," 79 and 82.
23. Barzen, "Materialization of Memoria," 82.
24. Frankfurt am Main, University Library, MS hebr. oct. 256, 55v–57r, https://tinyurl.com/yc5y88as.
25. Barzen, "Materialization of Memoria," 79, The synagogue complex and situation of the inscriptions is discussed at length in Cluse, "Jews," 157–63.
26. Petrucci, *Public Lettering*, 5–7.

or statutes, they often include messages of hope for the future salvation of the community.

The following two examples, while not directly concerned with the motif of stones central to this chapter, are critical to understanding the tradition of inscription poetry evidenced in Worms, both for their literal content and the themes suggested by the biblical quotations they referenced.[27] As we have shown elsewhere, a key technique employed in the medieval inscriptions from Worms was the intentional use of fragments of biblical quotes to reference the wider significance of the biblical sections from which the quotes were taken.[28] The first example, a foundation inscription from 1034, uses quotes from 1 Kings 8–9 regarding Solomon's Temple to ecuate the Worms synagogue with the lost Temple in Jerusalem, a motif found in other genres of literature produced in medieval ShUM (Speyer, Worms, and Mainz).[29] It also incorporates three idioms from Isaiah 56:5, a verse that promises a monument and an everlasting name within the temple that will endure forever. The biblical quotes from Kings and Isaiah support the definition of the synagogue as a votive gift "more pleasing to their creator than uprasing sacrifices" (line 5):

Foundation inscription, Worms Synagogue (1034)

1 May the "hearer of supplications" forever be praised (1 Kings 8:30, 45, 9:3)
   He who "endowed the heart" of his "servant" with faith (1 Kings 8:30, Exodus 35:35, Esther 7:5, 1 Kings 3:9)
2 Jacob son of David, a "man of prudence" (Proverbs 11:12)
   To build a "house for His great name" (1 Kings 8:17, 42)

---

27. For details of all the inscriptions from Worms, including stone sizes, state of preservation, history, and translation, see the annexes volume of Cluse, Fischer, Hahn et al., *ShUM Sites*.

28. Neta Bodner and Ariella Lehmann, "The Dedication Inscription of the Worms Mikveh, 1185/6," *Zion* 88, no. 1 (2023): 7–40 (Hebrew).

29. Scholars have shown a recurring motif of connections between the medieval Rhineland communities and Jerusalem in chronicles, for example Israel Jacob Yuval, "Heilige Städte, heilige Gemeinden—Mainz als das Jerusalem Deutschlands," in *Jüdische Gemeinden und Organisationsformen von der Antike bis zur Gegenwart*, ed. Robert Jütte and Abraham P. Kustermann (Vienna: Böhlau Verlag, 1996), 91–101. Jerusalem was also made present through liturgy, see Jeffrey Woolf, *The Fabric of Religious Life in Medieval Ashkenaz 1000–1300* (Leiden: Brill, 2015), 26–32 and 81–105, as well as in visual art, see Sarit Shalev-Eyni, "Reconstructing Jerusalem in the Jewish Liturgical Realm: The Worms Synagogue and Its Legacy," in *Visual Constructs of Jerusalem*, ed. Bianca Kühnel, Galit Noga-Banai, and Hanna Vorholt (Turnhout: Brepols, 2014), 164–65.

3 And his companion [=wife], lady Rachel, counted among the "untroubled" (Isaiah 32:9, 11, 18)
For His pleasure, they "honored the Lord with their wealth" (Proverbs 3:9)
4 They beautified "a lesser temple" [=synagogue] with treasures (Ezekiel 11:16)
And it was completed in the month of Elul, in the year 794 to the counting
5 More pleasing to their creator than uplifting sacrifices
They were privileged to buy "an everlasting name" (Isaiah 56:5)
6 "A monument and a name" and graceful acclaim (Isaiah 56:5)
"Better than sons or daughters" (Isaiah 56:5)
7 May they be recollected in favorable memories[30]
The reader should heed to answer, "Amen."

The same strategy was used more than a hundred and fifty years later in an inscription from the 1174/5 renovation.[31] The inscription, which runs the length of the capital on the eastern of the two internal columns, likewise uses biblical references to equate the Worms synagogue with Solomon's Temple, and the two interior columns with Yakhin and Boʻaz—the monumental columns in the sanctuary in Jerusalem. The cheerful inscription (which rhymes in Hebrew) seems to generally laud an unnamed person who put up the two columns, added decorative capitals, and hung lamps.

Column inscription, Worms synagogue (1174/5)
1 The splendor "of the two columns" (1 Kings 7:41)
2 He made "without sloth" (Ecclesiastes 10:18)
3 Also "the bowls of the capitals" (1 Kings 7:41)
4 He also "hung up the lamps" (1 Kings 7:49)

The content seems straightforward, but it masks the sophistication of the inscription. First, all the letters in the inscription are marked above with a circle, indicating that their sum should be calculated according

---

30. Although not a biblical quote, this line echoes parts of the High Holidays liturgy. See note 54 below.
31. The original inscription was destroyed in 1938, but some fragments are still extant. The stone is a copy made by a local stonemason in 1959 from documentation. Cluse, Fischer, Hahn et al., *ShUM Sites*, Annexes, 18–9.

יהי רצון מלפניך אדני
אלהינו ואלהי אבותינו
שתשכן שכינתך בבית הזה
"פי בגללו ברא יעקב בכרנתו
לבנותו ועזרו שמעון ויהודית
אשתו עד תום מלאכתו
בחדש אייר שנת ד'אלפים

תשצ"ד לבריאת העולם
אנא אדני אלהי ישראל
הקשיבה לתפילת עבדך
יעקב בן דוד ואשתו
רחל בת יצחק ובנם
שמעון ואשתו יהודית
אשר נדבו הון לבניינו

פָּאֳרֵי הָעַמּוּדִים שְׁתַּיִם
עָשָׂה בְּלִי עֲצַלְתַּיִם
גַּם גּוֹלַת הַכּוֹתָרוֹת
גַּם תְּלָה הַנֵּרוֹת

FIGURES 7.2 and 7.3 Column inscription, Worms synagogue, commemorating a renovation of the Worms synagogue, original written in 1174/5, current stone carved in twentieth century. Photograph by Neta Bodner.

to the numeric value of each Hebrew letter, thereby indicating the year of the inscription. The chronogram in the column inscription marks the Hebrew year 4935 from the creation of the world, equivalent to 1174/5. This indicates that the words of the inscription were calculated not only to make sense, to rhyme, and to fit the physical length of the capital side, but also to record the date of foundation.

This small textual unit also includes strategic references to the building of Solomon's Temple by incorporating quotes from 1 Kings 7

FIGURES 7.4 and 7.5 Column inscription, Worms synagogue, commemorating a renovation of the Worms synagogue. Original written in 1174/5, current stone carved in twentieth century. Photograph by Neta Bodner.

(the chapter that precedes the verses cited in the 1034 inscription).³² The second sentence of the inscription states that the synagogue was built without laziness. This line embeds a quote from Ecclesiastes 10:18: "By slothfulness a building shall be brought down, and through the weakness of hands, the house shall drop through." The

---

32. Katrin Kogman-Appel, *Visual Arts in the Jewish World* (Raanana: Open University Press, 2019), 272 (Hebrew).

author of the inscription implies that the synagogue, as opposed to the house in Ecclesiastes, will not sag or drop. This inscription, therefore, substantiates the image of the local synagogue as the Temple, an even bolder comparison than the "lesser temple" defined in the inscription from 1034.

After demonstrating how the use of biblical quotes supported the literal interpretation of the text found in the above two inscriptions, we now turn to five inscriptions at the heart of this chapter that refer, we argue, directly to stones. We suggest that the use of stones was inserted as a major theme and how biblical references to stones and carving are recruited to strengthen the significance of these actions.

Stones as Witnesses: Worms, 1034

Like the foundation inscription discussed above, the first inscription in our study is perhaps also from 1034.[33] Now situated south of the *Aron Kodesh* (the niche for storing the Torah scroll and marking the direction of prayer), it begins by identifying the stone itself on which the words are incised: "'this stone' 'beside the ark'" (line 1) and its important role—to serve as a witness.

Inscription, south of the Aron Kodesh, Worms synagogue (1034)

1 "This stone," "beside the Ark" (Genesis 28:22, Joshua 24:27, Deuteronomy 31:26)
2 "is a witness" to Jacob, a talented man (Deuteronomy 31:26)
3 Every "Shabbat after Shabbat," in memory (Isaiah 66:23)
4 To remember him with those sleeping in Hebron

The first sentences "This stone . . . is witness to Jacob" animate, or at least call attention to, the object on which the epigraphy is found, giving a voice to the material from which the words were read by whoever chose or managed to read them. The reference to "this stone" is a recurring trope found in other Hebrew inscriptions, such as an example from the Hagenau synagogue dated to 1492, which reads: "This stone we have set as a cornerstone." There are also roughly one hundred

---

33. The fragment was dated by Böcher to the eleventh century on stylistic grounds. According to Cluse, Fischer, Hahn et al. the original had once been replaced by a copy, which remained in its place until 1942. A fragment of the original stone was found in 1959. Cluse, Fischer, Hahn et al., *ShUM Sites,* Annexes, 10.

הא]בן הז]את שבצד הארון
עדה ל]מר יעקב] איש כשרון
כל שבת ושבת לזכרון
[ל]הזכירו עם י]ש]יני חברו[ן]

FIGURE 7.6 Inscription from 1034 situated south of the Aron Kodesh in the Worms synagogue, stone probably a sixteenth-century copy. Photograph by Neta Bodner.

tombstones from Germany from the eleventh to the fourteenth centuries that have a similar format.[34] While natural enough for an inscription on a stone marker, this phrasing reminds us to think about the practicalities undergirding the inscription, such as how much the stones cost and who could afford to commission one.

This literal reading coexists with a symbolic one: the stone as a representation of the entire community, their buildings, and their covenant with God. The symbolic reading rests on the biblical references within the inscription. The phrase "this stone," used to specify a particular stone, appears twice in the Bible. In both cases the isolated stone stands as a material witness to a covenant. In Genesis 28, Jacob took the stone on which he slept and dreamt of the ladder, stood it up vertically, anointed it with oil, and vowed that if he returned home safely, "this

---

34. Based on the tombstones contained in the Steinheim database, EPIDAT: http://www.steinheim-institut.de/cgi-bin/epidat#opt.

stone, which I have set up . . . shall be God's abode" (Genesis 28:22). The stone concretized the miraculous event and was used as a physical marker serving as a witness to the covenant between God and Jacob, embodying the memory for him and his descendants.

The second biblical appearance of the phrase appears in Joshua, and also connects stones, testament, and memory. Toward the end of his days, Joshua erected a stone as a witness to Israel's past and their promise to adhere to their covenant with the Lord: "See, this very stone shall be a witness against us, for it heard all the words that the Lord spoke to us" (Joshua 24:27).[35] Thus, in beginning with "this stone," the 1034 inscription from Worms is building on this cultural heritage by using the same language to articulate a comparable idea—that a specific stone stands as witness and perpetual reminder to the community: "'This stone' 'beside the ark' 'is a witness' to Jacob."

Inscribing Markers: Worms 1174/5

An inscription formerly on the lintel above the main synagogue portal in the north commemorates the 1174/5 renovation (from the same time as the column inscription discussed above).[36] Here the emphasis is not on the stone on which the words were incised, but rather on the person doing the inscribing.

Lintel inscription, north portal, Worms synagogue (1174/5)

1. Verses I "erected as markers"[37] (Jeremiah 31:21)
2. "Enduring" as long as the "counted days" (Psalms 90:12, Psalms 93:5)
3. In the reckoning 935 "the buildings were built" (1 Kings 8:13)
4. From the "opening of the gate," proving for years (Isaiah 26:2)
5. "Enter a righteous nation that keeps faith" (Isaiah 26:2)

---

35. Having been witness to all the events, the stone was a reminder to the people not to break their faith in God. The stone near the ark in Worms is also defined as a witness and perpetual marker of memory. The inscription itself states that 'this stone' is a witness and reminder to commemorate the patron's name (Jacob, incidentally) every week.

36. The determination of the location of the inscription as above the portal is according to Eli'ezer ben Shmu'el's transcription from 1559. See note 25 above.

37. Böcher reads *hatsavti*, as "I chiseled." Böcher, *Die alte Synagoge*, 101. However, the biblical reference from Jeremiah uses the word *hetsavti*, "I erected." Eli'ezer ben Shmu'el's transcription reads 'hetsavti' as well. See note 24 above.

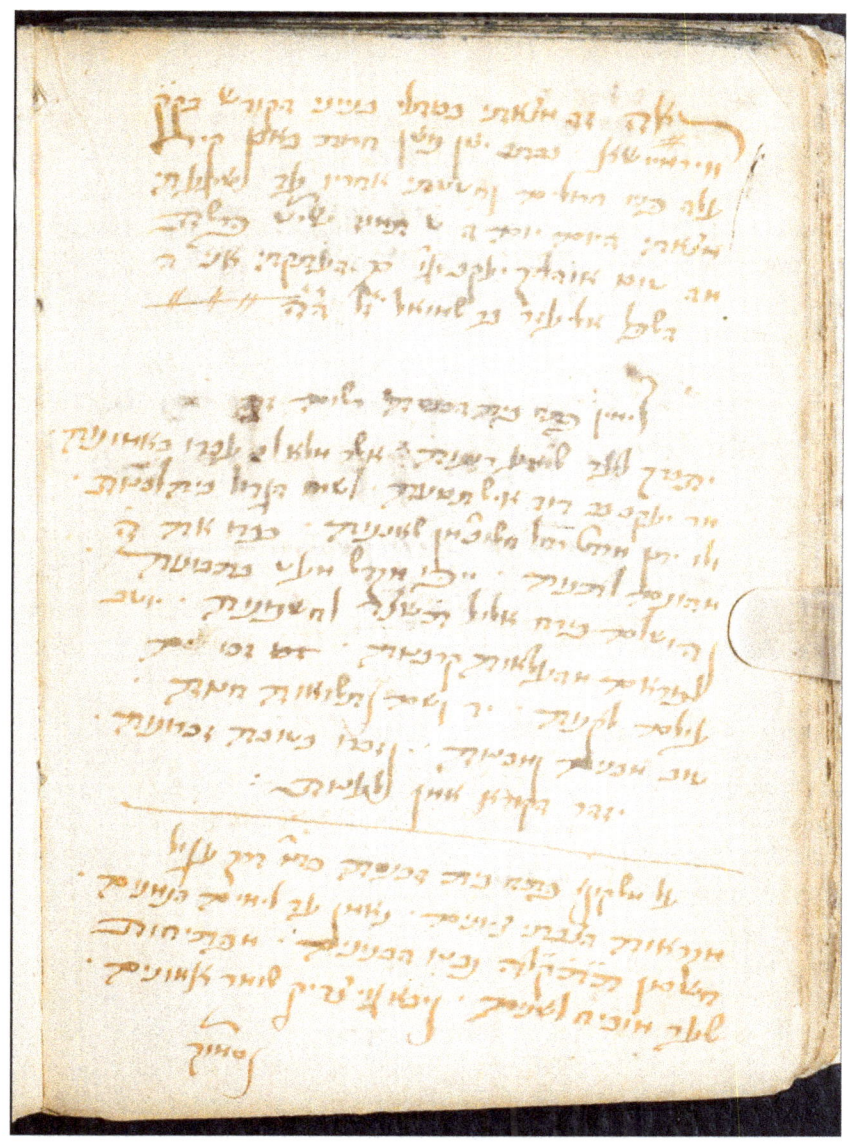

מקראות הצבתי ציונים . נאמן עד לימים הנמנים .
חשבון תִּתְקֹלֹהֹ נבנו הבניינים . מפתיחות
שער מוכיח לשנים . ויבא גוי צדיק שומר אמונים .

FIGURE 7.7   Manuscript transcription of an inscription from 1034 formerly situated south of the Aron Kodesh in the Worms synagogue, recorded by Eli'ezer ben Shmuel in 1559. MS hebr. oct. 256, fol. 055 verso, anthology in six parts (manuscripts). Digitized by the University library J.C. Senckenberg Frankfurt/Main University Library, 2011.

The anonymous author begins the poem by stating that he himself incised (*hatzavti*) or placed (*hetzavti*) the words to serve as "markers" (*tziyunim*) that he trusts will endure (line 2). The inscription does not include a donor name, only a date in a chronogram—the Hebrew year 4935 from the creation of the world, translating to year 1174/5. The poem spotlights the act of inscribing (placing or incising words) to commemorate the year in which the buildings were completed and to communicate the hope that the newly completed space will serve as the entryway for a righteous nation (lines 3 and 4). This gate through which the righteous nation will enter can be understood as both physical and conceptual: the inscription was positioned above the lintel of a real gateway while, by quoting from Isaiah 26:2, it evoked the gates of a victorious and redeemed Zion at the end of days. A similar idea can be found in an inscription from above the door of the synagogue in Rouffach (1290–1300), which begins with the words "the stones of the everlasting doors," referencing Psalms 24:7 and 9. The act of erecting the building or etching the inscriptions promotes redemption for those who walk the straight path, as the congregation (it is implied) do by beautifying and strengthening their physical house of prayer.[38]

Stone as Foundation: Worms, 1185/6

The redemption promised to the entire "righteous nation" of the community in the last inscription emphasizes that although individuals liberally donated funds and were commemorated personally for their contributions, these places of worship belonged to and were used by the whole community. The biblical contexts alluded to in this next inscription, which we discuss below, highlights the commonality of the community members: their heritage, their shared texts, and their aspirations for the future. Here too, the inscription exploits the duality of the literal stones and a metaphorical interpretation. The stones of the public buildings, hewn separately but all from the same quarry, are akin to the members of the community drawing their identity from a common source.

This inscription, found in the complex of the Worms synagogue, was probably originally set in a wall perpendicular to the main portal

---

38. The opening words of the inscription draw attention to the inscription itself: *verses I erected as markers* (line 1). The biblical context is Isaiah's prophecies of redemption and the future return: "Erect markers, set up signposts; keep in mind the highway, the road that you travelled. Return, Maiden Israel! Return to these towns of yours!" (Isaiah 31:21).

THE MEDIEVAL STONE REVOLUTION IN HEBREW INSCRIPTIONS 191

in the north.[39] Round marks over each Hebrew letter in line six of the inscription indicate the year of the inscription should be calculated from the numerical value of each letter, coming out to the Hebrew year 4946 from the creation of the world, or 1185/6. The inscription appears to commemorate the construction of a *mikveh*, a Jewish ritual bath (a building intended for ritual purification through immersion in water not drawn by human effort), built behind the synagogue in the southeastern part of the plot.[40] While the attribution to the mikveh cannot be fully demonstrated, there is supporting evidence for this conclusion: the date matches the architectural details of the ritual bath,[41] the inscription references water, wells, and pits in different ways, and we know of no other construction work in 1185/6, only a decade after the massive rebuilding of 1174/5, that would warrant such a long and intricate inscription.[42]

The mikveh of Worms is a monumental structure, constructed underground. It reached a pool of naturally welling ground water about eight meters under the medieval street level.[43] The digging of the pool itself and the building of a shaft above it, including large ashlar blocks of quarried stone at the base, would have presented significant multiple challenges. Water seeps into the pool from a crack intentionally left between large, quarried stone blocks that floor the bottom of the pool and line its bottom walls. Bringing the stones to the site and laying them as flooring in wet surroundings, with underground spring water perpetually seeping in, was a feat of engineering worth celebrating, as we argue this inscription does. The structure also contains a stairwell, an antechamber with a niche for derobing, and a second, semicircular stairwell leading to ground water. The shaft is roofed by a barrel vault, today with an opening which lights it from above.

---

39. Barzen, "Materialization of Memoria." The inscription is currently mounted in the west wall of the synagogue courtyard. It extends across two red sandstone plaques measuring 0.8 by 0.4 meters (right plaque) and 1 by 0.4 meters (left plaque). Cluse, Fischer, Hahn et al., *SchUM Sites*, Nomination Dossier, 132. See also Cluse, Fischer, Hahn et al., *ShUM Sites*, Annexes, 20–22.

40. We argue that the language of the inscription and the chosen biblical quotes support the connection to the foundation of the ritual bath. See Bodner and Lehmann, "The Dedication Inscription."

41. Krautheimer, *Medieval Synagogues*, 113.

42. Bodner and Lehmann, "The Dedication Inscription."

43. An important publication on the mikveh of Worms is Stefanie Fuchs, "Die Mikwen von Speyer und Worms: Aktueller Forschungsstand," in *Die Jüdische Gemeinde von Erfurt und die SchUM-Gemeinden: Kulturelles Erbe und Vernetzunz* (Jena/Quedlinburg: Bussert & Stadeler, 2012), 61–69.

The virtuosity and skill evinced, and the resources invested in the mikveh warranted the length, tone, and content of the inscription, which seems to include references to all the architectural details mentioned above within a generally enigmatic rhyming poem whose meaning is hard to decipher. Unlike most inscriptions commemorating donations, which specify names, the purpose of the donations, the dates, and often the sums donated, this inscription is strangely lacking in such detail. Only by unravelling the various biblical references can one begin to piece together its purpose. Delving deeper into the biblical quotes brings to the fore references to construction works that, already in their original biblical context, simultaneously refer to a physical building and to a conceptual architectural order. These references reflect both the literal and symbolic layers of meaning, which, we argue, are common to all the inscriptions we discuss.

Mikveh foundation inscription, Worms (1185/6)
1. "To erect witness" "upon Joseph" (Psalms 78:5, 81:6)
   It was done: "yearning for the courts" (Psalms 84:3)
   "Look to the rock hewn" (Isaiah 51:1)
2. "Those who revere the Lord" are "written at his behest" (Malachi 3:15)
   And the action validates: shall "cry out" and "answer" (Habakkuk 2:11)
   "A stone from the wall" and "a rafter from the woodwork" (Habakkuk 2:11)
3. He "dug a well" and "set the rafters" (Numbers 21:18; Psalms 104:3)
   And there "leveled" "a straight way" (Isaiah 40:3)
   And a wall "abode by its bays" (Judges 5:17)
4. In exchange for the money he commanded (Ecclesiastes 7:12)
   In the "shelter of wisdom" he made his haven (Ecclesiastes 7:12)
   "Sitting under the tamarisk tree, standing on the height" (1 Samuel 22:6)
5. "As the sun comes out," its light an arm (Judges 5:31)
   To shade him in the hut of skin (Job 40:31, Jonah 4:5, Isaiah 4:6)
   He shall be known by friends and branched with the noble (Job 40:30)
6. "He will feast on rich fare" of his "refreshments" (Psalms 36:9)
   "Justice shall be the girdle of his loins" (Isaiah 11:5)
   "And faithfulness the girdle of his waist" (Isaiah 11:5)

FIGURE 7.8 Mikveh Foundation Inscription, 1185/6, currently situated on a low wall between the Worms synagogue and mikveh, formerly situated above a portal on a wall perpendicular to the northern synagogue wall. Photograph by Neta Bodner.

In its opening sentence the poem invites the reader to "look to the hewn rock," perhaps the water pool itself, and notes that "he" (we don't know from the inscription who he is, except perhaps a certain Joseph mentioned in the opening line) "dug a well," "set the vaulting rafters" and "lay down a straight path" to stabilize a wall on all sides of the waters (line 3). By virtue of his work, he shall be known by friends and nobles and be girdled in justice and faith (lines 5-6). Here too the act of building is both a physical action—digging, roofing, building a wall, paving a path—and a means to achieve the conceptual gain of being girdled with justice and faith, and recognized by all.

The inscription also refers to the symbolic meaning of the stones and wood of construction. Once built, the very stones and wooden beams will speak out to express the meaning of the action (line 2), perhaps meaning the act of building. Here the inscription treats the stones as animated: it is the stone from the wall that will cry out and answer, the wooden rafters that will express the proof of action (line 2). The reference is from Habakkuk 2:11: "For the stone shall cry out of the wall, and the beam out of the timber shall answer it." There, it is the buildings of Babylon that decry its evil, its towns and cities built on a foundation of crime and iniquity, witnessed by the stones and walls that will not remain silent about what they have seen. In both the biblical reference and the inscriptions, the depiction of the stones as able to speak is congruent with the framing of stones as witnesses, a theme that runs through the different inscriptions analyzed in this chapter and which opens the mikveh inscription itself.

The phrase "to erect a witness to Joseph" uses a verb associated with building: *lehakim*, meaning to erect or construct. This line is an amalgamation of Psalm 78 and Psalm 81, both of which describe the covenant between God and the people of Israel and the building of the Temple as a sign of that covenant. The reference to the construction of the Temple links this inscription with the others and continues the trope of equating physical local buildings with the destroyed Temple of Solomon.

We have seen that the end of the first line, "Look to the rock hewn," can be read literally: the reader is being invited to look at a rock that has been hewn or quarried, which we suggest is the ritual bath dug into the ground at the end of the path whose entryway the inscription marks. At the same time the phrase is also a metaphor. The context of the original biblical verse (Isaiah 51:1) is a call to recognize the roots of the people of Israel.[44] According to Isaiah, the righteous who seek the Lord are the ones who need to remember the covenant and trust in the future restoration: "Look to the rock from which they themselves were cut and the quarry from which they were hewn, to Abraham their father and Sarah their mother." The verse uses rock and quarry as metaphors for the source or root of the righteous people, which also functions as their basis for comfort and hope for future salvation. Inscribed on actual stone and referring to a specific building dug out of the ground, the inscription manipulates both the literal and the metaphorical meanings of the phrase "look to rock hewn," suggesting that the reader should reflect on both the community's buildings and their shared heritage—part of which is their shared corpus of biblical texts familiar from the liturgy.

These verses from Isaiah are recited in one of the readings (*haftorah*) from the Books of the Prophets that follows the weekly Pentateuch reading during the seven weeks between the Ninth of Av, the day of mourning commemorating the destruction of the Temple, and the High Holidays. The verses would therefore be relatively well known to people who frequented the synagogue, even beyond the learned elite. In past decades, scholars of Jewish liturgy and *piyyut* have challenged the assumption that only the very learned could actively understand liturgical poetry. They point out that the structure of some *piyyutim*, their annual repetition, the space of the synagogue, and the performative aspects of the liturgy, were all designed to address and serve a wider group of active and informed congregants.[45] While this is not

---

44. "Listen to Me . . . you who seek the Lord: Look to the rock you were hewn from, to the quarry you were dug from. Look back to Abraham your father and to Sarah who brought you forth. . . . Truly the Lord has comforted Zion, comforted all her ruins; he has made her wilderness like Eden, her desert like the Garden of the Lord. Gladness and joy shall abide there, thanksgiving and the sound of music" (Isaiah 51:1-3).

45. Elisabeth Hollender, "Zur Verwendung der Bibel im frühen ashkenasischen Pijjut," in *Bibel in jüdischer und christlicher Tradition: Festschrift für Johann Maier zum 60. Geburtstag*, ed. Helmut Merklein, Karlheinz Müller, and Günter Stemberger (Frankfurt am Main: Anton Hain, 1993), 441-54; Shulamit Elizur, "The Congregation in the Synagogue and the Ancient Qedushta," in *Knesset Ezra: Literature and Life in the Synagogue, Studies Presented to Ezra Fleischer*, ed. S. Elizur et al. (Jerusalem: Yad Izhak Ben Zvi, 1994), 189-90 (Hebrew); Shulamit Elizur, "The Use of Biblical Quotes in Hebrew Liturgical Poetry," in *Prayers That Cite Scripture*, ed. James L. Kugel (Cambridge: MA: Harvard University Press, 2006), 83-100; Wout van Bekkum, "Hearing and Understanding Piyyut in the Liturgy of the Synagogue," *Zutot* 1 (2001): 58-63, https://doi.org/10.1007/978-94-017-3730-2_8; Laura S. Lieber, "The Rhetoric of Participation: Experiential Elements of Early Hebrew Liturgical Poetry," *Journal of Religion* 90, no. 2 (2010): 119-47, https://doi.org/10.1086/649845. See also Erez Shahar Rochman's contribution in chapter 10 of this book.

definitive evidence that the intended readers of the inscription poems were the congregation at large, nor how they were read, scholarship on the lived aspects of liturgy raises the possibility that the biblical quotations and allusions in piyyutim and on inscriptions were not as obscure as they may seem to a modern reader. Therefore, the words "look to the rock hewn" could have resonated with a relatively wide audience as a reminder to always bear in mind their shared past and heritage. "Look to the rock hewn" also appears in a synagogue inscription from Mainz and in tombstones from Worms, where, as we have argued elsewhere, it was used in the same way.[46] Those highly versed in the full biblical passage would immediately infer its broader context, namely trusting the covenant of the people of Israel with God, and Isaiah's promise of a better future when the Creator will turn wilderness into a thriving place and "Gladness and joy shall abide there, thanksgiving and the sound of music" (Isaiah 51:3).

The Engraver's Tools: Worms 1212/3

In 1212/3 major construction was once again carried out in the Worms synagogue, with the addition of a rectangular building, 9.2 by 12 meters large, appended to the eastern part of the northern synagogue wall, separated from the main synagogue by a wall pierced with windows and a door.[47] According to its foundation inscription, this new structure was meant to accommodate women who wanted to attend prayers: "And this house which he [Me'ir ben Rabbi Yo'el] built to pray in / For the 'women confident in the Lord' and his goodness" (lines 7–8). Its function as a prayer hall for women is well documented from the early modern period, and it became known as the "women's synagogue."[48] In the seventeenth century much of the roofing of this annex was

---

46. Bodner and Lehmann, "The Dedication Inscription," 35–39.

47. The first buildings known as women's synagogues in Ashkenaz in the Middle Ages are those found in the ShUM communities. The oldest preserved women's synagogue is the one in Worms, followed by the one built in Speyer around 1250. A women's synagogue in Mainz is mentioned in 1283 and in Cologne and Vienna in the second half of the thirteenth century. There are women's synagogues recorded in the fourteenth century in Prague, Regensburg, Hainberg a.d. Donau, Bruck a.d. Leitha. See Cluse, Fischer, Hahn et al., *ShUM Sites*, Nomination Dossier, 400.

48. Juspe Schammes attested to its use as a prayer hall for women in the seventeenth century. See Juspe Schammes, *Customs of the Holy Community of Worms*, ed. Binyamin Shlomo Hamburger and Eric Zimmer (Jerusalem: Makhon Yerushaliyim, 1988), vol. 2, 69–70 (Hebrew).

changed, along with the windows,⁴⁹ and a new entrance to the women's synagogue and a chamber for the Jewish council was built in the 1620s on its northern end, at which point it appears the inscription was removed.⁵⁰ In 1843 the wall separating the women's synagogue from the main synagogue was taken down,⁵¹ and the inscription was reengraved on a new stone, perhaps indicating its continued significance for the community.⁵²

The final sentences of the inscription spotlight the iron stylus as the engraver's tool for leaving a lasting memory in stone: "For remembrance, in an 'iron stylus' his 'writing was written' / 'So that it can be read easily'" (lines 9-10):

Women's Synagogue foundation inscription, northern annex of Synagogue, Worms (1212/3)

1. This "house" was "built" "for the name of the Lord" by (1 Kings 3:2, 5:17, 19, 8:17, 20)
2. R. Me'ir ben Rabbi Yo'el a scion of "my priests" (Lamentations 1:10)⁵³
3. In the year 973 to the creation, in the reckoning of my count
4. May he be remembered in good memory before the Lord⁵⁴

---

49. Krautheimer, *Medieval Synagogues*, 103.
50. Cluse, Fischer, Hahn et al., *ShUM Sites*, Nomination Dossier, 118. There are two surviving fragments of the inscription stone. The first was found in circa 1855 by Lewysohn and rediscovered in 1959. The second was found in the ruins of the synagogue in 1957. For more details, see Cluse, Fischer, Hahn et al., *ShUM Sites*, Annexes, 24.
51. Krautheimer, *Medieval Synagogues*, 113.
52. Cluse, Fischer, Hahn et al., *ShUM Sites*, Nomination Dossier, 118
53. This is the only place in the Bible where priests are referred to in the first-person possessive. Along with the references in line 1, this seems to be another comparison between the medieval synagogue and the temple. "God's house" (line 5) is used throughout the Bible to refer to the temple, and the idea of the synagogue as a house to pray in (line 7) is the keynote of Solomon's speech after the building was completed (1 Kings 8).
54. This seems like a reference to parts of the liturgy of the High Holidays, as well as an echo of line 7 in the 1034 inscription commemorating the foundation of the Worms synagogue. This line may refer particularly to the *Avinu Malkenu* prayer for Rosh Hashanah and Yom Kippur ("Our Father, our King, remember us favorably before You"). Although that specific blessing does not appear in the early versions of *Avinu Malkenu* in *Seder Rav Amram Gaon* or in *Mahdezor Vitry*, it can be attested in the second part of the Worms *Maḥzor* from ca. 1280 (Jerusalem, The National Library of Israel, Ms. Heb. 4°781/2, fol. 46r, https://tinyurl.com/3cnyfvzw). The verse is brought by Goldschmidt as part of the Ashkenazi rite in his Maḥzor: Daniel Goldschmidt, *Mahzor for the High Holidays According to the Customs of all the Branches of Ashkenaz* (Jerusalem: Koren, 1970), 131 (Hebrew). For a comparison between different versions of the *Avinu Malkenu* prayer, see: Lawrence A. Hoffmann, *Naming God: Avinu Malkeinu—Our Father, Our King* (Woodstock, VT: Jewish Lights Publishing, 2015) 264-75.

5   And when entering God's house
6   He will "respond and say, 'Amen, Lord!'" (Jeremiah 11:5)
7   And this house which he built to pray in
8   For the "women confident in the Lord" and his goodness (Isaiah 32:9, Proverbs 16:20, Psalms 118:8-9)
9   For remembrance, in an "iron stylus" his "writing was written." (Jeremiah 17:1, Job 19:24, Exodus 32:16)
10 "So that it can be read easily." (Habakkuk 2:2)

The inscription mentions the process of its own engraving: the writing (*mikhtavo*) was done using an iron stylus ('*et barzel*) in order to be remembered (line 9). The idea that words on stone are used to incise a lasting memory has been a common motif in most of the inscriptions discussed thus far. On the literal level, the text references the types of tools required to ensure an enduring inscription. It also utilizes the symbolism of the specific terms, taken from the Book of Job: "O that my words were written down; would they were inscribed in a record, incised on a rock forever with iron stylus and lead" (Job 19:23-24), in which writing in stone with an iron stylus serves as a metaphor for ensuring that a memory will be retained over time.

The words used in Job, "incised on a rock" (*betsur yeḥatsvun*) echo the opening line of the 1185/6 inscription: *tsur hutsav*, "the rock hewn." The only two instances in the Bible in which the root *hatsav*, to hew or cut, and *tsur*, rock, appear together are Isaiah 51:1 and Job 19:24, both quoted in medieval inscriptions in Worms. In both, the clear context is memory and lasting commemoration enabled by the durable material of quarried stone. In this inscription from the women's synagogue, the act of inscribing the stone with words reflects the actual process by which the poem was cut into the stone and, by using language borrowed from Job, adds further weight to the act—writing with an iron stylus to ensure its significance is conveyed onwards and not forgotten.

Considering aspects of daily life, it is worthwhile pondering the work that necessarily went into engraving words in stone. Inscribing such long poems into ashlar or other masonry blocks was a risky business. Mistakes could prove to be costly errors requiring an entirely new stone. Careful calculation had to be made regarding the size of the block and the size of the letters in relation to the length of the sentences and the full length of the poem relative to the height of the stone. The letters had to be legible and yet not too large, deep enough to survive weather

[בנה הבי]ת הזה לשם אדוני . ר מאיר בר יואל מזרע כהוני
[בתתק]עג ליצירה למנין חשבוני . יזכור בזכרון טוב לפני אדוני
יען ויאמר אמן אדוני .
[הב]ית הזה אשר בנה להתפלל בו . לנשים הבוטחות אל ה׳ ואל טובו
לזכון בעט ברזל נכתב מכתבו . למען ירוץ הקורא בו :

ובת מלך בת נדיב כבודה . פנימה נכנסה בית מנוחה .
לבית [ח]בר סגן כהן חמודה . לשם עזר מאיר נלקחה .
שמה מרת יהודית החסידה . בידה לקחה צידה ארוחה .
אשר אנה אלוה כל בידה . להכין בית נוה זה לו למנחה .
להשלים בו עד ערב עבודה . ת[פי]לה ועתירה ורון ושיחה .
חכמה בנתה בית בחמדה . בכך תהיה כאם בניה שמחה .
אלהים זכרה לה זאת לתודה . ולצדה סגולה ולשמחה :

נתחדש בשנת תרנא לפק

FIGURE 7.9 Women's Synagogue Foundation Inscription, northern annex of Synagogue, Worms, originally written in 1212/13, current stone a nineteenth-century reconstruction remounted in the twentieth century on the northern wall of the woman's synagogue annex. Photograph by Neta Bodner.

damage but at the same time not so wide as to impede reading. The technical act of cutting the words onto the stone by the person holding the chisel was never a stand-alone endeavor. The poem was likely composed by someone other than the person tasked with incising it, raising questions about the level of erudition needed by the engraver. If low, then perhaps the process required the oversight of the writer, or other types of cooperation between individuals.

The "iron stylus" is also found in Jeremiah, where it is used to describe just how pervasive the sins of Judea are, again expressing the idea that words inscribed with an iron stylus endure: "The guilt of Judah is inscribed with a stylus of iron, engraved with an adamant point on the tablet of their hearts and on the horns of their altars" (Jeremiah 17:1). The rest of the prophesy threatens the people of Israel who had enflamed the wrath of God but also promises blessings for those who trust in the Lord, as do the women for whom the 1212/3 women's synagogue in Worms was established.

The women's synagogue inscription ends with the words "so that it can be read easily," a reference to a verse from Habakkuk, in which God tells the prophet to inscribe his prophecy on tablets: "The Lord answered me and said: Write the prophecy down, inscribe it clearly on tablets, so that it can be read easily" (Habakkuk 2:2). The prophecy to be inscribed and made legible to all refers to the downfall of the Babylonians and, thus inscribed on tablets, it stands as a witness to the promise of future redemption and eventual salvation. These tablets are the inverse of the ones on which Jeremiah inscribes with an "iron stylus": Jeremiah's tablets are a witness to Judea's guilt, while Habakkuk's tablets are a witness their future salvation. The metaphors used in the women's synagogue inscription point to the physical act of engraving, of carving words that are not easily erased into the unyielding stone surface. Not surprisingly, the types of materials in the metaphors correspond to the function of the words: these inscriptions become associated with memory that was meant to last.[55]

From Quarry to Construction: Mainz, 1283

Using biblical allusions to highlight the material aspects of the inscription was not unique to Worms, as can be seen in at least one comparable example from nearby Mainz. In an inscription from the Mainz

---

55. Petrucci, *Public Lettering*, 2.

synagogue to commemorate repairs made in 1283, attention is called to the different stages of the construction process, including the quarrying and transportation of the stones. The Mainz inscription, of which only a fragment has survived, was documented by Siegmund Salfeld at the beginning of the twentieth century.[56]

Inscription, Mainz synagogue (1283)

1 "Rock was hewn" (Isaiah 51:1)
 For the "Diaspora" "set up." (Nahum 2:8)[57]
 For the ending[58]
2 Shaped.
 To transport with sorrow (Ecclesiastes 10:9)
 "Quarry stones" (1 Kings 5:31, 2 Kings 12:13, 22:6, 2 Chronicles 34:11)
3 "For the dwellers of the planted and the enclosed"—to make a floor. (1 Chronicles 4:23)
 R. Isaac
4 Son of Abraham, in his piety and sorrow,
 And his wife
5 Mistress Sarah,
 Their donation, three marks, for one "as fleet as a gazelle."[59] (Mishnah Avot 5:20)
6 And R. Abraham son of Isaac, in heaven now placed, gave three

---

56. Siegmund Salfeld, *Zur Geschichte der Mainzer Synagogue* (Mainz: Hofdruckerei Philipp von Zabern, 1908), 6-7. A photograph of the surviving fragment can be found in Andreas Lehnardt, *Eine Krone für Magenza: die Judaica-Abteilung im Landesmuseum Mainz* (Hesse: Michael Imhof Verlag, 2015), 197.

57. The biblical verse is unclear, but the use of the root H.TS.B and G.L.H together appears nowhere else in the Bible.

58. Line 1: Salfeld reads: "for the ending" (*lesiyum*) and translates "for the keystone," as do Barzen and Lehnardt, although Lehnardt transcribes *lehizam*—which is a word unknown in Hebrew. Lehnardt, *Eine Krone für Magenza*, 196. Cluse takes issue with Lehnardt's reconstruction, which often ignores biblical quotes and sometimes creates meaningless words. Cluse, "Jews," 157. It is further possible to read *lehayyim niqtsav*—to life numbered or shaped—or *lehayom niqtsav*—for today shaped.

59. Lehnardt reads "Fifty marks" (*N zaquq*). *Ein Krone für Magenza*, 196. However, in Baumgarten's analysis of the Nuremburg Memorbuch, she notes that "prior to 1298, couples gave an average of three silver coins each, whereas the average individual (man or woman) gave less than one." See Elisheva Baumgarten, *Practicing Piety in Medieval Ashkenaz: Men, Women, and Everyday Religious Observance, Jewish Culture and Contexts* (Philadelphia: University of Pennsylvania Press, 2014), 126. Fifty marks seems therefore overly high for the renovation of a floor, especially if compared to the sum of eight marks recorded for a roof renovation in a second inscription from Mainz (1281/1283).

7 Marks and the Rabbi R. Joseph gave one mark [? L? T? V][60]
8 May they be remembered in their turn [N[?]ZV]

Like the inscription from the Worms ritual bath, the inscription from Mainz begins with a reference to the verse discussed extensively above, "Look to the rock you were hewn from, to the quarry you were dug from" (Isaiah 51:1). However, by removing the word *look*, the Mainz inscription diverts the focus from the viewer of the inscription to the stone itself, which was "transported with sorrow" (line 2) to the construction site. The narrative of the inscription is hard to follow and the inscription is badly damaged, but the rhyming verbs of the surviving text seem to be imparting something of the following sequence: a rock was hewn: (*tsur hutsav*, line 1); it was placed or was cut for the Diaspora (*lagolah hutsav*, line 1); it was transported or heaved with hardship from the quarry to be laid as paving (*lehasiʿa beʿetsev avney mehtsav . . . leratsaf*, lines 2–3).

Eric Fernie has demonstrated that the development of the Romanesque style depended on an expansion in the provision of cut stone from quarries, which became a major industry in Latin Europe. The availability of high-quality ashlar blocks was crucial for the construction of the straight, regular walls typical of the Romanesque style of clarity and articulation.[61] The quarries, both above ground and below, from which the stones were cut and shaped, were a ubiquitous part of the medieval landscape from the eleventh century onward. The stately Romanesque buildings seen today in Europe were the product of an industrial revolution, at the heart of which was stone quarrying.[62]

The Mainz inscription's focus on the rocks and the quarrying process is indicative of the Jewish community's awareness of and knowledge about the difficulties of building with stone, and of their participation in the building innovations of the Romanesque period. Take, for example, the specific mention of the sorrows of transportation (line 2): stones needed to be loaded and unloaded from wagons or barges using ingenious machines, and transportation was expensive. Jean Gimpel estimated that transporting cut stone by land for some twenty

---

60. The last words in the final lines were badly damaged. We have guessed some of the letters as indicated with question marks based on the extant evidence and the rhyming scheme.
61. Eric Fernie, "Romanesque Architecture," 300.
62. Gimpel, *The Medieval Machine*, xv and 59.

kilometers was nearly equivalent to the cost of the material itself,[63] and although conveying the stone by water was cheaper and easier,[64] this method had its own risks and hazards, from sinking to tax stations.[65]

However, the general innovations and struggles of the European building industry may not have been the only association intended by the inscription. The term *quarry stones* (*avney mehtsav*, line 2) appears in the Bible only three times, all in the context of renovations of the First Temple:[66] one from the time of King Jehoash (2 Kings 12:13) and another associated with King Josiah's reform (622 BCE), which appears in the Book of Kings and is retold in Chronicles: "To the carpenters, the laborers, and the masons, and for the purchase of wood and quarried stones for repairing the House" (2 Kings 22:6). Much of the biblical description of Jehoash's renovation focuses on the fiscal, rather than the architectural, aspects of the renovation: the involvement of the priests in collecting the funds for the renovation and the fact that there was no need to keep checks on the priests who delivered the money to the workmen, "for they dealt honestly" (2 Kings 12:16). The focus of the biblical description on the honesty of the priest-overseers who paid the workers, in addition to the actual, physical construction, is echoed in the Mainz inscription's focus on the construction of the synagogue (hewing and transporting quarried stone) and the specific amounts donated by the members of the Jewish community, mentioned in the second half of the inscription.

The choice in the Mainz inscription to use the specific term *avney mehtsav*, quarry stone, not only reflects the actual source of the building materials, but also cleverly utilizes the biblical sources as an additional indication of the type of construction being commemorated: not the foundation of a synagogue, but its renovation. These references add another layer to the comparison between Mainz and Jerusalem found in other literary genres.[67] The inscription depicts the synagogue as a tangible stone-and-mortar building requiring pricey upkeep, but by framing these mundane renovations within the biblical contexts

---

63. Gimpel, *The Medieval Machine*, 61–62.
64. Gimpel, *The Medieval Machine*, 61–62.
65. See Tzafrir Barzilay's chapter 4 in this book.
66. Perhaps it is noteworthy that all three references relate to temple renovations rather than its initial construction, although it should be noted that transporting or carrying of stone is mentioned in the latter context: "The king ordered huge blocks of choice stone to be carried, so that the foundations of the house might be laid with hewn stones" (1 Kings 5:31).
67. See note 29 above.

referenced in the inscription, it also declares these efforts to be votive acts of piety.

Another reference to the quotidian aspects of building, the transportation of stones: "to transport with sorrow" (line 2) also has biblical roots. The quote is a reference to Ecclesiastes 10:9, in the context of a series of aphorisms pointing to the toil and hardships involved in any endeavor, even for a good cause. Quarrying stone and splitting wood, digging pits and breaching fences, are inescapable and necessary parts of life, and the hardships one encounters in the process are inevitable. This seems a rare instance of recognition of the highly skilled workmen—likely not Jewish—involved in the arduous act of construction.[68] Craftsmen are further alluded to in line 3, "dwellers of the planted [*Neta'im*] and the enclosed [*Gederah*]," taken from 1 Chronicles 4:23: "These were the workmen who dwelt at Neta'im and Gederah; they dwelt there in the king's service." The dwellers of the two settlements, Neta'im (literally, the planted) and Gederah (literally, the enclosed), are specified as workmen, descendants of Shelah son of Judah. The inclusion of this verse in the inscription may be a further reference to the craftsmen, or perhaps to the beneficiaries of the repairs, the dwellers of the walled city of Mainz, as well as, perhaps, visiting Jews from the surrounding countryside.[69]

We have argued that the inscriptions discussed in this chapter are evidence of the recognition on the part of two Jewish communities of the shift in building materials and techniques in the twelfth and thirteenth centuries, from brick walls and wooden ceilings to stone vaulting. This architectural shift had a profound impact on their urban surroundings. A literal reading of the inscriptions calls attention to the quotidian aspects of these changes, highlighting how the actual stones were quarried, transported, and incised.

Interwoven with the literal reading is a symbolic one, which utilizes the biblical quotes scattered throughout the inscriptions to invite deeper layers of reading, depending on the readers' level of erudition and recall of the biblical passages referenced. Many of the biblical quotes embedded in the different inscriptions are taken from biblical

---

68. Gimpel, *The Medieval Machine*, 113.
69. Cluse, "Jews," 138–40 and 157.

passages read as part of the liturgy, which would have made them more accessible to wider circles of the Jewish community.[70]

The inscriptions provide chronological information about the Jewish communal buildings, their founders, and their donors. They are also intricate poems containing a wealth of religious ideas, cleverly and aesthetically couched within the biblical references. Many of the inscriptions utilize the architectural and material elements of the building itself as a means of metaphoric interpretation. When, for example, the column inscription equates the physical double columns of the Worms synagogue with Yakhin and Boʻaz in Solomon's Temple, it offers the community of Worms a physical memory-aid for imagining momentarily (perhaps at certain liturgical high-points of the year) that their sanctuary, their "lesser temple," was akin to the original Temple. The inscription located in the synagogue courtyard (1185/6) that cites the prophet's yearning for the lost Temple courts, enables erudite readers to meditate on the act of building the synagogue courts and its intersection with hopes and yearnings to rebuild the Temple courts in the future.

A study of recurring themes shows that these were carefully chosen and full of purpose. The inscriptions in Worms refer to Solomon's Temple, specifically the descriptions of construction and consecration from 1 Kings 7–8. Such references can be found in the 1034 dedication, the 1174/5 renovation inscription on the pillars, and the 1212/3 inscription of the women's synagogue. This is also apparent in the choice made by the author of the Mainz inscription (1283), to draw his references to the Temple from different chapters (2 Kings 12 and 13), which describe its renovation, rather than foundation. The use of a similar, specific biblical corpus as a source for different inscriptions can also be seen in the choice of Habakkuk 2:2 and 11 in both the 1185/6 mikveh inscription: "'a stone shall 'cry out' and a rafter shall 'answer' from the woodwork'" and the 1212/3 women's synagogue inscription. Both quotes allude to the physicality of the inscription and the building. It is thus tempting to suggest that the earlier inscriptions informed the authors' choice of references in the later inscriptions.

In this chapter, we have demonstrated the various ways in which the very stones of the medieval synagogue and ritual bath inscriptions from Worms and Mainz "cry out" both to their readers and to each other

---

70. Bodner and Lehmann, "The Dedication Inscription," 21.

and highlight the efforts of the Jewish communities to construct their buildings: quarrying stone, transporting it, erecting it, and inscribing it—actions often overlooked in discussions of the everyday life of Jewish communities. This mixture of the ideological and the material shows how the ShUM communities, although noted for their scholarly output and the learned men of letters who led them, were also part of the material world. They invested significant financial and logistical efforts to build the kind of prayer spaces they believed they deserved. Though often funded by individuals, the inscriptions marking these efforts tell us of communities proud of their common achievements and shared ideologies. They speak to the hopes, concepts, and religious ideals of the Jews of Mainz and Worms and to the fiscal, artistic (and perhaps even physical) pains they took to embody them in stone.

Further Readings

Barzen, Rainer J. "Materialization of Memoria: Memory and Remembrance of Benefactors in Building Inscriptions in Medieval Ashkenaz." In *Perception and Awareness: Artefacts and Imageries in Medieval European Jewish Cultures*, edited by Katrin Kogman-Appel, Elisheva Baumgarten, Elisabeth Hollender, and Ephraim Shoham-Steiner, 77–116. Turnhout: Brepols, 2023.

Böcher, Otto. *Die alte Synagoge zu Worms: Festschrift zur Wiedereinweihung der Alten Synagoge zu Worms*. Frankfurt am Main: Verlag Stadtbibliotek, 1961.

Cluse, Christoph, Florence Fischer, Stefanie Hahn et al. *ShUM Sites of Speyer, Worms and Mainz: Nomination for the UNESCO World Heritage List*. State of Rhineland-Palatinate, 2020.

Elitzur, Shulamit. "The Use of Biblical Quotes in Hebrew Liturgical Poetry." In *Prayers That Cite Scripture*, edited by James L. Kugel, 83–100. Cambridge: MA: Harvard University Press, 2006.

Fernie, Eric. "Romanesque Architecture." In *A Companion to Medieval Art: Romanesque and Gothic in Northern Europe*, edited by Conrad Rudolph, 295–313. Lynchburg, VA: Blackwell, 2006.

Gimpel, Jean. *The Medieval Machine: The Industrial Revolution of the Middle Ages*. London: Wildwood House, 1988.

Hollender, Elisabeth. "Zur Verwendung der Bibel im frühen ashkenasischen Pijjut." In *Bibel in jüdischer und christlicher Tradition: Festschrift für Johann Maier zum 60. Geburtstag*, edited by Helmut Merklein, Karlheinz Müller, and Günter Stemberger, 441–54. Frankfurt am Main: Anton Hain, 1993.

Kogman-Appel, Katrin. *A Mahzor from Worms: Art and Religion in a Medieval Jewish Community*. Cambridge. MA: Harvard University Press, 2012.

Krautheimer, Richard. *Medieval Synagogues*. Jerusalem: Mossad Bialik, 1993 (Hebrew).

Paulus, Simon. *Die Architektur der Synagoge im Mittelalter: Überlieferung und Bestand*. Petersberg: Imhof, 2007.

Petrucci, Armando. *Public Lettering: Script, Power, and Culture*, trans. Linda Lappin. Chicago: University of Chicago Press, 1993.
Shalev-Eyni, Sarit. "Reconstructing Jerusalem in the Jewish Liturgical Realm: The Worms Synagogue and Its Legacy." In *Visual Constructs of Jerusalem*, edited by Bianca Kühnel, Galit Noga-Banai, and Hanna Vorholt, 161–70. Turnhout: Brepols, 2014.
Toman, Rolf, ed. *Romanesque: Architecture, Sculpture, Painting*. Köln: Ullmann & Könemann, 2007.
Yuval, Israel Jacob. "Heilige Städte, heilige Gemeinden—Mainz als das Jerusalem Deutschlands." In *Jüdische Gemeinden und Organisationsformen von der Antike bis zur Gegenwart*, edited by Robert Jütte and Abraham P. Kustermann, 91–101. Vienna: Böhlau Verlag, 1996.

CHAPTER 8

The Objects of Others

The Risks of Non-Elite Debtors in Jewish-Christian Credit Exchange

Aviya Doron

> The same Kalman has claimed from the goldsmith *zum Schildknecht* 105 pearls, two gold rings, four solders of silver and one grey men's coat for 14 gulden and the interest.
>
> —*Urkundenbuch zur Geschichte der Juden in Frankfurt am Main von 1150–1400*, ed. Isidor Kracauer

Sometime during November 1372, the Jew Kalman arrived at the imperial jury court in Frankfurt, known as the Frankfurter Schöffengericht, to claim the transfer of several pawns into his possession following the default of his debtors.[1] Among two claims he made on that day, he received a court verdict to officially transfer to his possession several valuable objects: pearls, gold rings, and solders of silver. While medieval Jewish moneylenders are often recognized as having handled such luxurious objects, these are usually associated with a very particular clientele: princes, bishops, and other members of the

---

This chapter was written under the auspices of the Beyond the Elite: Jewish Daily Life in Medieval Europe Project, PI Elisheva Baumgarten, from the European Research Council (ERC) under the European Union's Horizon 2020 research and innovation program, grant agreement No. 681507, and prepared for publication with funding from the Israel Science Foundation Grant 2850/22, Contending with Crises: The Jews of XIVth Century Europe, PI Elisheva Baumgarten.

1. The imperial jure court in Frankfurt is evidenced as of the twelfth century and was tied to the commercial activities around the biannual interregional fair; see Michael Rothmann, *Die Frankfurter Messen im Mittelalter* (Stuttgart: Franz Steiner Verlag, 1998). While the original manuscript containing the court verdicts, known as the *Frankfurter Gerichtsbücher*, was destroyed during the Second World War, a summary of all the cases involving Jews has survived in Isidor Kracauer's 1914 edition of sources on the Jews of Frankfurt. Isidor Kracauer, ed., *Urkundenbuch zur Geschichte der Juden in Frankfurt am Main von 1150–1400* (Frankfurt a. M.: J. Kauffmann, 1914).

medieval ruling elite.[2] However, in the case recorded in the Frankfurt court, the debtor, not identified by name, was not one of the highest echelons of society, but was, instead, simply recognized as a goldsmith. Even though goldsmiths readily had access to valuable objects that could be pawned with Jewish moneylenders, one thing in the court record stands out as unusual: the value of the loan these objects were used to secure. By comparison, two different loans that were claimed that same year in court, involving similarly lavish objects, were estimated at double or triple the value.[3] This raises the question, why was the goldsmith willing to part with these objects for such a low sum of money?

Although goldsmiths, along with other craftspeople, had regular access to raw materials, unfinished objects, tools, and other valuables, these were not necessarily their property to sell, pawn, or transfer. Furthermore, these materials and objects were often far more valuable than the income earned by the various people working in crafts who were not themselves workshop masters. This situation also applied to servants, maids, porters, and other workers in medieval cities who handled objects that were out of their personal financial reach. As Valentin Groebner demonstrated in his study of the working poor in fifteenth-century Nuremberg, the costliness of certain raw materials often led to misuse and abuse by textile workers, metal workers, and other craftspeople with access to them.[4] This problem was not a fifteenth-century novelty. The fourteenth-century credit market already provides rich evidence of the potential misuse of objects by Christian craftspeople and workers in their credit transactions with Jews. While the ubiquity of the phenomenon raises questions regarding the extent of delinquency associated with it, it nonetheless sheds light on various aspects of the social dynamics within urban households and workshops, and the engagement of Jews in these dynamics.

---

2. Birgit Wiedl, "Do hiezen si der Juden mesner ruefen. Jüdisch-christliche Geschäftsurkunden als Quellen zur Alltagsgeschichte," in *Abrahams Erbe*, ed. Ludger Lieb, Klaus Oschema, and Johannes Heil (Berlin: De Gruyter, 2015), 437–53; Joseph Shatzmiller, *Cultural Exchange: Jews, Christians, and Art in the Medieval Marketplace* (Princeton: Princeton University Press, 2017); Markus J. Wenninger, "Geld und Politik. Spezialprivilegien für jüdische Großbankiers des 14. Jahrhunderts im Südostalpenraum," *Aschkenas* 20, no. 2 (2012): 305–28, https://doi.org/10.1515/asch-2010-0012.

3. Kracauer, *Urkundenbuch*, 521.

4. Valentin Groebner, *Ökonomie ohne Haus: Zum Wirtschaften armer Leute in Nürnberg am Ende des 15. Jahrhunderts* (Göttingen: Vandenhoeck & Ruprecht, 1993), 179–80.

The relationships between Jews and craftspeople in the German lands have mostly been studied in the context of anti-Jewish violence, detailing the local dynamics leading to the involvement of craftspeople in instigating and driving violent acts against Jews, often during times of crises.[5] These violent events were thus framed as the culmination of ongoing anti-Jewish resentment, stemming from Jews' function as moneylenders. While there is ample evidence that Jews provided credit to members of different craft groups,[6] the ever-growing body of literature on credit across the medieval economy suggests that credit relationships did not necessarily result in hostilities.[7] In these quotidian, widespread credit transactions, objects often acted as stores of value, with household, industrial, and commercial objects frequently used as collateral for loans, and even as the eventual value exchanged in the transaction.[8]

---

5. Jörg R. Müller, "Judenverfolgungen und Vertreibungen zwischen Nordsee und Südalpen im hohen und späten Mittelalter, " in *Geschichte der Juden im Mittelalter von der Nordsee bis zu den Südalpen*, vol. 2, ed. Alfred Haverkamp (Hannover: Hahn 2002), 189–222; Frantisek Graus, *Pest–Geißler–Judenmorde. Das 14. Jahrhundert als Krisenzeit* (Göttingen: Max-Planck-Instituts für Geschichte, 1987); Markus J. Wenninger, *Man bedarf keiner Juden mehr. Ursachen und Hintergründe ihrer Vertreibung aus den deutschen Reichsstädten im 15. Jahrhundert* (Wien: Böhlau, 1981).

6. David Schnur, "Wirtschaftliche Beziehungen zwischen jüdischen Geldverleihern und christlichen Handwerkern im spätmittelalterlichen Frankfurt am Main," in *Ökonomische Glaubensfragen: Strukturen und Praktiken jüdischen und christlichen Kleinkredits im Spätmittelalter*, ed. Gerhard Fouquet and Sven Rabeler (Stuttgart: Franz Steiner Verlag, 2018), 63–98.

7. Daniel Lord Smail, *Legal Plunder: Households and Debt Collection in Late Medieval Europe* (Cambridge, MA: Harvard University Press, 2016); Daniel Lord Smail, "Interactions between Jews and Christians in Later Medieval Provence," *Medieval Encounters* 27, no. 4-5 (December 22, 2021): 410–33. https://doi.org/10.1163/15700674-12340114; Martha C. Howell, *Commerce before Capitalism in Europe, 1300–1600* (Cambridge: Cambridge University Press, 2010); Monika Gussone, "Informelle Kreditbeziehungen im spätmittelalterlichen Kalkar," *Annalen des historischen Vereins für den Niederrhein, insbesondere das alte Erzbistum Köln* 223 (2020): 53–123; Gabriele B. Clemens, ed., *Schuldenlast und Schuldenwert. Kreditnetzwerke in der europäischen Geschichte, 1300–1900* (Trier: Kliomedia, 2008); Gerhard Fouquet and Sven Rabeler, eds., *Ökonomische Glaubensfragen. Strukturen und Praktiken jüdischen und christlichen Kleinkredits im Spätmittelalter* (Stuttgart: Franz Steiner Verlag, 2018); Gabriela Signori, *Schuldenwirtschaft. Konsumenten- und Hypothekarkredite im spätmittelalterlichen Basel* (Konstanz: UVK Verlagsgesellschaft, 2015); Gabriela Signori, "Gelihen Geltz. Christliche Geldleihe aus dem Blinckwinkel spätmittelalterlicher Gerichtsbücher," in *Ökonomische Glaubenfragen. Strukturen und Praktiken jüdischen und christlichen Kleinkredits im Spätmittelalter*, ed. Gerhard Fouquet and Sven Rabeler (Stuttgart: Franz Steiner Verlag, 2018), 21–42.

8. Smail, *Legal Plunder*. The value stored in luxury objects has been especially stressed, as they were portable and easily fungible. See Daniel Lord Smail, "Persons and Things in Marseille and Lucca, 1300-1450," in *Oxford Handbook of History and Material Culture*, eds. Ivan Gaskell and Sarah Anne Carter (Oxford: Oxford University Press, 2020), 378–96; Katherine L. French, *Household Goods and Good Households in Late Medieval London: Consumption and Domesticity after the Plague* (Philadelphia: Pennsylvania University Press, 2021).

Likewise, most of the loans Jews extended at the time were backed by pawns: objects given by debtors to creditors at the time of the extension of the loan, which were supposed to secure the value of the loan and interest. Previous literature has often stressed the two extremes of Jewish moneylending—elite bankers[9] or loan sharks[10]—thus also aligning the objects Jews received as pawns along similar classifications: either magnificent works of art and ornate manuscripts,[11] or rags and simple household goods.[12] Focusing on two extremes, both these approaches have overlooked the intricacies of the full spectrum of the urban credit market and the Jews' role within it. Seeing that craftspeople and service workers enjoyed regular access to objects they did not own, tracing the different objects Jewish moneylenders received as pawns thus allows us to uncover and re-create the social relationships and complications that arose in the daily exchange of Jews and Christians. By tracking these relationships and the legal norms that framed them, this chapter exposes the risks involved in lending money to non-elite debtors and demonstrates that similar objects carried different implications of risk

---

9. Markus J. Wenninger, "Geld und Politik. Spezialprivilegien für jüdische Großbankiers des 14. Jahrhunderts im Südostalpenraum," *Aschkenas* 20, no. 2 (2012): 305-28. https://doi.org/10.1515/asch-2010-0012; Robert Stacey, "The English Jews under Henry III," in *The Jews in Medieval Britain: Historical, Literary, and Archeological Perspectives*, ed. Patricia Skinner (Rochester: Boydell Press, 2003), 41-54. On the Jews as bankers of the elite, Julie Mell, *The Myth of the Medieval Jewish Moneylender*, vol. 1 (New York: Palgrave Macmillan, 2017).

10. In his book on the credit activities of medieval women, William Chester Jordan raises the theory of a pariah group lending in relation to Jewish moneylenders. Accordingly, those ostracized from society were forced into moneylending, "usually servicing the least creditworthy among the borrowers." William C. Jordan, *Women and Credit in Pre-Industrial and Developing Societies* (Philadelphia: University of Pennsylvania Press, 1993), 19. On the medieval association of Jews with distress loans, see Giacomo Todeschini, "Christian Perceptions of Jewish Economic Activity in the Middle Ages," in *Wirtschaftsgeschichte der mittelalterlichen Juden: Fragen und Einschätzungen*, ed. Michael Toch (Berlin: De Gruyter, 2008), 1-16; Giacomo Todeschini, "Jewish Usurers, Blood Libel, and the Second-Hand Economy: The Medieval Origins of a Stereotype (from the Thirteenth to the Fifteenth Century)," in *The Medieval Roots of Antisemitism. Continuities and Discontinuities from the Middle Ages to the Present Day*, ed. Jonathan Adams and Cordelia Heß (New York: Routledge, 2018), 341-51.

11. Jörg R. Müller, "Zur Verpfändung sakraler Kultgegenstände an Juden im mittelalterlichen Reich: Norm und Praxis," in *Pro multis beneficiis—Festschrift für Friedhelm Burgard: Forschungen zur Geschichte der Juden und des Trierer Raumes*, ed. Sigfrid Hirbodian (Trier: Kliomedia, 2012), 179-204; Birgit Wiedl, "Sacred Objects in Jewish Hands: Two Case Studies," in *Jews and Christians in Medieval Europe: The Historiographical Legacy of Bernhard Blumenkranz*, ed. Philippe Buc, Martha Keil, and John Victor Tolan (Turnhout: Brepols, 2016), 57-78; Joseph Shatzmiller, "Church Articles: Pawns in the Hands of Jewish Moneylenders," in *Wirtschaftsgeschichte der mittelalterlichen Juden: Fragen und Einschätzungen*, ed. Michael Toch (Berlin: De Gruyter, 2008), 93-102; Joseph Shatzmiller, *Cultural Exchange: Jews, Christians, and Art in the Medieval Marketplace* (Princeton: Princeton University Press, 2017).

12. These objects are mostly mentioned in relation to Jews' provision of distress loans.

according to the identity of the person pawning them. Throughout the article I will attempt to contextualize Jews' credit exchange with non-elite debtors within the wider scope of the urban economy, allowing for a more nuanced understanding of their interactions with their Christian non-elite clients. An exploration of the different objects Jews received as pawns and the relationships they wove between Jews and Christians provides an opportunity to uncover several of the hitherto unexamined aspects of Jews' involvement in the urban credit market, going beyond the dichotomies that characterized their credit activities.

Between Provenance and Fair Use

As the court case from Frankfurt cited at the beginning of this chapter implied, a major question in the circulation of goods and materials in the urban economy was who had possession and usage rights over these goods, and the possibility that people, sharing the same household, workshop, or through some other commercial interaction, might pawn valuables to which they had access but which they did not own. As a result, urban legislators introduced laws attempting to prevent such abuse. An example for such legislation has survived from Nuremberg. As of the late thirteenth century, the city of Nuremberg issued extensive regulations regarding Jews' credit transactions and handling of pawns, which have been preserved in the city's *Judenordnungen* (regulations of Jews). These attempted to regulate nearly all aspects of Jews' interactions with Christians involving credit—from the space where the extension of credit for a pawn could take place, through the different objects Jews were allowed to accept as pawns, to the different possibilities for court interventions if something went wrong in the exchange.[13] The set of Nuremberg's Judenordnungen from the 1330s include a specific clause addressing the objects that craftspeople possess, but do not own:

> It is forbidden for any tailor, coat maker, or any other craftsman, that works on a wage, to pawn to either a Christian or a Jew any

---

13. The importance of these regulations in setting the tone for interactions between Jews and Christians is attested to by the fact that these were continuously updated, reinterpreted, and reissued, as well as transferred and adopted by neighboring towns. See Gottfried Michelfelder, "Die wirtschaftliche Tätigkeit der Juden Nürnbergs im Spätmittelalter," in *Beiträge zur Wirtschaftsgeschichte Nürnbergs*, ed. Stadtarchiv Nürnberg (Nuremberg: Stadtarchiv Nürnberg, 1967), 236–60. Zvi Avneri, ed., *Germania Judaica*, vol. 2: von 1238 bis zur Mitte des 14. Jahrhunderts, part 1 (Tübingen: Mohr Siebeck, 1968), 600–601.

good that is not his, worth more than the wage he earned on it. Whoever takes such an object as a pawn or lends upon it, must return it to its owner in return for the wage that he earned, and no more than that.[14]

This regulation mentions both Jews and Christians as engaging in moneylending, and forbids them from accepting such objects. The regulation also emphasizes the value of the object that craftspeople might seek to pawn. It states that the restriction applies to objects that workers do not own, *and* which are worth more than the value of their wage. Thus, the regulation attempted to guarantee a financial threshold for workers above which they could not further leverage themselves through credit. At the same time, the designation of the wage as the threshold of legitimate activity perhaps indicates that urban authorities recognized that craftspeople and other workers constantly made use of objects or raw materials they did not own, or possibly even received their wage in the form of such objects. As a result, attempting to completely ban these activities was either unenforceable, or simply an unnecessary restraint on the steady flow of the market.

Furthermore, while instating the prohibition, the regulation does not include any punishment for the misuse of objects. That is, in the event of violation, workers were not punished for abusing the access they had to valuable objects. Rather, moneylenders, whether Jews or Christians, had to absorb the losses arising from the difference between the wage that craftspeople earned and the money lent against the particular pawn. Directing the regulatory effort toward those who lent money placed a burden on them at the time of accepting a pawn, presumably requiring them to verify that any person involved in crafts actually owned the object offered as security for a loan, or at least had fair rights to use it for these purposes. At the same time, as debtors often reneged on loans and pawns were forfeited, moneylenders who valued the pawned objects accordingly could acquire valuable objects at low prices, as evidenced in the opening case from Frankfurt.

The issue of provenance and the potential abuse of access to materials was of great concern for municipal authorities in Nuremberg at the time. In the same set of regulations, a further clause forbids Jews,

---

14. Moritz Stern, ed., *Die israelitische Bevölkerung der deutschen Städte. Ein Beitrag zur deutschen Städtegeschichte mit Benutzung archivalischer Quellen*, vol. 3: *Nürnberg im Mittelalter* (Kiel: H. Fiencke, 1894–1896), 228.

specifically mentioning both Jewish men and women, from receiving any pawn from small peddlers, servants, or maids that is worth more than one pound.[15] Additionally, these peddlers and servants must be able to verify that the pawned object belongs to them: "It is also decreed, that no Jew or Jewess should lend more than one pound heller on a pawn to a peddler (male or female), nor to a servant or maid, which should occur with a promise, who is [the owner of] the pawn [by its owner]. Whoever disobeys this must be fined 60 heller on the pound, and return the pawn."[16] Similar to the previous restriction on craftspeople and workers, this regulation sought to prevent people from using objects they did not own but had access to through their occupation, specifically from using them to leverage themselves through loans. Here too, the target of the legislation is not those who might abuse their access to objects they did not own, but rather those who accepted them as pawns. While the previous restriction on lending to workers set a certain limit to the return Jewish moneylenders could receive if violating the prohibition, this regulation includes a double punishment: the creditor must both pay a fine to the city and return the pawn. If the risk moneylenders were exposed to remained between the creditor and debtor in the case of craftspeople and workers, when regulating servants and small peddlers, Jewish moneylenders were exposed to sanctions from the council.

The difference in consequences may also express the council's outlook as to the extent of delinquency caused by the misuse of objects by distinct labor groups. Craftspeople's interaction with the discussed objects was not simply a matter of access; rather, it involved a transformative process that, under certain conditions, could confer a legitimate basis for using the objects as collateral. In contrast, servants or small peddlers, who had access to valuable objects primarily through proximity or the possibility of theft and deceit, did not have the same basis to assert rights over these items. The council's regulation thus implicitly differentiated between forms of labor and their associated claims to property. While regulating Jewish moneylending practices, the city council revealed its perspective on what constituted legitimate versus

---

15. These small peddlers, named in the sources as *käufel* for men and *käuflin* or *keuferschen* for women, often dealt with secondhand objects, and even with pawns. Deutsches Rechtswörterbuch, "Käufel," https://drw-www.adw.uni-heidelberg.de/drw-cgi/zeige?index=lemmata&term=Kaeufel.

16. Stern, *Die israelitische Bevölkerung*, 226–27.

illegitimate assertions of rights to objects, and which types of misdeeds were considered within the tolerable grey zone.

Nuremberg was not the only city where urban authorities attempted to prevent workers of different kinds from abusing the access they had to valuable objects. A similar restriction has survived from Cologne, addressing the possibility that contract workers in the textile industry would pawn raw materials unlawfully. In a decree from April 14, 1332, the brotherhood of the city's patricians (Richerzeche) authorized the brotherhood of the woolen officials of the Griechenmarkt in Cologne to reclaim unlawfully pawned raw cloth, wool, or yarn.[17] It states that in the event that some person who was given raw materials by the brotherhood for further processing would pawn them with bakers, beer brewers, and Jews, then the brotherhood could take back the raw material without compensating those who received it as pawn.[18] The regulation further alludes to the possibility that the pawning was not done innocently, but in the context of some kind of illicit activity (*anderre behendicheyde of argelijst an sij braicht würde*). However, it does not clearly specify if they considered the party committing the misdeed to be the contract worker who abused their access to raw materials, or those who accepted the materials as pawns. Regardless of which party was responsible for the offense, the decree's outcome did not focus on punishing the contract workers or demanding repayment from them. Instead, it mandated the confiscation of the raw materials from whomever held them as pawn. This response underscores the high intrinsic value of the materials, which the guild prioritized over the uncertain repayment that might be extracted from the contract workers, who were likely financially incapable of adequately compensating the brotherhood. At the same time, by reclaiming the pawned goods, the guild was not simply securing its assets but was also reinforcing its legal authority over these items. This action highlights a broader effort to maintain control over the circulation of valuable resources within the economic system, rather than merely pursuing compensation from individual workers, and to remove the economic incentive for such transactions. This strategy is evident in the decree's stipulation that holders of pawned goods

---

17. As wool and cloths were a particularly prominent part of Cologne's production, the guilds associated with these crafts likewise wielded significant political power in the city. See Franz Irsigler, *Die wirtschaftliche Stellung der Stadt Köln im 14. und 15. Jahrhundert: Strukturanalyse einer spätmittelalterlichen Exportgewerbe- und Fernhandelsstadt* (Wiesbaden: Steiner, 1979), 11–112.

18. Heinrich von Loesch, ed., *Die Kölner Zunfturkunden nebst anderen Kölner Gewerbeurkunden bis zum Jahre 1500*, vol. 2 (Bonn: P. Hansteins Verlag, 1907), 481–82 no. 735.

could not seek compensation. By threatening the uncompensated confiscation of pawned goods, the decree sought to deter potential recipients of pawned objects from accepting questionable goods, thereby curtailing market demand of unlawfully pawned materials.

While legislative efforts from both Cologne and Nuremberg sought to inhibit the same unwanted practice by targeting the same economic actors, that is, receivers of pawned objects, the context of these efforts is different. In Nuremberg, the regulations were legislated in the context of various restrictions on Jews' economic activities, with the council attempting to prevent them from engaging in what they deemed to be problematic behavior. In order to inhibit Jews from taking part in unwanted exchange, the municipality sought either to impose fines or to expose them to financial losses. In contrast, the decree from Cologne came to remedy a problem of the city's wool guild, which clearly found itself at a loss as contract workers pawned valuable raw materials to different groups in the city. In order to protect themselves from future losses and assert their authority, the guild was able to receive legal power to confiscate these wrongfully pawned textiles. Thus, the inclusion of Jews in this decree was simply in the context of those groups in the city who relied on pawns for their exchange and did not necessarily suppose any wrongdoing on their part. Nonetheless, although the context of these two regulatory efforts is quite different, they both emphasize the same normative predicament—the use of objects by people who did not own them. Likewise, for Jewish moneylenders the exposure to risks remained similar, with the possibility of confiscation close at hand.

Know Your Debtor

The restrictions on workers' ability to pawn objects were instituted not only to establish the item's provenance but also to navigate the complexities surrounding its fair use. While provenance played a crucial role, it did not always dictate an individual's legal right to pawn the item. As the regulations reveal, the concept of fair use was often intricately linked to the identity of the person pawning the item, requiring lenders to exercise careful judgment in each case. Consequently, personal acquaintance or familiarity became central to these credit transactions, as lenders were tasked with determining both the item's provenance as well as whether the individual in question possessed the requisite legal authority to pawn it. Returning to the opening case from

Frankfurt, at times the court documented the profession of the individuals appearing in front of it, and occasionally, as the specific record with the Christian goldsmith, omitting the individual's name altogether and only documenting his profession. Of the more than 10,000 court records from Frankfurt during 1330-1400, 2,693 involve an individual who is identified through a professional designation.[19] Among these cases, many deal with craftspeople pawning objects related to their crafts, whether raw materials, tools, or finished products.[20] Each of these categories of objects carried a different potential suspicion of misconduct, according to the labor group that pawned it; a dayworker could pawn work tools that belonged to the master of the workshop, and both a master and any other worker could pawn raw materials that belonged to a client.

Furthermore, there were certain crafts that were more prone to misconduct than others. As the legal efforts from both Cologne and Nuremberg suggest, the issue of determining provenance of items pawned by craftspeople was especially pertinent in textiles, which was likewise the most common category of objects appearing as pawns in the Frankfurt court records, and widely evidenced as pawns in sources from throughout the German territories at the time. With evidence of Jews receiving a wide variety of textiles, ranging from raw uncut cloth, scraps of fabric, and finished garments, to household textiles, the provenance of textiles was an extremely acute problem. However, out of nearly one thousand cases in the *Frankfurter Gerichtsbücher* from the periods before and after the Black Death that involve the transfer of some sort of pawned textile, remarkably, only thirty mention a craftsperson engaged in the textile industry. In only six of these did textile workers pawn unfinished textiles or raw cloth. In all the rest they instead pawned finished coats,[21] skirts,[22] sheets,[23] and the like, objects found in any household and therefore not strictly related to their craft. Tailors, weavers, fabric shearers, and coat makers all appear on the lists,

---

19. Data based on my own database of the court records. David Schnur mentions similar estimations in David Schnur, "Wirtschaftliche Beziehungen zwischen jüdischen Geldverleihern und christlichen Handwerkern im spätmittelalterlichen Frankfurt am Main," in *Ökonomische Glaubensfragen: Strukturen und Praktiken jüdischen und christlichen Kleinkredits im Spätmittelalter*, ed. Gerhard Fouquet and Sven Rabeler (Stuttgart: Franz Steiner Verlag, 2018), 75.
20. David Schnur, "Wirtschaftliche Beziehungen," 63-98.
21. Kracauer, *Urkundenbuch*, 466, 496, 516, 547, 554, 557, 631, 658, 701, 765.
22. Kracauer, *Urkundenbuch*, 466, 520, 521, 531, 547, 554, 557, 631, 742, 765, 807.
23. Kracauer, *Urkundenbuch*, 495, 520, 521, 549, 761.

featuring as the highest represented craft. However, most of the cases involving them do not specify what the pawn was, a common practice in the court records, or simply noted that it involved other objects, such as pots and pans, grain, paternosters, or even armor. Contrary to the general tendency reflected in the court records of craftspeople pawning objects related to their crafts, it seems that textile workers refrained from this practice. Thus, it is possible that issues of provenance either prevented textile workers from pawning objects related to their craft, or provided a disincentive for Jewish moneylenders to accept such pawns from textile workers, or perhaps made those who did engage in this practice find ways to conceal it before the court.

Unlike textile workers, one profession that tended to pawn objects associated with their craft was goldsmiths. Out of the fifty cases in the Frankfurt court records that involve goldsmiths, twenty specifically mention a pawn. Of these, fifteen involve pawned objects that are related to their craft: a gilded belt,[24] silver belt,[25] silver cup,[26] silver jewelry,[27] or simply silver.[28] Interestingly, other than goldsmiths, these objects are mostly mentioned in the lists in relation to lords and nobles, and once a noble servant.[29] While the value of the loans these similar objects secured varied tremendously, it does raise questions as to the goldsmiths' legal possession of the items they pawned, which they eventually defaulted on, leading to the intervention of the court. Furthermore, in many cases the court records also evidence that the goldsmiths were not local to Frankfurt, thus raising the question whether Jewish moneylenders who extended these craftspeople credit had the ability or the desire to verify whether they were the rightful possessors of the raw materials they pawned with them.[30]

An early fifteenth-century responsum sent to R. Israel Isserlein, preserved in his book *Terumat ha-Deshen*, provides further insight into the possible consequences for moneylenders who received problematic pawns from goldsmiths. This example demonstrates that even in the

---

24. Kracauer, *Urkundenbuch*, 784.
25. Kracauer, *Urkundenbuch*, 798.
26. Kracauer, *Urkundenbuch*, 864.
27. Kracauer, *Urkundenbuch*, 533.
28. Kracauer, *Urkundenbuch*, 852.
29. Kracauer, *Urkundenbuch*, 833.
30. Kracauer, *Urkundenbuch*, 798, 533, 864, 801, 841.

case of previous acquaintance between the creditor and debtor, questions of provenance could pose a challenge to the exchange:

> Reuven gave a Christian smith a silver belt to have it fixed, and the Christian, after fixing it, pawned the belt with Shimon, and Shimon already had other pawns from that smith. And the smith said to Shimon: "take out all the pawns you have [from me] and calculate the principal and interest, and on top of these lend me more in coin and this belt will be pawned to you for everything because it is worth so and so [the value of all the loans together]" and so Shimon did. After this the smith ran away [from town] for he had so much debt, and when Reuven came to inquire after his belt, he found it pawned with Shimon. And Reuven came to Shimon to claim his belt, and Shimon replied "it is true that I have a belt in pawn from that smith, but I did not know that it belonged to you."[31]

As this case indicates, the smith abused the access he had to a valuable object, embezzled the belt, and took advantage of his longstanding relationship with Shimon to relieve himself of his debts. Through his access to Shimon and their prior acquaintance, he was able to pawn this valuable belt, which was worth more than all the other pawns that Shimon already had from him, and receive an additional loan. We may wonder whether Shimon had any suspicions regarding the origin of this belt, and how was it that this indebted smith was suddenly able to pawn such a valuable object. In this case, we see that previous acquaintance with the debtor did not protect this Jewish moneylender from receiving an object that was of illegitimate origin. Quite the contrary, perhaps his previous acquaintance with the smith is what made Shimon throw caution to the wind and enter into a perilous business exchange. Furthermore, the longstanding relationship between Shimon and the smith suggests that Shimon was not necessarily functioning under the assumption or expectation that the smith would repay his loans. The fact that the smith already had several pawns on hold with Shimon, that is, that he had taken out several loans that he had not yet repaid, did not prevent Shimon from extending him further credit. This raises many questions as to the creditworthiness of the smith, and what indicators were used to gauge the potential risks, or success of the

---

31. Israel Isserlein, *Terumat ha-Deshen*, ed. Shmuel Avitan (Jerusalem: Avitan, 1990), §309.

exchange. Most of all, this case demonstrates that for this moneylender default was not the decisive factor in determining to whom to extend credit.

While trying to adjudicate the conflict between the two Jews, both deceived by the smith, R. Isserlein provides illuminating details to his understanding of the current legal system, and of the risks of receiving pawned goods from craftspeople:

> And even if Shimon had to return the belt to Reuven according to the laws of the land, as the laws now are that anything that is stolen from the owners needs to be returned to them, the same of all [objects] that craftspeople or the custodians sell on their own that is of another. In any case, if following the laws of the land, Reuven must give Shimon the interest as well as the principal, as it is common law for Jews from the kingdom in some lands that when lending on a stolen object and the owner [of the object] comes to reclaim it they [the owner] must pay the principal and interest.[32]

At the conclusion of the reply, after discussing the different interpretations according to Jewish law and whether the craftsperson acquired property rights in the belt due to the work he had done on the object,[33] R. Isserlein established that the belt should be treated as stolen property.[34] He then moved on to discuss how even if this case had been addressed through Christian customary law, the final outcome for the disputing parties would be the same. He thus begins by detailing his knowledge of two prevalent legal practices. First, if someone is found with property that belongs to another, it must be returned to its rightful owner without compensation. That is, according to his previous interpretation that the belt should be treated as stolen property, this legal conclusion required that the belt be returned to Reuven, its rightful owner. In a similar vein, the second legal practice R. Isserlein discussed states that if someone is found with property that was sold by

---

32. Isserlein, *Terumat ha-Deshen*, §309:

33. In Bava Kama tractate 78b–79a, the question is discussed whether a craftsperson or artisan acquires property rights over the object which they worked on until they receive payment for the work which they had done. The Talmudic sages were in disagreement over this question, and what extent of possession rights the artisan held over the object.

34. According to the Talmudic market regulation (*Takannat ha-Shuk*), if a person unknowingly bought or received as pawn a stolen object, and if the original rightful owner were to place claims on that object, then the original owner must compensate the person who unknowingly bought or received that item as pawn for all they had paid for it.

craftspeople or custodians who did not own them, they must also return the property to the rightful owner without compensation. Thus, in both these cases Reuven was to have his belt returned to him according to customary law.

However, once introducing a discussion of customary law, R. Isserlein stated that it is necessary to address a third legal custom, which applied directly to Jews, referring to the unusual trade privilege known as the *Marktschutzrecht*. This privilege, first appearing in Jews' 1090 settlement privileges from Emperor Heinrich IV, allowed Jews in the German Empire to receive compensation for stolen items found in their possession from the rightful owner, contrary to the prevailing legal situation which considered individuals who possessed stolen goods as thieves.[35] According to R. Isserlein's interpretation of the law, the Marktschutzrecht eclipsed the prevailing legal practices attached to craftspeople's unlawful pawning of objects. This is because the Marktschutzrecht was a privilege that excluded Jews from the general legal conditions applicable to all in the empire. Accordingly, the person who had to absorb the losses was not Shimon, who did not take sufficient measures to

---

35. Dietrich von Gladiss and Alfred Gawlik, eds., *Monumenta Germaniae Historica: Diplomata Regum et Imperatorum Germaniae VI: Heinrici IV*, vol. 2 (Weimar: Harrassowitz, 1952): for Speyer: 543–47, no. 411; for Worms: 547–49, no. 412. This privilege has been the topic of intense scholarly research and great debate since the early twentieth century. Initial research into this privilege and its Talmudic origin was undertaken as part of anti-Semitic argumentations by Herbert Meyer, "Das Hehlerrecht der Juden und Lombarden," *Forschungen zur Judenfrage* 1 (1937): 92–109; Herbert Meyer, "Das jüdische Hehlerrecht," *Deutsche Rechtswissenschaft* 2 (1937): 97–111. These were later rebutted by Guido Kisch and Boaz Cohen, see Guido Kisch, "The Jewish Law of Concealment," *Historia Judaica* 1 (1938): 1–30; Boaz Cohen, "The So-Called Jüdisches Hehlerrecht in the Light of Jewish Law," *Historia Judaica* 4 (1942): 145–53. More recent studies have drawn attention to a variety of issues stemming from the privilege: Friedrich Lotter reexamined the question of Talmudic origin and the privilege's scope of influence in the German Empire, Friedrich Lotter, "Talmudisches Recht in den Judenprivilegien Heinrichs IV?" *Archiv für Kulturgeschichte* 72 (1990): 23–62, and Friedrich Lotter, "The Scope and Effectiveness of Imperial Jewry Law in the High Middle Ages," *Jewish History* 4 (1989): 31–58. https://doi.org/10.1007/BF01669755. Christine Magin has considered this privilege in relation to the legal position of Jews in the German Empire, in Christine Magin, *Wie es umb der iuden recht stet: Der Status der Juden in spätmittelalterlichen deutschen Rechtsbüchern* (Göttingen: Wallstein Verlag, 1999), 354. Jörg Müller delved into accusations against Jews for dealing in stolen goods, Jörg Müller, "'Gestolen und ainem juden versetzt,' Jüdische Pfandleiher zwischen legaler Geschäftspraxis und Hehlereivorwurf," *Aschkenas* 20, no. 2 (2010): 439–78, https://doi.org/10.1515/asch-2010-0019. Furthermore, many of the studies dealing with Jews' access to ecclesiastic objects discuss this privilege, as several of its later iterations in territorial and urban law involve specific limitations of the pawning of ecclesiastic objects. Müller, "Zur Verpfändung sakraler Kultgegenstände an Juden im mittelalterlichen Reich"; Wiedl, "Sacred Objects in Jewish Hands: Two Case Studies."

ensure that the belt was of proper origin, but rather Reuven, who had simply given his belt to be fixed.

The risks of craftspeople misusing the materials they had received for repairs, or even the raw materials they were given for producing new goods, extended beyond the risks to moneylenders.[36] The responsum details how, essentially, any economic exchange with those engaging in crafts posed risks stemming from the possibility that these individuals would misuse the access they had to objects they did not own. Thus, the boundary between theft, misuse, abuse of power, or simply getting by in the urban economy was often quite blurry. While these questions are discussed in the responsum within the context of a conflict between two Jews and through the Jewish legal system, legal authorities throughout the empire attempted to restrain these practices. However, the prevalence of these practices across different places and long periods of time actually demonstrates that objects were often expected to be repurposed and reused for temporary amounts of time, allowing people much necessary credit lines during times of shortages. Within these expectations, the question remains what delimited the boundary between licit and illicit use of objects. Narrowing down to the individual exchange between a particular Jew and a certain craftsperson, the responsum demonstrates how in daily transactions, people often chose to disregard risks and in fact operated within a grey zone, leaving them to rely on other compensation mechanisms in their businesses.

Objects on the Move

In a market where objects were constantly in circulation, being repurposed and reconfigured, there were many opportunities to mishandle and abuse goods. These opportunities were readily available to those whose professional occupation provided them with constant access to objects that were far beyond their own financial abilities: tailors, goldsmiths, workers, and service people. Yet, as objects were such fluid stores of value, routinely used for temporary purposes to cover different

---

36. Such a case is discussed in Andreas Lehnertz's article on Shofar production, where Christian craftspeople allegedly replaced valuable and ritually preferable ram's horns with buck goat horns. Andreas Lehnertz, "Dismantling a Monopoly: Jews, Christians, and the Production of Shofarot in Fifteenth-Century Germany," *Medieval Encounters* 27, no. 4–5 (2021): 360–86, https://doi.org/10.1163/15700674-12340112. Likewise, Valentin Groebner mentions similar difficulties in fifteenth-century Nuremberg; see Groebner, *Ökonomie Ohne Haus*, 179–80.

costs, the boundary between abuse of access to goods and legitimate recycling of purposes was often indistinct. For the debtors using these highly valuable objects as security for loans, which most likely were not their own, this was either a way to stretch beyond their financial means or a routine strategy for managing periods of shortage. It is difficult to determine whether these attempts were related to times of personal economic hardship, or whether they reflect much broader attitudes toward objects circulating in the market, and individuals' ability to benefit from objects in their temporary possession.

For Jewish moneylenders, who often relied on pawns in their credit exchange, ensuring that the object they received as pawn was properly and rightfully transferred to them was often crucial to their ability to profit from the transaction, as debtors frequently defaulted on loans. At the same time, in a reality of objects constantly in flux, debtors of certain social and professional groups were immediately suspect of mishandling objects. Such suspicion is also reflected in the regulatory efforts of urban authorities. Nonetheless, as the evidence from the Frankfurt court records demonstrates, such regulatory efforts did not prevent Jews from extending credit to dayworkers, craftspeople, and similar social groups, which accounted for nearly a quarter of all the claims in the court records. On the contrary, the questionable origin of certain objects, or of certain debtors, may have offered opportunities for moneylenders to enjoy access to objects of much higher value than the loan they secured, meaning that the risk premium could, at times, have paid off.

These dynamics highlight the law's active role in shaping economic behavior, as regulations did not merely reflect social practices but worked to define and stabilize categories of ownership and use. By establishing what constituted legitimate possession and proper use, these laws influenced not only the actions of debtors and moneylenders but also shaped the perception of risk associated with various objects. In this way, the legal framework functioned as an active force, seeking to impose order on the inherently fluid circulation of goods. Examining the objects that Jewish moneylenders received as pawns, and the social dynamics attached to the debtors who transferred them, reveals the complex world of credit relations. From high-ranking clergy and nobles to dayworkers and unknown peasants, the same Jewish moneylenders often supplied credit to a range of clients. What is more, the same objects offered as pawn by different social groups, say a golden belt offered by a nobleman versus that offered by a goldsmith, although presumably of equal monetary value, involved a very different set of risks. Thus, the function of pawned objects was far more abstruse than providing security or insurance for a loan by acting as a physical replacement for its monetary value. Rather, the value of pawned objects was constantly being renegotiated by the dynamics between social knowledge, legal norms, and the object's actual monetary value. Further research is required to fully comprehend the function of pawns in credit transactions, and particularly in Jewish-Christian exchange. At the same time, examining the credit relationships between Jewish moneylenders and non-elite debtors through the risks associated with the particular objects they provided as pawns reveals the wide range of relationships Jewish moneylenders maintained across medieval society, going beyond the elite moneylenders and their business concerns.

Further Readings

Clemens, Gabriele B., ed. *Schuldenlast und Schuldenwert. Kreditnetzwerke in der europäischen Geschichte, 1300–1900.* Trier: Kliomedia, 2008.

French, Katherine L. *Household Goods and Good Households in Late Medieval London: Consumption and Domesticity after the Plague.* Philadelphia: Pennsylvania University Press, 2021.

Groebner, Valentin. *Ökonomie ohne Haus: Zum Wirtschaften armer Leute in Nürnberg am Ende des 15. Jahrhunderts.* Göttingen: Vandenhoeck & Ruprecht, 1993.

Howell, Martha C. *Commerce before Capitalism in Europe, 1300–1600.* Cambridge: Cambridge University Press, 2010.

Irsigler, Franz. *Die wirtschaftliche Stellung der Stadt Köln im 14. und 15. Jahrhundert: Strukturanalyse einer spätmittelalterlichen Exportgewerbe- und Fernhandelsstadt.* Wiesbaden: Steiner, 1979.

Lotter, Friedrich. "The Scope and Effectiveness of Imperial Jewry Law in the High Middle Ages." *Jewish History* 4 (1989): 31-58. doi.org/10.1007/BF01669755.

Magin, Christine. *Wie es umb der iuden recht stet: Der Status der Juden in spätmittelalterlichen deutschen Rechtsbüchern.* Göttingen: Wallstein Verlag, 1999.

Michelfelder, Gottfried. "Die wirtschaftliche Tätigkeit der Juden Nürnbergs im Spätmittelalter." In *Beiträge zur Wirtschaftsgeschichte Nürnbergs,* edited by Stadtarchiv Nürnberg, 236-60. Nuremberg: Stadtarchiv Nürnberg, 1967.

Müller, Jörg R. "Zur Verpfändung sakraler Kultgegenstände an Juden im mittelalterlichen Reich: Norm und Praxis." In *Pro multis beneficiis—Festschrift für Friedhelm Burgard: Forschungen zur Geschichte der Juden und des Trierer Raumes,* edited by Sigfrid Hirbodian, 179-204. Trier: Kliomedia, 2012.

Rothmann, Michael. *Die Frankfurter Messen im Mittelalter.* Stuttgart: Franz Steiner Verlag, 1998.

Schnur, David. "Wirtschaftliche Beziehungen zwischen jüdischen Geldverleihern und christlichen Handwerkern im spätmittelalterlichen Frankfurt am Main." In *Ökonomische Glaubensfragen: Strukturen und Praktiken jüdischen und christlichen Kleinkredits im Spätmittelalter,* edited by Gerhard Fouquet and Sven Rabeler, 63-98. Stuttgart: Franz Steiner Verlag, 2018.

Shatzmiller, Joseph. "Church Articles: Pawns in the Hands of Jewish Moneylenders." In *Wirtschaftsgeschichte der mittelalterlichen Juden: Fragen und Einschätzungen,* edited by Michael Toch, 93-102. Berlin: De Gruyter, 2008.

Shatzmiller, Joseph. *Cultural Exchange: Jews, Christians, and Art in the Medieval Marketplace.* Princeton: Princeton University Press, 2017.

Signori, Gabriela. "Gelihen Geltz. Christliche Geldleihe aus dem Blinckwinkel spätmittelalterlicher Gerichtsbücher." In *Ökonomische Glaubenfragen. Strukturen und Praktiken jüdischen und christlichen Kleinkredits im Spätmittelalter,* edited by Gerhard Fouquet and Sven Raveler, 21-42. Stuttgart: Franz Steiner Verlag, 2018.

Signori, Gabriela. *Schuldenwirtschaft. Konsumenten- und Hypothekarkredite im spätmittelalterlichen Basel.* Konstanz: UVK Verlagsgesellschaft, 2015.

Smail, Daniel Lord. *Legal Plunder: Households and Debt Collection in Late Medieval Europe.* Cambridge, MA: Harvard University Press, 2016.

Smail, Daniel Lord. "Persons and Things in Marseille and Lucca, 1300-1450." In *The Oxford Handbook of History and Material Culture,* edited by Ivan Gaskell and Sarah Anne Carter, 378-96. Oxford: Oxford University Press, 2020.

Todeschini, Giacomo. "Christian Perceptions of Jewish Economic Activity in the Middle Ages." In *Wirtschaftsgeschichte der mittelalterlichen Judenn: Fragen und Einschätzungen,* ed. Michael Toch, 1-16. Berlin: De Gruyter, 2008.

Todeschini, Giacomo. "Jewish Usurers, Blood Libel, and the Second-Hand Economy: The Medieval Origins of a Stereotype (from the Thirteenth to the Fifteenth Century)." In *The Medieval Roots of Antisemitism: Continuities and Discontinuities from the Middle Ages to the Present Day,* edited by Jonathan Adams and Cordelia Heß, 341-51. New York: Routledge, 2018.

Wenninger, Markus J. "Geld und Politik. Spezialprivilegien für jüdische Großbankiers des 14. Jahrhunderts im Südostalpenraum." *Aschkenas* 20 (2012): 305-28. doi.org/10.1515/asch-2010-0012.

Wiedl, Birgit. "Sacred Objects in Jewish Hands: Two Case Studies." In *Jews and Christians in Medieval Europe: The Historiographical Legacy of Bernhard Blumenkranz,* edited by Philippe Buc, Martha Keil, and John Victor Tolan. 57-78. Turnhout: Brepols, 2016.

CHAPTER 9

Beyond Kiddushin
The Medieval Ashkenazic Betrothal Ring

Ido Noy

One of the most familiar and iconic moments of the Jewish wedding, both in the Middle Ages, as well as today, is the *kiddushin* ceremony, during which the groom presents his bride with a betrothal ring, known in Hebrew as a kiddushin ring, as an act of sanctification.[1] The Mishnah lists three ways to sanctify a woman as one's wife, one of which is "purchasing" the bride by presenting her with money or any valuable object.[2] By the early Middle Ages, there is evidence that Jews in the Land of Israel began to use rings for this purpose, likely absorbing the custom from the Romans and early Christians.[3] Nevertheless, it is only later that rings become the conventional

---

1. Mishnah Kiddushin 2:1.
2. Mishnah Kiddushin 2:1.
3. Explicitly mentioned in the *Book of Disputes between East and West*, which was probably written in the eighth century in the Land of Israel: "A ring does not sanctify marriage according to people of the East. Residents of the Land of Israel consider it [sufficient to] fully sanctify a marriage." For the English translation based on the Mordekhai Margaliot edition, see Leor Jacobi, *The Book of Disputes Between East and West or A Treasury of Alternate Customs from the Land of Israel and from Babylon* (Jerusalem: Leor Jacobi, 2012), 4, §25. On the similarities and differences between the customs of the Roman and Jewish weddings, see Daniel Sperber, *The Jewish Life Cycle: Custom, Lore and Iconography* (Ramat Gan: Bar-Ilan University Press, 2008), 931–32; Boaz Cohen, "On the Theme of Betrothal in Jewish and Roman Law," *Proceedings of the American Academy for Jewish Research* 18 (1948–49): 67–135.

object for kiddushin. One can assume that when Jews emigrated from Italy to Germany and northern France in the ninth century, they presumably brought this custom with them, but the earliest evidence of its adoption among the Jewish communities in Europe dates to no earlier than the eleventh century, with examples from Italy,[4] Germany,[5] northern France,[6] Spain, and Provence.[7] From this evidence it would appear that the use of the ring as part of the sanctification ceremony (kiddushin) was still in flux during this period. Initially, the kiddushin (betrothal ceremony, also known as *erusin*) and *nissuin* (nuptial/marriage ceremony) were two separate events, sometimes taking place a full year apart. The ring was given as part of kiddushin. By the eleventh century the two ceremonies had been combined into one, and the kiddushin ring was given to the bride under the marriage canopy (*huppah*) as part of the wedding ceremony.[8]

Since the act of kiddushin was sometimes performed by messengers, one may speculate as to whether the kiddushin ring was meant to be placed on the bride's finger by the groom during the ceremony. In cases such as when the bride is *niddah* (ritually impure as a result of menstruation) the groom is instructed to "not touch her [the bride] but let the ring fall on her finger."[9] There are also stories of boys who would throw a ring on a girl's lap as a joke.[10] These examples suggest that there was no real obligation for the groom to actually place the ring

---

4. Among the earliest evidence for this practice is a piyyut attributed to Amittai son of Shephattiah from Oria in southern Italy who lived in the second half of the ninth century. See *Megillat Ahimaaz*, ed. Benjamin Klar (Jerusalem Tarshish, 1974), 52–4, §107 (Hebrew); *Shirei Amitai*, ed. David Yona (Jerusalem: Achshav, 1975), 23, 51 (Hebrew).

5. *Ma'aseh ha-Geonim*, ed. Abraham Epstein and Jacob Freimann (Berlin: Mekitze Nirdamim, 1909), 61, §66 (Hebrew).

6. E.g., in writings attributed to Rashi. See *Sefer ha-Orah*, ed. Shlomo Buber (Lvov: Shlomo Buber, 1905), vol. 2, 178–79 (Hebrew); *Teshuvot Rashi*, ed. Israel S. Elfenbein (New York: Israel S. Elfenbein, 1943), 222, §198, 206, §232 (Hebrew).

7. As appear in a question sent to the Rashba (Shlomo ben Avraham ibn Aderet, 1235–1310). *She'elot u-Teshuvot ha-Rashba*, 7 vols (Jerusalem: Makhon Yerushalaim, 1997), 1:530, §166 (Hebrew).

8. In Ashkenaz in the eleventh century and then later in Provence and most of Spain. See Aaron H. Freimann, *Seder Kiddushin ve-Nissuin* (Jerusalem: Mosad Harav Kook, 1945), 29–31 (Hebrew). Avraham Grossman, *Pious and Rebellious—Jewish Women in Medieval Europe* (Waltham, MA: Brandeis University Press, 2004), 49–51; Zeev Falk, *Marriage and Divorce: Reforms in the Family Life of German-French Jewry* (Jerusalem: Mifal Hashikhpul, 1961), 32–95 (Hebrew).

9. Jacob ben Moses ha-Levi Moellin, *Sefer Maharil, Minhagim*, ed. Shlomo Spitzer (Jerusalem: Makhon Yerushalaim, 1989), 467, §5 (Hebrew).

10. Meir ben Baruch of Rothenburg (Maharam, thirteenth century), *Teshuvot Maharam* (Prague Edition), eds. Jacob Farbstein et al. (Jerusalem: Makhon Yerushalaim, 2014), 542, §993 (Hebrew).

on the bride's finger in order for the act of sanctification to take place. However, as some of other sources in this chapter suggest, over time the act of placing the ring on the bride's finger in fact gained ceremonial significance. This is likely due to the role that rings played in the marriage ceremony within the broader society. When worn in public during the ceremony and later throughout their lifetime, the ring also had a distinct social role in publicizing the couple's (and their families') consent to the marriage and the formation of a new conjugal family.[11]

Given the numerous references to it in medieval Jewish literature, along with depictions of it in illustrations of weddings and love scenes found in illuminated medieval Hebrew manuscripts from Germany and elsewhere, as well as material evidence gathered from medieval treasure troves, it would appear that the kiddushin ring eventually came to take on greater meaning and importance beyond its halakhic significance and ceremonial function.[12] The rich and complex picture arising from the sources compels us to look beyond the confines of the kiddushin ceremony to consider these additional levels of meaning, by determining how Ashkenazic women wore, used, and kept their kiddushin rings throughout their lives. Furthermore, by reading between the lines, we can uncover a range of non-elite voices, each contributing to a more nuanced understanding of everyday life.

This article is divided into two. The first section deals with symbolic perceptions of the kiddushin ring and the development of traditions and practices revolving around it. In this section I will suggest possible reasons for why such rings continued to be in use by their owners throughout their marital life, not only as a valuable piece of property but also as a means for both increasing the likelihood of a successful marriage, and broadcasting the marital, social, and economic status, and piety, of its owner. The second part of the article will discuss the ceremonial, functional, and symbolic roles of a distinct type of ring often referred to as a Mazal Tov ring.[13] I further suggest that in addition

---

11. On consent in Jewish marriage see Falk, *Marriage and Divorce*, 92–98; Grossman, *Pious and Rebellious*, 55–63.

12. Including sources from regions outside of Ashkenaz highlights the interconnectedness of medieval Jewish communities through cross-regional exchanges of goods and practices, which helps explain the similarities in their material culture and reveals shared customs and traditions relating to the Kiddushin ring.

13. Ido Noy, "The Mazal Tov Ring and the Ketubbah," in *In and Out, Between and Beyond: Jewish Daily Life in Medieval Europe*, eds. Elisheva Baumgarten and Ido Noy (Jerusalem: The Hebrew University of Jerusalem, 2021), 89–94.

to their function as a kiddushin ring, these objects were likely to have served other purposes as well.

Earthly and Divine Marriage

The fact that some grooms not only presented their brides with kiddushin rings but also physically placed the ring on their finger, led to halakhic discussions over the specifics of this ceremonial act. Various sources indicate that the Jews placed the ring on the index finger of the right hand, as indeed, they still do today. R. Elazar ben Yehuda of Worms (Rokeach. ca. 1160–1230) noted that the groom must "give the bride a ring on the second finger adjacent to the thumb and say: 'with this ring you are consecrated to me.'"[14] Maharil (Yaakov ben Moshe Levi Moellin of Mainz, ca. 1365–1427) also writes that the groom should place the ring on the finger near the thumb.[15] The same idea appears in non-Jewish sources as well.[16] Visual findings, however, do not necessarily align with the textual evidence. For example, in the Second Nuremberg Haggadah, produced in Franconia between 1470 and 1480, an illustration of the wedding of Moshe and Tziporah (figure 9.1) appears in which Moses is depicted taking a massive gold ring in his right hand and placing it on Tziporah extended index or middle finger.[17] Hovering above the couple is the Hebrew inscription: "Accept this betrothal

---

14. Elazar ben Yehuda of Worms, *Sefer ha-Rokeah*, ed. Baruch S. Shneorson (Jerusalem: S. Sheinfeld, 1960), 238, §351 (Hebrew). The same idea appears in *Sefer ha-Asufot* a collection of halakhot written by anonymous Ashkenazic sages. See Shmuel E. Stern, *Erusin ve-Nisuin le-Rabboteinu ha-Rishonim* (Bnei-Berak: Pardes, 1990), 38.

15. Moshe ha-Levi Moellin, *Sefer Maharil*, 467, §5. A similar custom is mentioned much later in seventeenth-century Worms by Juspa Schammes. See Erik Zimmer, "Minhagim shel R. Yuzpa Shammash," *Sinai* 86 (1979/80): 42 (Hebrew); Juspa Shammes, *Minhagim d-KK Wormeise*, 2 vols., eds. Shlomo B. Hamburger and Erik Zimmer (Jerusalem: Makhon Yerushalaim, 1992) 2:37, §231 (Hebrew); and Daniel Sperber, *Minhagei Yisrael: Mekorot ve-Toldot*, 8 vols. (Jerusalem: Mosad Harav Kook, 2003), 4:92–93, 57–58 (Hebrew).

16. E.g., Victor von Carben (1422–1515), a rabbi who converted to Christianity in 1476–77 and later became a priest and a Hebraist, gave another explanation for choosing the index finger. In his essay "Dem durchleuchtigsten hochgebornen Fursten und Herren," von Carben notes that Jewish grooms place the ring on the bride's index finger while being careful not to place it on the middle finger by accident, giving the explanation that this is because Joseph sanctifies Mary by placing a ring on her middle finger. See Von Carben, "Dem durchleuchtigsten hochgebornen Fursten und Herren" (Köln, 1508), chapter 8. On Von Carben and other Hebraists, see Yaacov Deutsch, *Jews and Judaism through Christian Eyes in Early Modern Europe: Close Yet Different* (New York: Oxford University Press, 2011), 25.

17. This scene does not refer only to the biblical text (Exod. 2:21) but also to the midrash; see "Moses," in Judah D. Eisenstein, *Otzar Midrashim* (A Treasury of Midrashim), 2 vols. (New York: Resnik, Menshael & Co., 1915), 2:359 (Hebrew).

FIGURE 9.1 The wedding of Moses and Zipporah (detail). Second Nuremberg Haggadah, 1470–80, Franconia, David Sofer Collection London 12v. Photo courtesy of Prof. Shalom Sabar.

and with a ring we are betrothed."[18] The different customs reflected in Ashkenazic manuscripts thus suggests that several traditions existed at the same time.[19] It is also possible that contemporary illustrators sometimes paid little attention to small details or, in the case of non-Jewish illuminators, might have had limited knowledge or understanding of Jewish wedding customs.

---

18. Unfortunately, Tziporah's hand in the "sister" Haggadah, the Yehuda Haggadah (9. 2) was not well preserved. Compare the Krems Ketubbah dated to the Jewish year 5152 (1391-92) made for the marriage of Zemah, daughter of R. Aaron, and Shalom, son of R. Menahem in Krems an der Donau (?) (9.11). Vienna, ÖNb Cod. Hebr. 218. The illustration depicts the focal point of their engagement, when Shalom is reaching out with his right hand in which there is a massive gold ring set with a red gemstone that he is apparently about to give to his bride, who stands ready on the other side of the ketubbah. Even though the palm of her hand is now difficult to make out, an error made by the illustrator, who drew Zamah's right hand once, then erased it and tried again, teaches us that her middle finger was the one intended for kiddushin.

19. Some wedding illustrations from fifteenth-century northern Italy also indicate that there were different customs regarding on which finger to place the kiddushin ring—whether on the middle finger or other fingers such as the index finger and the ring finger: Parma miscellany produced in the third quarter of the fifteenth century. Parma, Biblioteca Palatina Ms. Parm. 3596, fol. 275r; The Rothschild Miscellany produced in Ferrara ca. 1470. Jerusalem, Israel Museum, Ms130/51, fol.120v; Jewish prayer book (siddur) produced in 1481 in Pesaro, Budapest, Library of the Hungarian Academy of Sciences, Ms. A380, fol. 231r (9.7); the Life Cycle Miscellany, Produced in Italy in 1452. Zurich, René Braginsky collection (previously Montefiore library collection), Ms. 259, fol.11v; Arba'ah Turim produced in Mantua in 1435. Vatican, Biblioteca Apostolica Vaticana, Cod. Ross 555, fol.220r.

FIGURE 9.2 The wedding of Moses and Zipporah (detail). Yehudah Haggadah, 1470–80, Franconia, Israel Museum, Ms.180/50, fol.11v. Photo © The Israel Museum, Jerusalem, by Ardon Bar-Hama.

Medieval Hebrew sources from different genres shed more light on where to place the kiddushin ring, as well as the symbolic reasons behind it. For instance, in Exodus Rabbah (33:7), God is portrayed as a groom and Israel as his bride, with the giving of the Torah at Mt. Sinai perceived as a festive marriage ceremony and the Torah itself standing in for the marriage contract (*ketubbah*; pl. *ketubbot*) or the kiddushin ring.[20] This link between the heavenly and earthly marriage, noted in the name of the Maharam of Rothenburg (ca. 1215–93), explains the development of the kiddushin blessing during the Middle Ages: "The Maharam, may his soul rest in peace, says that [the reason] for the groom to say "Behold, you are consecrated to me according to the law of Moses and Israel," is because we find in many places that God

---

20. According to another set of allegories based on the Book of Proverbs, the groom symbolized the people of Israel (or Moses, who also functions as a bridegroom), while the Torah symbolized the bride, who is described as the daughter of God. See Sarit Shalev-Eyni, "Human Aspects of the Torah and Art in the Middle Ages," *Zion* 73 (2008): 153–62 (Hebrew). See also Shalev-Eyni, "Iconography of Love: Illustration of Bride and Bridegroom in Ashkenazi Prayerbooks of the Thirteenth and Fourteenth Century," *Studies in Iconography* 26 (2005): 27–57; Ruth Bartal, "Medieval Images of 'Sacred Love': Jewish and Christian Perspectives," *Assaph: Studies in Art History* 2 (1996): 93–110; Naomi Feuchtwanger-Sarig, "The Coronation of the Virgin and of the Bride," *Journal of Jewish Art* 12/13 (1986/87): 213–24.

betroth Israel via the Torah."²¹ The text goes on to explain that beginning the blessing with the Hebrew letter *heh* was meant to symbolize the kiddushin ring as well as the five books of the Torah.²² A similar notion was stated earlier, in the eleventh-century Ashkenazic exegesis for *Ar'a Raqdah* (And the Earth Danced) an Aramaic *piyyut* for Shavuot that appears in the Vitry Mahzor: "Five rings on the five fingers of her right hand to betroth and sanctify her to him, and these are the five books of Torah."²³ The commentary then goes on to explain that the right hand is used because the Torah was given to the children of Israel by the right hand of God.²⁴

Apart from the theologically symbolic linkage between the earthly and the divine marriage, the use of the number five and its Hebrew numerological equivalent "heh" were believed to have apotropaic power and were therefore incorporated into amulets and other talismans. In the Kabbalah, the monogrammaton, or one-letter name *heh* is one of the ineffable names of God and often appears on protective objects.²⁵ The association of the hand and its five fingers with the might of God is even more ancient, appearing in the Bible, where, for example, the Fourth Commandment relates that God redeemed the Children of Israel from Egypt with "a mighty hand and an outstretched arm."²⁶ Examples of Jewish and Christian art from Late Antiquity often use an open palm to depict the invisible God, referring to it as "the hand of God."²⁷ In an example from the Birds' Head Haggadah (produced in

---

21. Shimshon ben Tzadok, *Sefer Tashbetz Katan: Piskei Maharam mi-Rutenberg*, ed. Shlomo Angel (Jerusalem: Machon Yerushalayim, 2011), 263–68, §466–7 (Hebrew).

22. That is, the first letter *heh* at the first word of the blessing "You are hereby betrothed unto me . . ." ("Harei at mekudeshet li . . .").

23. Simhah ben Samuel of Vitry, *Mahzor Vitry*, ed. Simon H. Horowitz 2 vols. (Nürnberg, 1889), 1:336, §302 (the piyyut), 1:311, §287 (the interpretation) (Hebrew). Simhah ben Samuel of Vitry, *Mahzor Vitry*, ed. Aryeh Goldschmidt, 3 vols. (Jerusalem: Mekhon Otsar Haposekim, 2004), 2:492, §7 (Hebrew). See Israel M. Ta-Shma, *Keneset Mehkarim* 4 vols. (Jerusalem: Mosad Bialik, 2004), 1:77–87 (Hebrew).

24. "Velama beymina. Mishum shene'emar 'miyemino esh dat lamo'." Compare with BT, Berakhot.62a: "Rava said: Because the Torah was given with the right hand, as it is stated: "At His right hand was a fiery law unto them" (Deuteronomy 33:2).

25. Shalom Sabar, "The Khamsa in the Synagogue: A Meeting of Opposites? The Evolution of the Khamsa in Judaism and Jewish Folk Culture," in *Khamsa Khamsa Khamsa: The Evolution of a Motif in Contemporary Israeli Art*, eds. Ido Noy and Shirat Miriam Shamir (Jerusalem: The Museum for Islamic Art, 2018), 162–69.

26. Deut. 5 14.

27. An open palm also calls to mind the priestly blessing over the congregation that was also seen as powerful protection against demons and other pests. The use of the number five and the open palm in an apotropaic context also recalls the figure of Joseph and his father Jacob's blessing to him: "Ben porat Yosef ben porat alei ayin" ("Joseph is a fruitful vine, a fruitful vine by a fountain") (Gen. 49:22). The content of the blessing as well as its structure,

FIGURE 9.3 Receiving the Torah at Mount Sinai. The Birds' Heads Haggadah, Franconia, circa 1300. Jerusalem. The Israel Museum, MS 180/57, fol. 23r. Photo © The Israel Museum, Jerusalem, by Ardon Bar-Hama.

southern Germany in ca. 1300) an illustration of Moses on Mt. Sinai shows him receiving the Ten Commandments from (the hand of) God (figure 9.3).

---

namely the first five words, led to the popular belief that Joseph's figure was connected to fertility and protection against the evil eye (e.g. BT, Berakhot 20a). See Sabar, Shalom, "'Ben Porat Yosef': The Image of Joseph in the Folklore and Art of Sephardi Jews and the Jews in the Lands of Islam," *Beit Mikra: Journal for the Study of the Bible and Its World* 55, no. 1 (2010): 169–92 (Hebrew).

In the marital context, the embodiment of God via the letter *heh* and the number five not only had a protective aspect but was also aimed at enhancing a couple's fertility, so that they could fulfill the first positive commandment in the Bible, namely to "Be fruitful and multiply" (Gen 1:28). The Bible (Gen. 17:5–6) explains that adding the letter *heh* to Abram's name symbolizes his becoming the fruitful father of a multitude of nations. A midrash in Numbers Rabbah (18:21) uses gematria and numerology to give a more "scientific" explanation.[28] The midrash states that the numerical value of the Hebrew letters of Abram's name with the addition of *heh* equals 248, precisely the number of organs in the human body.[29] Thus, only once Abraham's name was completed by God, could he father children. A similar notion appears in the fourteenth-century *Sefer Kushiot*, where the anonymous writer addresses the reasons for choosing the index finger over the other fingers: "Since it has been said that [the tablets of the law were written by] 'the finger of God' (Exodus 31, 18), we are therefore accustom to betroth with the index finger ... and another reason because 'the finger of God' in gematria is 252, which stands for the 252 organs in a woman, therefore, we are accustom to betroth with the index finger."[30] The numerological link between the couple's fertility and the Hebrew letter *heh* is also illustrated in a source that quotes the Maharam as saying that the numeric value of "be fruitful and multiply" is the same as that of "bride and groom."[31] Thus it would appear that this use of numerology was not only intended to clarify the logic and origins of the customs but also provided the new couple with magical protection, the promise of fertility, and the assurance of divine favor for a strong and lasting relationship.[32]

---

28. *Sefer Gematriot of R. Judah the Pious*, introduction by Daniel Abrams and Israel M. Ta-Shma (Los Angeles: Hotsaat Keruv, 1998), 1–21.

29. Mishnah Oholot 1:6.

30. See BT, Bekhorot 45a. *Sefer Kushiot*, ed. Jacob I. Stahl (Jerusalem: Jacob I. Stahl, 2007), 11–12, §18 (Hebrew). In fact, the numeric value is 251, and not 252, however as *Sefer Gematriot* attributed to R. Judah the Pious teaches us—a difference in one letter does not matter. See *Sefer Gematriot of R. Judah the Pious*, ed. Jacob I. Stahl, 2 vols. (Jerusalem: Jacob I. Stahl, 2004), 1:71, §4, note 25 (Hebrew).

31. However, the numeric value of "Be fruitful and multiply" is 518 while "groom and bride" is 519. The same difference in the numeric value is found in 'ring' 486 and 'kiddushin' 485. See Shimshon ben Tzadok, *Sefer Tashbetz Katan*, 268, §467.

32. For other magical practices related to marriage and love, see Ortal P. Saar, *Jewish Love Magic: From Late Antiquity to the Middle Ages*, in *Magical and Religious Literature of Late Antiquity*, vol. 6 (Leiden: Brill, 2017). For a general overview of Jewish magic, see Yuval Harari, "Jewish Magic—An Annotated Overview," *El Prezente* 5 (2011): 13–85 (Hebrew).

The Kiddushin Ring—Sentimental, Social, and Moral Value

The apotropaic benefits that the kiddushin ring was perceived to provide had the potential to affect the couple for the rest of their lives, so long as the ring remained in their possession. Although, ideally, the kiddushin ring should be owned by the groom prior to the ceremony, in Ashkenaz it was often the case, as Rosh (Asher ben Yehiel 1250–1327) attests, that poor grooms who were unable to afford such rings would instead borrow them from friends or family members. However, since borrowed objects must necessarily be returned at some point to their owner, their use in the ceremony raised doubts as to the validity of the act of kiddushin. R. Asher, for example, recommended that as a rule one should be careful not to marry with a borrowed ring, yet when circumstances required, he ruled that the groom could borrow the ring but must inform the bride that this is the situation.[33] He also stipulated that the groom is obliged to buy the ring back from his bride or, alternatively, pay the lender a fee so that it will be as if the groom invested his own money in the kiddushin (albeit much less than the full value of the ring).

The groom's ownership of the kiddushin ring became a particularly acute halakhic issue in the thirteenth and fourteenth centuries in light of the relatively new role that Jews began to play in the European economy as suppliers of secured loans.[34] At least some Hebrew texts indicate that Jewish pawnbrokers believed that they were permitted to use items put up as collateral before their foreclosure, as I have expounded on elsewhere.[35] Even though halakhah permits using a pawned ring

---

33. R. Asher ben Yehiel, *Sheelot u-Teshubot le-Rabbenu Asher ben Yehiel*, ed. Yitzhak S. Yudlov (Jerusalem: Machon Yerushalayim, 1993/4), 156, §2; Isaac ben Abba Mari from Marseille, *Sefer ha-Ittur*, 2 vols., ed. Meir Yona (Vilna: Tzilum Yerushalayim, 1884), 2:4 §76. On Davidovich's suggestion that kiddushin rings were borrowed from the synagogue, see David Davidovich, "Jewish Marriage Customs that Disappeared in the Last Generations," *Yeda-'am: Journal of the Israel Folklore Society* 18 (1976): 107-8 (Hebrew). Others, led by the Rashba, were much more determined than the Rosh regarding the use of borrowed rings. Rashba, *She'elot 'u-Teshuvot ha-Rashba* 6:2§1.

34. Regarding the role of Jews in the economy of thirteenth- and fourteenth-century Germany, see Michael Toch, "Between Impotence and Power: The Jews in the Economy and Polity of Medieval Europe," in *Poteri economici e poteri politici secc. XIII–XVIII*, ed. Simonetta Cavaciocchi (Florence: Le Monnier, 1999), 221-43. On practical aspects of moneylending, see Michael Toch, "Geld und Kredit in einer spätmittelalterlichen Landschaft: Zu einem unbeachteten hebräischen Schuldenregister aus Niederbayern (1329-1332)," *Deutsches Archiv für Erforschung des Mittelalters* 38 (1982): 506-28.

35. Ido Noy, "The Fleuron Crown from Neumarkt in Silesia (Środa Śląska): Christian Material Culture in a Jewish Context," *Ars Judaica: The Bar-Ilan Journal of Jewish Art* 12 (2016): 33.

for kiddushin, it nevertheless resulted in some unpleasant situations.[36] Consider, for example, the question sent to R. Moshe ben Yitzhak Mintz (Maharam Mintz 1415–80) about an incident that took place in Landau. One Jewish man gave a ring as collateral for a loan from another Jewish man. The lender decided to send the pawned ring to a goldsmith in order to "make the ring beautiful and to color it as if it was new, so that [his son] could betroth his wife with this ring." He then gave it to his son as a gift, even though he knew that the borrower intended to redeem the ring in the near future. Maharam Mintz's answer was unambiguous—the groom must return the ring to its original owner and sanctify the bride once again, this time with another ring.[37]

Ownership of the kiddushin ring changes during the kiddushin ceremony, becoming the property of the bride after the groom hands it to her. Contemporary sources indicate that as such the ring continues to be of significance throughout a woman's life. *Sefer ha-Hinukh*, an anonymous thirteenth-century halakhic treatise, states: "It was the custom of Israel to betroth a woman with a ring, that was then in her hand always as a memento."[38] David ben Levi of Narbonne, a thirteenth-century Provençal sage, recorded that "women go out [in public] with kiddushin rings." Although the text refers specifically to this custom during the Sabbath, it is safe to assume that women wore kiddushin rings during the weekdays as well.[39] Maharil states that women kept their kiddushin rings because of their sentimental value: "[Women] are accustomed to keep the kiddushin ring for many days because of their affection [for it]."[40] The fact that women wore the ring in public demonstrates that it must have had not only a personal but also a social role, reflecting not just the marital status but also the wealth of the owner and her spouse. Together with other physical features and objects the ring could also broadcast to others that the woman was no longer an active participant in the matchmaking market.[41]

36. BT, Kiddushin 8b.
37. Moses son of Isaac haLevi Mintz, *She'elot u-Teshuvot Rabbenu Moshe Mintz* (Maharam Mintz), ed. Jonathan Shraga Domb (Jerusalem: Machon Yerushalayim, 1991), 1:213, 217, §49a (Hebrew).
38. *Sefer ha-Hinukh*, ed. Chaim Dov Chavel (Jerusalem: Mossad Harav Kook, 2001), 661, §539 (Hebrew).
39. Aaron ben Jacob ha-Cohen, *Kol Bo,* ed. David Abraham (Jerusalem: D. Abraham, 2008/9), 66, §31. Aaron ben Jacob ha-Cohen, *Orhot Hayyim*, ed. Joseph D. Stizberg (Jerusalem: Joseph D. Stizberg and Son 1955/6), 116, §261.
40. Moshe ha-Levi Moellin, *Sefer Maharil*, 50, §52.
41. On matchmaking as a social and religious institution as well as an economic market, see Jacob Katz, "Marriage and Sexual Life among the Jews at the Close of the Middle Ages," *Zion* 10, no. 1–2 (1945): 21–54, esp. 33–36 (Hebrew); Grossman, *Pious and Rebellious*, 64–67.

In addition to the sentimental and social value of the kiddushin rings, Maharam Mintz mentions another good reason for keeping it safe—to ensure good fortune. The responsum addresses a dispute over the distribution of property in a case where both the wife and her husband died a few days apart. At the heart of the discussion is the legal status of the woman's possessions prior to her marriage, especially the wedding gifts (*sivlonot*) and the kiddushin ring she received from her husband.[42] This responsum clearly indicates that women used to keep their kiddushin ring in their possession throughout their life. Maharam then continues and makes a fascinating argument regarding the ownership of the ring. He rules that the husband (now deceased) was not allowed to sell his wife's kiddushin ring, partly because "he who sells the kiddushin ring it is as if he sold his luck, and some will say that it is as if he invalidates the love and covenant between them, and it is not customary to sell unless there is great [economic] hardship."[43] According to this perception, the kiddushin ring was not only a symbol of the act of kiddushin, but also a kind of promise to preserve the marital framework. Losing the ring, or worse, selling it, meant that the couple's good fortune could be jeopardized, their love harmed, and their covenant with each other broken. Maintaining good marital luck had a unique meaning for medieval Jews, given that, unlike their Christian neighbors for whom divorce was simply not an option, Jews had to use all means available in order to stay married, including placing their faith in the "hands" of good luck.[44] It is therefore not surprising that, according to this responsum, the responsibility for keeping the kiddushin ring (and hence for keeping the marital bond) rested not only on the woman but on her partner as well.

While it would not be surprising to modern Jews that medieval Jewish women kept their kiddushin rings all their lives, what is interesting is the importance attached to these rings even after their deaths, and the use to which they were put in order to communicate personal and communal messages. In his work *Evel Rabbati*, Jacob ben Solomon ha-Sarfti, a fourteenth-century Jew who moved from northern France to Provence, offers a heartbreaking description of the last hours of his daughter Esther, who died of the Black Plague in 1382. The essay combines his own lamentation together with some of her final wishes,

---

42. Items such as Sivlonot girdles and rings (not for kiddushin) were bestowed between the couple. See, for example, Moshe ha-Levi Moellin, *Sefer Maharil*, 464–65, §2.
43. *She'elot u-Teshuvot Rabbenu Moshe Mintz*, 2:472, §76.
44. Grossman, *Pious and Rebellious*, 231–40, esp. 239–40.

including her desire to be buried with specific personal objects: "And you, my father, please take from me my rings, that are on my fingers. But on my small finger, leave the ring with which my husband sanctified me to be his betrothed among all other women. This you will do and furthermore, place the pure turban upon my head, to serve as an example and good sign for the life of my man my husband."[45] Esther's desire to broadcast her marital status as well as her devotion to her husband and her estimation of their love and relationship via two objects of halakhic significance should be understood in light of contemporary burial customs.[46] As noted by Maharam of Rothenburg, the final wish of R. Gershom Me'or ha-Golah (ca. 960–1028) was to be buried with his *tallit* (prayer shawl) as a symbol of his piety.[47]

Esther's final wish to symbolize her piety via her headgear and the kiddushin ring, has its opposite echo in a case where a woman's piety requires them to remove the ring from their fingers. Jewish women (and men) are required to fully immerse themselves in a body of water as an act of ritual purification. Halakhah mandates that all clothes and jewelry that comes between their "flesh" and the water must be removed. Detailed instructions regarding the performance of this ritual practice can be found in *Sha'arei Dura* written in the thirteenth century by Issac Ben Meir from the city of Düren. In the section dealing with familial purity, the author instructs women preparing for ritual immersion to

---

45. Paris, Bibliothèque Nationale de France, Ms. Heb. 733, 61r–67r, especially on 64r. Nati Barak, "The Early Ashkenazi Practice of Burial with Religious Paraphernalia," in *Death in Jewish Life: Burial and Mourning Customs among Jews of Europe and Nearby Communities* [*Studia Judaica* 78], eds. Stefan C. Reif, Andreas Lehnardt, and Avriel Bar-Levav (Boston: De Gruyter, 2014), 187–95; Ron Barkai, "A Medieval Hebew Text on the Death of Children," in *Women, Children and the Elderly: Essays in Honour of Shulamit Shahar*, eds. Miri Eliav-Feldon and Issac Hen (Jerusalem: The Zalman Shazar Center, 2001), 76–84 (Hebrew); Susan L. Einbinder, *No Place of Rest: Jewish Literature, Expulsion, and the Memory of Medieval France* (Philadelphia: University of Pennsylvania Press, 2008), 130–33.

46. Women's cut hair was also considered an object of personal significance that they treasured and which was often buried with them. See *Sefer Leket Yosher le-Rabbi Yose bar Moshe*, ed. J. Freimann (Berlin: Mekize Nirdamim, 1904), 82 (Hebrew).

47. Maharam, *Responsa, Rulings and Customs*, ed. I. Z. Cahana (Jerusalem: Mossad Harav Kook, 1957–62), 2:36 (Hebrew). On broadcasting piety in life and the afterlife via objects and appearances, see Elisheva Baumgarten, *Practicing Piety in Medieval Ashkenaz: Men, Women, and Everyday Religious Observance* (Philadelphia: University of Pennsylvania Press, 2014), 154–68; 173–89. For contemporary burial customs in Christian society, see R. W. Scribner, "Elements of Popular Belief," in *Handbook of European History: 1400–1600 Late Middle Ages, Renaissance and Reformation*, eds. T. A. Brady, Heiko A. Oberman, and J. D. Tracy (Leiden: Brill, 1994–95), 244–49.

be sure they enter the *mikveh* (ritual bath) only after removing their rings, as these would be a "barrier to their immersion."[48] A copy of *Sha'arei Dura* included in the Hamburg Miscellany, which was produced in Padua in 1477, contains an illuminated opening page with the initial Hebrew word: All [women who want to marry]. A man and woman are standing in what seems to be a typical landscape of the north Italian countryside (figure 9.4). The man is holding the woman's left hand while placing, or removing, two golden rings on her left thumb and middle finger. A third ring, most probably the woman's kiddushin ring, appears on her right index finger. Surprisingly, scholars interpreted this scene as an outdoor marriage ceremony, even though the man is occupied with the woman's left hand.[49] I would argue that this scene illustrates one of two possible practices relating to female immersion practices—the removal of the rings for safekeeping before going to the mikveh, or replacing the jewelry afterward. Looking at this scene from a wider perspective this illustration tells the story of an intimate moment between a married couple, a bond reinforced by the figure of the small lapdog in the background, a contemporary symbol of fidelity.[50]

The kiddushin ring retained its symbolic and practical significance as long as the married couple lived in peace with each other. However, when a marriage was facing difficulties or came to an end, the kiddushin ring lost its value as a symbol for marriage. Medieval sources attest that woman continued to wear kiddushin rings right up until the last moments of their marriage. As part of the divorce ceremony, for example, women were required to receive the *get* (bill of divorce) and hold it in their bare hands, and were therefore required to remove any rings in advance.[51] The very act of the removal of the kiddushin ring also visually broadcast the fact that the woman was now no longer in a relationship. A similar practice was required during the *halitzah* ceremony, when a childless widow undergoing a Levirate marriage had to

---

48. Issac Ben Meir, *Shaarei Dura*, ed. David Deblitzky (Bnei Brak: David Deblitzky, 2016), 281, §12.

49. Bezalel Narkiss, *Hebrew Illuminated Manuscripts* (Jerusalem: Encyclopedia Judaica/Amiel, 1984), 185, pl. 59 (Hebrew).

50. Ido Noy, "Amor Vincit Omnia: Medieval Jewish Love and Romance in Light of the Erfurt Girdle," *Erfurter Schriften zur jüdischen Geschichte*, vol 6, *Ritual Objects in Ritual Contexts* (Jena: Bussert & Stadeler, 2020), 80–93.

51. As implied in Maharam Mintz's *Get* order: "and if she [wears] a ring she must remove it" ("Veim yesh taba'at beyada tsrikha lahasir"). See *She'elot u-Teshuvot Rabbenu Moshe Mintz*, 2:576.

240 CHAPTER 9

FIGURE 9.4 Portrait of an Italian Jewish couple, painted in Padua in 1477. Hamburg Miscellany, Padua 1477. Staats- und Universitätsbibliothek Hamburg, Cod. in scrin. 132, fol. 75v.

remove the kiddushin ring given to her by her late husband prior to the wedding ceremony.[52]

The Mazal Tov Ring and the Ketubbah

The success of medieval Jewish marriages depended, first and foremost, on a couple's consent (and that of their families), and the affection and attraction they felt for each other. Yet, as we have seen, a marriage was also believed to be influenced by the degree of good fortune (mazal tov, literally: good constellation [of stars] / good luck) the couple had.[53] The earliest mention of reciting the popular blessing of "mazal tov" in

---

52. As implied in Maharam Mintz's halitzah order: "she must be warned from having a ring on her right hand." See *She'elot u-Teshuvot Rabbenu Moshe Mintz*, 2:593.

53. Moshe Idel, "The Zodiac in Jewish Thought," in *Written in the Stars: Art and Symbolism of the Zodiac*, ed. Ariel Cohen, Moshe Idel, and Iris-Fishof (Jerusalem: Israel Museum, 2001), 20–27.

the framework of the kiddushin ceremony, by the community, dates to fourteenth-century France, in an anonymous comment on *Sefer ha-Niyar*: "And they [the grooms] say: 'Behold you are consecrated to me with this ring according to the laws of Moses and Israel' and they [family and guests] answer 'mazal tov!'"[54] A similar custom is later attested to by Maharam Mintz in Ashkenaz: "And then when [the bride] was betroth all who stand there will say "Mazal Tov"!"[55]

The role of astrology in the couple's marital destiny is reflected in a variety of wedding objects replete with symbols and inscriptions.[56] One example is the ketubbah (the marriage contract), which was often decorated with the Hebrew inscriptions *Mazal Tov* (good fortune) and *Siman Tov* (good sign).[57] The cloth used as the huppah (wedding canopy), was often decorated with astral symbols and the inscription *Mazal Tov*, thus alluding to God's promise to Abraham: "I will multiply thy seed as the stars of the heaven" (Genesis 22:17) (figure 9.5).[58] Similar iconography and inscriptions decorated the "wedding stone" often set on the north wall of synagogues in southern Germany.[59] Their magical-apotropaic role is manifested immediately after the act of kiddushin, when the groom would throw a glass goblet full of wine onto it. This symbolic act had multiple meanings. The shattering of the vessel and the pouring of the (red) wine hints at the breaking of the (virgin) bride's hymen; breaking the glass was also intended to protect the newlywed against demons

---

54. *Sefer ha-Niyar*, ed. Gershon Appel (New York: Sura, 1960), §30.

55. *She'elot u-Teshuvot Rabbenu Moshe Mintz*, 2:538, §109.

56. See, for example, a matchmaking formula for successful marriage, including gematria and astrology, which appears in Isaac ben Isaac's book of magical practice, copied in Chinon, France, in ca. 1250. See Amit Shafran, "Match-Making Magic among Medieval French Jews," in *In and Out, Between and Beyond: Jewish Daily Life in Medieval Europe*, ed. Elisheva Baumgarten and Ido Noy (Jerusalem: The Hebrew University of Jerusalem, 2021), 83–87.

57. Shalom Sabar, "Words, Images, and Magic: The Protection of the Bride and Bridegroom in Jewish Marriage Contracts," in *Jewish Studies at the Crossroads of History and Anthropology: Authority, Diaspora, Tradition*, ed. Raanan S. Boustan et al. (Philadelphia: Pennsylvania University Press, 2011), 102–32.

58. Appears in JT, Sota 9:16, 24b, "what are huppot for grooms [?]. Painted sheets with golden crescents hang from them." On the huppah design in halakhah, custom, and art see Joseph Gutmann, "Jewish Medieval Marriage Customs in Art: Creativity and Adaptation," in *The Jewish Family: Metaphor and Memory*, ed. D. Kraemer (New York: Oxford University Press, 1989), 47–62; and Sperber, *The Jewish Life Cycle*, 220–64.

59. Known as Huppahstein, Traustein, or Hochzeitstein in German. Many examples also consist of the Hebrew inscription, "the voice of joy and the voice of gladness, the voice of the bridegroom and the voice of the bride" based on Jeremiah 33:11. Davidovich, *Jewish Marriage Customs That Disappeared in the Last Generations*, 108–112; Naomi Feuchtwanger-Sarig, "Interrelations Between the Jewish and Christian Wedding in Medieval Ashkenaz," *Proceedings of the Ninth World Congress of Jewish Studies, Division 2* (1986): 31–36.

FIGURE 9.5 Decorated Huppah with betrothed couple. Customs book, Nuremberg Miscellany, southern Germany, 1589. Germanisches Nationalmuseum Nürnberg, Bibliothek, 8° Hs. 7058, fol.12v.

and other harmful beings that might disrupt the wedding.[60] A twelfth-century text by Ephraim ben Jacob of Bonn (1132–97/98) provides a different reason for this custom, explaining that the breaking of the glass was an act of commemoration of the destruction of the Temple. In the Laws of Kiddushin in the *Mahzor Vitry* it is stated that the custom is to throw the glass cup against the wall.[61] Maharil gives a more detailed description of this custom and explains that the groom must stand "facing north and throw the cup [backward] so that it breaks against the wall."[62] This custom continues at Jewish wedding to this day, when,

---

60. Jacob Z. Lauterbach, "The Ceremony of Breaking a Glass at Weddings," in *Beauty in Holiness: Studies in Jewish Ceremonial Art*, ed. Joseph Gutmann (New York: KTAV, 1970), 340–69. On the breaking of the glass in the *shidduchin* (matchmaking) ceremony, see Sperber, *The Jewish Life Cycle*, 151–57.

61. *Mahzor Vitry*, 2:589, §470. See also *Sefer ha-Rokeah*, §355.

62. Because "Out of the north the evil shall break forth" ("Mitsafon tipatah haraha"). Jeremiah 1:14. See also *Pirke de-Rabbi Eliezer*, ed. Michael Higger, *Horev* 8 (1943/4): 82–119. See Moshe ha-Levi Moellin, *Sefer Maharil*, §5.

at the conclusion of the ceremony the groom stomps on a glass with his right foot, to cries of "Mazal Tov!" from the guests.

The chronological proximity between the kiddushin ceremony and the custom of saying "Mazal Tov!" to the newlywed couple in public led to the design of a unique type of ring, engraved with the Hebrew letters M-A-Z-A-L-T-O-V on the top of a miniature architectural structure at the top of the ring's bezel. While the many Mazal Tov rings that appeared in the antiquity market during the nineteenth century have a somewhat unclear provenance,[63] three rings, dating to the early fourteenth century, were discovered in archaeological excavations respectively, in Weisenfels,[64] Colmar,[65] and Erfurt (figure 9.6),[66] each with elaborate decorations and startling dimensions.[67] There is significant contention, among scholars, over whether these objects were in fact used for kiddushin. Abrahams, for example, argued emphatically that wearing such a large ring would be painful to the point of

---

63. For instance, a Mazal Tov ring from Munich (Schatzkammer der Residenz, inventory number: 52), is described in an entry from 1589 as: "Ein Alter guldiner Ring, umb und umb mit Herbäyschen Buchstaben, auf dem Castn steht ein Tabernacul einem Sacramentheußl gleich." See *Die Münchner Kunstkammer*, eds. Dorothea Diemer, Peter Diemer, and Lorenz Seelig, 3 vols. (Munich: Bayerische Akademie der Wissenschaften, 2008), 1:308. Many other unclear Mazal Tov rings are found in Jules M. Samson, *The Jewish Betrothal Ring (or Mazal Tov Rings)* (1982, unpublished). On the history and historiography of Mazal Tov rings, see Ido Noy, "Medieval Ashkenazi Wedding Jewelry and Love Tokens: Christian Material Culture in Jewish Context" (PhD diss., Hebrew University of Jerusalem, 2018), 53–61.

64. Halle (Saale), Kunstmuseum Moritzburg, inventory number: Mo-LMK-E-162. See Friedrich Wiggert, "Ueber einen in Weißenfels im J.1826 gemachten Fund goldner und silberner Schmucksachen aus dem vierzehnten Jahr-hunderte," *Neue Mitteilungen aus dem Gebiet historisch-antiquarischer Forschungen* 7, no. 2 (Halle, 1846): 89–90, pl.4 no. 4; Max Sauerlandt, "Ein Schmuckfund aus Weißenfels vom Anfang des 14. Jahrhunderts," *Der Cicerone* 11, no. 16 (1919): 520n3.

65. Paris, Musée national du Moyen Âge, inventory number: Cl.20658. Elisabeth Taburet-Delahaye and Michel Dhénin, "Le trésor de Colmar," *La Revue du Louvre et des Musées de France* 34, no. 2 (1984): 93; Elisabeth Taburet-Delahaye, "Les bijoux du Trésor de Colmar," in *Le trésor de Colmar* (Colmar, Musée d'Unterlinden, 1999), 19–30.

66. Weimar, *Thüringische Landesamt für Denkmalpflege und Archäologie*, inventory number: 5067/98. Maria Stürzebecher, "Der Schatzfund aus der Michaelisstraße in Erfurt," in *Die mittelalterliche jüdische Kultur in Erfurt*, ed. Sven Ostritz, vol. 1 (Weimar: Thüringische Landesamt für Denkmalpflege und Archäologie, 2010), 1:94–99, 220n5. Christine Descatoire, ed., *Treasures of the Black Death* (London: Wallace, 2009), 60–61n1. Two other rings that appeared in the nineteenth century, one from the collection of the Municipal Museum in Cologne and another in the Hermitage Museum in St. Petersburg, show a complete or partial resemblance to the Erfurt Mazal Tov ring, which may indicate continuity in its medieval design up to modern times.

67. Some scholars argue that these rings are too large and bombastic for use as a kiddushin ring. Nevertheless, measuring the dimensions of the medieval Mazal Tov rings mentioned above reveal that the inner diameters of the hoops are between 17-18mm, surely an average size for a woman's finger.

244   CHAPTER 9

FIGURE 9.6 Mazal Tov ring, part of the Erfurt Treasure, second quarter of the fourteenth century. Courtesy of the Thuringian State Office for Heritage Management and Archaeology, inventory number: 5067/98. Photograph by Brigitte Stefan.

torturous.[68] This was supported by earlier scholars, from the nineteenth century, who claimed that Mazal Tov rings were never intended for kiddushin but rather were designed to hold bouquets of myrtles or flowers,[69] or were even originally used as bishop's rings.[70] Seidman also suggested that the Mazal Tov rings were not used for kiddushin but rather filled a symbolic role of wishing the couple good fortune: the

---

68. Israel Abrahams, *Jewish Life in the Middle Ages* (New York: Macmillan Company, 1917), 183.

69. Anglo-Jewish Historical Exhibition, *Catalogue of Anglo-Jewish Historical Exhibition, 1887, Royal Albert Hall, and of Supplementary Exhibitions Held at the Public Record Office* (London: British Museum, South Kensington Museum, 1887), 115.

70. Presumably because Kabbalistic inscriptions, such as A.G.L.A.—which stands for the Hebrew formula "You are mighty forever, Lord," included in Tefilat HaAmidah, the central Jewish prayer—were often used in Christian magic as a means of protection against fire ("Allmächtiger Gott, Lösche Aus"). See George F. Kunz, *Rings for the Finger* (Philadelphia: J. B. Lippincott, 1917), 214.

ring was first worn on the groom's finger and then removed and worn on the bride's finger.[71] Sperber, for his part, posited that brides wore such rings to recall the destruction of the Temple in Jerusalem,[72] while Guttman suggested a practical-economic explanation, namely that the rings belonged to the synagogue and were borrowed (for a fee) for the wedding ceremony by those members who could not afford a ring of their own.[73]

How can we determine if in fact Mazal Tov rings were used for kiddushin? From a halakhic standpoint any ring (or any valuable object for that matter) could be used, provided that their value was properly assessed by an appraiser.[74] Medieval Hebrew sources also attest to the using of inscribed rings for kiddushin. Aaron ben Jacob ha-Cohen, who lived in Provence in the late thirteenth and early fourteenth centuries, quoted a ruling of David ben Levi of Narbonne regarding whether it is permissible to wear jewelry on the Sabbath: "And now when women wear kiddushin rings surely these must be understood to have the same ruling as jewelry rather than seal rings. Since the letters [on the rings] are not [used as] seals at all, even though the engraved letters or their shapes in relief can be used for signing."[75] A responsum of Maharam Mintz, dealing with the mundane issue of loans and pledges, also appears to support the use of Mazal Tov rings for kiddushin: "And he came before us, the honorable R. Jacob of Ulm, may he live, and told us that he has pawns of silver, a gold-plated belt, and two golden rings from you. In each of these rests a rock called a diamond, along with another kiddushin ring, which was engraved with M"T [mazal tov]. And he said that for many days you have not redeemed your deposit and that he is in need of his payment."[76]

---

71. Gertrud Seidmann, "Marriage Rings in the Jewish Museum, London," in *The Jewish Museum: Annual Report* (London, 1982) (without pagination).
72. Sperber, *Minhagei Yisrael*, 4:143–48.
73. Joseph Gutmann, *The Jewish Life Cycle* (Leiden: Brill, 1987), 15–16.
74. The roots of this ruling can be found in Tosafot. Rashi's grandson, Jacob ben Meir, also known as Rabbeinu Tam (1100–71), explains that the reason why "the world is accustomed to betroth with a stoneless ring" is because precious materials such as stones and pearls can sometimes hold great discrepancy in their value. Rabbeinu Tam therefore rules that such material must be properly assessed by an appraiser in order to prevent situations where a bride will feel mistaken or even deceived by the value of the kiddushin ring. BT, Kiddushin 9a. For a discussion on the use of decorated rings for kiddushin, see Sperber, *Minhagei yisrael*, 4:143–48 (Hebrew).
75. *Kol Bo*, 116, §261.
76. *She'elot uTeshuvot Rabbenu Moshe Mintz*, 1:179, §70.

246 CHAPTER 9

Despite the seemingly incontrovertible proof provided by the above text, this is challenged by two illustrations of the "Order of the Bride and Groom" included in a Jewish prayer book (*siddur*) produced in 1481 in Pesaro (now Italy), which appear to indicate that Mazal Tov rings may have served an additional function other than betrothal.[77] The first illustration depicts the apex of the Jewish marriage ceremony, in which the bridegroom places a plain gold ring on the bride's index finger (figure 9.7). The second illustration portrays the moment in which the bridegroom gives the ketubbah to his bride (figure 9.8). A close look at the second illustration shows that the ketubbah is rolled up and fastened by a golden ring with a raised element on its bezel, an object reminiscent of the Ashkenazic Mazal Tov ring. The Italian illustrator clearly distinguished between these two gold rings—an unadorned ring for betrothal, and a heavily decorated one for the ketubbah holder— suggesting that their respective designs are tailored to their ritual uses. Marriage contracts, like Torah scrolls and other ritual documents and letters, were written on paper or parchment and then rolled into scrolls. Such documents were then often tied using various materials and techniques, such as circles and hoops that also served as magical protection.[78] A metal ring such as the one depicted in the illustration above could have served this purpose. Given that only a handful of Italian marriage contracts dating to before the sixteenth century have survived, we cannot determine whether this was common practice among Italian Jews. However, many of the Mazal Tov rings of Italian origin do have extraordinary inner diameters.[79]

---

77. Budapest, Library of the Hungarian Academy of Sciences, Ms. A380, fols. 231r, 231v. This manuscript was stolen from the library's collection at the beginning of the 1980s.

78. Another ritual object used as a scroll folder is the wimple, a long strip of cloth used as a baby diaper in circumcision. Known already in sixteenth-century southern German communities, the wimple was often decorated with the name of the baby, his birth date, and the blessing: "May God raise him up to [the study of the] Torah, to the [wedding] canopy, and to good deeds, Amen Selah." The wimple was brought together with the newborn to the synagogue and was donated to the synagogue and used to tie the Torah scroll. See Binyomin S. Hamburger, *Shorshei Minhag Ashkenaz: Sources and Roots* 4 vols., trans. David Silverberg (Beni Brak: Machon Moreshes Ashkenaz, 2016), 2:328–67 (Hebrew). Shalom Sabar, "Wedding Scenes on Wrappings of the Torah Scrolls from Germany," *Rimonim* 6 (1999): 47-49 (Hebrew); Sperber, *The Jewish Life Cycle*, 143–151. For a more general perspective see Don C. Skemer, *Binding Words: Textual Amulets in the Middle Ages* (University Park: Penn State Press, 2006).

79. A rolled ketubbah is illustrated in a Hebrew manuscript from fifteenth-century northern Italy (Florence). See Princeton University Library, Garrett Ms.26, 17r. Don C. Skemer, *Medieval & Renaissance Manuscripts in the Princeton University Library* (Princeton: Princeton University Press, 2013). Compare to the ketubbah depicted in the Yehudah Haggadah fig. 2. On the handing of the ketubbah in Early Modern Italy, see Roni Weinstein, *Marriage Rituals*

FIGURE 9.7 Kiddushin, Siddur, Pesaro, Italy, 1481. Formerly from the David Kaufmann Collection, Library of the Hungarian Academy of Sciences. MS A380, Vol. II, fol. 230r. Courtesy of the Center for Jewish Art, Hebrew University of Jerusalem.

FIGURE 9.8 The ring and the ketubbah, Siddur, Pesaro, Italy, 1481. Formerly of the David Kaufmann Collection, Library of the Hungarian Academy of Sciences. MS A380, Vol. II, fol. 231v. Courtesy of the Center for Jewish Art, Hebrew University of Jerusalem.

Alternatively, Mazal Tov rings may have functioned as an adornment of the ketubbah. One finds similar metal rings in the Große Heidelberger Liederhandschrift, a corpus of illuminated medieval German love poems (*Minnelieder*) that was produced in 1300-40 for the Manesse family in Zurich. Many images in the codex depict iconography typical of the ideas of courtly love popular during this period, including the bestowing of gifts and exchanges of documents, most likely letters and love poems. An illustration in a collection of poems by Wilhelm von Heinzenburg (before 1262-93), reveals additional details. It depicts a young man bestowing three gifts on his beloved: a roll of parchment, a wallet, and a gold ring set with a stone (figure 9.9).[80] A similar notion for using a ring attached to a text appears in the Rothschild Haggadah, which was produced in northern Italy, ca. 1450 (figure 9.10). Here the well-known illustrator Joel ben Simeon drew a golden ring set with a blue stone, and attached it to the Hebrew initial "Great, mighty" (*Ve'rav*), likely a reference to the description of the children of Israel, who, after settling in Egypt, became "fruitful and increased abundantly, and multiplied and became very, very mighty, and the land became filled with them" (Deuteronomy 26:5). Based on the context it seems likely that this ring refers to marriage, and possibly also allude to the illustrations of Moses and Tziporah above (figures 9.1-9.2), which illuminate the same part of the Haggadah.

There is a pronounced similarity between the ketubbah holder shown in the Italian prayer book and the three Mazal Tov rings from Germany. But did medieval German Jews also use metal ring holders to fasten their rolled-up marriage contracts? Or were these rings in fact used as part of the wedding ceremony? An indication that German Jews used to roll their ketubbot appears in the wedding scene in the Yehuda Haggadah (9. 2).[81] However, a simple test of the hypothesis that Mazal Tov rings were used to fasten these documents, can be made by comparing the measurements of any of the Ashkenazic Mazal Tov rings described above to the measurements of contemporaneous illustrated marriage contracts from Germany. One example is the Krems ketubbah dated to

---

Italian Style: A Historical Anthropological Perspective on Early Modern Italian Jews (Leiden: Brill, 2004), 245-48, 278-81. For the large diameter Italian Mazal Tov rings, see Samson, *The Jewish Betrothal Ring*.

80. See Noy, "The Mazal Tov Ring and the *Ketubbah*," 92.

81. The rolled ketubbah is missing in the similar wedding scene in the Second Nuremberg Haggadah (see figure 9.1 of this chapter).

Figure 9.9 Bestowing love gifts. Miniature for Herr Wilhelm von Heinzenburg, Codex Manesse. Heidelberg, Universitätsbibliothek, CPG. 848, fol. 162v.

FIGURE 9.10 An illustration for the Hebrew initial ורב (Great, Mighty). The Rothschild Haggadah (formerly Murphy Haggadah), northern Italy, ca. 1450. Jerusalem, National Library of Israel, Ms. 6130°24, fol.20v.

1391–92 (figure 9.11).[82] The original dimensions of this document were approximately 600 by 740 mm. It would therefore have been impossible to insert it into any of the Ashkenazic Mazal Tov rings, which have an inner diameter of approximately 20 mm. However, the illuminated Krems ketubbah is exceptional, since most medieval Ashkenazic marriage contracts were not adorned, and it can be assumed that their average size was significantly smaller. Therefore, in theory, it is still possible that smaller, plain ketubbot could have fit (tightly rolled) into such rings.[83]

Whether or not Ashkenazic Jews used Mazal Tov rings only for kiddushin or as ketubbah holders, as the fifteenth-century Italian Jews did, their typical design suggests that they also played a visual and aesthetic role within the marital context. The architectural structure

---

82. This is in contrast to other Ashkenazi wedding contracts, which were customarily unadorned. The reason Ashkenazi Jews did not place great value on the ketubbah (which is why it was customarily undecorated) had to do with the ruling of R. Gershom ben Yehuda Me'or ha-Golah (ca. 950–1028) that forbade divorce without the consent of the woman. Furthermore, the Ashkenazi ruling for a fixed amount in the ketubbah decreased public interest in hearing the contract read aloud, so it had less importance. See Shalom Sabar, "The Beginning of Ketubbah Decoration in Italy: Venice in the Late Sixteenth to the Early Seventeenth Centuries," *Journal of Jewish Art* 12–13 (1986–87): 101; Shalom Sabar, *Ketubbah: Jewish Marriage Contracts of the Hebrew Union College Skirball Museum and Klau Library* (Philadelphia: Jewish Publication Society, 1990), 89.

83. Sabar, *Ketubbah*, 289–91.

FIGURE 9.11 A painting from the four fragments of the Krems (?) Ketubbah, 1391–92. Vienna, Österreichische Nationalbibliothek, Cod. hebr. 218. Courtesy of the Center for Jewish Art, Hebrew University of Jerusalem.

on the bezel top perhaps symbolized the building of the couple's new home.[84] Alternatively, it may have represented contemporary depictions of the Temple in Jerusalem,[85] thus commemorating the Temple's destruction, and prefiguring, together with other features in the ceremony, its future reconstruction.[86] Similar to church towers, the architecture on top of the ring's bezels contained a miniature bell that could

---

84. It may also symbolize the bride according to the concept that "his house" that is—his wife" ("Beyto zo ishto"). Mishnah Yoma 1:1.
85. Or, for that matter, other building and architectural elements representative of the Temple, such as the synagogue, the Holy Ark, or the *bimah*. See also Shalom Sabar, *Mazal Tov: Illuminated Jewish Marriage Contracts from the Israel Museum Collection* (Jerusalem: The Israel Museum, 1994), 43-78. Sabar, "Messianic Aspirations and Renaissance Urban Ideals: The Image of Jerusalem in the Venice Haggadah, 1609," *Jewish Art* 22/23 (1998): 295-312; Pamela Berger, *The Crescent on the Temple: The Dome of the Rock as Image of the Ancient Jewish Sanctuary* (Leiden: Brill, 2012), 197-223.
86. On the commemorating of the Temple's destruction as part of Jewish wedding rituals, including fasting, breaking the glass, wearing certain jewelry and cloths, and ash, see Ta-Shma, "Huppah venissuin behalakhah," *Mahanaim* 83 (1962-63): 24-27; Daniel Sperber, *Minhagei Yisrael*, 4:143-48.

produce a unique soft sound. Such tinkling could draw the attention of the participants and guests, while also, according to popular beliefs, protect the newlyweds against demons that might disrupt the joy of the wedding. The apotropaic role of the bells complements the function of the Hebrew blessing "Mazal Tov" in increasing the likelihood of a successful marriage.

As a ceremonial object, the kiddushin ring was significant, first and foremost, for its role in the betrothal ceremony. And yet, as many contemporary historical, visual, and material sources suggest, the meaning and importance of the kiddushin ring also extended beyond its halakhic and ceremonial function. It became one of the most important objects owned by a married woman, simultaneously broadcasting the marital bond between the wedded couple and symbolizing the covenant between God and the people of Israel. Kiddushin rings were also perceived as objects that could potentially predetermine and maintain marital good fortune, and fend off hazards that might harm the young couple. It is thus not surprising that kiddushin rings came to hold increasing sentimental and amuletic value and were cherished by their owners for the rest of their lives, and sometimes even into the afterlife. The individuals mentioned in these sources, along with the esoteric aspects of everyday life, reveal a range of non-elite perspectives, each offering unique insights. Together, these perspectives provide a more comprehensive and profound understanding of daily life, shedding light on experiences and interpretations related to the kiddushin ring specifically and to Jewish marriage more broadly. This expanded view helps us appreciate the intricate ways in which such a seemingly small object can intersect with and reflect the lives of Jews in the Middle Ages.

Further Readings

Abrahams, Israel. *Jewish Life in the Middle Ages.* New York: Macmillan, 1917.
Bartal, Ruth. "Medieval Images of 'Sacred Love': Jewish and Christian Perspectives." *Asaph: Studies in Art History* 2 (1996): 93–110.
Davidovich, David. "Jewish Marriage Customs that Disappeared in the Last Generations." *Yeda-'am: Journal of the Israel Folklore Society* 18 (1976): 107–112 (Hebrew).
Descatoire, Christine, ed. *Treasures of the Black Death.* London: Wallace, 2009.
Falk, Zeev. *Marriage and Divorce: Reforms in the Family Life of German-French Jewry.* Jerusalem: Mifal Hashikhpul, 1961 (Hebrew).

Feuchtwanger-Sarig, Naomi. "The Coronation of the Virgin and of the Bride." *Journal of Jewish Art* 12-13 (1986-87): 213-24.
Freimann, Aaron H. *Seder Kiddushin Ve'Nissuin*. Jerusalem: Mosad Harav Kook, 1945.
Gutmann, Joseph. "Jewish Medieval Marriage Customs in Art: Creativity and Adaptation." In *The Jewish Family: Metaphor and Memory*, edited by D. Kraemer, 47-62. New York: Oxford University Press, 1989.
Katz, Jacob. "Marriage and Sexual Life among the Jews at the Close of the Middle Ages." *Zion* 10 (1945): 21–54 (Hebrew). jstor.org/stable/i23547023
Noy, Ido. "Amor Vincit Omnia: Medieval Jewish Love and Romance in Light of the Erfurt Girdle." *Erfurter Schriften zur jüdischen Geschichte, Ritual Objects in Ritual Contexts*, 6: 80-93. Jena: Bussert & Stadeler, 2020.
Noy, Ido. "The Fleuron Crown from Neumarkt in Silesia (Środa Śląska): Christian Material Culture in a Jewish Context." *Ars Judaica: The Bar-Ilan Journal of Jewish Art* 12 (2016): 23-38. muse.jhu.edu/article/687166.
Noy, Ido. "The Mazal Tov Ring and the Ketubbah." In *In and Out, Between and Beyond: Jewish Daily Life in Medieval Europe*, edited by Elisheva Baumgarten and Ido Noy, 89–94. Jerusalem: The Hebrew University of Jerusalem, 2021.
Sabar, Shalom. *Ketubbah: Jewish Marriage Contracts of the Hebrew Union College Skirball Museum and Klau Library*. Philadelphia: Jewish Publication Society, 1990.
Sabar, Shalom. "Words, Images, and Magic: The Protection of the Bride and Bridegroom in Jewish Marriage Contracts." In *Jewish Studies at the Crossroads of History and Anthropology: Authority, Diaspora, Tradition*, edited by Raanan S. Boustan et al., 102-32. Philadelphia: Pennsylvania University Press, 2011.
Samson, Jules M. *The Jewish Betrothal Ring (or Mazal Tov Rings)* (1982, unpublished).
Sauerlandt, Max. "Ein Schmuckfund aus Weißenfels vom Anfang des 14. Jahrhunderts." *Der Cicerone* 11 (1919): 519-26.
Seidmann, Gertrud. "Marriage Rings in the Jewish Museum, London." In *The Jewish Museum: Annual Report*. London, 1982.
Shalev-Eyni, Sarit. "Iconography of Love: Illustration of Bride and Bridegroom in Ashkenazi Prayerbooks of the Thirteenth and Fourteenth Century." *Studies in Iconography* 26 (2005): 27-57. https://www.jstor.org/stable/23923658.
Stürzebecher, Maria. "Der Schatzfund aus der Michaelisstraße in Erfurt." In *Die mittelalterliche jüdische Kultur in Erfurt*, edited by Sven Ostritz, vol. 1, 94–99, 220n5. Weimar: Thüringische Landesamt für Denkmalpflege und Archäologie, 2010.
Taburet-Delahaye, Elisabeth. "Les bijoux du Trésor de Colmar." In *Le trésor de Colmar*, 19-30. Colmar, Musée d'Unterlinden, 1999.
Ta-Shma, Israel. "Huppah ve-Nissuin be-Halakhah." *Mahanaim* 83 (1962-63): 24-27.

Weinstein, Roni. *Marriage Rituals Italian Style: A Historical Anthropological Perspective on Early Modern Italian Jews*. Leiden: Brill, 2004.

Wiggert, Friedrich. "Ueber einen in Weißenfels im J.1826 gemachten Fund goldner und silberner Schmucksachen aus dem vierzehnten Jahr-hunderte." *Neue Mitteilungen aus dem Gebiet historisch-antiquarischer Forschungen* 7 (Halle, 1846): 86–95.

PART IV

Rituals

Hannah Teddy Schachter, Elisheva Baumgarten,
Erez Shahar Rochman, and Amit Shafran

The study of rituals is a rich interdisciplinary lens through which to explore Jewish life in medieval Europe. Rituals structure both exceptional and routine aspects of life, from ceremonies marking birth or death to practices embedded in politics, health, or daily social interactions. While definitions for ritual abound,[1] it has been most recently defined as a "metacategory" for ceremonially communicative *doings* and *thinkings*, typically prescribed based on a constellation of religious and nonreligious customs, as well as any number of cultural norms.[2] Any mundane activity can be ritualized, as Barry Stephenson recently commented: "Just as theater takes the drama of everyday life, condenses it, formalizes it, and puts it on stage for view, ritual is cobbled together out of ordinary acts and gestures

---

1. See Catherine Bell, *Ritual: Perspectives and Dimensions* (New York: Oxford University Press, 1997), 3–13, for an overview of definitional and theoretical variations of ritual. On the conceptual plurality and cross-cultural variability of definitions, see Michael Stausberg, "Ritual: A Lexicographic Survey," in *Theorizing Rituals: Issues, Topics, Approaches, Concepts*, ed. Jens Kreniath et al. (Leiden: Brill, 2006), 51–100.

2. Roberto Gronda et al., "Histoires Pragmatiques: A Conversation with Simona Cerutti and Yves Cohen," *European Journal of Pragmatism and American Philosophy* 8, no. 2 (2016): 11, 10.4000/ejpap.654.

made extraordinary."³ Studying past rituals requires attention to how they construct, rather than merely express, religious worldviews, symbolic systems, and communal identities through embodied and material practices.⁴

The repetitive nature of rituals made them a central feature of everyday life. All the rituals examined here are collective. They include more than one person, are performed in specific and defined spaces, and have practices that include actions, words, and objects associated with them. The spaces were situated within the medieval urban landscapes; the objects were sometimes shared by Jews and Christians; and the words recited and the actions performed expressed the values and beliefs of those who performed them. As scholars of medieval Jewish rituals have long argued, examining these specific moments in Jewish life provides a deeper understanding of the way Jews themselves understood the world around them. They also offer a more profound conception of the complex ways Jews simultaneously belonged to and separated themselves from the Christian world within which they lived.⁵

Scholars have examined ritual as a lens through which social groups express, reinforce, or challenge prevailing values and expectations. A ritual can both express consent with prevailing conventions and norms and push back against them. In the context of our joint work, one of our goals was to better understand the extent to which ideas recorded by the erudite were shared by members of the Jewish community at large. Since in many instances all members of the community participated in a given ritual, they allow insight into the workings of the medieval Jewish communities and their entanglement with their surroundings. Moreover, while contrasting recommended behaviors and rituals allows us to trace the ongoing reformulation of Jewish customs, comparing the performance of rituals over time provides a window into aspects of change and continuity in these communities.⁶

---

3. Barry Stephenson, *Ritual: A Very Short Introduction* (Oxford: Oxford University Press, 2015), 54, 76.

4. On ritual as a site of meaning-making through embodied practice, see Catherine Bell, *Ritual Theory, Ritual Practice* (New York: Oxford University Press, 1992), 19–29.

5. Ivan G. Marcus, *Rituals of Childhood: Jewish Acculturation in Medieval Europe* (New Haven, CN: Yale University Press, 1996); Harvey E. Goldberg, *Jewish Passages: Cycles of Jewish Life*, The S. Mark Taper Foundation Imprint in Jewish Studies (Berkeley: University of California Press, 2003); Elisheva Baumgarten, "Annual Cycle and Life Cycle," in *Cambridge History of Judaism*, ed. Robert Chazan, 1st ed. (Cambridge: Cambridge University Press, 2018), 416–39.

6. One example of this is tournaments at weddings. See Eyal Levinson, "Tournaments and Medieval Jewish Weddings," in *Jewish Everyday Life in Medieval Northern Europe, 1080–1350* :

Based on three examples from the everyday domains of worship, medicine, and festival, the chapters in this section show a variety of avenues through which rituals impacted the lives of Jews in medieval France and Germany, and how they both blur and demarcate the lines between Jews and their Christian neighbors. In the first of these contributions, Erez Shahar Rochman discusses the use of *piyyutim*, Hebrew liturgical poetry. Contrary to the prevailing scholarly assumption that such poetry was a strictly elite ritual form, Shahar Rochman demonstrates how piyyutim were actually geared toward the general Jewish community and served as an effective ritual channel for the construction of communal identity. His chapter underlines the involvement of the community members in the performance of the prayers and how ideas and messages long considered elitist were in fact part of more common practice.

Elisheva Baumgarten and Amit Shafran explore a particular medicinal ritual from the thirteenth century, an Hebraico-French incantation to ward off fever. The authors trace this remedy to a Christian mass that was then adapted and appropriated for Jewish health practices. Examining the process by which a Christian prayer was transformed into a Jewish one, they further demonstrate how shared and differing understandings of foodstuffs and medical processes came into play.

In the final contribution of this section, Hannah Teddy Schachter considers the role of Jews in urban processions, that is, ritualized marches during certain liturgical and civic occasions throughout the year. By highlighting the contrast between Jewish visibility in liturgical and civic processions, Schachter argues that the performative power of medieval processions as a ritual reflects the nuanced significance of Jewish life in medieval Christian society that both Jews and Christians at times embraced.

The various source materials mined in this section—Hebrew prayer books and liturgical poems, responsa literature, Latin chronicles and mass liturgy, illuminations, material culture, and more—each offer some detail as to the everyday activities of medieval Jews. Who did medieval Jews interact with and what practices did they adapt and adopt from their neighbors? How did they make these practices their own? Did learned and less learned Jews observe the same daily routines and practices and use the same narratives of explanation? How did Jews differ from their Christian neighbors even when performing similar

---

A Sourcebook, eds. Elisheva Baumgarten, Tzafrir Barzilay, and Eyal Levinson (Kalamazoo : Medieval Institute Publications, Western Michigan University, 2022), 1R, 33.

actions? These are some of the larger issues probed in these chapters. The methods discussed in the following chapters relate to religious practice, material culture, spacial and anthropological theories, as well as comparative history. These are all examples of the array of avenues by which we can trace how everyday rituals shaped the experiences of medieval European Jews.

Chapter 10

Not Only for the Learned

Piyyutim *as Part of Public Prayer*

By Erez Shahar Rochman

This chapter deals with the subject of *piyyutim* (liturgical poems, sing. *piyyut*) and their recitation by the crowd of worshippers in the synagogues of medieval Ashkenaz. During the High Middle Ages, hundreds of piyyutim of various subgenres were composed in Ashkenaz and were incorporated into daily and holiday prayers. They were also recited on Shabbat and in private events during which prayers and celebrations were held.[1] These poems have already received a fair amount of scholarly attention, focusing mostly on the historical contexts in which they were written, the theological attitudes of their composers (the *payytanim*), their literary style, and the manner in which they were incorporated into the main body of prayer.

This chapter is based on an M.A. thesis submitted in the summer of 2022 to Professor Elisheva Baumgarten at the Hebrew University of Jerusalem. It was written under the auspices of the Beyond the Elite: Jewish Daily Life in Medieval Europe Project, PI Elisheva Baumgarten, from the European Research Council (ERC) under the European Union's Horizon 2020 research and innovation program, grant agreement No. 681507, and prepared for publication with funding from the Israel Science Foundation Grant 2850/22, Contending with Crises: The Jews of XIVth Century Europe, PI Elisheva Baumgarten.

1. Shulamit Elitzur, "Ha-Hazarah el ha-Mahzor," *Madae'i ha-Yayahadut* 35 (1995): 137; and Yitzhak Moshe Elbogen, *Ha-Tefillah be-Yisrael be-Hitpatthutah ha-Historit* (Tel Aviv: Dvir, 1972), 165.

Two important questions, however, have yet to be extensively discussed and will be addressed in this chapter: (1) Who was the target audience of the piyyutim? and (2) What meanings was this audience meant to draw from their recitation?[2] Despite the fact that piyyutim were composed by learned members of the elite, usually rabbis, their authors knew that prayer in the medieval Ashkenazic synagogue was a communal activity, and that it did not always depend on a leader. These payytanim lived and operated within a reality in which the community played a central role in the shaping of prayer practices and were aware that it was this public that would ultimately either accept or reject their poems.[3] Evidence of this can be found in the rabbinical literature of the time, which describes many cases in which the order and nature of prayer in the synagogue ran contrary to the preferences of the rabbinical elite. One such example, specifically pertaining to piyyutim, is found in *Sefer Maharil, Hilkhot Tefilah*:

> [Maharil] was careful to recite the *krovetz* and would be mad at his students who would study *tosafot* or other matters in the synagogue while the public was reciting *krovetz*, and they did care to say them.[4] He used to carry a book of *Arba'ah Turim* with him to synagogue, and he would study it whenever the cantor would prolong his melodies, or during *kedusha* and *kaddish*. Nevertheless, when the crowd would recite *krovetz*, he was careful to also say them with them.[5]

---

2. A parallel scholarly discussion regarding the classical piyyutim of the Byzantine era in the Holy Land is found in Shulamit Elitzur's article, "Kahal ha-Mitpalelim ve-ha-Kedushta ha-Kedumah," in *Knesset Ezra: Literature and Life in the Synagogue—Studies Presented to Ezra Fleischer*, ed. Shulamit Elizur, Moshe David Herr, Gershon Shaked, and Avigdor Shinan (Jerusalem: Ben-Zvi Institute, 1994), 171. Elitzur is here following Ezra Fleischer's claim that these early piyyutim were written to be used by a mixed crowd, which included the unlearned population as well.

3. It should be noted that many rabbinical texts normally considered as intended only for the scholarly elite were in fact affected by the ways of life of people who belonged to other circles within the Jewish community. For this reason, with careful analysis they too may be considered as sources bearing witness to daily life in these communities. See Elisheva Baumgarten, *Practicing Piety in Medieval Ashkenaz: Men, Women, and Everyday Religious Observance* (Philadelphia: University of Pennsylvania Press, 2014), 13–14.

4. A subgenre of piyyutim, also known as *kerovot*, which are incorporated into the *Amidah* prayer.

5. Yaakov ben Moshe Levi Moelin, *Sefer Maharil: Minhagim shel Rabbenu Yaakov Moellin*, ed. Shlomo Shpitzer (Jerusalem: Jerusalem Institute, 1989), 437–38.

Maharil (R. Yaakov ben Moshe ha-Levi Moellin) was the leading rabbinical authority of Ashkenazic Jews in the fourteenth and fifteenth centuries, especially its western communities. The book of customs named after him was compiled by his student, R. Zalman of St. Goar. This passage suggests that during Maharil's lifetime piyyutim were recited by the public in synagogue, even though scholars did not always consider them to be particularly important. It demonstrates the inclination of his rabbinical students to see piyyutim as an unnecessary extension of prayer, and so rather than recite them along with the community, they preferred to focus on their studies. The students have generally followed the example of their rabbi, who also used to study during prayer, as the quote above explicitly states. However, unlike them, Maharil made a point of not neglecting to recite the piyyutim, and his angry reaction toward his students makes it clear that he expected them to honor them too. It seems that despite their years of learning, during which they surely gained a high level of liturgical proficiency, recitation of piyyutim was not a well-established socioreligious norm for these members of the learned elite. It also implicitly demonstrates that the community at large did not rely on such scholars for leading the performance of prayer, including the piyyutim, and in fact, ignored their disdain for them.

In medieval Ashkenaz, Jewish prayer customs, including the recitation of piyyutim, were considered to be a part of every community's *minhag hamakom*—the local tradition. Rabbinical literature from the period broadly supports the notion that every community should develop and cherish its own customs.[5] There is evidence to suggest that in unusual cases, in which there was a dispute between the worshippers and a rabbinical authority regarding prayer customs, the former

---

6. For an extensive survey of the early historical background that led to the rise of the exceptional importance of customs in medieval Ashkenaz, see Israel M. Ta-Shma, *Minhag Ashkenaz ha-Kadmon: Heker ve-Iyyun* (Jerusalem: Magnes, 1992), 13–14, 85–105. One typical example for this is seen in the introduction to the book of customs written by R. Isaac Tyrnau, a contemporary of Maharil and one of the consolidators of the eastern Ashkenazic rite. Relying on a rule appearing several times in various tractates of the Mishnah, he wrote: "And the late sages instructed that everything (should be conducted) according to the local customs . . . and if you do not have a good hold in halakhah for the matter, follow the customary tradition." See Yitzhak Isaac Tyrnau, *Sefer ha-Mingahim*, ed. Shlomo Shpitzer (Jerusalem: Jerusalem Institute, 1979), 2.

overrode the latter.⁷ One such example, again pertaining to the recitation of piyyutim, is found in *Sefer Maharil, Hilkhot Yom Kippur*:

> Mahari Segal said that *minhag hamakom* must not be changed in any matter, even the melodies that they are used to over there.⁸ And he told us of one time when he himself was cantor in the Regensburg community during the High Holidays, and he would recite the whole prayer according to the customs of Osterreich, as is established there. . . . And he said that at that time, he would recite the *seliha* called *"Ani ani hamedaber"* that R. Ephraim wrote for the *musaf* prayer,⁹ and he believed it be of merit to say it there in honor of R. Ephraim, who is buried there. And the leaders told him that it is not their custom to recite it, and he did not heed them due to his own belief. Later, the rabbi's daughter died on Yom Kippur, and the righteous rabbi justified this sentence suffered by his daughter due to his changing of *minhag hamakom*.¹⁰

This source describes a case in which the Mainz-born Maharil was a guest cantor during the High Holidays in the Regensburg community. During the *musaf* prayer on Yom Kippur, he began reciting the *seliha* "Ani ani hamedaber," written by R. Ephraim Bar Yitzhak in commemoration of the 1096 persecution. His reason for incorporating this piyyut in the prayer was the fact that its composer had lived in Regensburg during the twelfth century and was buried in the local cemetery. Maharil was surprised to find that the crowd was not accustomed to reciting it, and although the community members voiced their opposition, he decided to continue its recitation. The lesson conveyed by the story's morale emphasizes the high personal price supposedly paid by his daughter, due to what he considered his own transgression. The passage thus reflects

---

7. The tradition that the community plays an active role in determining the order and nature of prayer in synagogue can first be identified in texts from the twelfth century and into the Early Modern period. See, for example, the overruling of the local rabbi by the worshippers in Mainz, around the time of Ra'aavan (late eleventh-mid-twelfth centuries), in *Sefer Ra'avan*, ed. Yehoshua Ehrenreich (New York: Grassman, 1958), 49.

8. Another name for Maharil.

9. Pl. selihot, a subgenre of penitential piyyutim, recited especially during and between the High Holidays of Rosh Hashanah and Yom Kippur.

10. *Sefer Maharil*, 339–340. In an early manuscript of this same book, University Library Johann Christian Senckenberg, Frankfurt am Main, Germany, Ms. Oct. 94, fol.106r–106v, it is written that those who objected to Maharil's decision were 'the residents of the city' [*toshavei ha-ir*], rather than its leaders.

Maharil's understanding of the importance of the local prayer customs, which should not be changed "in any matter, even the melodies." Considering this liturgical dynamism and the role of the community in its shaping, the following part of this chapter is dedicated to a brief review of some of the characteristics of the crowd of worshippers in the medieval Ashkenazic synagogue, before turning back to treating the subject of piyyutim more specifically.

Liturgical Literacy Among the Synagogue Crowd

In his research on learning and literacy in medieval Jewish communities, Ephraim Kanarfogel makes a distinction, important for the purpose of this chapter, between full literacy, namely a mastery of reading and writing skills, and basic literacy, sufficient for the reading and memorization of liturgical text. Kanarfogel uses the term *literal memory*, or *memoria ad verba*, originally coined by literary scholar Mary Carruthers,[11] to emphasize the correlation between the relatively high memorization capabilities of liturgical texts and biblical verses by the Jews of medieval Ashkenaz, and their generally higher level of liturgical literacy when compared to the Jews of Spain.[12] This ability evolved in the Ashkenazic communities in part due to the daily repetition of the same texts of daily prayer beginning in childhood, evidence of which practice can be found as early as the twelfth century.[13]

Surviving textual sources indicate that alongside experiential learning and the development of liturgical skills during the prayers themselves, liturgical literacy was also developed through dedicated opportunities for learning. For most men, formal religious tutoring centered on preparing and enabling them to perform the obligatory *mitzvot* (positive

---

11. Mary Carruthers, *The Book of Memory: A Study of Memory in Medieval Culture* (Cambridge: Cambridge University Press, 2008), 116.
12. Ephraim Kanarfogel, "Levels of Literacy in Ashkenaz and Sepharad as Reflected by the Recitation of Biblical Verse Found in the Liturgy," in *From Sages to Savants: Studies Presented to Avraham Grossman*, eds. Joseph R. Hacker, Yosef Kaplan, and B. Z. Kedar (Jerusalem: Zalman Shazar Center for Jewish History, 2010), 200 (Hebrew).
13. Ephraim Kanarfogel, "Prayer, Literacy and Literary Memory in the Jewish Communities of Medieval Europe," in *Jewish Studies at the Crossroads of Anthropology and History: Authority, Diaspora, Tradition*, ed. Ra'anan S. Boustan et al. (Philadelphia: University of Pennsylvania Press, 2011), 265, 250–52. For a similar examination of the liturgical literacy displayed by the wider Christian public in the Middle Ages and early modern era, see Virginia Reinburg, *French Books of Hours: Making an Archive of Prayer, c. 1400–1600* (New York: Cambridge University Press, 2012), 88–89, 109–12, 237.

commandments), one of which was prayer.[14] Additional learning opportunities existed in medieval Ashkenaz independent of the activity of the great sages and were held either in the community's *beit midrash* (study hall) or synagogue, particularly during the evening hours. These were designed to help deepen the knowledge and understanding among the broader populace and promote the observing of the *mitzvah* (positive commandment) of Torah study.[15] Ordinary worshippers therefore had a considerable degree of familiarity with biblical verses, as well as with rabbinical legends (*aggadah*), and homiletical exegesis (midrash).[16]

As for women, although not obligated by halakhah to perform the three daily prayers as men were, they were expected to pray once a day,[17] and there is evidence to suggest that they took part in daily or Sabbath prayers and those during the holidays, which took place in synagogue.[18] Women heard the Shabbat sermons delivered by rabbis, first sitting in the same physical space as the men,[19] and then, from the thirteenth century on, in the women's synagogues (*Frauenschule*).[20] Other sources also attest to the religious education received by women throughout their lives.[21] This was intended to help them understand and perform

---

14. Current scholarly literature indicates that tutors were central for the advancement of learning among children. Reading was one of the earliest skills pursued, mostly by practicing reading biblical verses. See Ephraim Kanarfogel, "Schools and Education," in *Cambridge History of Judaism: The Middle Ages—The Christian World*, ed. Robert Chazan (Cambridge: Cambridge University Press, 2018), 403–9, as well as Kanarfogel, "Prayer, Literacy and Literal Memory," *Cambridge History of Judaism*, 267–68. The debate quoted there revolves around the responsibility of fathers to teach children the basics of reading, as well as the form of instruction enacted by the tutors, which included the weekly Torah portion, *haftarot, targum onkelos,* and *peirush rashi*.

15. Ephraim Kanarfogel, "Between the Tosafist Academies and the other Battei Midrash in Ashkenaz in the Middle Ages," in *Yeshivot and Batei Midrash*, ed. Immanuel Etkes (Jerusalem: Zalman Shazar Center, 2006), 95–105 (Hebrew).

16. It is worth emphasizing that these skills paved the way to a greater understanding of piyyutim as well, since these are mostly based on biblical verses or terminology, and often make reference to aggadah and midrash.

17. The obligation of women to pray once daily is noted in *Siddur Rashi*, compiled by Rashi's students. See *Siddur Raschi: Ritualwerk*, Salomo Buber ed. (Berlin: Hevrat Mekitzei Nirdamim, 1910), 44. See also the extensive scholarly discussion on the matter of women's voluntary performance of additional mitzvot in Baumgarten's *Practicing Piety*, 139–71.

18. Baumgarten, *Practicing Piety*, 49.

19. This is in accordance with the words of Ra'avyah as quoted in *Sefer Maharil, Hilkhot Shabbat*: "This is the ground for Ra'avyah ruling that it was permitted during the *shabbat* sermon to spread prayer shawls to separate between men and women for the sake of modesty." See *Sefer Maharil*, 220–21.

20. See Elbogen, *Ha-Tefillah be-Yisrael*, 351. See also Baumgarten, *Practicing Piety*, 48.

21. For two examples of this approach, see the words of Maharil, quoted in *Sefer Ha-'Agur*, composed by R. Yaakov ben Barukh Landa in the fifteenth century, see *Sefer Ha-'Agur ha-Shalem*,

the mitzvot expected of women, including prayer. In addition, a few outstanding women were known as educated communal leaders and cantors, whose erudition and religious devotion promoted the inclusion of their female peers as active participants in the public prayers in synagogue.[22] Women are also mentioned as philanthropic donors who supported the establishment and maintenance of synagogues, further demonstrating their involvement in matters of communal spirituality.[23]

Alongside textual sources, material evidence also provides clues to the connection between female worshippers and the synagogue.[24] Tombstones of Jewish women, found in the cemetery of Worms, mention their dedication to praying at the synagogue, and their promotion of women's participation in public prayer. One of these was Golda, daughter of R. Shmuel, whose tombstone states that she passed away while in synagogue:

> This tombstone was erected at the head of the honorable Mistress Goldah bat R. Shmuel, who passed away at the Synagogue on Monday evening the 4th of Tevet, and was buried on Tuesday in the year 5052. May her soul be bound in the bundle of the living with the rest of the righteous women in heaven. *Amen* and *amen sela*.[25]

The abovementioned date is significant, since the fourth of Tevet was an ordinary weekday, a few days after Hannukah, attesting to this woman's presence in synagogue on regular days rather than only on special occasions or during holidays. Women such as Goldah bat R. Shmuel might also have developed a significant level of liturgical literacy.

As the above discussion indicates, there is a need for further updated scholarly examination of the community of worshippers in medieval Ashkenaz. Such a discussion, based on the latest research and a renewed

---

ed. Moshe Herschler (Jerusalem: Moznaim, 1960), 16–18; and see also in *Sefer Hasidim*, ed. Judah Wistinetzky (rept. Frankfurt: Wahrmann, 1925), 211.

22. Avraham Grossman has identified sources attesting to the existence of female cantors, pointing out the relationship between these women and the rest of the female attendees. He goes so far as to claim that the female cantors should be seen as representing the whole medieval Ashkenazic female praying audience. See Avraham Grossman, *Hasidot u-Mordot: Nashim Yehudiot be-Eyropa be-Yemei ha-Beinayim* (Jerusalem Zalman Shazar Center, 2003), 315 (Hebrew).

23. Grossman, *Hasidot u-Mordot*, 320.

24. Such testimonies are especially important in tracking the liturgical behavior and religious practices of women who did not belong to the learned elite. See Elisheva Baumgarten, "Who Was a Hasid or Hasidah in Medieval Ashkenaz? Reassessing the Social Implications of a Term," *Jewish History* 34 (2021): 134–39, https://doi.org/10.1007/s10835-021-09378-3.

25. steinheim-institut.de/cgi-bin/epidat?id=wrm-537&anzeige=classic&inv=0537.

reading of medieval sources, could also reopen the scholarly debate on whether men and women outside the circle of scholarly elite were an integral part of the audience for whom piyyutim were intended. The relative complexity of these texts and the fact that for the most part they were not part of daily prayer, must have posed a significant challenge for ordinary worshippers. Below I explore possible ways in which this challenge was met.

Recitation of the High Holidays Piyyutim

In medieval Ashkenaz special emphasis was placed on the active participation of the community in synagogue during the High Holidays. Thus, in comparison to the daily prayers, those of the High Holidays are known to have drawn larger than usual numbers of worshippers into the synagogue. This despite the fact that they were more challenging for participants, given that large portions of them were recited either only once, or at most, two or three times, during the year. On Yom Kippur, for example, during which all as one were expected to atone for both individual and collective sins, a number of relatively less familiar piyyutim were incorporated into the liturgy.[26] It thus appears that at least some worshippers would spend the days leading up to the holiday rehearsing and (re-)learning the liturgy, in order to fulfill their personal religious obligation to recite the piyyutim. This appears to be the intention behind the explicit instructions that appear in *Hilkhot Rosh Hashanah* in *Sefer Maharil*:

> Mahari Segal demanded that every person should get accustomed to the *krovetz* of Rosh Hashanah and pray intently by himself, and must not rely on the cantor, for he fulfills the obligation only in the stead of the ignorant and dwellers of villages and settlements who do not know how to pray. . . . And even if one says that he will direct his attention and hear the cantor, that is impossible in those days in which long piyyutim are recited, and every now and then he will not hear the cantor, and thus he cannot fulfill his obligation. And every person should rehearse and learn the prayer and the *krovetz* in advance so that they would be familiar to him

---

26. Sarit Shalev-Eyni, "The Aural-Visual Experience in the Ashkenazi Ritual Domain of the Middle Ages," in *Resounding Images: Medieval Intersections of Art, Music, and Sound*, ed. Susan Boynton and Diane J. Reilly (Turnhout: Brepols, 2015), 193.

during prayer. And he shall also teach his sons and the members of his household the order of prayer.[27]

Maharil appears to assume here that at least some of attendees at synagogue for the Rosh Hashanah service had a limited degree of familiarity with the krovetz piyyutim of this liturgy, and that they apparently did have access to written texts to study from, even before the holiday itself. This aligns with research suggesting that special effort was made to write prayer books for the High Holidays, and we know that by the twelfth century these were becoming more widely available to those who gathered at the synagogue.[28] However, this source also seems to indicate that at least some people could not have simply read them directly from the prayerbook in real time, or fully understand them. Considering their recitation an integral part of every individual's personal obligation, Maharil thus expects everyone to devote time before the holiday to rehearse the entire liturgy, including the piyyutim, and teach them to their families. This implies that when they finally came to synagogue, assisted by prayerbooks, they could put their recently sharpened skills of liturgical literacy more efficiently to use. In general, it is likely that Maharil's approach regarding the need to prepare for the recitation of piyyutim was not exclusive to Rosh Hashanah, and probably encompassed all prayers recited individually that could not be performed only by the cantor.

While the first half of this chapter focused on demonstrating the importance of a renewed discussion of *who* read piyyutim and *how*, the second half concentrates on the complimentary questions of *why* and *what for*—why these liturgical texts were written in the first place, and what communal purposes they ultimately served.

Shaping Communal Memory and Identity

Medieval Ashkenazic payytanim saw themselves as heirs of the classic piyyut tradition, which began in the Holy Land during the Byzantine

---

27. *Sefer Maharil*, Shpitzer, 271–72.
28. See, for example, Eliezer ben Yoel ha-Levi, *Sefer Ra'avyah*, 2nd. ed. Avigdor Aptowitzer (Berlin: Mekitze Nirdamim, 1929), 190. For an analysis of this source, see Kanarfogel, "Prayer, Literacy and Literal Memory," 258. Other evidence also suggests that on Yom Kippur the worshippers held prayer books in their hands. See Kanarfogel, "Levels of Literacy in Ashkenaz," 199. Material evidence for this is scant, since almost none of these books have survived. Elbogen also asserted that prayer books for the High Holidays were common until religious persecutions brought about their destruction See Elbogen, *Ha-Tefillah be-Yisrael*, 279.

period. Significantly, one of the traditions characteristic of these ancient piyyutim was the incorporation of (presumably) historical accounts of the plights of the Jewish people during the period of their composition, in the form of *selihot* and *kinnot* (lamentations).[29] This tradition continued in medieval Ashenkaz, and by the time of Rabbeinu Gershom (ca. 960–1040), many selihot and kinnot had already been composed there, some with similar memorial characteristics. As a result, as the years went by, the prayers of the liturgical calendar, including the High Holidays and the shabbatot before Shavuot and Tisha B'Av, came to function as a sort of communal memorial book. One prominent example of such a corpus is the more than twenty piyyutim written during the twelfth century, in the aftermath of the First Crusade,[30] which I shall use as a demonstrative case study.

Aware of the memorial attribute of piyyutim, earlier historical research examined them as potential sources relating the tragic events that befell the Jewish communities of medieval Ashkenaz and sought to reconstruct historical events out of these surviving shreds of evidence. More recently however, a different scholarly approach has emerged that focuses on these texts as representing attributes of a certain culture and identity, regardless of their facticity. So, for example, with regards to the Hebrew Chronicles of the First Crusade, Robert Chazan has argued they should not be treated as historical documents of record, despite the fact that they are written in prose and provide numerous details pertaining to historical events, places, and persons.[31] This contrasts with piyyutim, for example, which are normally much more obscure in style. Ivan Marcus views the Chronicles primarily as texts created for religious and educational purposes, aimed at shaping a certain

---

29. On this issue see Shulamit Elitzur, "Evel Ishi ve-Nehamat ha-Am ba-Piyyutim ha-Kedumim," *Ganzei Kedem* 7 (1991): 9, as well as Elbogen, *Ha-Tefillah be-Yisrael*, 172, 238. On the subject of the development of the selihot genre, see Elbogen, *Ha-Tefillah be-Yisrael*, 247–48, as well as Lucia Raspe, "The Migration of German Jews into Italy," in *The Jews of Europe around 1400: Disruption, Crisis and Resilience*, eds. Lukas Clemens and Christoph Cluse (Wiesbaden: Harrassowitz Verlag, 2018), 183–84, 186.

30. For a summary of the matter, see Susan L. Einbinder, *Beautiful Death: Jewish Poetry and Martyrdom in Medieval France* (Princeton: Princeton University Press, 2002), 10. A useful parallel summary of the scholarly discussion regarding the usage of the more ancient classical piyyutim as historical sources is found at Shulamit Elitzur, "Galut al Admat ha-Moledet," *Mehkarei Yerushalayim ba-Sifrut ha-Ivrit* 27 (2004): 21–27.

31. See, for example, the marginal treatment accorded to them by Robert Chazan, *Masa ha-Tzlav ha-Rishon ve-ha-Yehudim: Tatnu 1096* (Jerusalem: Zalman Shazar Center, 2000), 10–12.

communal self-perception based on shared values.³² Building on these observations, further research has more broadly defined the ideology of *kiddush hashem*/Jewish martyrdom that evolved in Ashkenaz post-1096, and identified its various themes and patterns.

This research has focused almost exclusively on the Hebrew Chronicles.³³ It seems that the very unusual and exciting fact of the survival of these Chronicles has drawn so much attention to them that the importance of piyyutim as parallel textual sources has consequently been neglected in scholarly debate. During the course of this current research, the corpus of the 1096 piyyutim was thoroughly surveyed, and was found, rather unsurprisingly, to represent the same sort of ideology and theology observed in the prose text of the Chronicles.³⁴ Strikingly however, nowhere in the Ashkenazic customs literature (*Sifrut ha-Minhagim*), nor in fact anywhere else, do we find mention of the Chronicles being used in a liturgical context, while the 1096 piyyutim, which essentially contain the same messages, were widely present in public prayer.³⁵ This fact, alongside the renewed examination of the levels of liturgical literacy of the congregation and ways of crowd participation in public prayer, offers a fresh starting point from which to reconsider what could be the central role piyyutim played in the minds of medieval Ashkenazic Jews.

This renewed examination also aligns with and makes use of current trends in the study of liturgy. Earlier liturgical study, based mostly on

---

32. The research done by Ivan Marcus went in this direction. See, for example, "From Politics to Martyrdom: Shifting Paradigms in the Hebrew Narratives of the 1096 Crusade Riots," *Prooftexts* 2 (1982): 42–43, http://www.jstor.org/stable/20689021.

33. One important exception is the work of Yisrael Yuval, who situates the piyyutim in a central position, alongside the Chronicles: "Ha-Nakam ve-ha-Klalah, ha-Dam ve-ha-'Alilah—me-'Alilot Kedoshim le-'Alilot Dam," *Zion* 58 (1993): 33–90. Yuval expansively points to the theological similarity between the piyyutim and the Chronicles.

34. One of the conclusions of this chapter is that the liturgical memory represented by the 1096 piyyutim serves what Marcus describes in his "From Politics to Martyrdom," 46, as the second paradigm in the consciousness of the Ashkenazic Jews regarding the events of the First Crusade, which seeks to portray the martyrs as a holy generation. The first paradigm, which appears in the Chronicles but not in the piyyutim, describes those who were murdered as ordinary Jews who tried to save their lives using conventional methods. This approach apparently had no place within the collective memory shaped by the liturgy. It is therefore also apparent that Marcus's suggestion that the piyyut was not considered an accepted genre for the portrayal of innovative and daring acts, such as the large-scale martyrdom of the First Crusade, is incorrect.

35. Marcus suggests that as prose literature, the very complex and detailed account they contain rendered such incorporation impossible. See Marcus, "From Politics to Martyrdom," 43–44.

philological methodologies, tended to concern itself primarily with the discovery of the ways in which prayer was shaped, over time, as a compound traditional text. More recent studies have shifted their focus to the ways in which prayers were performed as a living ritual, experienced in a myriad of ways by its diverse participants. The liturgical text is seen as the basis for a wide range of ritual activities through which individuals and communities could express shared identities, values, and religious attitudes.[36] One of the starkest attributes of liturgical activity is its juxtaposition of traditional content, concerned predominantly with the past, and the performance of ritual in the present. Worshippers thus experience a certain repetition of both a mythical and an actual past, despite the progression of time since the events themselves (which may or may not have in fact occurred). This feature of liturgical activity was widely present in the culture of medieval Europe, in both Christian and Jewish settings, and was utilized for the dramatic re-creation of collective memory.[37] Liturgy was intended to transmit knowledge of the past that was deemed important for individuals and communities, and had the dual role of containing and disseminating collective memory. This makes liturgy a rich source for the study of social history, which seeks to examine the lives of people and social circles beyond the scholarly elite.

Examining piyyutim as part of the evolution of the local liturgical tradition thus can potentially shed light on the perceptions of both the

---

36. The study of Jewish liturgy has also followed these trends, encouraged by the work of scholars such as Ivan Marcus, Yosef Hayim Yerushalmi, Laurence Hoffman, Elisabeth Hollender, and others. Their studies are characterized by an increased usage of sociological and anthropological methodologies, which indicate that shared rituals signify a shared identity. The evolution of the scholarly discussion regarding liturgy as part of Judaic studies is summarized by Lawrence A. Hoffman in "Jewish Liturgy and Jewish Scholarship: Method and Cosmology," in *Oxford Handbook of Jewish Studies*, eds. Jeremy Cohen, Martin Goodman, and David Jan Sorkin (Oxford: Oxford University Press, 2004), 260–65. See especially 254–64, regarding the connection between prayer, ritual, and the shaping of identity and culture in the Jewish context. For a concise summary of the development of research on ritual and its relevance as a social tool for the shaping of consciousness, beyond the specific Jewish context, see the third chapter of the book by Gerald A. Klingbeil, *Bridging the Gap: Ritual and Ritual Texts in the Bible* (Winona Lake, IN: Eisenbrauns, 2007).

37. The perception of the liturgical ritual as a dramatic performance enacted by its participants was first developed by Victor Turner. See Klingbeil, *Bridging the Gap*, 39–40. In general, the liturgical experience promotes the linkage of memory and activity through reading, singing, motion, and the use of dedicated objects. See Katie Ann-Marie Bugyis et al., *Medieval Cantors and their Craft: Music Liturgy and the Shaping of History, 800–1500* (Woodbridge, Suffolk, UK: York Medieval Press, 2017), 1–2. For a direct reference to the Ashkenazic piyyutim as a means of dramatic reenactment, see Einbinder, *Beautiful Death*, 9.

scholars who wrote them, and the crowd that performed them over the generations. More specifically, in the context of the 1096 piyyutim, it is hereby suggested that greater importance should be ascribed to the practicalities of remembrance and transmission of messages that were in fact carried out through liturgical means.[38] The next section of this chapter provides an example of the liturgical context in which a part of the corpus of the 1096 piyyutim was recited, in an attempt to further demonstrate the specific role these played in service of the community as a whole.

Liturgical Context and Public Performance of the 1096 Piyyutim

A close examination of medieval Ashkenazic *mahzorim* reveals that following the destruction of the First and Second Temple, the First Crusade was the central traumatic historical event of these communities, and the one that had the greatest impact on their prayers.[39] In fact, an examination of the liturgical sources indicates that for the people who followed the western, and to a lesser extent the eastern, Ashkenazic rite, the First Crusade was perceived as a foundational event as catastrophic as the destruction of the First and Second Temples.[40] This attitude, as well as the role played by piyyutim in its formation, is demonstrated most clearly in the following passage from *Sefer Minhagim de-bei Maharam*, regarding the Tisha B'Av prayer:

> And the Torah scroll is put back in place and everyone sits on the ground. And immediately the cantor begins reciting the *kinnot* written by the Kaliri ... and there are those who skip some of the *kinnot* of the Kaliri and say others in their place which were established by other sages about the persecutions. And there is no need

---

38. In discussing the advantage of liturgical texts for facilitating public ritual expression, Ivan Marcus writes, "Rituals also evoke shared values that are experienced in public.... And so if we would understand a culture as a whole, we should study its rituals, customs, and gestures in addition to its narratives and other types of collective expression." See Ivan G. Marcus, *Rituals of Childhood: Jewish Acculturation in Medieval Europe* (New Haven, CT: Yale University Press, 1996), 5. This view of liturgy as a primary agent for the shaping of public memory was expressed earlier by Yosef Hayim Yerushalmi, *Zakhor: Jewish History and Jewish Memory* (Seattle: University of Washington Press, 1982), 41–42.

39. Prayer books, which contained the entire annual liturgy of a community.

40. This equation of the devastation that took place in 1096 with the destruction of Jerusalem and the Temple is also seen in the Hebrew Chronicles. See Marcus, "From Politics to Martyrdom," 49.

for concern because their killing is equivalent for grieving and for being covered in dirt as much as the burning of the house of our Lord, the chamber and the capital.[41]

These instructions appear in the book of customs named after the Maharam of Rothenburg and his students (thirteenth–fourteenth centuries). The passage supports the custom of replacing some of the classical kinnot written by the Byzantine-era poet Eleazar ha-Kalir on the destruction of the Temple, with kinnot written about the persecution experienced by recent generations. This justification is directly related to the persecution of 1096, since it itself is a direct quote from the *kinah* "Mi yi'tten roshi ma'yim," written by R. Kalonymus ben Yehuda ha-Bahur, a survivor of the 1096 persecution. This poem remains a regular part of the liturgy for Tisha B'Av and is still recited:

> Their killing is equivalent for grieving and for being covered in dirt
> As much as the burning of the house of our Lord, the chamber and the capital,
> And because we must not add occasions of lamentation and burning
> And one must not precede such a day, rather only to delay it
> Thus today I will arouse my mourning
> And I shall eulogize, wail and cry with bitter soul

These words demonstrate the manner in which piyyutim were used as a way to incorporate the specific historical memory of the Ashkenazic communities into the larger historical narrative of the Jewish people, particularly the trials and suffering that they have endured. This is seen in both the thematic comparison between the destruction of Jerusalem and the killing of the martyrs in the First Crusade, as well as in the identification of Tisha B'Av as the appropriate time to commemorate both events. A link is thus established between these events within the collective memory. Similarly, by incorporating piyyutim into the prayers of other major holidays, such as Shavuot, Rosh Hashanah, and Yom Kippur, a further link was made between the contemporary experiences of the medieval Ashkenazic communities and the ancient collective memories of the Jewish people.

---

41. Meir ben Barukh of Rothenburg, *Sefer Minhagim de-bei Maharam*, ed. Yisrael Shenhav Elfenbein (New York: Jewish Theological Seminary, 1938), 34.

The liturgy for Tisha B'Av, in which the largest portion of the 1096 piyyutim is read, offers a clear example of how this sort of prayer was conducted. The accounts of it preserved in *Sefer Minhagim de-bei Maharam* and in *Sefer Maharil* paint a vivid picture of the public ritual that took place on this fast day and the ways in which the community gathered in the synagogue participated in reciting the kinnot. A paragraph in the first of these two books regarding the prayer on the day of Tisha B'Av itself, reads as follows: "And when the cantor is done reciting the 21 kinnot, then every person will say kinnot as they wish, and when they finish all the kinnot, then the cantor would start . . . and then the crowd would start reading Job and Jeremiah and the portion starting 'Come near, you nations.'"[42] This passage demonstrates Maharam's division between those kinnot recited by the *shaliah tzibur* (cantor) and those said by the congregation. According to the quote just given, the cantor would lead the recitation of the twenty-one piyyutim written by Eleazar ha-Kalir both on the eve of Tisha B'Av and on the day itself, following which kinnot were recited privately by the worshippers, and then the congregants read together from Job, prophecies of destruction in Jeremiah, and a few verses from Isaiah. This is indicative of a generally high level of liturgical and biblical literacy among the members of the congregation, specifically with the verses on which many of the piyyutim are based. A paragraph in *Sefer Maharil* completes the picture, providing an even more detailed description of the order of the kinnot recited on the day of Tisha B'Av, and how they were divided between the cantor and the worshippers:

> And the cantor sits on the ground to say kinnot. And here you have the order which Maharil has set for the cantor: *shabbat suro. eicha atzta.* . . . These are the 17 kinnot set by the Kalir. . . . and when the cantor is done, then the exceptional among the crowd begins, and thus did Maharil, and says *tziyon halo tishali lishlom asirayich* etc., and all the people say many *tziyonim*. And also the cantor, if he would like, would say many kinnot and tziyonim. One time the people have finished kinnot and one of them thought that they no longer say kinnot, since they were late to do so, and he jumped ahead, and said one tziyon. And when he was done, Maharil did

---

42. Based on Isaiah 34:1. *Sefer Minhagim de-bei Maharam*, 34–35.

not care for it and kept saying kinnot, and all of the people said many more kinnot after him.[43]

The paragraph above makes it clear that the first kinah said by anyone other than the cantor was "Amarti sheu meni," also written by Kalonymus ben Yehuda ha-Bahur following the First Crusade. It was said by "the exceptional among the crowd," meaning, in this case, Maharil himself. Yet, significantly, the text also refers to the congregants as active participants in the recitation and even as leading the recital of the piyyutim. The case reported above, in which an individual mistakenly began reciting one of the piyyutim of the tziyonim subgenre, which were said following the kinnot, also demonstrates that the piyyutim after the one started by "the exceptional" were led by others in the congregation, and everyone could hear at least the beginning of their recitation. This seems to accord with a comment found in the Hamburg Cod. Hebr. 37 manuscript, a prayerbook (*siddur*) of the Western Ashkenazic rite written in 1434, where it says: "And there is also a custom in Magentza that whoever says kinnot will start by saying the last verse [of the previous kinah, E.S.R.] aloud so that it will be known that the kinah is done.[44] So I have heard from the mouth of Maharil and from the elderly homeowners."[45] As these two sources suggest, for the most part, the kinnot were recited by the entire congregation together, with each member saying it quietly to themselves, except for the verses at the beginning and end. To ensure coordination, the ending of each kinah was recited aloud, in the same manner as the verses of Lamentations were read. Another short comment, appearing on folio 156v of the same manuscript reads: "Here anyone who would like to shall start whichever tziyonim they wish, but the youth should not prod the elderly." The comment attests to the fact that much of the public prayer on this day was led by individuals from the congregation. It also seems to suggest there even was some concern that the younger congregants would finish reading before the older, and would then get impatient and hurry their elders along.

As mentioned earlier, the piyyutim written after the First Crusade were incorporated into the liturgy of a significant portion of the holidays throughout the Jewish year, including the High Holidays and Shavuot,

---

43. *Sefer Maharil*, 254–55.
44. Magentza is the Jewish name of the city of Mainz.
45. The Hamburg State and University Library Carl von Ossietzky, Hamburg, Germany Cod. Hebr. 37, f.154v.

as well as several special Shabbatot. On each of these occasions, their recitation played the dual role of recalling moments of ancient Jewish history and giving place to more recent congregational memory. The evidence presented above indicates that those in the synagogue were active participants in the performance of this ritual, including in the leading of the liturgy. When considered in light of the previous sections of this chapter, which showed that it is possible that these worshippers had a greater understanding of these texts than previously thought, it is possible to conclude that the piyyutim played an important role in the shaping of public memory and the creation of a shared identity.

The large number of the piyyutim composed during this period and the various surviving liturgical sources that describe their usage, leave little doubt regarding the importance of these compositions within the body of liturgy. Although written by members of the rabbinic elite, these texts elicited the active engagement of the congregation and played an important role in the formation and preservation of their collective memory and identity. Thus, by examining the role of piyyutim in liturgical texts and the ways in which they were performed, this chapter uncovers a trace of the lives of ordinary Jewish men and women in medieval Ashkenaz and expands our knowledge of their quotidian experiences. Due to the nature of surviving sources, comprised mostly by rabbinical texts, we might never arrive at a conclusive understanding of the relationship between the worshippers and the piyyutim. Nevertheless, this chapter aimed to demonstrate that by thoroughly reading the extant sources with eyes turned toward the crowd, much still remains to be explored in order to broaden our knowledge of the quotidian experiences of ordinary Jewish men and women during this period. This is a reading based on the accumulation of the largest possible number of sources, stemming from a variety of scholarly and literary fields. In this case, an examination of liturgical texts and the ways in which they were performed was employed in attempt to find traces to the lives of ordinary people and provide clues for the writing of social history.

This chapter focused on two different aspects relating to liturgy: (1) Our understanding of the behavior of the congregation of worshippers and the ways they actively participated in prayer in general, and in the recitation of piyyutim in particular; and (2) an exploration of the context in which piyyutim were incorporated into the main body of prayer, looking at the ways they were intended to be performed and connected in the minds of worshippers to broader meanings associated with various holidays.

Regarding the worshippers, this chapter supports the claim that those who gathered in the synagogues were a diverse group, yet one able to understand a significant part of the Hebrew prayers. The language of the piyyutim in particular was largely based on biblical verses and paraphrases, and required a familiarity with the Bible as well as rabbinic legends and homiletic exegesis. There is also evidence suggesting that a concerted effort was made, or was expected to be made, to rehearse the piyyutim prior to the holidays.

The 1096 piyyutim were incorporated into some of the most of important holidays in the Jewish calendar, becoming associated with the broader meanings of each holiday, such as the memory of the destruction of the First and Second Temples during the fast day of Tisha B'Av, as well as several other related occasions. In this manner, the local memory of many Ashkenazic communities regarding the persecution of the First Crusade was juxtaposed and linked to the broader historical and religious Jewish narrative and to values already embedded in Jewish tradition. Evidence from Ashkenazic customs literature leaves little doubt that piyyutim were not exclusively recited by cantors, and that the public played an active role in reciting them. They repeated the recitation and performance of the same liturgical texts and rituals year after year, with only slight changes incorporated over the centuries. A powerful meeting point between worshippers, the liturgical texts, and the accepted rituals of their performance, piyyutim thus gave shape to communal memory and identity. The piyyutim of the First Crusade are therefore a key example of the role played by text and liturgy in the creation of the self-image and the world of values that defined Ashkenazic Jewry, beginning in the High Middle Ages and throughout the centuries to follow.

Further Readings

Baumgarten, Elisheva. *Practicing Piety in Medieval Ashkenaz: Men, Women, and Everyday Religious Observance*. Philadelphia: University of Pennsylvania Press, 2014.

Baumgarten, Elisheva. "Who Was a Hasid or Hasidah in Medieval Ashkenaz? Reassessing the Social Implications of a Term." *Jewish History* 34 (2021): 125–54. doi.org/10.1007/s10835-021-09378-3.

Bugyis, Katie Ann-Marie, et al. *Medieval Cantors and Their Craft: Music Liturgy and the Shaping of History, 800–1500*. Woodbridge: York Medieval Press, 2017.

Carruthers, Mary. *The Book of Memory: A Study of Memory in Medieval Culture.* Cambridge: Cambridge University Press, 2008.

Chazan, Robert. *Masa ha-Tzlav ha-Rishon ve-ha-Yehudim: Tatnu 1096.* Jerusalem: Zalman Shazar Center, 2000.

Einbinder, Susan L. *Beautiful Death: Jewish Poetry and Martyrdom in Medieval France.* Princeton: Princeton University Press, 2002.

Elbogen, Yitzhak Moshe. *Ha-Tefillah be-Yisrael be-Hitpatthutah ha-Historit.* Tel Aviv: Dvir, 1972.

Elitzur, Shulamit. "Evel Ishi ve-Nehamat ha-Am ba-Piyyutim ha-Kedumim." *Ginzei Kedem* 7 (1991): 9-24.

Elitzur, Shulamit. "Galut al Admat Ha-Moledet." *Mehkarei Yerushalayim ba-Sifrut ha-Ivrit* 27 (2004): 21-27.

Elitzur, Shulamit. "Ha-Hazarah el ha-Mahzor." *Madae'i ha-Yayahadut* 35 (1995): 137-40.

Elitzur, Shulamit. "Kahal ha-Mitpalelim ve-ha-Kedushta ha-Kedumah." In *Knesset Ezra: Literature and Life in the Synagogue—Studies Presented to Ezra Fleischer*, edited by Shulamit Elizur, Moshe David Herr, and Gershon Shaked, 171-90. Jerusalem: Yad ben Zvi, 1994.

Grossman, Avraham. *Pious and Rebellious: Jewish Women in Medieval Europe.* Jerusalem: Zalman Shazar Center, 2003 (Hebrew).

Hoffman, Lawrence A. "Jewish Liturgy and Jewish Scholarship: Method and Cosmology." In *The Oxford Handbook of Jewish Studies*, edited by Jeremy Cohen, Martin Goodman, and David Jan Sorkin, 733-55. Oxford: Oxford University Press, 2004.

Kanarfogel, Ephraim. "Between the Tosafist Academies and the other Battei Midrash in Ashkenaz in the Middle Ages." In *Yeshivot and Batei Midrash*, edited by Immanuel Etkes, 95-105. Jerusalem: Zalman Shazar Center, 2006 (Hebrew).

Kanarfogel, Ephraim. "Levels of Literacy in Ashkenaz and Sepharad as Reflected by the Recitation of Biblical Verse Found in the Liturgy." In *From Sages to Savants: Studies Presented to Avraham Grossman*, edited by Joseph R. Hacker, Yosef Kaplan, and B. Z. Kedar, 187-211. Jerusalem: Zalman Shazar Center for Jewish History, 2010 (Hebrew).

Kanarfogel, Ephraim. "Prayer, Literacy and Literary Memory in the Jewish Communities of Medieval Europe." In *Jewish Studies at the Crossroads of Anthropology and History: Authority, Diaspora, Tradition*, edited by Ra'anan S. Boustan et al., 250-68. Philadelphia: University of Pennsylvania Press, 2011.

Kanarfogel, Ephraim. "Schools and Education." In *The Cambridge History of Judaism: The Middle Ages—The Christian World*, edited by Robert Chazan, 393-415. Cambridge: Cambridge University Press, 2018.

Klingbeil, Gerald A. *Bridging the Gap: Ritual and Ritual Texts in the Bible.* Winona Lake, IN: Eisenbrauns, 2007.

Marcus, Ivan G. "From Politics to Martyrdom: Shifting Paradigms in the Hebrew Narratives of the 1096 Crusade Riots." *Prooftexts* 2 (1982): 452-60. www.jstor.org/stable/20689021.

Marcus, Ivan G. *Rituals of Childhood: Jewish Acculturation in Medieval Europe.* New Haven, CT: Yale University Press, 1996.

Raspe, Lucia. "The Migration of German Jews into Italy." In *The Jews of Europe around 1400: Disruption, Crisis and Resilience,* edited Lukas Clemens and Christoph Cluse, 173-93. Wiesbaden: Harrassowitz Verlag, 2018.

Reinburg, Virginia. *French Books of Hours: Making an Archive of Prayer, c. 1400–1600.* New York: Cambridge University Press, 2012.

Shalev-Eyni, Sarit. "The Aural-Visual Experience in the Ashkenazi Ritual Domain of the Middle Ages." In *Resounding Images: Medieval Intersections of Art, Music, and Sound,* edited by Susan Boynton and Diane J. Reilly, 189-204. Turnhout: Brepols, 2015.

Ta-Shma, Israel M. *Early Franco-German Ritual.* Jerusalem: Magnes, 1992 (Hebrew).

Yerushalmi, Yosef Hayim. *Zakhor: Jewish History and Jewish Memory.* Seattle: University of Washington Press, 1982.

Yuval, Israel Jacob. "Vengeance and Damnation, Blood and Defamation: From Jewish Martyrdom to Blood Libel Accusations." *Zion* 58 (1993): 33–90 (Hebrew). https://www.jstor.org/stable/i23561945.

CHAPTER 11

Curing Fevers, Sharing Prayers
Jews, Christians, and Conjurations
Elisheva Baumgarten and Amit Shafran

A well-known passage in the thirteenth-century compilation, *Sefer Hasidim,* tells of a Jewish woman whose child was sick.[1] Seeking a cure for his illness, this woman consulted with her non-Jewish neighbor. She (the neighbor) advised her to concoct a brew and steep a stone in it, as this stone was a known and proven cure.[2] The Jewish woman refused to use this stone when she found out that it was in fact a relic, a stone that had been brought to Europe from the

---

We are most grateful to the readers for the press and Judah Galinsky for their helpful comments on this chapter. The origin of this chapter is in Shafran's MA thesis: "'To Me, Isaac son of Isaac': Magical Techniques and Rituals among Medieval Jews in Thirteenth-Century Northern France" (MA Thesis, Hebrew University of Jerusalem, 2021). The chapter is an expansion and addition to some of the work in the thesis. This chapter was written under the auspices of the Beyond the Elite: Jewish Daily Life in Medieval Europe Project, PI Elisheva Baumgarten, from the European Research Council (ERC) under the European Union's Horizon 2020 research and innovation program, grant agreement No. 681507, and prepared for publication with funding from the Israel Science Foundation Grant 2850/22, Contending with Crises: The Jews of XIVth Century Europe, PI Elisheva Baumgarten.

1. *Sefer Hasidim* (Parma), ed. Jacob Wistenetski (Frankfurt: Mekize Nirdamim, 1924), §1332.

2. The expression "known and proven" (*yadu'a u-menuseh*) is a common one in medieval medical manuscripts as was this technique, steeping stones in brews. While it does not appear in this source, it is alluded to and typical of medical writings. See Elisheva Baumgarten, "Ask the Midwives: A Hebrew Manual on Midwifery from Medieval Germany," *Social History of Medicine* 32 (2019): 1–22.

Holy Land, and said to be from Jesus' grave.[3] She said: "Since she [the Christian neighbor] said that it belongs to Jesus, I do not wish that my son drink from it and she did not want to make any cure out of this stone. And this is 'with all your soul' 'love the Lord, your God' (Deut. 6:5; 19:9)."[4] In this tale, the cure, is a standard medical practice of the time—a medical brew, intermingled with a relic.[5] The use of religious objects as part of medical cures was one of many options, among them the use of everyday foodstuffs or the recitation of verses and conjurations. Some of these cures were religiously "neutral," whereas others were steeped in faith-based symbols and ideas.

This story is but one example of how illness, a universal phenomenon, was treated in a religious-specific way. This vignette also explains some of the suspicions voiced by the rabbis, from late antiquity through medieval times, concerning the employment of healers and doctors from other faiths.[6] At the same time, the willingness of the Jewish mother to consider using her Christian neighbor's cure is noteworthy. It was only the religious nature of the stone/relic that caused her to reject the cure. Implied in this story is that the sharing of cures, medical practices, and practitioners between Jews and their Christian neighbors was a given; this was part of the complexities of living in and sharing the same spaces.[7]

---

3. This source is discussed from different perspectives; see Julia M. H. Smith, "Portable Christianity: Relics in the Medieval West (c. 700–1200)," *Proceedings of the British Academy 181* (2012): 143–68, https://doi.org/10.5871/bacad/9780197265277.003.0006; Elisheva Baumgarten, "'A Separate People'? Some Directions for Comparative Research on Medieval Women," *Journal of Medieval History* 34 (2010): 212–28; Ephraim Shoham-Steiner, "Jews and Healing at Medieval Saints' Shrines: Participation, Polemics, and Shared Cultures," *Harvard Theological Review* 103 (2010): 114–15, https://www.jstor.org/stable/40390064.

4. *Sefer Hasidim* (Parma), §1332. This is the standard verse cited for one's willingness to die rather than worship idolatry (BT Pesahim 25a). See also Haym Soloveitchik, "Religious Law and Change: The Medieval Ashkenazic Example," *AJS Review* 12 (1987): 205–21, https://doi.org/10.1017/S0364009400002014; Judah D. Galinsky, "Different Approaches Towards the Miracles of Christian Saints in Medieval Rabbinic Literature," in *Ta Shma: Studies in Judaica in Memory of Israel M. Ta-Shma*, ed. Avraham (Rami) Reiner, vol. 1 (Alon Shvut: Tevunot - Mikhlelet Hertsog, 2011), 196 and 215–16.

5. About such practices, already in antiquity, see Jason Sion Mokhtarian, *Medicine in the Talmud* (Berkeley: University of California Press, 2022). For other medieval recipes, see Ron Barkai, *A History of Jewish Gynaecological Texts in the Middle Ages*, Brill's Series in Jewish Studies, v. 20 (Leiden: Brill, 1998); Baumgarten, "Ask the Midwives."

6. About such suspicions, see Joseph Shatzmiller, *Jews, Medicine, and Medieval Society* (Berkeley: University of California Press, 1994); Naama Cohen-Hanegbi, "Special Cluster Learning Practice from Texts: Jews and Medicine in the Later Middle Ages," *Social History of Medicine* 32 (2019): 659–69 and the articles in this special issue, https://doi.org/10.1093/shm/hkz076.

7. Shatzmiller, *Jews, Medicine, and Medieval Society*.

R. Isaac b. Isaac of Chinon's Prayerbook

The prayer against *bon malon* (carbuncle), written in French using Hebrew letters, appears in a manuscript belonging to Isaac son of Isaac, who lived in Chinon in the Loire Valley during the mid-thirteenth century.[8] This Isaac is a figure who is well known to scholars; the scion of an elite family of rabbis and scholars, he was also a prolific writer of beautiful Hebrew hymns (*piyyutim*).[9] Less is known, however, about the town of Chinon or its Jewish community during the period of time that Isaac lived there. The modicum of archaeological evidence extant from the period indicates that during the thirteenth century a small Jewish community was concentrated near the marketplace, on the rue de la Juiverie, which was known as "the most commercial street" in town. A Jewish cemetery has also been identified beyond the walls of the town.[10] In any case, the life of this community came to an abrupt end in 1306, when all the Jews in the Kingdom of France, including those in Chinon, were expelled by King Philip IV, and their property confiscated.[11]

The prayer appears in a small easily portable booklet, part prayerbook, part personal notebook, in which the author wrote down different cures and prayers and copied various passages from other Hebrew and Aramaic sources. The manuscript, now housed in the National Library of France, MS BnF héb.633, measures 9 cm by 7.2 cm, and is

---

8. Henri Gross, *Gallia Judaica: Dictionnaire geographique de la France d'apres les sources rabbiniques* (Paris: L. Cerf, 1897), 580–81.

9. Collette Sirat, "Un rituel Juif de France: Le manuscrit hébreu 633 de la bibliothèque nationale de Paris," *Revue des études juives* 119 (1961): 7–40; Ephraim Elimelech Urbach, *The Tosaphists: Their History, Writings and Methods*, 4th ed. (Jerusalem: Bialik Institute, 1980), 636, 720–721, and more recently Ephraim Kanarfogel, *The Intellectual History and Rabbinic Culture of Medieval Ashkenaz* (Detroit: Wayne State University Press, 2013), 432–34, 454–55, 480.

10. Henri Grimaud, "Le quartier juif à Chinon au XIVe siècle," *Bulletin de la société archéologique de la Touraine* 10 (1895–1896): 137–41. For additional scholars from Chinon, see note 9 above.

11. In 1315, the Jews were allowed to return to France, but those who returned to Chinon did not remain for long. The few historical sources that have come down to us about Jewish Chinon refer mostly to its bitter end—in a massacre that occurred on October 2, 1321, as part of the events surrounding the "Lepers' Plot," in which French Jews were accused of ordering lepers to poison Christian wells. In the 1321 massacre, about 160 Jews from Chinon were burned alive on the outskirts of the city. See William Chester Jordan, *The French Monarchy and the Jews: From Philip Augustus to the Last Capetians* (Philadelphia: University of Pennsylvania Press, 1989), 245–46; Simon Shwarzfuchs, *A History of the Jews in Medieval France* (Tel Aviv: Hakibbutz Hameuchad Publishing House, 2001), 293–94; Tzafrir Barzilay, *Poisoned Wells: Accusations, Persecution, and Minorities in Medieval Europe, 1321–1422* (Philadelphia : University of Pennsylvania Press, 2022), 38–70.

crafted from a mixture of vellum, parchment, and paper. It consists of 35 quires and 9 single pages bound to the middle of the codex. Despite being pocket-sized, it contains almost 300 folios, most of them densely filled on both sides with liturgical texts of diverse kinds.[12] Colette Sirat has identified 16 different scripts in the manuscript, among them writings by two identified scribes, Isaac himself, and Jacob, Isaac's teacher and mentor, who copied the first part of the codex sometime at the beginning of the thirteenth century.[13] Jacob wrote down in the book a number of customs and liturgical rituals of the community to which he and Isaac belonged. The 11 quires in his handwriting deal with daily prayers similar to those found in *Mahzor Vitry*. Jacob signed his name to f.50V, and his work ends at f.104V, where the hand of his student—Isaac—appears for the first time.[14]

Unlike Jacob, Isaac's quires are eclectic, and contain a wide variety of texts. In fact, as part of her work on the text, Sirat created an index of Isaac's writings, which she divided into over a dozen different topics.[15] It appears that Isaac simply wrote down whatever he deemed interesting or useful, leading to a peculiar pagination and assemblage of topics and texts, even on the same folio.[16] The manuscript lacks any systematic or thematic organization, so that midrash, personal prayers and rituals, poems, blessings for different occasions, and prayers for Rosh Hashanah and Yom Kippur are all mixed together.[17] For example, a poem that creates an acrostic of divine names, with a marginal note on a ritual for the health of the scribe's wife and daughter, all appear on fol.206r. These are followed on fol. 206v by a poem by Meir of Rothenburg (d. 1293); another poem by Judah he-Hasid (1150–1217) on fol.207v; and afterward, a personal "grace and favor" prayer on fol.209.[18] Isaac then goes on to another poem by Judah ha-Levi (1075–1141) on fol.210. Subsequently, on fol.211v, Isaac copied two adjurations for protection,

---

12. This manuscript was studied by Colette Sirat in the sixties and described in broad terms. It deserves further study. Amit Shafran, in her M.A. thesis, "To Me, Isaac son of Isaac," wrote about three folios from the manuscript, concentrating in particular on what she defined as magic. In the third chapter of the thesis, she focuses on the conjuration under discussion here and a large part of the first part of this chapter summarizes her thesis.
13. Sirat, "Un rituel juif de France," 9–10.
14. Sirat, "Un rituel juif de France," 9–11.
15. Sirat, "Un rituel juif de France," 13–23.
16. Sirat, "Un rituel juif de France," 13–14.
17. Sirat, "Un rituel juif de France," 22–24.
18. For more information on "grace and favor" charms, see Gideon Bohak, "Jewish Magic in the Middle Ages," in *The Cambridge History of Magic and Witchcraft in the West*, ed. David J. Collins, S. J., 1st ed. (Cambridge: Cambridge University Press, 2015), 268.

followed by a passage from Tractate Berakhot 17a (fol.212). Among the different formulae, there are arithmetic calculations and calendars,[19] as well as prayers for different purposes such as travel and disease.[20] Other themes include hymns, fortune-telling, and matchmaking, along with more routine texts such as holiday prayers, medicinal recipes, and a personal prayer to be recited after studying Torah.[21] All these were part of everyday activities. Some of these prayers and recipes can be found in other manuscripts, whereas others are known only from this manuscript.[22]

Isaac's work has been described as a kind of personal notebook that gathers useful prayers and formulae for various occasions annually and different phases of a person's life.[23] A number of the prayers and adjurations include his name rather than a generic reference to so-and-so son or daughter of so-and-so (*ploni ben* or *bat ploni*).[24] This collection of prayers and formulae add to what is known about Isaac as a scholar and allow a glimpse of other aspects of his life. It is possible that the recipes and rituals he chose to sign were those close to his heart.[25] It is also likely that these prayers were used not only for himself and his family but also for members of his community, as this was a well-known additional position often held by rabbis, much like some churchmen were medical experts in medieval Christian culture.[26] This was perhaps one of the ways he made a living, by reciting such personal prayers for others or teaching these to them.

---

19. National Library of France, MS BnF Heb.633, fol. 256v.
20. National Library of France, MS BnF Heb.633, fol. 206v.
21. Sirat, "Un rituel juif de France," 24.
22. Some of these are discussed by Ephraim Kanarfogel, *Peering through the Lattices: Mystical, Magical, and Pietistic Dimensions in the Tosafist Period* (Detroit: Wayne State University Press, 2000). Kanarfogel discusses Isaac and his prayers on p. 73n112; 174–76 where he compares between some of R. Isaac's prayers and those of Ashkenazic rabbis and other French rabbis, such as Rabbenu Tam. Kanarfogel is not interested in the medical matters at hand but in the prayers themselves and their place in traditions of piety, mysticism, and magic. More work is needed to create a fuller index of prayers for medical situations. See the work of Katelyn Mesler, "The Three Magi and Other Christian Motifs in Medieval Hebrew Medical Incantations: A Study in the Limits of Faithful Translation," *Latin-into-Hebrew: Texts and Studies*, ed. Resianne Fontaine and Gad Freudenthal (Leiden: Brill, 2013), 161–218.
23. On this genre, see Simcha Emanuel, *Fragments of the Tablets: The Lost Library of Ba'alei ha-Tosafot* (Jerusalem: Magnes Press, 2007), 250–54 (Hebrew).
24. National Library of France, MS BNF héb. 633, fol. 1.
25. Shafran made this suggestion, "To Me, Isaac son of Isaac," 19–20.
26. Naama Cohen-Hanegbi, *Caring for the Living Soul: Emotions, Medicine, and Penance in the Late Medieval Mediterranean* (Leiden: Brill, 2017).

Prayers Against Fever and Carbuncles

Three prayers against disease appear on folios 149v–150. The first prayer (149v–150r), which will be our focus, is in vernacular French, written in Hebrew script. It is followed by a prayer in Hebrew and Aramaic against fever (150r), and a prayer that is partly in French and partly in Hebrew entitled *hamaria hafukhah* (150v). Whereas the Hebrew is legible, the French is very hard to decipher and requires future attention. These are then followed by two cures, one for a sick child (151r) and the other for quartan fever (151r). This section of the notebook concludes with *Pitum ha-Ketoret* (151v– 154r), a prayer often recited in relation to plague and fever.[27] While the Hebrew prayer sequence deserves further attention, for the purpose of this chapter we will focus only on the first prayer.

FIGURE 11.1. The prayer in Hebraico-French in the prayerbook/personal notebook of Isaac son of Isaac. ©BNF héb. 633, fol. 150r.

---

27. Susan L. Einbinder, *Writing Plague: Jewish Responses to the Great Italian Plague* (Philadelphia: University of Pennsylvania Press, 2022), 4–5; 104–5; 115–24.

The text in its original Hebraico-French,[28] along with a French transliteration, was published by Menahem Banitt.[29]

For good health (*li-refu'ah shlemah*)

I conjure you, Bon Malon (carbuncle), by the Lord God who neither should nor [does] disappoint, who neither sleeps nor slumbers;

I conjure you, by God the mighty king, since you are here, [that you] no longer progress;

I conjure you, by God the Great, since you are here, not to profit anymore;

I conjure you, by God who is in Heaven, since you are here, not to remain [in my body] anymore;

I conjure you by the Living God, since you are here, not to withdraw like the famous tide of the sea,[30] abandoning your misery behind you and [not] letting your evil remain; to no longer wrench his gut or infect his flesh;

I conjure you by the Lord God: take away your cruelty; and by bread and salt, by wine and water, and by all that God has created;

I conjure you by the Living God and by the true health that inspire the doctor; and by bread and wine, and by all that God created, not to stay here;

I conjure you by all the prayers that exist and have ever existed;

I conjure you with all the prayers that have been and all those that will see the light of day;

I conjure you by all the men who ever came into the world and by Abraham, the great man, who was ready to sacrifice his son for the love of God [and to] make him suffer martyrdom; and actually heal, in the same way that God restored [health] to the prophetess Miriam after she had had leprosy; and actually

---

28. "Hebraico-French," following Fudeman's suggestion in her book: Kirsten A. Fudeman, *Vernacular Voices: Language and Identity in Medieval French Jewish Communities* (Philadelphia: University of Pennsylvania Press), 2011.

29. Menahem Banitt, "Une formule d'exorcisme en ancien français," in *Studies in Honor of Mario A. Pei*, ed. John Fisher and Paul A. Gaeng (Chapel Hill: University of North Carolina Press, 1972), 43–44; See also Shafran, "To Me, Isaac," 31–44.

30. Perhaps a reference to the Red Sea.

healed; drive out this evil from here and relieve this pain; so be it from all (to) eternity.

Three times and it will help (the sick), with God's aid (*ve-yo'il, be'ezrat hashem*).[31]

The formula starts with a Hebrew headline, stating its purpose: "For good health." It ends again with Hebrew words "Three times and it will help, with God's aid." The body of the formula includes ten adjurations, all in Hebraico-French. In the first half of the cure, the user conjures the illness itself, the bon malon. Menachem Banitt, based on the analysis of other medicinal texts and their linguistic features, posited that bon malon means fever and carbuncle, a boil or sore, symptomatic of the fever.[32] The second half of the prayer calls on God through a series of adjurations. We will begin our examination with one of the most outstanding aspects of the prayer, the adjurations. How common were such adjurations? What was their history in medieval European Jewish settings?

Adjurations

Adjurations were a common method of dealing with illness and are a feature in many medieval medical and magical traditions. This mechanism presents illness as a demon who, like any other creature, is subject to God, and must obey Him, and must even respond to a request made in His name. Therefore, adjurations, and especially adjurations using God's names and titles, were considered to be something the illness had no choice but to obey.[33] Virginia Reinburg defined such prayers as belonging to a type of prayer she called colloquy-style, one that is structured like a conversation being spoken between God and the interlocutor. She states, "Colloquy-style prayers begin with an invocation, and sometimes a request to be heard, followed by a request for assistance.... The devotee then makes a request, usually followed by a promise to devote self or life to God or the saint."[34]

---

31. National Library of France, MS BNF 633, fol. 149v. The entire last line is in Hebrew.
32. Banitt, "Une formule d'exorcisme en ancien français," 39–40.
33. Harari, "Religion, Magic, and Adjurations," 53–56; Swartz, "Scribal Magic and Its Rhetoric," 174–79; Avigail Manekin-Bamberger, *Intersections between Law and Magic in Ancient Jewish Texts* (Tel Aviv: Tel Aviv University, 2018), 111–13; Gideon Bohak, *Ancient Jewish Magic* (Cambridge: Cambridge University Press, 2008), 82.
34. Virginia Reinburg, "Oral Rites: Prayer and Talk in Early Modern France," in *Spoken Word and Social Practice*, ed. Thomas V. Cohen and Lesley K. Twomey (Leiden: Brill, 2015), 382–83.

Adjurations of this sort can be found in many Jewish and Christian texts. Bohak, for example, has traced its existence from the Babylonian Talmud through the medieval period.[35] Examples from the Babylonian Talmud include conjurations of God using coins, vessels, salt, water, lentils, dates, beets, fish, animal parts, wine, vinegar, and living creatures, such as ants.[36] More specifically for our purposes, among the different cures are those recommended for fevers, including one for an *"ishta tzemirta,"* which Rashi explains is a very high fever (*kadahat*).[37]

A quick review of the cures recorded in the Talmud allows a better appreciation of how the Hebraico-French cure in Isaac's notebook is exceptional, especially in comparison to more traditional ones. Of the cures for fever that appear in the Talmud one includes laying sand on the sick person's body; another recommends capturing an ant, sealing it in a tube and saying (to the ant!) "Your burden upon me and my burden upon you!" Yet another includes an incantation recited next to a river, which seeks to transfer the illness from the person to the river.[38] The most detailed cure in the Talmud includes the recitation of verses rather than conjurations. R. Yoharan recommends taking a strand of hair from the sick person, and an iron knife, and going to a place where there is a thornbush:

> On the first day he must slightly notch it [the bush] and say: "And the angel of the Lord appeared to him" (Ex. 3:2), On the following day he [again] makes a notch and says, "And Moses said I will turn aside now and see" (Ex. 3: 3). The next day he makes another small notch and says: "And when the Lord saw that he turned aside (*sar*) to see." (Ex. 3: 4)

This is a typical recitation of verses, using the meaning of the passage in the context of disease. Much like the bush was burning, the sick person is suffering from fever, and like Moses turned aside (*sar*), the fever is being encouraged or ordered to go away, using the double meaning of the word *sar*, in the sense of turning aside, like Moses did, but also in the sense of departing, as is the aspiration for the fever. Some of these cures were supposed to be recited multiple times (three, seven etc.). The

---

35. Bohak, "Jewish Magic in the Middle Ages"; Bohak, *Ancient Jewish Magic*, 152. See also Yuval Harari and Batya Stein, *Jewish Magic before the Rise of Kabbalah* (Detroit: Wayne State University Press, 2017), 220–21.
36. BT Shabbat 66b, BT Gittin 70a.
37. BT Shabbat 67a, BT Gittin 69a and b.
38. "River, river. Take back the water that you gave to me for the routine that has come upon me, it came upon me in its day and it has now left me in its day." BT Shabbat 66b.

Talmud continues with a discussion of the most appropriate verses for the fever, with R. Aha suggesting alternatives to those of R. Yohanan, including an adjuration to the thorn:

> Oh thorn, oh thorn,[39] not because you are higher than all the other trees did the Holy One, Blessed is He, cause his *shekhinah* to rest upon you, but because you are lower than all the trees did he cause his *shekhinah* to rest upon you. And even as you saw the fire [kindled] for Hananiah, Mishael and Azariah, and fled from before them, so look upon the fire [fever] of so and so and flee from him.[40]

Evident from these Talmudic examples is that common foodstuffs and verses or adjurations were often employed in order to deal with illness, particularly fevers. Furthermore, these methods were used not only by the Jews of late antiquity but were an accepted part of general medical practices and approaches to healing during this period.[41] Medieval Christian books of hours and missals also include adjurations against disease that use foodstuffs and appeals to God and to the saints.[42]

R. Isaac's Adjuration

Returning to the prayer in R. Isaac's notebook, one can see some similarity to the type of Talmudic precedents mentioned above. Recited three times, the Hebraico-French prayer demands that the fever leave the sick person's body, it refers to foodstuffs, and it calls on biblical figures. Yet if we compare this adjuration to other prayers that appear in Isaac's book, its uniqueness stands out. As noted above, appearing in the same folio is a Hebrew prayer against fever (kadahat), which uses

---

39. Here hinting to the burning bush, the *sneh*.
40. BT Shabbat 67a. It would seem that Mishael, Hananiah, and Azariah are invoked here because they withstood fire and thus can fight against the fever. These figures are often mentioned in medieval prayers, in liturgy for Shavuot. For a story about them, see Rella Kushelevsky, *Tales in Context: Sefer ha-Ma'asim in Medieval Northern France* (Detroit, MI: Wayne State University Press, 2017), 122–23, story § 10.
41. Dorothea M. Salzer, *Die Magie der Anspielung: Form und Funktion der biblischen Anspielungen in den magischen Texten der Kairoer Geniza* (Tübingen: Mohr Siebeck, 2010).
42. See Adolf Franz, *Die Kirchlichen Benediktionen im Mittelalter* (Freiburg: Herdersche Verlagshandlung, 1909), 2:481–84; Edina Bozóky, *Charmes et prières apotropaïques* (Turnhout: Brepols, 2003), 49–65.

a familiar format of divine names, often found in Jewish amulets from Late Antiquity until the medieval period.[43]

An amulet against fever:

ABRKA ABRKA AB AB ACAB ABR ABRA BRACY AMBKA AB ABRKAL ABRKAL ABRKAL YH YH YH YHWH YH YHWH
Lord, Lord, God, God, God, Ts, Tsva'ot, Tsva'ot
Metatron, Gabriel and Michae[l]
And Raphael he will cure Ploni son of Plonit from the fi[re] And fever inside him, Amen
and for a woman Plonit daughter of Plonit from the fire and fever inside her Amen.[44]

It starts with letter combinations of the word ABRKA, which is a paraphrase of the divine name Abraxas (sometimes spelled Abrasax). This mystical term originated in the system of the Gnostic Basilides, and was common in Greco-Egyptian magic during Late Antiquity.[45] It appears on objects ranging from Babylonian incantation bowls to amulets found in the Cairo Genizah as well as in Ashkenazic and Oriental texts.[46] Jewish practitioners believed Abraxas to be "the name of a very powerful angel or celestial power," or even one of the many names of God himself.[47] This prayer also displays common combinations of divine names and titles, especially the Tetragrammaton, and calls on archangels, a well-known practice in such texts.[48] Other examples would add

---

43. Bohak, *Ancient Jewish Magic*, 305–6; Bohak, "Jewish Magic in the Middle Ages."
44. National Library of France, MS Paris Heb.633, fol. 150r.

קמיע לקדחת אברקא אברקא אב
אב אכאב אבר אברא בראכי אמבקא אב
אברקאל אברקאל אברקאל יה יה יה יהוה יה
יהוה אדני אדני אדני אלהים אלהים אלהים צב
צבאות צבאות מטטרון גבריאל ומיכא[ל]
ורפאל הוא ירפא פלוני בר פלונית מהאי [אש]
ומהקדחת אשר בקרבו אמן ולאשה
פלונית בת פלונית מהאש ומהקדחת
אשר בקרבה אמן

45. Bohak, *Ancient Jewish Magic*, 247–50.
46. Bohak, *Ancient Jewish Magic*, 247–50.
47. Bohak, *Ancient Jewish Magic*, 247–50.
48. Swartz, "Scribal Magic and Its Rhetoric," 177; Bohak, *Ancient Jewish Magic*, 305–7.

the words "Amen Selah."[49] In contrast, the Hebraico-French adjuration does not use known formulas.

The prayer begins by calling upon the disease: "I conjure you, Bon Malon (carbuncle), by the Lord God who neither should nor [does] disappoint, who neither sleeps nor slumbers." It ends with this solicitation: "I conjure you by all the men who ever came into the world and by Abraham, the great man, who was ready to sacrifice his son for the love of God [and to] make him suffer martyrdom; and actually heal, in the same way: like God restored [health] to the prophetess Miriam after she had had leprosy; and actually healed; drive out this evil from here and relieve this pain; so be it from all (to) eternity."

Some of these examples can be found in other Hebrew prayers of the period. Miriam was typically called on in prayers for the sick recited in synagogues, where God was asked to heal the sick like he healed Miriam and Naaman from leprosy, and Hezekiah from his illness. Often such prayers called on the patriarchs and the matriarchs as well.[50] However, in this instance, the reference to "all the men" is not clear. Who is the prayer referring to apart from Abraham, who is singled out from "all the men"? It would seem that the text is referring to all the people of the world, which is highly unusual. In contrast, the reference to Abraham and Isaac is much more common, with the reference to the sacrifice and healing of Isaac being particularly popular in medieval literature after the First Crusade.[51]

The prayer also states: "I conjure you by the Living God, since you are here, not to withdraw like the famous tide of the sea,[52] abandoning your misery behind you and [not] letting your evil remain; to no longer wrench his gut or infect his flesh." In this case, it is unclear to which sea the prayer is referring, yet perhaps, like the request in the Talmud that the river take away the fever, so too, it is a general idea of the sea that is being referenced. It is also possible that sea in question is specifically the Red Sea. As Steve Weitzman has recently argued, the parting

---

49. Hermann Gollancz, *Clavicula Salomonis* (Frankfurt: M: J. Kauffmann, 1903).

50. Inbal Gabay-Zada, "The Ritual of Miriam's Well and the Jews of Ashkenaz and Provence: 11th–14th Centuries" (MA Thesis, Bar-Ilan University, 2017); Elisheva Baumgarten, *Biblical Women and Jewish Daily Life in the Middle Ages* (Philadelphia: University of Pennsylvania Press, 2022), 57–70.

51. Shalom Spiegel, *The Last Trial* (New York: Pantheon Books, 1967).

52. Perhaps a reference to the Red Sea.

of the Red Sea and the plague of blood in Egypt were often alluded to in medical tractates.[53]

In addition, like the cures found in the Talmud and especially within Christian traditions, R. Isaac's Hebraico-French cure also mentions foodstuffs.

> I conjure you by the Lord God: take away your cruelty; and by bread and salt, by wine and water, and by all that God has created;
>
> I conjure you by the Living God and by the true health that inspire the doctor; and by bread and wine, and by all that God created, not to stay here;

Bread, salt, wine, and water are basic foodstuffs but they are also staples of religious ritual, both Jewish and Christian. All Jewish festive and ritual meals begin with benedictions over bread and wine. They were also integral components of the Christian rite of mass. Salt was believed, from Biblical times, to ward off evil, and thus, for this reason, for example, babies were sprinkled with salt immediately after birth.[54] Water too was commonly used for cures but is also a basic and elemental source of life.

As is evident, the Hebraico-French prayer contains some features that are common in medieval Jewish prayers and cures. Yet, we would also argue that alongside these familiar themes, the conjuration itself and some of the expressions within it, are exceptional. Perhaps its most outstanding feature is its language. While Old French would have been spoken on a daily basis by the Jews living in France, few Jewish prayers in this language, or indeed in any vernacular, have reached us from the medieval period.[55] This became a much more common phenomenon during the Early Modern period, when prayers in Yiddish abound.[56]

---

53. Our thanks to Steven Weitzman, who related this as part of a talk at the Hebrew University of Jerusalem in spring 2023.
54. See Baumgarten, "Ask the Midwives."
55. See for example: Gideon Bohak, "Catching a Thief: The Jewish Trials of a Christian Ordeal," *Jewish Studies Quarterly* 13, no. 4 (2006): 344, https://doi.org/10.1628/0944 57006780130420; Colette Sirat, "Une formule divinatoire latine dans deux manuscrits hébreux," *Revue des études juives* (1966): 391-94; Katelyn Mesler, *The Three Magi and Other Christian Motifs in Medieval Hebrew Medical Incantations: A Study in the Limits of Faithful Translation* (Leiden: Brill, 2013), 161-218, https://doi.org/10.1163/9789004252868_012; Susan Einbinder, "The Troyes Laments: Jewish Martyrology in Hebrew and Old French," *Viator* 30 (1999): 201-30, https://doi.org/10.1484/J.VIATOR.2.300835.
56. See, for example, Tracy Guren Klirs, *The Merit of Our Mothers = [Bizkhus imohes]: A Bilingual Anthology of Jewish Women's Prayers* (Cincinnati: Hebrew Union College, 1992). See also

Moreover, the appeal to biblical figures other than the patriarchs and matriarchs, is also not common in Jewish medieval prayer, at least according to our knowledge to date. In contrast, such conjurations, including appeals to biblical figures and similar foodstuffs, are well known from medieval Christian rituals.[57]

Christian Adjurations for Fever

Given the language in which the prayer was written, it is important to seek comparisons not only in Jewish sources, but in Christian sources as well. One telling example is a prayer against fever, recited in a mass in honor of the Burgundian king St. Sigismund (d. 542). The prayer has survived in Latin but it is assumed that vernacular versions were also in circulation.[58] Sigismund was said to have come into conflict with Bishop Appolinaris of Valence over the rules of marriage, leading him to imprison the bishop. When, shortly after this, the king fell ill, he, realizing that the disease was a punishment for the imprisonment of the bishop, sent the queen to request that Appolinaris pray for him. According to early medieval legend, Sigismund was cured.[59] His near contemporary, Gregory of Tours, subsequently reported: "Whenever people suffering from chills piously celebrate a mass in his honor and make an offering to God for the king's repose, immediately their tremors cease, their fevers disappear, and they are restored to their earlier

---

prayers for the dead: Sylvie Anne Goldberg, *Crossing the Jabbok: Illness and Death in Ashkenazi Judaism in Sixteenth- through Nineteenth-Century Prague* (Berkeley: University of California Press, 1996).

57. Pierre Rézeau, *Les prières aux saints en français à la fin du moyen âge* (Geneva: Librairie Droz, 1982).

58. Frederick S. Paxton, "Liturgy and Healing in an Early Medieval Saint's Cult: The Mass 'In Honore Sancti Sigismundi' for the Cure of Fevers," *Traditio* 49 (1994): 23-43, https://doi.org/10.1017/S0362152900012988.

59. This story is described in National Library of France, MS BNF Lat. 1510 from the late fourteenth century or early fifteenth century. For Sigismund's life and early cult, see Robert Folz, "Zur Frage der heiligen Könige: Heiligkeit und Nachleben in der Geschichte des burgundischen Königtums," *Deutsches Archiv für Erforschung des Mittelalters* 14 (1958): 317-44; Robert Folz, *Les saints rois du moyen âge en occident* (Bruxelles: Sociéte des Bollandistes 1984), 23-25, 196-97. J. M. Wallace-Hadrill, *The Long-Haired Kings and Other Studies in Frankish History* (London: Methuen, 1962), 131, 200-201, where he explains that Gregory wanted Merovingian kings to have miraculous power and sanctity. Sigismund was the opponent of Arianism and curer of fevers. Frederick S. Paxton, "Power and the Power to Heal: The Cult of St. Sigismund of Burgundy," *Early Medieval Europe* 2 (1993): 95-110, https://data.isiscb.org/isis/citation/CBB000044525; Paxton, "Liturgy and Healing in an Early Medieval Saint's Cult." Sigismund later became a hero of sorts in Hungary and Bohemia, see Dragoș Gh. Năstăsoiu, "A New *sancta et fidelis sodetas* for Saint Sigismund of Burgundy: His Cult and Iconography in Hungary during the Reign of Sigismund of Luxemburg," *Hungarian Historical Review* 5 (2016): 587-617.

health."⁶⁰ In the centuries that followed, the saint day of St. Sigismund was celebrated across Europe on May 1,⁶¹ and the special mass said in his honor was copied and recopied numerous times, resulting in various versions and permutations.⁶² There are a number of variations of this mass and of prayers derived from it in Latin and in the vernacular languages.⁶³

The prayer against fever recited in this mass begins with the instructions: "Every day for three days [read this] three times over the fever-sufferer and he will be healed."⁶⁴ It then reads:

> In the name of the Father and the Son and the Holy Spirit, Amen. Behold the crosse of the triune Lord. Christ was born. On. Bon. Jon. Christ suffered. Don. Ron. Con. Christ rose from the dead. Ton Son. Yon. When the Lord Jesus had entered the house of Simon Peter, he saw Peter's mother-in-law lying ill with fever, and standing over her he commanded the fever and dismissed it and then immediately she ministered to him [Matt. 8:140–15; Luke 4: 38–39] Syon, Syon, Syon.⁶⁵

---

60. *Nam, si qui nunc frigoritici in eius honore missas devote celebrant eiusque pro requie Deo offerunt oblationem, statim, conpressis tremoribus, restinctis febribus, sanitati praestinae restaurantur, Liber in Gloria Martyrum*, ed. B. Krusch, rep. MGH (Turnhout: Brepols, 2010), 537; trans. Raymond Van Dam, *Glory of the Martyrs* (Liverpool: Liverpool University Press, 1988), 97.

61. Yitzhak Hen, *Culture and Religion in Merovingian Gaul, A.D. 481–751* (Leiden: Brill, 1995), 95, notes that prayer for kings was a standard part of early medieval liturgy, "missa pro principe." For an example, see Jonathan Black, "The Divine Office and Private Devotion in the Latin West," in *The Liturgy of the Medieval Church*, eds. E. Ann Matter and Thomas J. Heffernan, 2d ed. (Kalamazoo, MI: Medieval Institute Publications, 2005), 59; before the Carolingian reforms there was an insular tradition of prayerbooks containing personal prayers for protection, prayers of praise, prayers addressed to the saints, prayers of confession, and collections of psalm verses. See also Robert Bartlett, *Why Can the Dead Do Such Great Things? Saints and Worshippers from the Martyrs to the Reformation* (Princeton: Princeton University Press, 2013), 214–15.

62. The most detailed account remains Adolf Franz, *Die Messe im deutschen Mittelalter Beitr. Zur Geschichte der Liturgie und des religiösen Volkslebens* (Freiburg: Herder, 1902), 191–203.

63. This text was published by Ernest Wickersheimer, *Les manuscrits latins de médecine du haut moyen âge dans les bibliothèques de France* (Paris: Editions du centre national de la recherche scientifique, 1966), 32–33. For studies of the prayer, see Paxton, "Power and the Power to Heal"; Paxton, "Liturgy and Healing in an Early Medieval Saint's Cult"; Ian N. Wood, "Liturgy in the Rhone Valley and the Bobbio Missal," in *The Bobbio Missal: Liturgy and Religious Culture in Merovingian Gaul*, ed. Yitzhak Hen and Rob Meens (New York: Cambridge University Press, 2004), 206–18; Don C. Skemer, *Binding Words: Textual Amulets in the Middle Ages* (University Park, PA: Pennsylvania State University Press, 2006), 106–7, 189–90; Don C. Skemer, "Amulet Rolls and Female Devotion in the Late Middle Ages," *Scriptorium* 55, no. 2 (2001): 206–7, 226, http://dx.doi.org/10.3406/scrip.2001.1929.

64. Adolf Franz, *Die Messe im deutschen Mittelalter*, 191–203, and see the comparisons there.

65. Trans. by Faith Wallis, ed. *Medieval Medicine. A Reader* (Toronto: University of Toronto, 2010), 69–70.

This paragraph has no parallel in the Hebrew prayer discussed above. It is deeply infused with tales of sick sufferers taken from the New Testament. It also contains mnemonics in French (bon, jon, don, ron, etc.) indicating aids for remembering the prayer for those who could not read or were less fluent in Latin. Noting the figure to whom the prayer is devoted it continues: "For the commemoration of St. Sigismund, king, free your servant, Lord God." It is after these words that our comparison begins.

Mass for St. Sigismund	**Hebraico-French Prayer**
In the name of the Father, I speak to you, O fevers. In the name of the Son, I speak against you. In the name of the Holy Spirit, I conjure you, O fevers. You are seven sisters . . .⁶⁶	I conjure you, Bon Malon (carbuncle), by the Lord God who neither should nor [does] disappoint, who neither sleeps nor slumbers;
	I conjure you, by God the mighty king, since you are here, [that you] no longer progress;
	I conjure you, by God the Great, since you are here, not to profit anymore;
	I conjure you, by God who is in Heaven, since you are here, not to remain [in my body] anymore;

The Hebrew prayer does not call on the seven sisters, a common theme in Christian prayers,[67] but does conjure God in a way far more similar to the mass than to the abraxas prayer discussed above. The Christian and Jewish prayers both continue adjuring God, using different names:

---

66. In addition to the mass, a number of prayers against fever have also survived, some associated directly with St. Sigismund and others related to other familiar themes, such as the seven sisters and the seven sleepers, as well as prayers that include writing amulets on apples, bread, cheese, and other foodstuffs. See Lea T. Olsan, "Writing on the Hand in Ink: A Late Medieval Innovation in Fever Charms in England," *Incantatio. An International Journal on Charms, Charmers and Charming* 7 (2018): 9–45, htps://doi.org/10.7592/Incantato_2018_7_Olsan.

67. Olsan, "Writing on the Hand in Ink."

Mass for St. Sigismund	Hebraico-French Prayer
I conjure you and join issue with you by the Father and the Son and the Holy Spirit... the Holy Trinity and by St. Mary... St. Michael... Gabriel, Raphael who is called the medicine of God... holy angels... Matthew, Mark, Luke and John... by those powers which contain heaven and earth and by St. John the Baptist who baptized the Lord God in the River Jordan...[68]	I conjure you, Bon Malon (carbuncle), by the Lord God who neither should nor [does] disappoint, who neither sleeps nor slumbers;
	I conjure you, by God the mighty king, since you are here, [that you] no longer progress;
	I conjure you, by God the Great, since you are here, not to profit anymore;
	I conjure you, by God who is in Heaven, since you are here, not to remain [in my body] anymore;

The Hebrew text does not refer to the same figures but expresses a similar sentiment.

The next part of the Latin conjuration calls on many different Christian figures asking them to use their powers:

Mass for St. Sigismund	Hebraico-French Prayer
I conjure you and join issue with you by the Father and the Son and the Holy Spirit... the Holy Trinity and by St. Mary... St. Michael... Gabriel, Raphael who is called the medicine of God... holy angels... Matthew, Mark, Luke and John... by those powers which contain heaven and earth and by St. John the Baptist who baptized the Lord God in the River Jordan...[69]	I conjure you by all the men who ever came into the world and by Abraham, the great man, who was ready to sacrifice his son for the love of God
	[and to] make him suffer martyrdom; and actually heal, in the same way: like God restored [health] to the prophetess Miriam after she had had leprosy; and actually healed; drive out this evil from here and relieve this pain; so be it from all (to) eternity.

---

68. This too is a common theme and one that can be found in Hebrew incantations as well. See Salzer, *Die Magie*, 100, 192, 408.

69. Salzer, *Die Magie*, 100, 192, 408.

In this part of the prayer, there are direct parallels between the Christian and Jewish prayers, despite the different figures called on. The Latin prayer ends in a manner quite similar to the Jewish prayer:

Mass for St. Sigismund	Hebraico-French Prayer
I conjure you fevers and join issue with you, that you be cast out of the servant of God. Amen, Amen, Amen, Our father.	drive out this evil from here and relieve this pain; so be it from all (to) eternity.
In the memory of the Holy King Sigismund, Lord God, free this your servant N. In the name of the father, I say to you fevers, in the name of the Son, I contradict you; in the name of the Holy Spirit, I conjure you.[70]	

These last conjurations are replete with Christian motifs yet the actual language is very similar to what appears in the Hebraico-French prayer. All in all, albeit the specific religious features, the two prayers share many common features and beliefs.

The Hebraico-French prayer also contains additional elements that can be found in other medieval Christian conjurations against fever, such as water, wine, bread, and salt. As Lea Olsan has documented, there were numerous formats for such practices. A common one was the use of foodstuffs as a way to ward off demons, a feature evident in the Hebraico-French version.[71] While bread and wine were central to the Mass as well as in Jewish rituals around meals, they were not used regularly in other, more traditional magical/medical rituals. Their use here in this prayer, more closely resembles their use in the Mass rather than in Jewish rituals.[72]

---

70. Dijon, Bibliothèque Municipale, MS 448, fol. 181r; translated by Faith Wallis in *Medieval Medicine*, 69–70.
71. Olsan, "Writing on the Hand in Ink."
72. Shafran, "For me, Isaac, son of Isaac," 39.

Can a Mass for a Saint be a Jewish Prayer?

Reexamining the Hebraico-French version at this point reveals that while there are many pronounced differences, the two prayers share a basic underlying structure or form, one that does not exist in other Hebrew adjurations. This raises the possibility that perhaps an unknown Christian text lurks behind this Jewish prayer. While we have not found an exact parallel, in what follows we will point to some possibilities. Moreover, the use of the vernacular makes this comparison all the more relevant. We argue that R. Isaac, or someone who preceded him, was familiar with Christian prayers of this sort, and adapted a version of the Latin prayer that already existed in the vernacular. Recent research indicates that this type of adaptation, most often of rituals, was quite common.[73] In such cases, the liturgy, or the words recited remained distinct, but the basic prayer mechanism was adapted. For example, if during the lying-in of a Christian woman the names Anna, Maria, and Elisabeth were called on, or a verse recited concerning the Holy Family's hasty departure to Egypt, during the lying-in of Jewish women a verse about the Jews' hasty departure from Egypt would be recited and Sarah, Leah, Rebecca and Hannah would be called on.[74]

Although examples of prayers recited in the vernacular, such as the one examined here, rather than in Hebrew are limited, there nevertheless are other known instances of this phenomenon, some of which are also cures for disease, while others are prayers for protection against thieves or for infants.[75] It is quite possible that this was in fact a more common practice, examples of which have not reached us. After all, Hebrew documents were preserved far more often than those in the vernacular.

We began this chapter with the anecdote from *Sefer Hasidim* about two neighbors consulting one another about cures. It seems plausible that Jews, who, as other chapters in this volume demonstrate, were more closely entangled with their Christian neighbors than previously assumed, could have come into contact with this prayer from them. Perhaps French Jews heard their neighbors reciting this prayer over their sick children. Their neighbors were probably reciting it in the vernacular rather than in Latin, as a stand-alone prayer, rather than

---

73. See note 36 above.
74. Baumgarten, "Ask the Midwives."
75. See note 55.

a mass, a development in the history of this prayer as it evolved over time. Appealing enough to make the jump to the Jewish community, the prayer was put to work curing Jews suffering from fever as well. Perhaps the existing Talmudic precedents contributed to a sense of legitimacy in appropriating it for this use.

What mechanism was at work here? Did Jews remove the blatantly Christian holy names, leave the material culture (bread, wine, water and salt), and replace Christian examples with Jewish ones so that the prayer, originally a mass, was transformed into a Jewish one?[76] If this was the case, the prayer can serve as a case study of sorts for the filtration process. What did Jews find overtly and overly Christian and remove and what did they leave in the prayer? Scholars who have examined other adaptations of this sort, particularly so-called magical and medical formulas, such as prayers against thieves, have shown that usually only the most overtly Christian features are removed, such as references to the three magi, Jesus, Mary, and other holy figures.[77]

If Jews consciously adapted this prayer from their neighbors for their own use were they comfortable doing so because it was associated with a Christian king rather than an actual saint? Was that a factor at all? Were certain Christian figures more offensive than others? Mary and Miriam are often paralleled in these prayers but other shared figures such as Raphael and Gabriel are lost in translation. Why weren't Hananiah, Mishael, and Azariah, well-known figures in Jewish liturgy and narratives written in medieval Ashkenaz, called on?[78] More adaptations of this sort need to be examined in order to reach firmer conclusions, but this seems to be a case where Christian figures and values are deleted and Jewish replacements are made to avoid overtly foreign religious content.

No less fascinating is the vehicle by which this prayer was preserved. Isaac was a learned man, yet this prayer was as much a part of his repertoire as the more traditional prayers. While few Jews would pray to Jesus, dead or resurrected, they would however direct their prayers to

---

76. See an additional example of such a mechanism as described with another adjuration, Gideon Bohak, "Catching a Thief: The Jewish Trials of a Christian Ordeal," 344. Similar methods can be seen in stories, for example the story of R. Johanan and the scorpion, Kushelevsky, *Tales in Context*, 468–50, story § 28.

77. See Bohak, "Catching a Thief"; Mesler, "The Three Magi"; Sirat, "Une formule divinatoire latine dans deux manuscrits hébreux."

78. Kushelevsky, *Tales in Context*, story § 10, 122–123. They also appear in the liturgy for Shavuot and Yom Kippur.

the more appropriate figures of Abraham and Miriam, and as this example shows, Jews, both learned and unlearned, were clearly comfortable conjuring God to cure fevers. Isaac's mélange of three prayers against disease, one in Hebraico-French; one part Hebrew and part Hebraico-French, and one on Hebrew is an apt reflection of his multiple affiliations.

Scholars who have studied conjurations against fever and other similar medical practices have remarked that in the Christian world, these prayers tacked on to the mass were tolerated rather than encouraged by the Church. However, as Lea Olsan has recently argued, these prayers were not just the province of less educated people. As she demonstrated, such prayers were known by learned men who recorded them for posterity,[79] Isaac included. His book, with its eclectic collection of styles, forms, and prayers, is a clear example of the mixing of high and low culture. It indicates that there was perhaps a less clear divide between elites and non-elites than we suppose, and that occasionally it is only through material left behind by elites that we can get a sense of less elitist practices.

Medicine, Prayer, Jews, and Christians

This example also sheds light on the intersection between medicine and prayer in the Middle Ages. Whereas the practice of medicine has long been understood to have been shared by Jews and Christians, albeit with its own set of complexities and cautions, prayer is almost always considered to be religion specific.[80] However, the prayer studied here illustrates that even specifically religious prayers could be shared, adapted, and appropriated. It is important to note, however, that this prayer is a private one and was not intended to be recited in a public or communal setting, but rather at the bedside of an ill person, either by a family member or a specialist. While some work on communal prayers and rituals appropriated from one religion to the other has been done,[81] the phenomenon of private prayer has yet to be robustly

---

79. Olsan, "Writing on the Hand in Ink"; Lea T. Olsan, "Charms and Prayers in Medieval Medical Theory and Practice," *Social History of Medicine* 16, no. 3 (2003): 343, https://doi.org/10.1093/shm/16.3.343.

80. See above, note 5.

81. For a number of examples, see Israel Jacob Yuval, *Two Nations in Your Womb: Perceptions of Jews and Christians in Late Antiquity*, trans. Barbara Harshav and Jonathan Chipman (Berkeley: University of California Press, 2006), 205–56.

addressed, both within Judaism or with an eye to Christian parallels.[82] Since Jews and Christians recited multiple prayers of this sort on a daily basis, they present a new avenue for future research. Certain medieval texts, such as those berating Jewish women for praying to the Virgin Mary, a known saint of childbirth, while giving birth,[83] seem to support the supposition that Jews were perhaps less reticent to recite prayers familiar to them from their Christian surroundings when doing so privately, even those expressly directed at Christian saints and motifs. Our prayer against fever, however, does not reflect a complete adoption, but rather a more subtle appropriation. The medieval Jews, seeking to use what they hoped was an effective cure, altered the overtly Christian elements of the prayer and omitted other elements that could not be adapted. As Edina Bozóky remarked:

> Charms circulated with rapidity and astounding adaptability. They had a great ability to pass from one linguistic context to another. . . . This phenomenon reveals the importance of the meaning of charms. In the case of comprehensible charms, the language was only the supporting structure, subordinated to the meaning.[84]

In light of this, one can perhaps expand her formulation. Isaac b. Isaac of Chinon considered this prayer so potent that he thought it worth recording in his manuscript alongside other Hebrew prayers for the sick. Language did not deter him and he, or someone who preceded him, perhaps a female member of his family, perhaps a fellow healer, after learning of this prayer, incorporated it within the Jewish repertoire.

Isaac's use of both Hebrew and French prayers is another example of the extent to which Jews were embedded in their local surroundings and shared countless aspects of practice and belief with their neighbors.[85]

---

82. See for example Yitzhak D. Gilat, "Two Bakashot of Moses of Coucy," *Tarbiz* 28 (1959): 54–58.

83. Elisheva Baumgarten, "Women's Rituals: The Sabbath of the Parturient in its Early Modern Cultural Context," *Festschrift in Honor of Prof. Eric Zimmer*, ed. Gershon Bacon et al. (Ramat Gan: Bar-Ilan University Press, 2008) 11–28 (Hebrew).

84. Bozóky, *Charmes et prières apotropaïques*, 108.

85. See for example, Ivan G. Marcus, "A Jewish-Christian Symbiosis: The Culture of Early Ashkenaz," in *Cultures of the Jews: A New History*, ed. David Biale (New York: Schocken Books, 2002), 449–516; Ivan G. Marcus, *Rituals of Childhood: Jewish Acculturation in Medieval Europe* (New Haven, CT: Yale University Press, 1996); Baumgarten, "Appropriation and Differentiation," 39–63; Elisheva Baumgarten, Ruth Mazo Karras, and Katelyn Mesler, "Introduction," in *Entangled Histories: Knowledge, Authority, and Jewish Culture in the Thirteenth Century*, ed. Elisheva Baumgarten, Ruth Mazo Karras, and Katelyn Mesler (Philadelphia: University of Pennsylvania Press, 2017), 1–20.

It must also be noted that Isaac was not only a collector of texts but is considered an accomplished poet and a Tosafist. Thus, this one small example allows us not only to place Jewish-Christian interactions along a spectrum rather than as a binary but also provides a new perspective on the rabbinic class, as it situates them closer to if not alongside their neighbors and provides a glimpse of the spaces that they moved in such as homes and markets, and their everyday activities.

Finally, the example analyzed in this chapter holds additional interest. In the 1990s, historian Peregrine Horden argued that early medieval stories of dragon slayers should possibly be read as stories about the successful control of diseases such as malaria.[86] If he is right, then the connection between Sigismund as healer of fevers, and medieval folk heroes and dragon slayers, such as Beowulf and St. George or Sigurd, takes on new significance. In that respect, it is interesting that in the thirteenth century, in northern France, not far from Isaac b. Isaac of Chinon's home, a collection of tales known as *Sefer ha-Ma'asim*, was copied, which included several tales of dragons.[87] Prayers, medicine, and dragons thus connect Jew and Christians, further embedding Jews in medieval European culture. This is another direction for future research. It is possible that we can learn about Christian healing practices no less than Jewish ones, through these surviving examples.

Arising from R. Isaac's notebook is the suggestion that the response of the Jewish woman to her neighbor's cure using a Jesus relic was both the exception and the rule. It was an exception, because Jews often used Christian *materia medica*, sometimes even the exact formulas used by their neighbors. It was the rule, because Jews also sought to remove overtly Christian symbols and saints from these prayers when borrowing them. Isaac's notebook alerts us to the importance of finding more examples of personal prayers in the vernacular and seeing how these adaptations were made. Such examples will help elucidate both the negotiation and the differentiation that were part of Jewish life in the Middle Ages among both the elite and those who were "beyond the elite."

---

86. Peregrine Horden, "Disease, Dragons and Saints: The Management of Epidemics in the Dark Ages," in *Epidemics and Ideas: Essays on the Historical Perception of Pestilence*, ed. Paul Slack and Terence Ranger, Past and Present Publications (Cambridge: Cambridge University Press, 1992), 70-71.

87. Kushelevsky, *Tales*, Story § 27.

Further Reading

Banitt, Menahem. "Une formule d'exorcisme en ancien français." In *Studies in Honor of Mario A. Pei*, edited by John Fisher and Paul A. Gaeng, 39–44. Chapel Hill: University of North Carolina Press, 1972.

Baumgarten, Elisheva. "Appropriation and Differentiation: Jewish Identity in Medieval Ashkenaz." *AJS Review* 42 (2018): 39–63. doi.org/10.1017/S0364009418000053.

Bohak, Gideon. "Catching a Thief: The Jewish Trials of a Christian Ordeal." *Jewish Studies Quarterly* 13 (2006): 344. doi.org/10.1628/094457006780130420.

Bozóky, Edina. *Charmes et prières apotropaïques*. Turnhout: Brepols, 2003.

Cohen-Hanegbi, Naama, ed. "Learning Practice from Texts: Jews and Medicine in the Later Middle Ages." *Social History of Medicine* 32 (2019), and the articles in this special issue. doi.org/10.1093/shm/hkz076.

Einbinder, Susan. "The Troyes Laments: Jewish Martyrology in Hebrew and Old French." *Viator* 30 (1999): 201–30. doi.org/10.1484/J.VIATOR.2.300835.

Franz, Adolf. *Die kirchlichen Benediktionen im Mittelalter*. Freiburg: Herdersche Verlagshandlung, 1909.

Franz, Adolf. *Die Messe im deutschen Mittelalters*. Freiburg: Herder, 1902.

Fudeman, Kirsten A. *Vernacular Voices: Language and Identity in Medieval French Jewish Communities*. Philadelphia: University of Pennsylvania Press, 2011.

Galinsky, Judah D. "Different Approaches Towards the Miracles of Christian Saints in Medieval Rabbinic Literature." In *Ta Shma: Studies in Judaica in Memory of Israel M. Ta-Shma*, edited by Avraham (Rami) Reiner, 1:195–219. Alon Shvut: Tevunot - Mikhlelet Herzog, 2011 (Hebrew).

Hen, Yitzhak. *Culture and Religion in Merovingian Gaul, A.D. 481–751*. Leiden: Brill, 1995.

Mesler, Katelyn. "The Three Magi and Other Christian Motifs in Medieval Hebrew Medical Incantations: A Study in the Limits of Faithful Translation." *Latin-into-Hebrew: Texts and Studies*, edited by Resianne Fontaine and Gad Freudenthal, 161–218. Leiden: Brill, 2013.

Mokhtarian, Jason Sion. *Medicine in the Talmud*. Berkeley: University of California Press, 2022.

Olsan, Lea T. "Writing on the Hand in Ink: A Late Medieval Innovation in Fever Charms in England." *Incantatio. An International Journal on Charms, Charmers and Charming* 7 (2018): 9–45. doi.org/10.7592/Incantato_2018_7_Olsan.

Paxton, Frederick S. "Liturgy and Healing in an Early Medieval Saint's Cult: The Mass 'In Honore Sancti Sigismundi' for the Cure of Fevers." *Traditio* 49 (1994): 23–43. doi.org/10.1017/S0362152900012988.

Reinburg, Virginia. "Oral Rites: Prayer and Talk in Early Modern France." In *Spoken Word and Social Practice*, edited by Thomas V. Cohen and Lesley K. Twomey, 373–92. Leiden: Brill, 2015.

Rézeau, Pierre. *Les prières aux saints en français à la fin du Moyen Âge*. Geneva: Librarie Droz, 1982.

Salzer, Dorothea M. *Die Magie der Anspielung: Form und Funktion der biblischen Anspielungen in den magischen Texten der Kairoer Geniza*. Tübingen: Mohr Siebeck, 2010.

Shafran, Amit. "'To Me, Isaac son of Isaac': Magical Techniques and Rituals among Medieval Jews in Thirteenth-Century Northern France." MA Thesis, Hebrew University of Jerusalem, 2021.

Shatzmiller, Joseph. *Jews, Medicine, and Medieval Society*. Berkeley: University of California Press, 1994.

Shoham-Steiner, Ephraim. "Jews and Healing at Medieval Saints' Shrines: Participation, Polemics, and Shared Cultures." *Harvard Theological Review* 103 (2010): 111–29. jstor.org/stable/40390064.

Sirat, Colette. "Une formule divinatoire latine dans deux manuscrits hébreux." *Revue des études juives* (1966): 391–94. doi.org/10.3406/rjuiv.1966.1552.

Sirat, Collette. "Un rituel juif de France: Le manuscrit hébreu 633 de la bibliothèque nationale de Paris." *Revue des études juives* 119 (1961): 7–40. doi.org/10.3406/rjuiv.1961.1381.

Skemer, Don C. *Binding Words: Textual Amulets in the Middle Ages*. University Park: Pennsylvania State University Press, 2006.

Wallis, Faith, ed. *Medieval Medicine: A Reader*. Toronto: University of Toronto, 2010.

CHAPTER 12

To See and Be Seen

The Role of Jews in Medieval Urban Processions

Hannah Teddy Schachter

> It happened once in Reims [France] that there was an intolerable drought.... For three days, [Christian] believers carried relics and reliquaries in procession through the town and countryside, but not even the smallest cloud appeared. Seeing their great activity, a certain Jew, the chief leader of the synagogue (*archisinagogus*) said: ... Allow us to carry around our [Torah] scrolls and codices. And many believers said: This is good, it is good indeed.
>
> —Peter the Chanter, *Verbum Adbreviatum*

Processions were a familiar feature of medieval life.[1] Defined by the ritual theorist Ron Grimes as "linearly ordered, solemn movements of a group through chartered space to a known destination," urban and rural dwellers took part in such ceremonial marches to celebrate life-cycle events, conduct public religious worship, welcome important officials, and even—as in the source above—to affect the weather.[2] This later twelfth-century work by Peter the Chanter (d.1197) describes how

---

Research for this chapter was supported by the European Research Council (ERC) project "Beyond the Elite: Jewish Daily Life in Medieval Europe," led by Elisheva Baumgarten, under the European Union's Horizon 2020 Research and Innovation Program (grant agreement no. 681507). I would like to thank Elisheva Baumgarten for her invaluable comments, as well as Gadi Algazi, Manon Banoun, Elisheva Carlebach, Moishi Chechik, Andreas Lehnertz, Ivan Marcus, Miri Rubin, and Birgit Wiedl for our engaging discussions on the present topic.

1. The quote given in this chapter's epigraph is from Peter the Chanter, *Verbum Adbreviatum: Textus Conflatus*, ed. Monique Boutry, CCCM, 196 (Turnhout: Brepols, 2004), 1:76, 505. For a full translation and discussion of this source, see Elisheva Baumgarten, "Shared Stories and Religious Rhetoric: R. Judah the Pious, Peter the Chanter and a Drought," *Medieval Encounters* 18 (2012): 36–54, esp. 41–42, 10.1163/157006712X634558.

2. Ronald Grimes, "Procession," in *The Encyclopedia of Religion*, ed. Mircea Eliade (New York: Palgrave Macmillan, 1987), 12:1–3.

some Jews of northern France not only watched their Christian neighbors march in procession in hopes of rainfall, but also followed suit with their own sacred objects, publicly unifying the two groups in a ritual geared toward a collective purpose. Although there were many occasions when Jews took part in the processional rituals led by local Christian authorities, at other times they were either excluded or chose to exclude themselves. Their reasons for both participation and exclusion shed light on the status of Jews and their relationship with the Christian majority. This chapter thus seeks to address the key question of how to interpret the different sociocultural and political roles played by Jews in various types of processions across France and the Holy Roman Empire.

Urban processions in medieval Europe have a long and fruitful historiography, broadly defined along two lines of inquiry: The first focuses on their liturgical functions, with studies dedicated to processions as performative movements "in demonstration to and contemplation of God," especially during religious feasts days like Palm Sunday, Corpus Christi, and saints' days.[3] Scholars including Anne Bagnall Yardley, Clifford C. Flanigan, and Miri Rubin have emphasized that liturgical processions were rich, multisensory dramas that both enacted the social structure of the religious community through ordered participation and reinforced communal identity through the display of powerful symbols like relics, crosses, and monstrances.[4]

---

3. Quoted in Sabine Felbecker, *Die Prozession: Historische und systematische Untersuchungen zu einer liturgischen Ausdruckhandlung* (Altenberge: Oros, 1995), 542. See Károly Goda, "Binding the Bonds: Metropolitan Modes of Eucharistic Confraternal and Processional Life in Late Medieval East-Central Europe," in *Practicing Community in Urban and Rural Eurasia (1000–1600)*, eds. Fabian Kümmeler, Judit Majorossy, and Eirik Hovden (Leiden: Brill, 2021), 384–402; Eberhard Isenmann, *Die deutsche Stadt im Mittelalter, 1150–1500: Stadtgestalt, Recht, Verfassung, Stadtregiment, Kirche, Gesellschaft, Wirtschaft* (Vienna: Böhlau Verlag, 2014), 659; Craig Wright, "The Palm Sunday Procession in Medieval Chartres," in *The Divine Office in the Latin Middle Ages: Methodology and Source Studies, Regional Developments, Hagiography*, eds. Margot Fassler and Rebecca A. Balzer (Oxford: Oxford University Press, 2000), 344–71; Miri Rubin, *Corpus Christi: The Eucharist in Late Medieval Culture* (Cambridge: Cambridge University Press, 1991); David Harris Sacks, "The Demise of the Martyrs: The Feasts of St. Clement and St. Katherine in Bristol, 1400–1600," *Social History* 11 (1986): 141–69, https://doi.org/10.1080/03071028608567649; Ludwig Remling, "Die 'Große Prozession' in Münster als städtisches und kirchliches Ereignis im Spätmittelalter und in der frühen Neuzeit," *Quellen und Forschungen zur Geschichte der Stadt Münster* 11 (1984): 197–233.

4. Anne Bagnall Yardley, *Performing Piety: Musical Culture in Medieval English Nunneries* (New York: Palgrave Macmillan, 2006), 113–15; Clifford C. Flanigan, "The Moving Subject: Medieval Liturgical Processions in Semiotic and Cultural Perspective," in *Moving Subjects: Processional Performance in the Middle Ages and the Renaissance*, eds. Kathleen Ashley and Wim Hüsken (Leiden: Brill, 2001), 35–51, here 46; Rubin, *Corpus Christi*, 213, 245, 266–67; Pierre André

The second line of inquiry regarding medieval processions deals with their civic functions. Much of twentieth-century scholarship focused on the political aspects of these rituals in honor of visiting monarchs, coronations, and high office to show how urban authorities of the late Middle Ages staged and consolidated their power.[5] Further studies have considered processions as the "practices of citizens" and forms of "civic religion among burghers,"[6] designed to communicate the unity of the urban commune, despite the apparent divisions and periodic unrest among its social groups.[7]

Sharing an understanding of processions as performative space practices in the construction of medieval urban community, these two lines of scholarly inquiry have considered the participatory and nonparticipatory roles among almost every social group—rulers, nobles, confraternities and guilds, clergy and parishes, slaves, women, and children[8]—in order to assess how these rituals encouraged social cohesion.[9] The

---

Sigal, "Les voyages de reliques aux onzième et douzième siècles," in *Voyage, quête, pèlerinage dans la littérature et la civilisation médiévales,* ed. Huguette Taviani (Aix-en-Provence: Presses universitaires de Provence, 1976), 73–104.

5. Mario Damen and Kim Overlaet, "Weg van de staat. Blijde Intredes in de laatmiddeleeuwse Nederlanden op het snijvlak van sociale, culturele en politieke geschiedenis," *BMGN – Low Countries Historical Review* 134 (2019): 3–44; Olivier Richard and Benoît-Michel Tock, "Des chartes ornées urbaines: les Schwörbriefe de Strasbourg (XIVe-XVe siècles)," *Bibliothèque de l'École des chartes* 169 (2011): 109–28; Jesse D. Hurlbut, "Processions in Burgundy: Late-Medieval Ceremonial Entries," in *Pageants and Processions: Images and Idiom as Spectacle,* ed. Herman du Toit (Cambridge: Cambridge Scholars Publishing, 2009), 93–106; Gerd Althoff, *Die Macht der Rituale: Symbolik und Herrschaft im Mittelalter* (Darmstadt: Wissenschaftliche Buchgesellschaft, 2003); Gordon Kipling, *Enter the King: Theatre, Liturgy and Ritual in the Late Medieval Civic Triumph* (Oxford: Clarendon Press, 1998); Bernard Guenée and Françoise Lehoux, *Les entrées royales françaises de 1328 à 1515* (Paris: Éditions du Centre national de la recherche scientifique, 1968).

6. Leslie Brubaker and Chris Wickham, "Processions, Power, and Community Identity: East and West," in *Empires and Communities in the Post-Roman and Islamic World, C. 400–1000 CE,* ed. Rutger Kramer and Walter Pohl (Oxford: Oxford University Press, 2021), 121–87; Andrew Brown, *Civic Ceremony and Religion in Medieval Bruges c.1300–1520* (Cambridge: Cambridge University Press, 2011); Charles Phythian-Adams, "Ceremony and the Citizen: The Communal Year at Coventry 1450–1550," in *Crisis and Order in English Towns 1500–1700: Essays in Urban History,* ed. Peter Clark and Paul Slack (London: Routledge and Kegan Paul, 1972), 57–85.

7. Tom Pettitt, "The Morphology of the Parade," *European Medieval Drama* 6 (2003): 1–30, 3; Meg Twycross, "Introduction," in *Festive Drama,* ed. Meg Twycross (Woodbridge: Brewer, 1996), 1–33, 5.

8. Sabina von Heusinger, "Die Handwerksbruderschaften in Straßburg," in *Städtische Gesellschaft und Kirche im Spätmittelalter,* ed. Sigrid Schmitt and Sabine Klapp (Stuttgart: Franz Steiner Verlag, 2008), 123–40; Debra Blumenthal, *Enemies and Familiars: Slavery and Mastery in Fifteenth-Century Valencia* (Ithaca: Cornell University Press, 2009), 120.

9. Thomas A. Boogaart, "Our Savior's Blood: Procession and Community in Late Medieval Bruges," in *Moving Subjects: Processional Performance in the Middle Ages and the Renaissance,*

importance and central role played by processional rituals in constructing medieval urban community amid a Christian majority thus raises the question of what parts were left for a religious minority to play within this context.

Interestingly, an exhaustive study on the role of Jews in urban processions of medieval Europe has not, as yet, been carried out.[10] Those who have engaged with the topic tend to conclude that processions were a means of ritual exclusion, an example of systematic municipal discrimination, as well as an occasion for Jews to show their submission and subjugation to Christian hegemony.[11] Such framing leaves less room for recognizing that, as the processional ritual was adapted for a range of purposes, the sources demonstrate evolving and nuanced roles for the Jewish community. In her discussion of the weather procession example cited above, Elisheva Baumgarten recently commented that this particular ritual for rainfall presented one urban occasion during which Jews and Christians could express neighborliness, familiarize themselves with each other's practices, but also compete religiously for divine outcomes.[12]

This chapter examines Jewish participation in urban processions, distinguishing between those enacted in the framework of Christian liturgical observances and those that served primarily civic functions. It will further the scholarly consideration of processions as ritual performances intended to stage and visibly symbolize urban community by

---

ed. Kathleen Ashley and Wim Hüsken (Leiden: Brill, 2001), 69–116; Mervyn James, "Ritual, Drama and Social Body in the Late Medieval English Town," *Past and Present* 98 (1983): 3–29.

10. See, for example, Emilie Amar-Zifkin, "Observing the Observers: Processions and Public Religion in Medieval Ashkenaz" (PhD diss., Yale University, 2023), which was finished after to the completion of the present chapter but is sure to be a further step in this endeavor.

11. Thomas Barton, "Non-Christian Service on the Public Stage: Artisans, Musicians, and the Implications of Ethno-Religious Difference in Late-Medieval Iberia," *Medieval Encounters* 29 (2023): 52–112, 78, 83; Reinhold S. Ruf-Haag, *Juden und Christen im spätmittelalterlichen Erfurt: Abhängigkeiten, Handlungsspielräume und Gestaltung jüdischen Lebens in einer mitteleuropäischen Großstadt* (Trier: Mikrofichepublikation, 2009), 346; Amnon Linder, "The Jews Too Were Not Absent . . . Carrying Moses's Law on Their Shoulders: The Ritual Encounter of Pope and Jew from the Middle Ages to Modern Times," *Jewish Quarterly Review* 99 (2009): 323–95, 323; Michael Toch, *Die Juden im mittelalterlichen Reich* (Munich: R. Oldenbourg, 1998), 44; Noël Coulet, "De l'intégration à l'exclusion: la place des Juifs dans les cérémonies d'entrée solennelle au Moyen Âge," *Annales. Économies, Sociétés, Civilisations* 34 (1979): 672–83, 680. In an attempt to provide a more balanced view, I argue against this narrative in Hannah Teddy Schachter, "When Rulers Came to Town: Jews and Civic Processions in Medieval Ashkenaz," *Medieval History Journal* 27 (2024): 353–81.

12. Elisheva Baumgarten, "Shared Stories and Religious Rhetoric: R. Judah the Pious, Peter the Chanter, and a Drought," *Medieval Encounters* 18 (2012): 36–54.

addressing the visibility of Jews.¹³ Tracing simultaneous ritual developments over the course of the thirteenth to the fifteenth centuries, the following will demonstrate that, while the *invisibility* of Jews was a basic feature of liturgical processions, their *visibility* in civic processions was significant and expected.

Liturgical Processions

The prohibition forbidding Jews to be seen on the streets whenever liturgical processions were in progress originated in the sixth century, when restrictions first stipulated at the Third Council of Orléans in 538 were later implemented by Frankish kings in the years 554 and 581.¹⁴ Not only were Jews to be invisible at these events, but any visible signs of Jewishness were also to be eliminated. Conflict erupted in 866, for example, between Pope Nicholas I (d. 867) and Arsenius, bishop of Orta, due to the latter's "effort to introduce Jewish furred garments (*iudaicae peluciae*)" into Good Friday processions, an occasion at which even the "clothes of the superstitious people" were not to be seen.¹⁵ Although Markus Wenninger has termed such early instances of prohibiting Jewish participation as "successless attempts to isolate Jews," in fact the same exhortations to avoid Christian liturgical processions echo within the works of Jewish leaders as well.¹⁶ In his legal work *Sefer Yereim* (Book of the Fearful), twelfth-century Tosafist Eliezer b. Samuel of Metz (died ca. 1165) commented that

> one should be wary of idolatry according to its form of worship so as not to falter, even if it is unintentional; for there are non-Jews who carry idols [lit. images] on their shoulders and those

---

13. Visibility has been increasingly used as a framework to explore interreligious relations in the Middle Ages. See Clara Almagro Vidal and Jörn Roland Christophersen, "Visibility of Religious Difference in Medieval Europe and the Mediterranean," *Hamsa: Journal for Judaic and Islamic Studies* 7 (2021): online https://doi.org/10.4000/hamsa.1049; Beth Williamson, "Sensory Experience in Medieval Devotion: Sounds and Vision, Invisibility and Silence," *Speculum* 88 (2013): 1–43, as well as the current research project led by Claire Soussen, "Visibilité et invisibilité des minoritaires dans l'espace public à la fin du Moyen Âge–VISMIN."

14. Heinz Schreckenberg, *Die christlichen Adversus-Judaeos-Texte (11.–13. Jh.) mit einer Ikonographie des Judenthemas bis zum 4. Laterankonzil* (Frankfurt: Peter Lang, 1991), 2:421–22.

15. Johannes Diaconus, ed. Jacques-Paul Migne, *Patrologia Latina*, vol. 75 (Paris: Garnier fratres, 1862), 159.

16. See Markus Wenninger, "Das gefährliche Fest: Ostern als zeitlicher Kristallisationspunkt antijüdischen Verhaltens," in *Feste und Feiern im Mittelalter. Paderborner Symposion des Mediävistenverbandes*, ed. Detlef Altenburg, Jörg Jarnut, and Hans-Hugo Steinhoff (Sigmaringen: Jan Thorbecke Verlag, 1991), 323–32, 324.

[other non-Jews] who follow them to the church [lit. to shame]. This walking (or processing) is the worship of idolatry, therefore one must take care not to follow them, even if he/she needs to go somewhere, because it is still walking, and walking is its [i.e., idolatry's] worship.[17]

Reminding his audience that they could find themselves unintentionally in the midst of Christian worship at any point while walking outside, Eliezer offers the Jewish perspective on the matter of exclusion from such liturgical Christian processions, namely, that Jews may have abstained for their own religious reasons—a type of cautious self-exclusion to avoid taking part in Christian liturgies. Furthermore, Eliezer's writings indicate that, by his time, any Christian statutes limiting Jewish visibility during liturgical processions were likely neither especially strict nor effective where he resided.

The visibility of Jews became of concern to churchmen once again in the early thirteenth century, specifically with regards to processions commemorating the Passion or Crucifixion. In 1205, Pope Innocent III (d. 1216) complained to King Philip II Augustus of France (d. 1223) that some Jews had allegedly watched liturgical processions on Good Friday, disrupting the sequence of religious events by "publicly running to and fro through the towns and streets, and everywhere laughing, as is their wont, at the Christians because they adore the Crucified One on the Cross."[18] Ten years later, this same pope passed various rulings at the Fourth Lateran Council in 1215, according to which Jews should be less visible in public on holy days, such as Passion Sunday, when processions were held.[19] The implementation of this ruling spread across France during the first half of the thirteenth century, appearing not only in the Decretals of Pope Gregory IX, which expressly stipulated that Jews "should not keep their doors and windows open during Good

---

17. R. Eliezer of Metz, *Sefer Yereim*, ed. Yisrael Goldblum and Shlomo Zalman Chaim Halberstam (repr. Jerusalem: Machon Chatam Sofer, 1973), no. 270. See Judah D. Galinsky, "Different Approaches Towards the Miracles of Christian Saints in Medieval Rabbinic Literature," in *Ta Shma: Studies in Judaica in Memory of Israel M. Ta-Shma*, eds. Avraham (Rami) Reiner, Joseph R. Hacker, Moshe Halbertal, Moshe Idel, Ephraim Kanarfogel, and Elchanan Reiner (Alon Shvut: Tevunot Press, 2011), 1:195–220, here 198 (Hebrew).

18. Solomon Grayzel, *The Church and the Jews in the XIIIth Century*, 2 vols (Philadelphia: Dropsie, 1933), 1:34, 104–9, no. 14.

19. *Constitutiones Concilii quarti Lateranensis una cum Commentariis glossatorum, Monumenta Iuris Canonici*, ed. Antonio García y García (Vatican City: Biblioteca Apostolica Vaticana, 1981), Canon 68.

Friday,"²⁰ but also in the statutes of French provincial councils, such as Rouen (1223), Avignon (1243), and Beziers (1246).²¹

Such ecclesiastical measures were also implemented by secular authorities, King Louis IX of France (d. 1270) and his mother, Queen Dowager Blanche of Castile (d. 1252). When the sacred relic of the Passion, the Crown of Thorns, was translated to Paris in 1239, the liturgical processions for the Crown's feast were designed to "let the entire French people, without distinction in sex, dignity, or status" share in sacred solemnities and communal joy.²² Yet, Parisian Jews were not to be seen. An order relating to the relic's processions, now lost, was summarized by a nineteenth-century historian: "The Jews were ordered not to leave the six little streets reserved for them in the Champeaux on that day, in their streets from the rue de la Fripperie to the rue Jean-de-Beauce. It is well understood that whoever sees [them] will have the right to run after them."²³ One cannot know if the six streets of the Jews were part of the original text that lay before the author or were his own elaboration. As the long-held assumption of the Juiverie in the Champeaux has been disproven, however, it is more likely that the original source mirrored the general prohibitions across Franco-German regions, merely outlawing Parisian Jews from leaving their houses or streets while the Crown of Thorns was carried.²⁴

Furthermore, it is evident that the liturgical procession routes themselves impacted urban Jewish settlement. To continue the example from Paris, Meredith Cohen recently discussed the network of parishes that framed the processional courses and transformed the greater city into a liturgical space many times throughout the year.²⁵ These routes

---

20. *Corpus Iuris Canonici*, Decretal. Greg., Lib. V, Tit. 6, cap. 4.

21. *Sacrorum conciliorum nova et amplissima collectio*, ed. Johannes Mansi, vol. 23, 229, 702; Solomon Grayzel, *The Church and the Jews in the XIIIth Century*, 1:34n70, 316–17, 332–33.

22. Cecilia Gaposchkin, "Between Historical Narration and Liturgical Celebrations: Gautier Cornut and the Reception of the Crown of Thorns in France," *Revue Mabillon* 30 (2019): 91–145, here 123.

23. Georges d'Avenel, *Les évêques et archevêques de Paris depuis Saint Denys jusqu'à nos jours avec des documents inédits* (Paris: Casterman, 1878), 1:177–79.

24. Anne Lombard-Jourdan, *Aux origines de Paris: La genèse de la rive droite jusqu'en 1223* (Paris: CNRS, 1985), 97, disproving Robert Anchel, "The Early History of the Jewish Quarters in Paris," *Jewish Social Studies* 2 (1940): 45–60, esp. 53; and Michel Roblin, *Les Juifs de Paris. Démographie, économie, culture* (Paris: A. et J. Picard, 1952), 14.

25. See Meredith Cohen, *The Sainte-Chapelle and The Construction of Sacral Monarchy: Royal Architecture in Thirteenth Century Paris* (Cambridge: Cambridge University Press, 2015), 164–67 and 197.

intersected and overlapped at various points with known streets of medieval Jewish residence (figure 12.1).

Sometime during the 1160s, while Parisian Jews still resided within three streets of the Île de la Cité under King Louis VII (d. 1180), the rue Neuve-Notre-Dame was newly built to connect the rue de la Juiverie and the rue du Parois, transforming all of these streets, especially the rue Vieille-Draperie of Jewish residence, into the most commonly traveled procession route in Paris between the palace and the cathedral.[26] A sixteenth-century engraving displays this street in processional use (figure 12.2), where the liturgical procession is returning from Notre-Dame de Paris via the rue Neuve-Notre-Dame, turning left toward Petit Pont with numerous people looking on from their windows on the street that was the Juiverie prior to the expulsion of the Jews from the royal domain in 1182. After their recall to Paris in 1198, Jews did not return to their former streets in the Cité but resettled either in those areas seldom traveled for liturgical procession—such as the rue de la Harpe and rue de la Huchette on the left bank—or in streets entirely untouched by liturgical travel—like rue Neuve-Saint-Merri on the right bank. By the time the Crown of Thorns and its Feast were celebrated during the mid-thirteenth century, then, it would have been possible for Jews to remain confined to certain streets and unseen during the urban ritual without necessarily having to shut their windows and doors.

As to why such efforts were taken, one reason for ensuring Jewish invisibility during liturgical processions was theological: liturgical processions were designed to "draw the greater commune towards the timeless lessons of salvation," as Andrew Brown recently demonstrated.[27] Exegetical discourse on salvation, which became a common motif specifically among Parisian theologians in the thirteenth century, maintained that Jews bore the guilt and shame for tormenting Christ by mocking him and crowning his head with thorns.[28] The proponents of these Jewish visibility regulations—e.g. Innocent III, Gregory IX, and

---

26. Jean Favier, *Le Bourgeois de Paris au Moyen Âge* (Paris: Tallandier, 2012), 466; Michel Fleury and Jeanne Pronteau, "Histoire de Paris," *Annuaires de l'École pratique des hautes études* 4 (1974): 633–69; Jean-Baptiste Renou de Chauvigne, *Recherches critiques, historiques et topographiques sur la ville de Paris: La Cité* (Paris Lottin, 1772), 91–92; L'Abbé Lebeuf, *Histoire de la ville et de tout le diocèse de Paris*, ed. Hippolyte Cocheris (Paris: Durand, 1865), 2:589.

27. Andrew Brown, *Civic Ceremony*, 71.

28. William C. Jordan, "Judaizing the Passion: The Case of the Crown of Thorns in the Middle Ages," in *New Perspectives on Jewish-Christian Relations*, eds. Elisheva Carlebach and Jacob J. Schacter (Leiden: Brill, 2012), 51–63, esp. 59, 63.

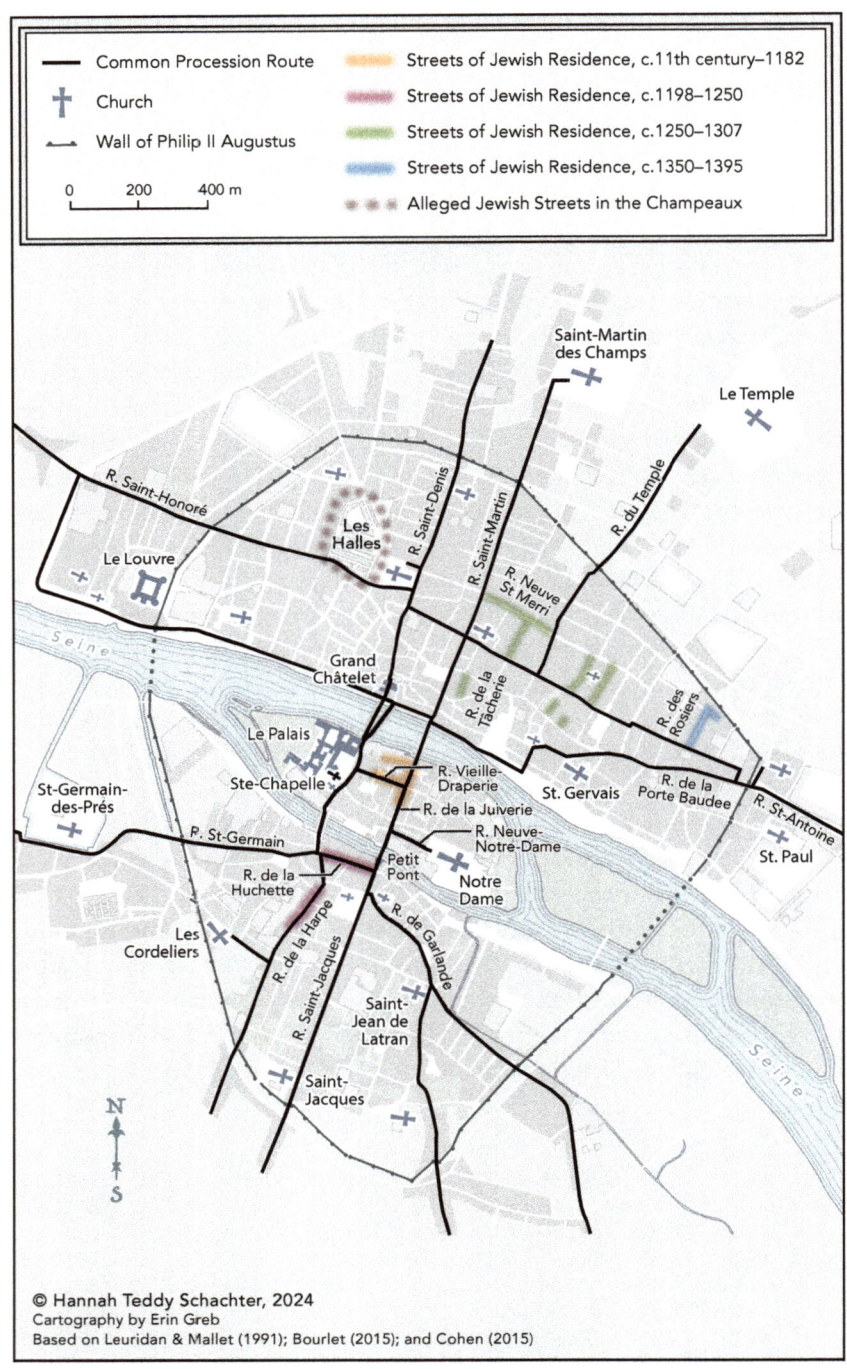

FIGURE 12.1. Procession routes and Jewish settlement in medieval Paris. © Hannah Teddy Schachter, 2024.

FIGURE 12.2. People watching from their windows and homes as the liturgical procession from the Notre-Dame de Paris passes. Sixteenth-century engraving. L. Gaultier (ca. 1560s) Bibliothèque historique de la Ville de Paris, EST 208.

in this case King Louis and Queen Blanche—had strong ties with the Parisian circles.[29] Citing risks of contemporary Jews mocking processional commemorations of the Passion was one mode of actualizing biblical scenes for the Christian populous. In addition, publicly outlawing Jews from being seen served as a further means of conveying the past and present threat of Jews to Christ and to create social cohesion among the Christian community.

This theory lends itself well to scholarly discussions about how Jews featured in narratives relating to Eucharistic events, especially in the Holy Roman Empire. As Miri Rubin has shown, public processions became prevalent sometime after the promulgation of the doctrine of transubstantiation, or "Real Presence," of Christ in the Eucharist at the Fourth Lateran Council, and sometime before the Feast of Corpus Christi was fully established in 1264 (and reaffirmed in 1311-12 and 1317).[30] The popular narrative of Jews as tormenters of the Host has been discussed at length by Rubin, and, more recently, by Birgit Wiedl and Eveline Brugger. Building on multiple reported cases of Jews allegedly attacking the Host, mocking Christians, and throwing stones precisely during these processions,[31] these scholars have argued that

---

29. Gaines Post, "Parisian Masters as a Corporation: 1200–1246," *Speculum* 9 (1934): 421–45, esp. 444; Lindy Grant, *Blanche of Castile, Queen of France* (New Haven: Yale University Press, 2016), 189, 156, 233.
30. Rubin, *Corpus Christi*, 85, 176-84.
31. Already in 1281, a Jew in Vienna was accused of attacking a priest and the monstrance he was carrying with dirt or a stone and was condemned to be stoned to death. Eveline Brugger and Birgit Wiedl, "Im Haus des Juden fand man eine blutbefleckte Hostie: Hostienschändungsvorwürfe und ihre Folgen für die jüdische Bevölkerung Österreichs im Mittelalter," *Jahrbuch für Landeskunde von Niederösterreich* 84 (2018): 35-57, 44. While one cannot be sure about the realities of such allegations, there are accounts of Jews "perceiving the sacrament

the narrative function of the Jews was to promote the credibility of the Host as the body of Christ and to knowingly reenact the Passion.³² One might add that, because the cornerstone of the processional ritual was to "see," "show," and "bring" the Host as the real body of Christ "before the eyes of all" for universal Christian celebration, barring the visibility of Jews became an essential aspect of this ritual reenactment.³³ The church councils of Breslau and Vienna in 1267 wrote that, when "the sacrament of the altar is carried in front of the houses of the Jews, the Jews themselves, upon hearing the sound, must retreat into their houses and close their windows and doors."³⁴ Thus, the simple act of banishing Jews from the sight of Eucharistic processions served to declare the likelihood of Jewish misdemeanors against the Host, implicitly reinforcing truths of Christ's "Real Presence" at these events. The role of Jews to be declared invisible was therefore a tool for communal piety and helped make the theories of the Eucharistic miracle of transformation all the more tangible to the religious Christian majority.

As the presence of the Host and general ambience during Holy Week significantly increased chances of interreligious violence, a second reason for Jewish invisibility during liturgical processions was as a precautionary measure to ensure peace and prevent disruptions.³⁵ Markus Wenninger has suggested this and gathered countless examples across German lands where Jewish residents were either required to stay indoors, to remain within a certain quarter, or to "flee into another alley whenever the procession [with the Host] comes, so as not to be

---

in processions as a joke." See David H. Price, "Johannes Pfefferkorn and Imperial Politics," in *Revealing the Secrets of the Jews: Johannes Pfefferkorn and Christian Writings about Jewish Life and Literature in Early Modern Europe*, ed. Jonathan Adams and Cordelia Heß (Berlin: De Gruyter, 2017), 27–42, 40.

32. Brugger and Wiedl, "Hostienschändungsvorwürfe," 51; Rubin, *Corpus Christi*, 126; Miri Rubin, *Gentile Tales: The Narrative Assault on Late Medieval Jews* (Philadelphia: University of Pennsylvania Press, 2004), 70–92, 135, 187. See below note 35.

33. Édouard Dumoutet, *Le désir de voir l'hostie et les origines de la dévotion au Saint-Sacrement* (Paris: Beauchesne, 1926), 85; Foucart-Borville Jacques, "Essai sur les suspenses eucharistiques comme mode d'adoration privilégié du Saint Sacrement," *Bulletin Monumental* 145 (1987): 267–89, esp. 272; Otto Nussbaum, *Die Aufbewahrung der Eucharistie* (Cologne: Peter Hanstein Verlag, 1979), 140, 333–35, 318.

34. Eveline Brugger and Birgit Wiedl, *Regesten zur Geschichte der Juden in Österreich im Mittelalter, 1: von den Anfängen bis 1338* (Innsbruck: Studien Verlag, 2005), 60n45.

35. On ritual stoning during Eastertide, see Daniel Jütte, "'They Shall Not Keep Their Doors or Windows Open': Urban Space and the Dynamics of Conflict and Contact in Premodern Jewish–Christian Relations," *European History Quarterly* 46 (2016): 209–37; Elliot Horrowitz, *Reckless Rites: Purim and the Legacy of Jewish Violence* (Princeton: Princeton University Press, 2006), 172.

harmed."³⁶ So stated the *Meissner Rechtsbuch*, a work compiled during the mid-fourteenth century, which enabled the Jews in the Margravate of Meissen to live peacefully for the following eighty years.³⁷ If processional rituals sought to promote social cohesion, then the visible absence of Jews among the Eucharist would have been one way to both quell tensions within the urban space, as well as to ensure communal religious unity while the ritual was underway.

By the later fifteenth century, the desire to ensure Jewish invisibility during Eucharistic processions grew to have much greater impact on Jewish life. In Frankfurt am Main, for example, the processional routes revolved around the imperial Cathedral of Frankfurt and parish church of St. Bartholomäus (figure 12.3), which was situated directly adjacent to the synagogue and school of Frankfurt Jews. According to Fritz Backhaus, this urban entanglement of Christian and Jewish sacred space ultimately contributed to mounting pressure across the fifteenth century, culminating in the Jews' eventual relocation to the area later known as the Frankfurt Ghetto.³⁸ Thus, the phenomenon described above in Paris, by which urban Jewish residence was impacted by commonly traveled procession routes, can be similarly seen in Frankfurt.

In 1442, the Frankfurt council received a letter from Frederick III, king of the Romans (d. 1493), who had previously spent some time in the city during the Feast of Corpus Christi. Complaining that the activities of the church had been disturbed by the proximity of the synagogue and Jewish homes to the parish church, the king ordered the council to demolish the synagogue and relocate the Jewish residences to another area.³⁹ In protest, the Jews of Frankfurt issued a letter to the council, citing the liturgical processions and agreeing to wall up

---

36. Friedrich Ortloff, *Das Rechtsbuch nach Distinctionen nebst einem Eisenachischen Rechtsbuch* (Jena: Crökersche Buchhandlung, 1836), 3:17, 34; Markus Wenninger, "Das gefährliche Fest," 329.

37. Zvi Avneri, ed., *Germania Judaica von 1238 bis zur Mitte des 14. Jahrhunderts* (Tübingen: Mohr Siebeck, 1968), 2:531-32.

38. Argued in Fritz Backhaus, "Die Einrichtung eines Ghettos für die Frankfurter Juden im Jahre 1482," *Hessisches Jahrbuch für Landesgeschichte* 39 (1989): 59-86, esp. 64-5. For a discussion of the local liturgical processions, see Luitgard Gedeon, "Prozessionen in Frankfurt am Main," *Archiv für mittelrheinische Kirchengeschichte* 52 (2000): 11-53, 27. Among the many examples of changing routes to avoid Jewish quarters by the later fourteenth century, see the discussion of the Corpus Christi procession in Valencia of 1350s in Abigail Agresta, *The Keys to Bread and Wine: Faith, Nature, and Infrastructure in Late Medieval Valencia* (Ithaca, NY: Cornell University Press, 2022), 75-80.

39. Dietrich Andernacht, *Regesten zur Geschichte der Juden in der Reichsstadt Frankfurt am Main von 1401-1519* (Frankfurt: Hahnsche Buchhandlung, 1996), 1:199n712. Backhaus, "Die Einrichtung eines Ghettos," 64.

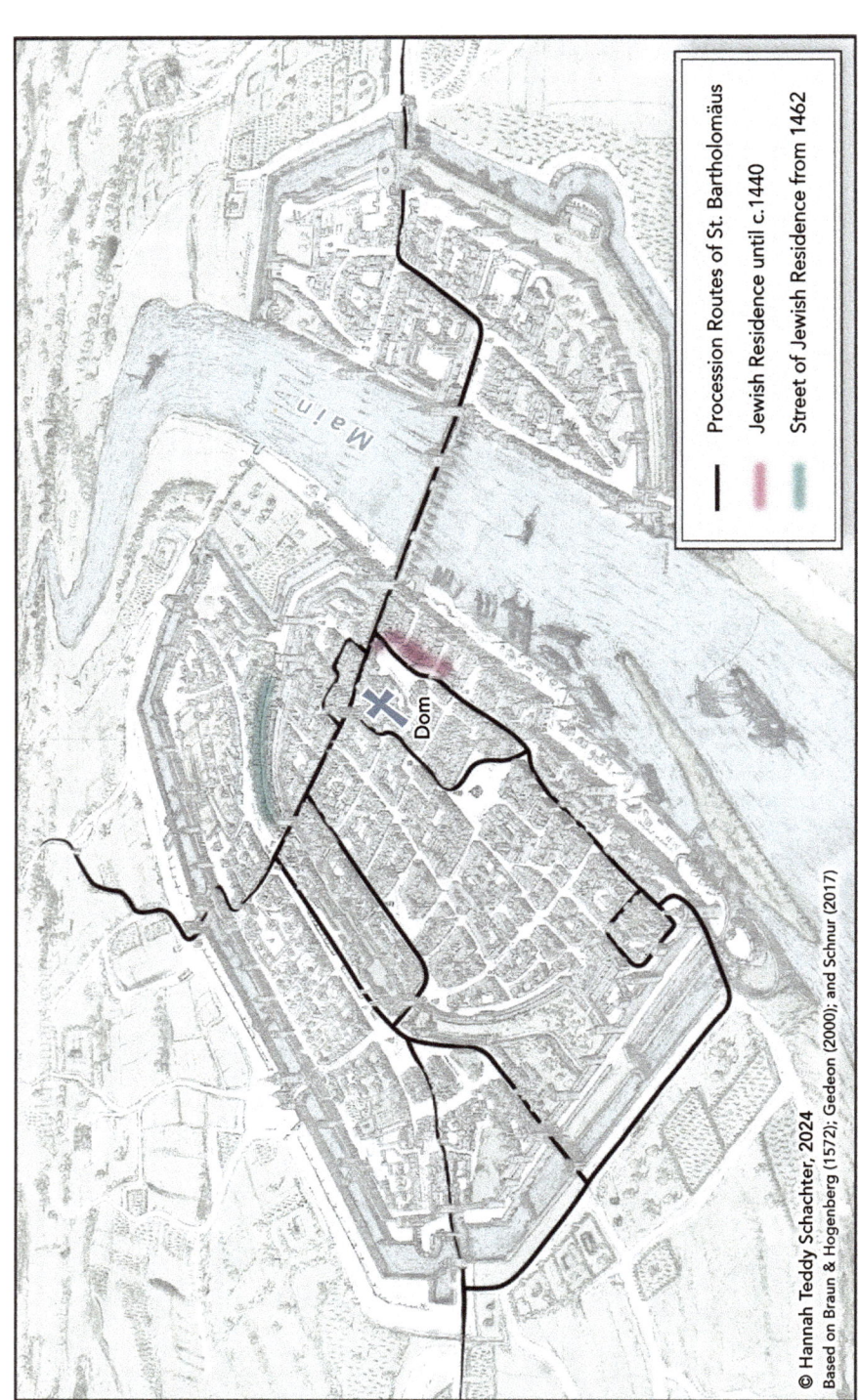

FIGURE 12.3. Procession routes and Jewish settlement in Frankfurt am Main, ca. 1440. © Hannah Teddy Schachter, 2024.

the gate, doors, and windows of the house in the schoolyard facing the church, to have all their houses inspected by representatives of the council and, wherever they took offense at the view, to proceed accordingly. As David Schnur has shown, such negotiations compelled the Jewish community to make architectural and spatial concessions in the early 1440s in response to Christian concerns about the visibility of sacred cites.[40] They added: "And at whatever times there are processions passing through the streets with the sacrament [*heilthum*], regardless of how often that may occur and be announced to us, we shall close our doors and windows at the same time and remain inside."[41] Subsequently, an affluent member of the Frankfurt Jewish community, who also lived on this street, agreed to close his house doors, wall up his windows, or evacuate on demand during the neighboring cathedral-lead processions in his street.[42] Having intensified markedly by the end of the fifteenth century, the terms of Jewish invisibility during liturgical processions were therefore known, upheld, and negotiated by local Jews on both an individual and collective basis with local Christian authorities.

Civic Processions

A trajectory of another kind can be traced for civic processions. One type of such a procession was the so-called royal entry. Rooted in the triumphal entry traditions of Hellenistic and Roman emperors in Late Antiquity,[43] these rituals became some of the most enduring and widely practiced ceremonial forms in medieval Europe, whose intention was to welcome secular rulers (kings, queens, or other officials) on their first arrival to a city. Often discussed as a dramatized staging of town-crown "political reciprocity,"[44] the royal entry included civic festivities and

---

40. David Schnur, *Die Juden in Frankfurt am Main und in der Wetterau im Mittelalter: Christlich-jüdische Beziehungen, Gemeinden, Recht und Wirtschaft von den Anfängen bis um 1400* (Wiesbaden: Kommission für die Geschichte der Juden in Hessen, 2017), 187–90.
41. David Schnur, *Die Juden in Frankfurt,* 188.
42. Dietrich Andernacht, *Regesten,* 1:199n734.
43. Neil Murphy, "Receiving Royals in Later Medieval York: Civic Ceremony and the Municipal Elite, 1478–1503," *Northern History* 43 (2006): 241–55; Sabine MacCormack, *Art and Ceremony in Late Antiquity* (Berkeley: University of California Press, 1981), 1–92; Carl Erdmann, "Kaiserliche und päpstliche Fahnen im hohen Mittelalter," *Quellen und Forschungen aus italienischen Archiven und Bibliotheken* 25 (1933): 1–48, 11.
44. Lawrence M. Bryant, *Ritual, Ceremony and the Changing Monarchy in France, 1350-1789* (New York: Routledge, 2009); Tess Knighton, "Royal Entries into Barcelona and the History of Emotions," in *Paisagens sonoras históricas: Anatomia dos sons nas cidades,* eds. Antónia Fialho

gestures of loyalty and homage,[45] intended to secure the goodwill of the entering sovereign and to signal the expectations of just governance.[46]

Additionally, royal entry processions took on significant religious connotations, closely modeled on the Bible.[47] The arrival of a king, *adventus regis,* was devised as a restaging of the *adventus Domini,* the triumphant arrival of Christ to Jerusalem on Palm Sunday. Thus, these processions ritually transformed any city into Zion, any male monarch into the likeness of Christ, and any female sovereign into the triumphant Virgin Mary, Queen of Heaven.[48] As a result, scholars have more recently described the performance of such civic processions as "civic religion," which sought to honor the city by borrowing symbols, themes, and motifs from religious rituals without themselves being necessarily sacred.[49] Considering these strong Christological associations, one might assume that here too the role of Jews would be their absence, as was the case during liturgical processions. Yet, while they are clearly related, an entirely different dynamic appears to have been at play.[50]

The first difference can be discerned in the sources themselves. There are almost no traces of royal edicts or ecclesiastical laws throughout the medieval period mandating Jewish absence from lay rulers' entry processions, and the vague indications we do have primarily date to the late twelfth century, when they were ignored by certain Jews of that area.[51] Likewise, there are no known edicts requiring Jewish presence in the

---

Conde, Vanda de Sá, and Rodrigo Teodoro de Paula (Évora: Publicações do CIDEHUS, 2021) online https://doi.org/10.4000/books.cidehus.16900.

45. André Holstein, *Die Huldigung der Untertanen: Rechtskultur und Herrschaftsordnung, 800–1800* (Boston: De Gruyter, 1991); Jean-Claude Schmitt, *La raison des gestes dans l'Occident médiéval* (Paris: Gallimard, 1990). Bernard Guenée and Françoise Lehoux, *Les entrées*, 65.

46. Joël Blanchard, "Le spectacle du rite: les entrées royales," *Revue Historique* 305 (2003): 475-519.

47. Josèphe Chartrou, *Les entrées solennelles et triomphales à la Renaissance (1484–1551)* (Paris: les Presses universitaires, 1928), 53-54; Ernst H. Kantorowicz, "The 'King's Advent' and the Enigmatic Panels in the Doors of Santa Sabina," *Art Bulletin* 26 (1944): 207-31, esp. 209-11.

48. Descriptions mirrored Matthew 21:9. See Kipling, *Enter the King,* 15, 222. For "The Queen's Advent," see Kipling, *Enter the King,* 293.

49. Caroline Bourlet and Boris Bove, "Religion civique ou affiliation communautaire? Le témoignage des testaments parisiens des XIIIᵉ-XVᵉ siècles," *Histoire urbaine* 60 (2021): 71-96; Brown, *Civic Ceremony and Religion,* 279.

50. Bernard Guenée, "Liturgie et politique. Les processions spéciales à Paris sous Charles VI," in *Saint-Denis et la royauté,* ed. Françoise Autrand, Claude Gauvard and Jean-Marie Moeglin (Paris: Sorbonne, 1999), 29-32.

51. Jews were forbidden from attending the coronation [perhaps processions] of Richard I in 1189 but approached the king after the ceremony to offer gifts *contra prohibitionem regis.* See Richard Fitz Nigel, *Gesta Regis Henrici Secundi Benedicti Abbatis,* ed. William Stubbs

geographical region in question.⁵² Instead, the most detailed evidence regarding Jewish participation in these processions to have survived is overwhelmingly in the Hebrew source material. This is likely because, contrary to liturgical processions, Jews had certain Jewish legal precedents and thus possible religious motivations for attending these civic events. The Babylonian Talmud describes how one should hurry to see the lavish entry of a worldly ruler, in order to differentiate it from the future magnitude with which the Messiah will come.⁵³ Similarly to that of Christians, then, the Jewish tradition inscribed royal entry with its own distinct messianic undertones.

Traditionally, the primary goal of this attendance was to see or watch, and from the start of the thirteenth century, Hebrew legal writings begin to engage in discussions about the frequency with which this obligation was to be met. One example can be found in the German collection of Jewish law and lore known as *Sefer Hasidim* (Book of the Pious): "If the king [arrives] with great military force and much splendor, then a righteous man, who already went toward him [once], should not disrupt his study to go toward the king another time."⁵⁴ This source conveys that medieval Jews often went to royal entry processions and could flexibly decide when to abstain. Given this freedom of choice, this author instructs that the act of seeing a royal entry once was probably enough. The prevalence of such discussions among more pietistic texts may have resulted from the clash some authors perceived between honoring Talmudic instructions and becoming embroiled in the Christian ritual acts of procession. Another passage of *Sefer Hasidim* tells of a pious man who refused to go toward the king on his ceremonious arrival, because "they [the Christians] bring their idols and incense of their idolatry";⁵⁵ while a fifteenth-century Hebrew moralistic work teaches that "when the events of the gentiles happen in your city, then

---

(London: Longmans, Green, Reader, and Dyer, 1867), 2:83. Samuel Singer, "Jews and Coronations," *Transactions: The Jewish Historical Society of England* 5 (1905): 79–114.

52. Demands for Jews to be present at papal inaugural processions in Rome present a genre unto themselves and will not be included here. See Linder, "*The Jews Too Were Not Absent*," 323. On the distinction between papal and royal processions, see Hannah Teddy Schachter, "When Rulers Came to Town," 365.

53. BT Brakhot 19b: the priests of Israel should hurry "even towards the kings of the nations of the world, so that if one will be privileged to witness the redemption of Israel, he will distinguish between kings of Israel and kings of the nations of the world." See Yehuda Zoldan, "Taking the Torah out for Kings," *Kingdom of Judah and Israel* 8 (2002): 131–46 (Hebrew), 142–43.

54. *Sefer Hasidim*, ed. Judah Wistenetzki (Frankfurt: Wahrmann, 1924), 3280n772.

55. *Sefer Hasidim*, ed. Reuven Margoliot (Jerusalem: Mosad Harav Kook, 1957), 304n435.

you should be careful not to watch them."⁵⁶ In these cases, however, the warnings are issued in response to questions posed by another member of the Jewish community, asking why one should ever *refrain* from attending. All of these sources indicate, therefore, that while these types of civic processions incorporated similar Christian ritual elements to liturgical processions, the royal entry was a lavish event that many Jews sought to attend, as a result of which Jewish pietists endeavored to encourage their students to prioritize religious study.

As for what Jews did at civic processions, it is abundantly clear that they went far beyond any Talmudic precedents of passively watching, but rather became physically involved and sought to be seen. In the anonymous later thirteenth-century rabbinic text, *Sefer ha-Hinukh* (The Book of Education) likely from northern Spain, but popular and copied across the geographic region in question, the author demonstrates that many Jews participated by parading the Torah for Christian rulers. The act can also be traced back to a Talmudic precedent by which the Torah was taken out of the synagogue for the kings of Israel in order to honor their appointment and to honor the Torah.⁵⁷ This later thirteenth-century source is among the earliest known instances in which the commandment was projected onto non-Jewish rulers as well. The author seeks to correct such conflations and temper the fervor of his Jewish audience, stating: "This act that [Jewish] people do out of custom in the diasporas today, to take out the Torah scroll for the gentile kings—is not this commandment [*mitzvah*] at all." Recognizing, however, that Jews will likely continue to perform this ritual, the author concedes: "But should [the Jews] choose a Levite to carry the Torah [for the kings today, as was done previously for kings of Israel], then blessings be upon them."⁵⁸ The author proclaims himself a Levite in his introduction to this work, however, thereby reserving this honor of parading the Torah before rulers for Jews like himself.⁵⁹

A similar sense of honor associated with being seen with the Torah during royal entry processions can be discerned from an early fourteenth-century theological composition, *Shulhan Kesef* (The Silver

---

56. Mordecai Menachem Honig, "Al Mahadurato ha-Hadashah shel Sefer ha-Maskil (Sefer Hasidim) le-R. Moshe b. R. Eleazar ha-Cohen," *Yerushateinu* 1 (2007): 225–26.

57. Derived from Talmudic discussions on Deuteronomy 17:18–19 and 19:19, see Yerushalmi Sota 16:5, Yoma 16:1, Babylonian Sota 2; Gitin 2; Taanit 2. See Yehuda Zoldan, "Taking the Torah out for Kings," 143.

58. *Sefer ha-Hinukh*, ed. Chaim Dov Chavel (Jerusalem: Mossad Harav Kook, 1961), 369.

59. I thank Judah Galinsky for bringing this to my attention.

Table), written by the Jewish intellectual Joseph ibn Kaspi (d. 1340) of Provence:

> Once an honored bishop of Provence asked me: Why should you [also] ask the kings . . . to honor and revere the Hebrew Bible [*Sefer Torat Moshe*] and present it in front of you when they come to town, when we [Christians] also present our icons before them? For what reason are we [and our kings and our great leaders] obligated to honor the Hebrew Bible in your hands when . . . our books . . . are like yours?[60]

This question expresses the bishop's dismay that the Hebrew Bible of the Jews was to take precedence over the Christian books, that is, the New Testament and Gospels, during royal entry and implicitly, possibly polemically, insinuates a subordinate position of Christians to Jews. The text also implies not only that the presentation of the Torah to rulers was the Jews' expected role in these rituals, but that the role of Christians and rulers was to actively venerate it. Ibn Kaspi goes on to provide his answer to the bishop:

> There is a clear advantage, holiness, and quality of our [the Jews'] books, especially the Hebrew Bible, over yours, due to the language and script in which it has been written from its origins. And there are two reasons [for why using the original language and script is important]: The first is because the script in which the Hebrew Bible was written is the script of God, and it was in this language that God gave it [to us]. For it is known that when one of the[se] kings issues us a privilege, then it will be far more valuable in our [the Jews'] eyes that he writes it in his script and language than in another. Even if this privilege will be copied exactly in what is called a *vidimus*, then the original will still be more valuable. And the proof of this is that if we were to bring the *vidimus* with the same seal to the court of the king, it would not be as official, nor as precious as the original, certainly not if it were received changed into another language and script that are not those of the king. And so, our books written in the language and script of the king of kings [i.e., God] are far more honored than the copies to another language and script. As for the second reason, [the act of translation leads to] alterations and losses in the

---

60. Yosef ibn Kaspi, *Shulhan Kesef*, ed. Hannah Kasher (Jerusalem: Ben-Zvi Institute, 1996), 58.

content in many places, until the meanings of the copied books are unintelligible to what was intended. And so, the Hebrew Bible copied into another language and order of script is not the same at all as that given by God. Thus, all the nations acknowledge that our Hebrew Bible is from heaven.[61]

There are two points to highlight from this answer: The first is that, from the perspective of the Provençal Jewish author, showing the Torah scroll played a theological role in the performance of royal entry. Jews were to present and display the true Hebrew word and script—the perceived origins of the Christian civilization—for veneration among the Christian majority and its officials. Various scholars have discussed the Christian doctrine upheld by numerous medieval theologians and commonly presented in ritual materials and art, according to which the Jews preserved the Hebrew Scriptures, despite their blindness to its meaning, and bore witness to Christian truth and triumph.[62] Medieval Jews were aware of this Christian doctrine, subverting and rejecting this narrative role in various contexts.[63] From what ibn Kaspi expresses here, however, I would argue that the royal entry processions presented one ritual occasion of city life when Jews voluntarily took up the position of being seen among the Christian majority as bearers of the Hebrew Truth and representatives of an integral phase of Christendom. It appears to be a point of pride for this Jewish author that these ritual processions provided a moment when the significant role of Jews within Christian society was ceremonially and visibly communicated to the entire urban commune.

The second important point ibn Kaspi makes is that showing the Torah was of political significance. Presenting the Torah to secular rulers is made analogous to the royal procedure of presenting privileges to Jews. Although this formulation is metaphorical, the context of the question remains the Jewish-royal encounter during entry rituals, where homage was typically given and confirmed. Thus, one could interpret

---

61. Kaspi, *Shulḥan Kesef*, 59.

62. Jeremy Cohen, *Living Letters of the Law: Ideas of the Jew in Medieval Christianity* (Berkeley: University of California Press, 1999), 23–66; and Paula Fredrikson, "Augustine and Israel: Interpretatio ad litteram, Jews, and Judaism in Augustine's Theology of History," *Studia Patristica* 38 (2001): 119–35; Aryeh Grabois, "The Hebraica Veritas and Jewish-Christian Intellectual Relations in the Twelfth Century," *Speculum* 50 (1975): 613–34.

63. For an example, see Rella Kushelevsky, *Tales in Context: Sefer ha-Ma'asim in Medieval Northern France, Bodleian Library, University of Oxford, Ms. Bodl. Or. 135* (Detroit: Wayne State University Press, 2017), 409.

that ibn Kaspi considered this encounter of homage, in a sense, reciprocal. Just as the original privilege of the king (in his language and script) is the authoritative basis for Jewish standing, so, too, the original Hebrew text and script of the Bible (in the God-given language) serves as an authoritative basis for kings. As kings were thought to be divinely appointed, ibn Kaspi implies that a king's reverence of the Torah during ritual processions was an expression of homage to God. This fits well within scholarly discussions of these royal entries as dramatized stagings of town-crown political reciprocity.[64] By presenting the Torah, the Jews saw their role as reciprocating political honor to their rulers and the greater commune. This helps to explain the readiness with which some Jews participated in these urban rituals, as evinced in the Hebrew sources.

Jewish participation in these processions often involved a hope for privileges or public recognition from the new ruler, as ibn Kaspi suggests. For example, in his journal entry on December 4, 1385, Jean le Fevre, bishop of Chartres and chancellor to the dukes of Anjou and counts of Provence (ca. 1330–1390), recorded that the Jews of Arles joined the city's processions to welcome the eight-year-old Louis II of Anjou (d. 1417), and his regent mother, Marie de Blois, Duchess of Anjou, Countess of Provence, and Queen of Naples (d. 1404):

> We arrived near the city [of Arles] and there were processions. . . . In a quarter of the city, the king gave florins to the people, and they shouted: "Long live [King Louis]" etc. . . . The king and his mother came to the cathedral church and saw the body of Saint Trophime. . . . In the city in one place, the Jews, holding their [Torah] scroll, showed it to the king and wanted him to kiss it. We countered by inclining [our heads toward] it.[65]

This brief depiction echoes a similar event from 1350, in which the clerics of Notre Dame Cathedral in Paris greeted the newly crowned King John II of France (d. 1364) upon his entry into the city by standing in a certain city square, dressed "as it should be" in silk capes, carrying crosses, candles, gilded books, in order to approach the ruler with the

---

64. Jesse D. Hurlbut, "Processions in Burgundy," 165–71.
65. Jean Le Fèvre, *Journal de Jean le Fèvre: chancelier des ducs d'Anjou et comtes de Provence (1381–1388)*, ed. Michel Hébert, Jean-Michel Matz, Noël Coulet, Philippe Genequand, Mathieu Lescuyer, Christophe Masson, and Thierry Pécout (Rennes: Presses universitaire de Rennes, 2020), 222.

book of the Gospels for his "oath to maintain [our] conical privileges, legal rights and to defend [us] to the utmost."[66] The king's response to the clerics was to bow humbly and reverently kiss the Holy Scriptures. Thus, as Jean le Fevre's description makes clear, Jews too joined the solemn processions, greeting their rulers with the Torah and asking for recognition of their rights similarly to the other groups of the city.[67] In this way, both the Torah and the Gospels were holy texts that represented or justified these groups' presence and performed the unity of the whole.

Although the previous two sources originate from Provence, which has been shown to possess a more geopolitically distinct community of Jews,[68] there was similar significance invested in Jewish visibility during processions in more northern French and northeastern Ashkenazic regions as well. Sources written by clerical and lay Christians convey that Christians expected to see the Jews perform actively with the Torah scroll. The most important chronicle from thirteenth- and fourteenth-century Bohemia relates how moved the clerical writer was to see this when the new king John of Bohemia (d. 1346) ritually entered to Brno in 1311:

> He was received magnificently not only by the clergy and all the Christian people, but also by the entire synagogue of the Jews, [who] had come rather far from the city of Brno to first greet the coming king. When I saw this unusual Jewish procession reverentially carrying the Torah-scroll wrapped in muslin and receiving the king with Hebraic song, my mind was liquified as much from amazement as from the ardor of their devotion, and my eyes led forth an issuing of tears.[69]

In this case, and in line with ibn Kaspi's description, the cleric was receptive and reverent in the presence of the Torah scroll, hinting toward its presence as a significant devotional element of the procession.

By the fifteenth century, this Jewish presence with the Torah was expected also among the Christian laity. Ulrich von Richental (d. 1437) chronicled how Jewish and Christian men and women filled the streets,

---

66. Archives Nationales de France, K. 47, no. 6; Bernard Guenée and Françoise Lehoux, Les entrées, 48–55.
67. See my extended discussion of these sources in Hannah Teddy Schachter "When Rulers Came to Town."
68. See Pinchas Roth, *In This Land: Jewish Life and Legal Culture in Late Medieval Provence* (Toronto: Pontifical Institute of Mediaeval Studies, 2021).
69. *Fontes rerum Bohemicarum*, ed. Josef Emler (Prag 1871), 4:178.

rooftops, and windows of Constance to watch the entry processions in honor of the Ecumenical Council that began in 1414. Ulrich also describes a designated group of Jewish representatives gathered for their own moment of fealty, "with many great burning candles and all wearing their religious dress as they do when they celebrate their long day [Yom Kippur]. Singing in Hebrew, the Jews approached and ... bowed down while offering the 10 commandments [Torah] and requesting the confirmation of their freedoms."[70] With slight admonition, the king received them declaring that "the commandments of Moses are good and right" (*Moyses gebott sind gut und recht*).[71] From both Christian and Jewish perspectives, then, it had become an expected and necessary part of these civic processions for Jews to perform their sociocultural and political role in Christian society by appearing before lay rulers, representing themselves as the bearers of precious Hebrew documents, to honor and pay homage and receive confirmation in return.

Ultimately, the different roles of Jews in both liturgical and civic processions in medieval France and the Holy Roman Empire demonstrate how the oscillation between presence and absence of this religious minority contributed to the definition of the Christian majority. The role of Jews to be absent in liturgical processions, particularly those related to the Passion, Crucifixion, and Host, served two functions. Theologically, drawing from the narrative role of Jews as antagonists to Christ, Christian authorities instrumentalized Jewish invisibility to reenact the real presence of Christ in the urban space and reinforce Christian understandings of biblical truths in communal ritual. Practically, Jewish invisibility tempered urban violence, enhancing the sense of peace and community while these rituals took place. Medieval Jews not only willingly opted out of these events, in part for their own religious reasons, but were also able to negotiate the terms of their invisibility at set times. I posit that the necessity of Jews' invisibility from these liturgical urban events increasingly factored into where Jews could reside within the city as the medieval period wore on. Conversely, the role of Jews to be present in royal entry civic processions also had clear theological and

---

70. *Chronik des Konstanzer Konzils 1414–1418 von Ulrich Richental*, ed. Thomas Martin Buck (Ostfildern: Jan Thorbecke, 2010), 114.

71. *Ulrich Richental: Die Chronik des Konzils von Konstanz*, ed. Thomas Martin Buck (MGH Digitale Edition, 2019), Aulendorfer Version (A), 267,1. https://edition.mgh.de/001/html/edition.html. At this moment of the procession, Jews sought confirmation from the pope, who initially refused them, later rebuking and summoning Jews to convert in line with the particular rituals of papal entry to Rome. See note 52 above.

practical functions. From a combination of their own religious, political, and economic reasons, Jews were eager and expected to fill their role as the bearers of the Torah, the original Hebrew documents central to both Judaism and Christendom, and to perform their part in the Christian conception of history. They also sought to represent themselves and to request and receive privileges in much the same ritual gesture as other social groups of the urban commune. In this case, the Jewish presence contributed to, rather than impinged on, the expression of Christian community and the wholeness of Christian society.

The two types of processions studied here thus prove to be parallel processes, both related and unrelated, in which Jewish (in)visibility was a defining component of ritual urban performance in medieval Christian contexts. Considering common discussions on how Jews were included and excluded from their civic communities, this chapter on medieval processions makes a case for how Jewish life was lived in vibrant and complex fluctuation between the two. Continuing to mine sources related to the performative power of processions and other urban rituals will likely shed further light on the dynamic realities of Jewish life in medieval Christian societies, offering yet another prism through which to nuance scholarly discussions of minority-majority relations in the premodern world.

Further Reading

Almagro Vidal, Clara, and Jörn Roland Christophersen. "Visibility of Religious Difference in Medieval Europe and the Mediterranean." *Hamsa: Journal for Judaic and Islamic Studies* 7 (2021). doi.org/10.4000/hamsa.1049.

Althoff, Gerd. *Die Macht der Rituale: Symbolik und Herrschaft im Mittelalter*. Darmstadt: Wissenschaftliche Buchgesellschaft, 2003.

Amar-Zifkin, Emilie. "Observing the Observers: Processions and Public Religion in Medieval Ashkenaz." PhD diss., Yale University, 2023.

Baumgarten, Elisheva. "Shared Stories and Religious Rhetoric: R. Judah the Pious, Peter the Chanter and a Drought." *Medieval Encounters* 18 (2012): 36–54. doi:10.1163/157006712X634558.

Blanchard, Joël. "Le spectacle du rite: les entrées royales." *Revue Historique* 305 (2003): 475–519.

Boogaart, Thomas A. "Our Savior's Blood: Procession and Community in Late Medieval Bruges." In *Moving Subjects: Processional Performance in the Middle Ages and the Renaissance*, edited by Kathleen Ashley and Wim Hüsken, 69–116. Leiden: Brill, 2001.

Bourlet, Caroline, and Boris Bove. "Religion civique ou affiliation communautaire? Le témoignage des testaments parisiens des XIIIe-XVe siècles." *Histoire urbaine* 60 (2021): 71–96.

Brubaker, Leslie, and Chris Wickham. "Processions, Power, and Community Identity: East and West." In *Empires and Communities in the Post-Roman and Islamic World, C. 400–1000 CE,* edited by Rutger Kramer and Walter Pohl, 121–87. Oxford: Oxford University Press, 2021.

Brugger, Eveline, and Birgit Wiedl. "Im Haus des Juden fand man eine blutbefleckte Hostie: Hostienschändungsvorwürfe und ihre Folgen für die jüdische Bevölkerung Österreichs im Mittelalter." *Jahrbuch für Landeskunde von Niederösterreich* 84 (2018): 35–57.

Coulet, Noël. "De l'intégration à l'exclusion: la place des Juifs dans les cérémonies d'entrée solennelle au Moyen Âge." *Annales. Économies, Sociétés, Civilisations* 34 (1979): 672–83. doi.org/10.3406/ahess.1979.294079.

Felbecker, Sabine. *Die Prozession: Historische und systematische Untersuchungen zu einer liturgischen Ausdruckhandlung.* Altenberge: Oros, 1995.

Flanigan, Clifford C. "The Moving Subject: Medieval Liturgical Processions in Semiotic and Cultural Perspective." In *Moving Subjects: Processional Performance in the Middle Ages and the Renaissance,* edited by Kathleen Ashley and Wim Hüsken, 35–51. Leiden: Brill, 2001.

Gaposchkin, Cecilia. "Between Historical Narration and Liturgical Celebrations: Gautier Cornut and the Reception of the Crown of Thorns in France." *Revue Mabillon* 30 (2019): 91–145.

Gedeon, Luitgard. "Prozessionen in Frankfurt am Main." *Archiv für mittelrheinische Kirchengeschichte* 52 (2000): 11–53.

Honig, Mordecai Menachem. "Al Mahadurato ha-Hadashah shel Sefer ha-Maskil (Sefer Hasidim) le-R. Moshe b. R. Eleazar ha-Kohen." *Yerushateinu* 1 (2007): 225–26.

Jütte, Daniel. "'They Shall Not Keep Their Doors or Windows Open': Urban Space and the Dynamics of Conflict and Contact in Premodern Jewish–Christian Relations." *European History Quarterly* 46 (2016): 209–237. doi.org/10.1177/0265691416630925.

Kipling, Gordon. *Enter the King: Theatre, Liturgy, and Ritual in the Late Medieval Civic Triumph.* Oxford: Clarendon Press, 1998.

Linder, Amnon. "The Jews Too Were Not Absent... Carrying Moses's Law on Their Shoulders: The Ritual Encounter of Pope and Jew from the Middle Ages to Modern Times." *Jewish Quarterly Review* 99 (2009): 323–95. 10.1353/jqr.0.0052.

Rubin, Miri. *Corpus Christi: The Eucharist in Late Medieval Culture.* Cambridge: Cambridge University Press, 1991.

Schachter, Hannah Teddy. "When Rulers Came to Town: Jews and Civic Processions in Medieval Ashkenaz." *Medieval History Journal* 27 (2024): 353–81. doi.org/10.1177/09719458241273726.

Wenninger, Markus. "Das gefährliche Fest: Ostern als zeitlicher Kristallisationspunkt antijüdischen Verhaltens." in *Feste und Feiern im Mittelalter. Paderborner Symposion des Mediävistenverbandes,* edited by Detlef Altenburg, Jörg Jarnut, and Hans-Hugo Steinhoff, 323–32. Sigmaringen: Jan Thorbecke Verlag, 1991.

Afterword

Beyond the Elite, and Much More

Miri Rubin

The image of the Wandering Jew came into being in Europe in the fifteenth century, and spread thereafter. Imagining a person who belonged nowhere, who had no place to call home, it was, like so many fictions about Jews, a fantasy; a story combining fear, speculation, and hate, with a touch of magic and the supernatural.[1] This was indeed a period of frequent movement for Jews, forced into peripatetic lives following repeated expulsions from cities and kingdoms. Yet it utterly fails to capture the reality of Jewish lives in the towns and cities of Europe during this period, as the contributions to this book so amply demonstrate.

For it is place that emerges most vividly from the pages you have just read. While this book is divided into four sections—people, spaces, objects, rituals—it is in fact place, in its fullest meaning, that best summarizes these contributions. Place is what people make of the spaces they inhabit and of the resources—natural and human—that those offer. Place contains what can be freely obtained, as well as what can be

---

1. Lisa Lampert-Weissig, *Instrument of Memory: Encounters with The Wandering Jew* (Ann Arbor: University of Michigan Press, 2024).

made and owned, by individuals surrounded by their kin, their neighbors, and their coinhabitants.[2]

The Jews most definitely made their places in hundreds of settings across Ashkenaz, the terrain explored in this book, a swath of settlement that extended in an arc from England, through northern France and Germany to Poland/Lithuania. In each of these lands Jews spoke both the local vernacular and a Jewish one, reserving Hebrew for ritual purposes only, and using a mixture of Hebrew and Aramaic for study. In each place they lived they quickly adapted to local realities—food stuffs and products, the climate, and the working of local communication. In each of these lands Jews participated in social networks of neighbors and business associates, and learned to understand the governing political structures; they became accustomed to aesthetic codes and contributed by making and using objects guided by them. Fully inhabiting these spaces, they knew intimately the local sights, smells, and sounds: the ringing of a bell, the smell of a river, the sight of a cathedral or a city wall, and the texture of local clothes, loaves of bread, masonry, or yarn.

People make spaces into places where identities are developed and expressed. And since identities are plural, multifaceted, and changing, all this is reflected in places, too. Jews shared among themselves a great deal of heritage and lore, but these were experienced in ways inflected for each person by gender, age, status, and education, in myriad individual combinations. Jews differed from each other even as they shared important, fateful bonds. In his discussion on *piyyutim* (liturgical poems recited in the synagogue during prayers), Erez Shahar Rochman makes clear that these adorned the liturgy with poetry of remembrance and commemoration in ways that were uniquely local, while suggesting that they also served to communicate to the vast majority, who were not members of the scholarly elite, important historical, theological, and devotional content.

So how might we imagine these non-elite Jewish lives? Perhaps by no longer characterizing them as being made of an "outer" shell of interactions with a Christian world and an "inner" core of Jewishness. A local sound or sight, the form of words or a melody, the savor of food and drink, could all be pleasing, moving, and meaningful to a Jew in any town or city in Ashkenaz, and incorporated into what we may consider to be their inner world.

---

2. *Making Place: Space and Embodiment in the City*, ed. Arijit Sen and Lisa Silverman (Bloomington: University of Indiana Press, 2014).

AFTERWORD

An example of the use of local knowledge by Jews in the intimate experience of prayer is offered in the chapter by Elisheva Baumgarten and Amit Shafran, in which they explore a prayer against boils (carbuncle) from thirteenth-century France, found in a miscellaneous manuscript that had belonged to Isaac ben Isaac of Chinon. The prayer is in French, copied out in Hebrew letters, and is one of a series of Hebrew prayers and poems. The prayer is an adjuration against the carbuncle (*bon malon*) in the name of God; an incantation aimed at bringing about a cure and preserving health by appealing to God's action, which was intended to be recited by a Jew just as his or her Christian neighbors might do using the same text.

We need not disentangle this practice as Jewish, or not. Situated in a mostly Hebrew manuscript, it was clearly no longer just Christian in any meaningful sense. A prayer such as this tells us a great deal about how French Jews lived, and sought to improve their lives.

I use the word *dis/entanglement* advisedly here, since it has served to conceptualize—and name—a book coedited by the leader of Beyond the Elite, Elisheva Baumgarten. Into that earlier book, *Entangled Histories: Knowledge, Authority, and Jewish Culture in the Thirteenth Century*, twelve chapters explore the intellectual activities of Jews and Christians, sometimes through mutual influence, other times through polemic.[3] It is pleasing to see in the current book the realization of the scholarly endeavor Beyond the Elite that aims to probe the lives of Jews who were not scholars, going about their daily lives, and doing so with a strong sense of place, and entangled with the lives of their Christian neighbors.

This change of perspective, or rather, this enhanced focus, means that the contributions you have just read aim to trace the structures of social relations rather than to signal achievements of individuals (though we do come across some fascinating characters along the way). A good example is the chapter on orphans by Andreas Lehnertz and Eyal Levinson, where we learn how common it was for families to accommodate an orphan in their midst. Support for fatherless children—and occasionally adults—was considered to be a core charitable endeavor for both Christian and Jews, inspired by biblical injunctions and made necessary by evident social need. This was particularly true of children and women, who depended on fathers and husbands to realize their legal rights and to enjoy their full social capacities. It is striking to note

---

3. *Entangled Histories. Knowledge, Authority, and Jewish Culture in the Thirteenth Century*, ed. Elisheva Baumgarten, Ruth Mazo Karras, and Katelyn Mesler (Philadelphia: University of Pennsylvania Press, 2017).

how the fair and generous treatment of orphans became a social norm by which people were judged. It is also evident that in relations with Christian authorities, say in the matter of settlement, orphans were considered to be full members of the families that had adopted them.

To say that this book deals with those who were "beyond the elite," does not mean that authoritative voices and normative experiences are absent from its chapters. The lives of artisans, children, women, orphans, and farmers, were all affected by attitudes and practices shaped by royal, urban, and religious authorities. The contributors expertly combine and contrast official sources to other types of writings and, notably, to objects and images. Together these reveal social realities and personal experiences. Such, for example, was Ido Noy's chapter on the use of rings as tokens of betrothal, nuptial gifts, and symbols of a fateful life-cycle transition. Attested to in Ashkenaz from the eleventh century on as a symbol of the bride's passage into the marital state, different versions of the ring developed, in keeping with local styles and materials, and communities saw to it that even poor bridegrooms owned the ring he used to marry his bride. Here is a close reading of an object entangled in webs of meaning, Jewish and other.

Aviya Doron addresses the use of materials in less felicitous contexts, sometimes unlawfully deposited—say wool for the making of cloth, or precious metals for the making of jewelry—as pawns to secure loans with lenders, Jews and others. This phenomenon was tantamount to theft as it meant the use of an object that belonged to another. If the debt failed, the lender reclaimed the pawned materials, but who was its owner? Noy cites both Christian and Jewish sources, and so reveals attempts to deal with the phenomenon: quoting both the *Nurenberg Judenordnungen* from the 1330s and R. Israel Isserlein (1390–1460), as he worked to pass judgment on pawning what one did not own. The city legislated, the rabbi advised, but the story here is of people beyond the elite bound by credit exchanges and labor, by the circulation of goods, and by neighborhood.

This urban landscape of moneylenders of differing ethnicities and religions is excellent terrain for comparative exploration of how Jews were different from other groups of "familiar strangers" in the cities.[4] Nureet Dermer traces the settlement of Jews and Lombards in fourteenth-century Paris and demonstrates the changes in neighborhood

---

4. I developed this concept when working on Miri Rubin, *Cities of Strangers, Making Lives in Medieval Europe* (Cambridge: Cambridge University Press, 2020).

locations following expulsions and return in 1315, 1322, and 1360. Highlighting what was similar and different as Jews resettled after each expulsion with more restricted permitted practices reflects the gradual replacement of their function in the city by Lombards. One can only imagine the regret felt at the loss of a well-established and conveniently located neighborhood that had served Jews for generations with its landmarks and associations. While Lombards also suffered expulsions and some restrictions, Paris was not their sole home, and that is where the difference lies.[5]

Jews were often inspired to act and create by local habits shared with non-Jews. Netta Bodner and Ariella Lehmann's chapter studies a series of dedicatory inscriptions carved in buildings in Mainz and Worms. These inscriptions celebrate the new or renewed buildings as communal achievements, but also delight in the very work of engraving, metal on stone. There is in them an appreciation for the durability as well as the malleability of stone, expressed in the quotation of verses from the Hebrew Bible associated with the building of Solomon's temple. And there is more, suggest the authors; Jews appreciated that the building and maintenance of synagogues and *mikveh*s was part of a broader process, the remaking of medieval cities in stone, for the first time since the Roman period. Stone was now the material of choice for religious as well as seigneurial and civic buildings in northern Europe, and so for Jewish buildings too.

All these buildings and objects were set in landscapes that non-elite Jews knew well. That meant the city streets they inhabited, where they regularly observed Christian processions. Hannah Teddy Schachter shows in her chapter that on occasion Jews participated in civic ceremonies, as part of the vision of the city that the ceremony sought to portray and celebrate. Vast stretches of rural lands were also familiar to Jews. Annika Funke analyses the effect on Jews of the proliferation of territorial lordships in the vicinity of Frankfurt in the fifteenth century, showing that it resulted in a multiplication of dues and payments exacted from Anschel of Münzenberg. His name, a German toponym, marks Anschel as belonging to a town held by several lords in condominium. In his petition to the Count of Hanau of 1512 with the request for alleviation in dues, Anschel names the lords and their territories,

---

5. The methodological study of Jews alongside other professionals has proven fruitful, as in Rowan Dorin, *No Return: Jews, Christian Usurers, and the Spread of Mass Expulsion in Medieval Europe* (Princeton: Princeton University Press, 2023).

clearly aware of the extent of their lands and dominium. Like Anschel, many Jews were obliged to acquaint themselves with the kinship ties and genealogies of the numerous lords who affected the well-being of their communities. Jewish diplomats worked hard to counter the many claims by territorial lords, by arguing that these would badly affect the local economy, and so the count and even the emperor. And if they were not heard, these well-embedded Jews could threaten to leave, and to make new homes elsewhere.

Alongside such local knowledge of seigneurial families and their territorial claims, Jews knew the land through extensive travel, often by rivers. However, settled and thriving their communities, Jews—like others—left home for a variety of reasons: commerce, education, or attendance at celebrations with family members; on diplomatic business for their community, or in service of a patron. Tzafrir Barzilay's chapter shows the regularity of river travel for Jews. Already in 903-6, the toll regulations of Raffelstetten on the Danube near Linz mentioned tolls paid by Jews. In 1190 Henry II exempted the Jews of Mainz and Worms of all tolls, and in the thirteenth century a Jewish married couple attempted to renegotiate the tolls paid at the important crossing at Koblenz. Along with the cost and inconvenience, there is here a familiarity with landscape, often far from home for days and even weeks. Travel was yet another context within which Jews were situated close to non-Jews sharing space, conversations, anxiety, and expectations.

Such movement in the landscape took Jews out of their habitual urban environment. The absence of a family member often forms the basis for the problems treated in responsa related to family life, marriage, and labor. On their travels, Jews—like others—sought arrangements that were safe and reassuring. Albert Kohn's chapter introduces us to the reality of the need to find a temporary home when away from home. He notes the involvement of Jews in running inns, especially in southern Europe, but also the existence of dedicated Jewish hostelries where most non-elite Jewish travelers stayed. Some Jews lodged with other Jews, and most guests of rank would have been hosted by locals. Hosting merchants might even give a person some advantage in trading with their guests. As Jews traveled they learned of the habits, markets, and methods of artisans and merchants elsewhere; they also encountered differences in Jewish life and worship styles. Travel was work, but it also allowed for melodies, rituals, practices, and strategies of survival to travel between Jewish communities.

AFTERWORD

Travel was not always a matter of choice. It was occasioned by expulsions from towns and cities, but also by the internal discipline of Jewish communities. Miri Fenton's chapter on excommunication (*herem*) treats the reality of chastisement by expulsion from a Jewish community. Some excommunication was limited in time, like the three years imposed on a murderer; others were a general withdrawal of neighborly relations from the offending Jew. In a few cases this punishment was for life, not unlike the move to a new city a convert to Christianity was often obliged to undertake. The application of *herem* tested the desire to maintain solidarity within the Jewish community, but it was an important deterrent, and a mark of rabbinical authority. It could affect every member of a community, elite and non-elite, by forcing individuals to adhere to the collective decree.

Reading this book, it strikes me that its chapters can be treated as a series of explorations, of instantiations of actor network theory (ANT). ANT sees social life as the collective and ongoing interaction between humans (and their ideas), objects, and technologies.[6] Just as we have seen, laws created frameworks that shaped Jewish lives, and religious teachings framed ethical choices, but the dramas of daily life were enacted by individuals in their places, with things, while creatively navigating life's vagaries and contingencies.

No individual is ever without things, outside place, devoid of ideas, and unaware of expectations. In the vast variety of social situations some rituals, habits, and structures—some pathways—help individuals make sense, work, and communicate. But there are also myriad situations that are less familiar, attractive, threatening, and inspiring, and Jews confronted them with words and things creatively. They borrowed and adapted effective prayers, they learned the landscape in order to travel safely, and studied the genealogies of lords in order to find a way through their predacious intentions. Jews used objects to bind themselves to others, as gifts, tokens, or pawns, creating the networks that are the essence of all social life. They moved through the streets with an array of sensibilities—some like, and some unlike those of their non-Jewish neighbors. Their contact with an ancient language and rituals offered solace, but may also have been a puzzling burden. Only close studies of Jewish places, leavened by broad concepts, can produce the

---

6. Bruno Latour, *Reassembling the Social* (Oxford: Oxford University Press, 2005).

histories—like the chapters assembled here—that explains Jews' resilience and their creativity, and their sense of belonging in Ashkenaz.

This book summarizes a project that is expert and imaginative in the identification of sources in different genres and materials, while also being aware of the breadth of approaches and methods that animate contemporary historical work. No chapter is bound by a sole approach: urban history is employed alongside the history of the emotions, religious experience with gender and family, as well as deft analyses of political structures and economic logic. There is a great deal more to learn about the resilience of non-elite Jews of Ashkenaz, and this book shows how we may do so.

Further Readings

Baumgarten, Elisheva, Ruth Mazo Karras, and Katelyn Mesler, eds. *Entangled Histories: Knowledge, Authority, and Jewish Culture in the Thirteenth Century*. Philadelphia: University of Pennsylvania Press, 2017.

Dorin, Rowan. *No Return: Jews, Christian Usurers, and the Spread of Mass Expulsion in Medieval Europe*. Princeton: Princeton University Press, 2023.

Lampert-Weissig, Lisa. *Instrument of Memory: Encounters with The Wandering Jew*. Ann Arbor: University of Michigan Press, 2024.

Latour, Bruno. *Reassembling the Social*. Oxford: Oxford University Press, 2005.

Rubin, Miri. *Cities of Strangers: Making Lives in Medieval Europe*. Cambridge: Cambridge University Press, 2020.

Sen, Arijit and Lisa Silverman, eds. *Making Place: Space and Embodiment in the City*. Bloomington: University of Indiana Press, 2014.

Acknowledgments

This book is the final product of the Beyond the Elite: Jewish Daily Life in Medieval Europe research project (2016–22), funded by the European Research Council. The work begun in the framework of this project is now being continued in Contending with Crises: The Jews of XIVth Century Europe project (2022–27) funded by the Israel Science Foundation. It is with gratitude that I acknowledge that it is through the support of both these grants that this book was able to come into being.

The Beyond the Elite project, based at the Hebrew University of Jerusalem, ran for six years, and its activities included more than a dozen international conferences held in Jerusalem, trips to Germany and France, numerous workshops, dozens of visiting scholars from around the world, and many visiting students. We cooperated with a wide variety of institutes for Jewish studies, in places such as Germany (Trier, Cologne, Frankfurt, Erfurt), France, England, the United States, and Canada.

Over the course of the grant period the members of the research group completed theses, dissertations, articles, and books. Working together in shared quarters, we developed new ways of collaboration, benefiting and enjoying studying together and learning from each other to ask new and different questions; each bringing his or her own skill set and knowledge of languages and genres. Together, we sought to better understand daily life among the Jews of medieval Ashkenaz, and developed social-historical methods of study. In some cases, group members chose to write articles together, as is evident in this volume. All in all, this model, which was new for all of us, resulted in tremendous progress in our individual work as well as novel types of joint study and publications. The fruits of our work, including a number of fascicles in journals, a sourcebook (published by Western Michigan University), a film about the project, as well as virtual tours of our exhibit in Jerusalem and in Erfurt, Germany, and so on, can be found on our website: https://beyond-the-elite.huji.ac.il/.

The core group members (in alphabetical order), Tzafrir Barzilay, Neta Bodner, Nureet Dermer, Aviya Doron, Annika Funke, Etelle Kalaora, Albert Kohn, Ariella Lehmann, Andreas Lehnertz, Eyal Levinson, Adi Namia-Cohen, Ido Noy, Erez Shahar Rochman, Hannah (Teddy) Schachter, and Amit Shafran, included postdocs, doctoral students, and master's students, some of whom spent the entire tenure of the project in the group and some joined only for a couple of years.

The essays in this book, written by most of the members listed above, were drafted during 2021–22, the final year of the project. We workshopped them with three colleagues: Gadi Algazi (Tel Aviv University), Elisheva Carlebach (Columbia University), and Miri Rubin (Queen Mary University of London) in September 2022. We then revised each article and the book as a whole. Many group members continued with me to a new, not unrelated project, funded by the Israel Science Foundation, Contending with Crises: The Jews of XIVth Century Europe. It was under the auspices of this project that the final stages of completing the book were carried out.

We are thrilled that Cornell University Press accepted this book for publication and are honored to be part of the Medieval Societies, Religions, and Cultures series. Great encouragement and important feedback were received from the editors of this series, Cecilia Gaposhkin and Anne E. Lester. The comments and suggestions made by the anonymous readers for the press were most helpful. All of this helped improve our final product. We would like to express our immense appreciation to those colleagues who provided us with invaluable advice and critique throughout the process. We would also like to express our gratitude to Miri Rubin, who has been a good friend and teacher to all of us throughout our years of working together, and who graciously agreed to contribute the epilogue to this book. Additional thanks go to Fray Hochstein who not only edited the essays but also asked many insightful questions, and to Sara Tropper who helped prepare the final manuscript. I also wish to thank editor Mahinder Kingra and the entire team at Cornell University Press for their support.

As the Principal Investigator of the project, I want to express my personal thanks to the colleagues from Israel and abroad who worked with us throughout the project and to the administrative staff at the Research Authority and the Faculty of Humanities of the Hebrew University of Jerusalem, especially Merav Yaacobi and Hani Ben Yehuda.

Most important, my gratitude to the group members knows no bounds. As I often said to them, and still say, working in a group and leading this project (and the one that has followed it) is the joy of my academic career. As a team, we dedicate this book to the one and only Audrey Fingherman. Audrey has been with us as the group coordinator from the start and it is her wisdom and organizational skills that have enabled us to work so successfully and productively together.

Our joint research and its products, among them this book, stem from our fascination with and desire to shed light on the realities of daily life and the lives of medieval women and men, Jews and Christians. This is not just an exercise in curiosity, but an integral part of our quest to understand human nature and to use this knowledge to try and make the world we live in a better place. As we complete this collection of articles, this world is in the midst of a turbulent and unsettling period, especially here in Israel. It is our hope that well before this book appears, we will be on a path to peace. As we seek to hear voices from the past, it is our hope that people will learn to listen and hear each other and seek life and understanding in the present, for all our sakes and those of the generations to follow.

Elisheva Baumgarten

Contributors

Tzafrir Barzilay is a senior lecturer of medieval history in the Department of History at Bar-Ilan University. He is interested in the social history of minorities, environmental and geographical factors, and religious movements in medieval Europe. He is currently investigating religious and quotidian practices pertaining to water in Jewish and Christian life in High and Late Medieval Europe. He is the author of *Poisoned Wells: Accusation, Persecution and Minorities in Medieval Europe, 1321–1422* (University of Pennsylvania Press, 2022) and coeditor with Elisheva Baumgarten and Eyal Levinson of *Jewish Daily Life in Medieval Northern Europe, 1000–1350: A Sourcebook* (Western Michigan University Press, 2022). Barzilay participated in the Beyond the Elite: Jewish Daily Life in Medieval Europe project as a postdoctoral fellow from 2016 to 2019.

Elisheva Baumgarten is the Yitzchak Becker Professor for Jewish Studies and teaches in the Departments of Jewish History and History at the Hebrew University of Jerusalem. Baumgarten is a social historian interested in Jewish-Christian relations and the daily lives of the Jews of medieval Ashkenaz in the High Middle Ages. Her books include *Mothers and Children: Jewish Family Life in Medieval Europe* (Princeton University Press, 2004); *Practicing Piety in Medieval Ashkenaz* (University of Pennsylvania Press, 2014), and *Biblical Women and Jewish Daily Life in the Middle Ages* (University of Pennsylvania Press, 2022) as well as many articles and edited volumes, among them *Jewish Everyday Life in Medieval Northern Europe 1080–1350*, coedited with Tzafrir Barzilay and Eyal Levinson (Western Michigan University Press, 2022). Baumgarten led the Beyond the Elite: Jewish Daily Life in Medieval Europe project from 2016 to 2022 and is currently heading the Israel Science Foundation research project, Contending with Crises: The Jews of XIVth Century Europe (2022-27).

Neta Bodner is a senior lecturer at the Open University of Israel in the Department of Literature, Languages, and the Arts. She is an architectural historian interested in religious architecture. Bodner has authored journal articles in *Viator, Jewish Studies Quarterly, Zion*, and *Arts* and chapters in edited volumes on Christian and Jewish architecture in German-speaking lands, Israel, and in Italy. She has coedited two books on religious architecture with Bianca Kühnel and Renana Bartal and is PI of a collaborative project on the mikveh of Cologne funded by the Israel Science Foundation. Bodner has recently completed a monograph on medieval Jewish ritual baths from Germany. She was a postdoctoral fellow in the Beyond the Elite: Jewish Daily Life in Medieval Europe project in 2016–18 and 2019–20.

Nureet Dermer holds a PhD in Jewish History from the Hebrew University of Jerusalem (2024) and was a fellow in the Beyond the Elite research team throughout its duration. She was a fellow in the Contending with Crises research team from 2022 to 2024. Her dissertation, "Between Expulsion: Jews and Christians in Fourteenth Century Northern France," as well as her postdoctoral research and publications focus on the lives and trajectories of northern French Jews (*Tzarfatim*) during the fourteenth and fifteenth centuries, with emphasis on Jewish-Christian relations, local identities, foreignness and belonging, the balance between expulsions and traumatic events and the everyday lives, and the dynamics of exclusion and inclusion of Jews, among other marginalized groups, during these centuries.

Aviya Doron is completing her PhD at the Department of Jewish History at the Hebrew University of Jerusalem under the supervision of Elisheva Baumgarten. Her research explores risk and trust in Jewish-Christian economic interactions in the German empire, and the institutions that supported interreligious economic exchange. Aviya Doron was a research fellow in the Beyond the Elite: Jewish Daily Life in Medieval Europe project between 2017 and 2022 and is currently a fellow in the Contending with Crises research team.

Miri Fenton completed her PhD in medieval history at the Hebrew University. Her work compares and contrasts the experience of community in the everyday life of Jews in the Crown of Aragon and Ashkenaz during the High Middle Ages. Miri holds a BA in history and an MPhil in philosophy of religion from the University of Cambridge. She was the Henry Fellow at Yale Graduate School in 2011–12, and studied at egalitarian yeshivot in New York and Jerusalem. Since completing her PhD, she left academia and is now a venture capital investor in Tel Aviv.

Annika Funke is a doctoral candidate at the University of Trier. Her research focuses on Jewish political agency in rural areas of Late Medieval Germany, particularly in the Wetterau region near Frankfurt. She has been a member of the research groups Beyond the Elite: Jewish Daily Life in Medieval Europe (2021–22) and Contending with Crises research group (2022–24) at the Hebrew University of Jerusalem.

Albert Evan Kohn is a doctoral candidate at Princeton University. Kohn studies how medieval religious ideas circulated between Jews and Christians and shaped their everyday lives. His dissertation is a social history of Jewish and Christian Sabbath observance in the cities of northern France and the Rhineland during the thirteenth and fourteenth centuries. He was a visiting research fellow at Beyond the Elite: Jewish Daily Life in Medieval Europe from 2019 to 2021.

CONTRIBUTORS

Ariella Lehmann is a doctoral student at the Hebrew University of Jerusalem. Her research focuses on lived religion and biblical literacy, and she is currently writing about how ordinary Jews in medieval Ashkenaz encountered and engaged with the book of Job. She wrote her master's thesis during her time in the Beyond the Elite team, between the years 2016–18, about the preparations for Shabbat in medieval Ashkenaz. She is currently part of the Contending with Crises team (2023–present). Drawing on her experience as a teacher in the Israeli school system, she also worked with the other Beyond the Elite team members to develop a website with resources for teaching about medieval Jewish life in Israeli junior high schools.

Andreas Lehnertz is junior professor of medieval history with a specialization in Jewish history at the University of Trier. He studies the social, cultural, and religious history of Europe. His academic pursuits focus on the nuanced dynamics of everyday Christian-Jewish relations, the study of marginal Hebrew and Yiddish deeds, the study of Jewish and general sealing practices, and the in-depth study of Jewish craftspeople. He wrote *Jewish Seals in the Medieval German Empire: The Authentication and Self-Representation of Jewish Men and Women* (Harrassowitz Verlag, 2020). He was a postdoctoral fellow in the Beyond the Elite: Jewish Daily Life in Medieval Europe research team and a member of the Martin Buber Society in the Humanities and Social Sciences, also at the Hebrew University of Jerusalem. Currently he is studying Jewish craftspeople in medieval Germany.

Eyal Levinson is a senior researcher in the Contending with Crises: The Jews in 14th Century Europe research group. He was a postdoctoral research fellow in the Beyond the Elite research group (2016–22). He researches youth, men, fatherhood, and masculinities in medieval Ashkenaz. His book *Gender and Sexuality in Ashkenaz in the Middle Ages* (in Hebrew) was published in 2022 by the Zalman Shazar Center and the Leo Baeck Jerusalem Institute. He also coedited with Tzafrir Barzilay and Elisheva Baumgarten, *Jewish Life in Medieval Northern Europe, 1080–1350: A Sourcebook* (Western Michigan University Press, 2023). Eyal is the author of several articles, among them "Situated Fathering in Medieval Ashkenaz"; "Male Friendship in Medieval Ashkenaz"; and "Eternal Love I Conceive for You: Traveling Jewish Men and Covenantal Bromances."

Ido Noy is researcher and a curator of Jewish art and Jewish history. His research interests cover various disciplines, geographies, and periods, including Hasmonean and Herodian numismatics in antiquity, Ashkenazi wedding jewelry and love tokens in the Middle Ages, Judaica from the Bezalel School, contemporary Jewish art, folklore, and 1980s popular culture. Noy was a member of the Beyond the Elite research team and published several articles are as part of the project. Noy curated the final exhibition of the project and coedited with Elisheva Baumgarten the catalog for the exhibition *In and Out, Between and Beyond: Jewish Daily Life in Medieval Europe*, which first opened in the Stern Gallery (2021) at the Hebrew University of Jerusalem, and later in the Old Synagogue Museum in Erfurt, Germany (2022–24).

Erez Shahar Rochman is a high school teacher at Keshet School in Jerusalem. He completed his MA in the Department of Jewish History at the Hebrew University of Jerusalem and was a member of the Beyond the Elite research group (2020–22).

Miri Rubin is a historian of medieval and early modern Europe (1100–1600) at Queen Mary University in London. Her work explores new approaches to the study of social relations in the predominantly religious cultures of Europe and seeks to understand issues of identity, community, and gender; the boundaries of cooperation; and the threat of violence. She is the author of many books and articles, among them *Corpus Christi: The Eucharist in Late Medieval Culture* (Cambridge University Press, 1992), *Gentile Tales: The Narrative Assault on Late Medieval Jews* (University of Pennsylvania Press, 1999), *Mother of God: A History of the Virgin Mary* (Yale University Press, 2009), and *Cities of Strangers: Making Lives in Medieval Europe* (Cambridge University Press, 2020). Since January 2020 she has also been president of the Jewish Historical Society of England.

Hannah Teddy Schachter is a doctoral candidate in Jewish history at the Hebrew University of Jerusalem, where she is a member of the ISF research group Contending with Crises: Jews in 14th Century Europe. She was a member of the Beyond the Elite research team from 2019 to 2022. She is also a Rotenstreich Fellow at the Jack, Joseph, and Morton Mandel School for Advanced Studies in the Humanities and an affiliated researcher of the Laboratoire de Médiévistique occidentale de Paris at the University of Paris Panthéon-Sorbonne. Her research focuses on the relations between Jews and Christian monarchies in the Middle Ages, with a particular focus on royal women. Her publications include "When Rulers Came to Town: Jews and Urban Processions in Medieval France and the Holy Roman Empire" (*Medieval History Journal*, 2024), and her dissertation is entitled "The Queens of France and the Jews in the Thirteenth Century."

Amit Shafran is an ASO account manager at YellowHead: Scaling made Simple in Jerusalem. She completed her MA in the Department of History at the Hebrew University of Jerusalem and was a member of the Beyond the Elite research group (2020–22).

Index

Abraham (biblical figure), 195, 234, 241, 285, 290, 295, 299
Abraham b. Isaac (Worms), 201–2
Abrasax, 289
Adelheid of Münzenberg, 79
adjurations, 282–83, 286–88, 297, 330
afterlife, 53, 238, 252
agency, 19, 27–29, 50, 61, 63, 67, 71, 95
Alexander Süslin of Frankfurt, 56
Altdorf, 67
Altona, 55
Amsterdam, 52, 53
amulets, 232, 246, 252, 289, 294n66
Anschel of Münzenberg, 28–29, 74–76, 80, 86, 93, 332–33
apotropaic powers, 232, 235, 241, 252
Appolinaris of Valence, 292
archbishops, 105, 109, 111
architecture, 176, 202, 243, 250, 251
arithmetic, 283
ark (*Aron Kodesh*), 186
astrology, 241
Augsburg, 52, 93
Austria, 57, 63, 110
Avignon, 310

Babylon, 194, 200
Balthasar Hubmair, 70
Bamberg, 112
Banitt, Menahem, 285, 286
Barukh ben Samuel, 61–62
Baumeister as administrator, 88, 90
beit din, 32n5, 34n9, 36, 39, 40–42, 44, 45–46, 51, 53, 54, 61, 63. See also courts
belts, 35, 208–9, 218, 223–24
beer brewers. See craftspeople
Benjamin of Tudela, 113, 154–55, 159–60

Beowulf, 301
Bernhard III of Solms-Braunfels, 74
betrothal. *See* marriage
Beziers, 310
Bird's Head Haggadah, 231–33
Black Death, 6, 75n2, 141n54, 150, 217, 221, 237
Blanche of Castile, 310, 313
Bohemia, 324
Bonn, 112, 115–17, 120
Boppard, 116, 121
bourgeois, 127–28, 131–32, 139, 142–43
Braunfels, 74
bread, 35, 51, 159, 163, 171, 285, 291, 296. *See also* food
Breslau, 314
bride and bridegroom. *See* marriage
Bristol, 52
Brnom, 324
Burgfrieden, 79–80, 88–91. *See also* condominium, *Ganerbschaft*
burial, 62, 110, 118, 238

calendar, 283
canon law, 49
cathedral, 109–10, 112, 311, 315, 323, 329
cemeteries. *See* burial; tombstones
charity, 14n38, 33, 41, 53, 147n6, 150, 162
Charles IV, 79–80, 133, 141
children. *See* guardians
Chinon, 281
citizenship, Jews as citizens, 21–23, 75n2, 121–22, 127–31, 141–42, 157, 306. See also *bourgeois*
collateral, 210, 214, 235, 236. *See also* moneylending
Colmar (Treasure), 243

Cologne, 108-10, 112-13, 115-17, 215-16
community affiliation, 10, 22-23, 27, 31, 35-36, 39, 42-43
communal authority, 8-11, 22, 24, 36-39, 40-42, 75n2, 262-62, 334
condominium, 74-80, 83, 88-92, 94. See also *Ganerbschaft*
conversion to Christianity, 44, 54, 152, 229n16, 325n71, 334
Corpus Christi, 305, 313, 315
Council of Constance, 325
Counts of Hanau, 74, 79-81, 84-88, 90-92
courts: Frankfurt imperial jury court (Frankfurter Schöffengericht), 75, 77, 77, 80, 81n18, 83, 85, 88, 208-22; parloir of Paris, 127, 137; court records, 12, 14, 208-9, 217-18, 223; royal court, 157, 231. See also *beit din*
courtly love, 248
craftspeople: bakers, 215; beer brewers, 215; goldsmiths, 208-9, 218-19, 236; textile workers, 217-18
credit. See moneylending
Crown of Thorns, 310-11
Crusades (First and Second), 2-3, 24, 115, 179, 268-69, 271-76, 290
curses, 34, 38n22

Danube River, 105, 110-13
David ben She'altiel, 62
demons, 232n27, 241-42, 252, 286, 292
disease, 283, 284-86, 287, 292-96
divorce, 39, 145, 237, 239, 250n82
dowries and inheritance, 40, 43, 55, 62. See also marriage
dragons, 301

Easter. See Holy Week
education, 51, 59, 68, 263-67
Elbe River, 112
Eleazar b. Judah of Worms (Rokeah), 34, 162
Eleazar ha-Kallir, 272, 273
Eliezer b. Joel ha-Levi (Ra'aviah), 45, 117, 120
Eliezer b. Samuel of Metz, 308-9
Eliezer b. Uri, 118
Eliezer bar Nathan (Ra'avan), 61, 115, 117-20
emperor, 75-76, 95, 105, 108, 110, 333
engagement (*erusin*). See marriage

Engelbert II (archbishop), 109
England, 5, 6, 112, 115-16, 157, 329
Ephraim of Bonn, 115-16, 120
epigraphy, 176, 180, 186, 171n11. See also tombstones
Eppstein, 78-79, 89
Erfurt, 112, 243
Eucharist, 305, 313-15
excommunication (*herem*): as communal punishment, 31-33; effectiveness of, 33-35; as legal mechanism, 31, 39-42; settlement bans (*herem ha-yishuv*), 32; *herem stam*, 32, 45-46. See also *nidui*
expulsion, 21, 77-78, 87-88, 93n69, 126n4, 127, 129, 131, 134-35, 137, 141, 143, 281, 311, 332

Falkenstein, 78-80
fertility, 234
fever, 285-86, 287, 288, 289, 292-94, 301
fingers (middle, index, thumb), 227-30, 234, 238, 239, 243-46
food, 114, 117, 287-88, 291, 296
fortune-telling, 283
Fourth Lateran Council, 18n48, 153, 309, 313
Frankfurt am Main, 65-66, 74-75, 80, 96, 118, 315-17
Frankfurter Schöffengericht. See courts
Fredrich II (duke), 110
Fredrich II (emperor), 110
Frederick III, King of the Romans, 315
Fürth, 53

Gabriel (angel), 289, 295, 298
Gambach, 74
Ganerbschaft, 78-80, 88. See also condominium
gematria, 234, 241
Gera, 112
Gershom b. Judah (*Me'or ha-Golah*), 40n33, 113-14, 238, 250n82, 268
Goitein, Shlomo Dov, 20
goldsmiths. See craftspeople
Good Friday. See Holy Week
Gospels, 321, 324
Götz von Fuderholz, 67-69
Gregory IX, 309, 311
Gregory of Tours, 292-93
guardians, 50, 52, 58-59, 61, 66-67, 72
guests, 147-48, 162, 164-65
guilds, 215-16

INDEX

Hagenau synagogue inscription, 186
Haggadah, 229, 230, 232, 246, 248, 250, 251
Haim b. Isaac Or Zaru'a, 38
halitzah, 239, 240
Halle, 112
Hamburg, 55
Hananiah, Mishael, Azariah (biblical figures), 288, 298
Hanau, 74, 76–77, 79–81, 84–88, 90–92
Hebraico-French, 285–86, 287, 291, 292
Hebrew Bible, 56, 187–90, 192–96, 276, 318, 321–23, 324, 326
heh (Hebrew letter), 232, 234
Heinrich II (archbishop), 111
Heinrich II (emperor), 105
Heinrich IV (emperor), 108, 110, 121, 178n12
herem. See excommunication
holidays, 118, 120, 282; High Holidays, 41, 182, 194, 197n54, 262, 266–67, 272, 282, 325
Holocaust, 4
Holy Week, 314; Crucifixion, 309, 325; Good Friday, 308, 309, 310; Palm Sunday, 305, 318
homage, 318, 322–23, 325
homes (Jewish), 24, 50, 62, 92, 148, 149n18, 157–64, 165–66
Horden, Peregrine, 301
hospices and hospitals, 150–51, 155–57
huppah (marriage canopy), 227, 241, 242. *See also* marriage

idolatry, 308–9, 319
Île de la Cité, 134, 137, 140
imperial court. *See* courts
Innocent III, 309, 311
inns, 149, 151–54
invisibility of Jews, 308, 311, 314–15, 317, 325
Isaac (biblical figure), 290
Isaac b. Joseph of Corbeil (Semak), 38, 42, 158–59
Isaac b. Samuel, 165
Isaac of Chinon, 281–300
Isaac of Meiningen, 103
Isaac son of Abraham (of Mainz), 201
Isenburg, 74, 76–77, 79–80, 82–87, 89–94
Israel Isserlein, 63, 218–22

Jacob (biblical figure), 187–88
Jacob ben Meir (Rabbenu Tam), 36, 41, 109, 161n83, 245n74, 283n22
Jacob ben Moses Moellin (Maharil), 49, 229, 236, 242, 260–64, 266–67
Jacob of Chinon, 282
Jean le Fevre, 323–24
Jehoash (biblical figure), 203
jewelry, 226–58
Jewish streets, 2–3, 16–17, 99–101, 133–37, 139, 178, 279, 281, 297, 310–12, 315, 325, 331–32
Joel ha-Levi (of Bonn), 120
John II of France, 323
John of Bohemia, 324
Josel of Rosheim, 91
Joseph ibn Kaspi, 321–23, 324
Joshua (biblical figure), 188
Josiah (biblical figure), 203
Judah ha-Cohen (of Mainz), 64, 117
Judah ha-Levi, 282
Judah he-Hasid, 58–60, 282. *See also* *Sefer Hasidim*
Judenregal, 75–77, 79–81, 88, 94
Juiverie. See Jewish streets

kaddish, 53
ketubbah, 64, 228, 230, 231, 240, 241, 246–48, 250, 251. *See also* marriage
kiddushin, 226–58. *See also* marriage
kings of France, 129, 131, 132, 281, 309
kissing, 323, 324
Koblenz, 105–6, 109, 111, 121; Koblenz toll, 103, 105–9, 111–13, 119
Königstein, 74
Krems an der Donau, 57

lachrymose history, 5–6
Late Antiquity, 55, 280, 288–89, 317
leprosy, 285
Levite, 320
Linz, 113
liturgical poetry. See *piyyutim*
living quarters. *See* Jewish streets
Loire Valley, 281
Lombards, 125–34, 140–43
London, 52, 54, 116
Louis II of Anjou, 323
Louis VII of France, 311
Louis IX of France, 310, 313
love, 228, 237, 238, 248
Low Countries, 106, 111–12
Lübeck, 52

INDEX

Magdeburg, 112
magic, 234, 241, 246
Maharam of Rothenburg. *See* Meir of Rothenburg
Maharil. *See* Jacob ben Moses Moellin
Mahzor Vitry, 45, 232, 242, 282
maids. *See* servants
Maimonides, 60
Main River, 106, 111–12, 118
Mainz, 1–3, 61–62, 64, 66, 112–15, 117–18, 120, 177–78, 196, 200–202, 205–6
Makhir brothers, 114, 119
malaria, 301
Marie de Blois, 323
markets, 17, 23, 92, 117, 122, 221–22, 333
Marktschutzrecht (Jewish Trade Privilege), 221–22. *See also* privileges
marriage, 39, 40, 43–44, 161–62, 226–58; betrothal (*erusin*) 172, 226, 227, 229, 246, 252, 290. See also *huppah*; *ketubbah*; *kiddushin*; matchmaking
Mary (Virgin), 298, 318
mass, 291, 292, 294–98. *See also* Eucharist; transubstantiation
matchmaking, 236, 241, 283. *See also* marriage
medical practice, 279–80, 283, 287–88, 299
Me'ir ben Joel, 196–97
Meir b. Barukh of Rothenburg (Maharam), 32, 36–39, 41–43, 56, 64–65, 109, 117, 231, 238, 265, 271–73
Meir Cohen (of Mainz), 1, 3
Meissner Rechtsbuch, 315
Memorbuch (of Nuremberg), 103, 109, 121, 147
merchants, 108–9, 117–20, 122, 125–26, 133, 140, 148–49, 156, 160–61, 170, 172, 333
Merseburg, 112
Meshulam ben Kalonymus, 2, 71
Messiah, 319
Metz, 112
Meuse River, 108, 111
mikveh (ritual bath), 191–94, 205, 239
Minnelieder (Love Poems), 248
Miranda do Doura, 54
Miriam (biblical figure), 285, 290, 299

moneylending, 9, 68–69, 125–26, 131, 140–41, 145, 208–10, 211, 213–16, 218, 223–24, 235, 245, 331–32
Mosel River, 105–6, 111–13, 116
Moses (biblical figure), 287
Moshe Mintz (Maharam Mintz), 236–37, 241, 245
Mt. Sinai, 231, 233
Munich, 69
Münzenberg, 28–29, 74, 76–77, 79–83, 85–86, 88–95

neighborhoods. *See* Jewish streets
New Testament, 321, 324
Nicholas I, 308
nidui, 31–32, 39. *See also* excommunication
ninth of Av, 195
Notre-Dame Cathedral, 311
numerology. See *gematria*
Nuremberg, 68, 103, 156, 209, 212–17, 223

Olsan, Lea, 296, 299
Orhot Tzadikim, 60

Palm Sunday. *See* Holy Week
Paris, 125–31, 133–43, 310–13
passengers, 104, 116
Passion Sunday, 309, 311, 313, 314, 325. *See also* Holy Week
Passover, 120. *See also* holidays
pawnbroking, 86–87, 214–15, 235, 236, 245. *See also* moneylending
pearls, 208–9
Perpignan, 53, 66
Peter the Chanter, 304
petitions, 81, 84, 86–87. *See also* courts
petit pont (Paris), 135, 137
Philipp, Count of Solms-Lich, 74
pilgrimage, 150, 155
piyyutim, 195–96, 205, 260–61, 271–75; among laymen, 263–64, 271–75; among women, 264–66, 275; preparation before holidays in the context of, 266–67, 276; as a source of social history, 227, 232, 259–60, 266–67, 269–71, 271–75; as shapers of communal memory and identity, 267–71; 1096 persecutions and, 268–73; Ninth of Av liturgy, 271–74, 276

Place du Grève, 137, 140
plague. *See* Black Death
Pont au change (Paris), 135
poor, poverty, 10, 24, 41, 55, 57, 62, 65, 67n51, 68n52, 79, 92, 128, 147, 150, 154–57, 162, 164, 235, 331
porters, 117–18, 209
ports, 115
Prague, 112
prayer book, prayers, 53, 260–62, 266–67, 273–76. See also *piyyutim*
privileges, 51, 108–11, 113, 121–22, 221–22, 321, 322, 323, 324, 325, 326
property, 40–41, 43, 79, 85, 86, 88, 91, 109, 113, 158, 209, 214, 220–21, 228, 236, 237, 281
Provence, 321–24
public shaming, 34–35

queens, 310, 313, 317–18, 323

Rabbenu Tam (Jacob b. Meir), 36, 40–42
Raffelstetten, 113
Ralf (Rodulf) Glaber, 175
Raphael (angel), 289, 295, 298
Rashi (Solomon b. Isaac), 59, 287
Red Sea, 290–91
Regensburg, 58, 67, 69–70, 87n42, 108, 111–13, 156, 262
Reinburg, Virginia, 286
Reinhard I of Hanau, 74, 79, 89
relics, 279–80, 301, 310
rentals, 61, 93, 114n43, 157–64
Rhine River, 105, 110–13, 115–17, 120
Rhineland, 110, 112–13, 115, 117, 121
rivers, 103–5, 108–22. See also *specific rivers*
roads and travel, 104, 146, 149–51, 153, 156
Rothschild Haggadah, 248
Rosh Hashanah. *See* holidays, High Holidays
rouelle (Jewish badge), 129n17, 132
Rouen, 310
Rouffach synagogue inscription, 190
Rudiger of Speyer, 2–4, 148
Rue de la harpe (Paris), 135–36
Rue de la tacherie (Paris), 135
Rue de rosieres (Paris), 137
Rue des juifs, 134, 137, 139
Rue des lombards, 125
Rycke of Frankfurt, 64–68

Saale, 112
Sabbath (Shabbat), 35, 103, 114–15, 118, 165–66, 171, 186, 236, 245, 246, 259, 264, 275
sacrament, 314, 317
sailors, 115, 118
saints, 150, 286, 288, 293n61, 298, 300, 301. *See also specific saints listed under St.*
salt, 285, 287, 291, 296. *See also* food
Samson b. Abraham of Sens, 165
Samuel b. Meir (Rashbam), 109
Sarah (biblical figure), 195
Sarah, Mistress (of Mainz), 201
seals, 12, 14, 65n45, 245, 321
Second Nuremberg Haggadah, 229–30, 248
Sefer ha-Dinim, 64
Sefer ha-Hinukh, 236, 320
Sefer ha-Ma'asim, 57, 68, 301
Sefer ha-Rokeah. See Eleazar b. Judah of Worms
Sefer Hasidim, 35–36, 41, 58, 59, 60, 279, 297, 319
Sefer Kolbo, 34, 42
Seine River, 126, 135, 137
seizures, 81–84, 86–87
servants, 16, 51, 55, 76, 80, 82, 84, 85, 87, 91–93, 106, 138, 209, 214, 218, 296. *See also* slaves
Shalom of Neustadt, 57
Shimon he-Hasid, 115
ships (*or* vessels), 103–5, 113–18
Shulkhan Kesef. See Joseph Ibn Kaspi
Sigismund, 292–93, 301
singing, 165, 270n37, 324–25
Sirat, Colette, 282
slander, 37–38
slaves, 106, 113. *See also* servants
Solms, 74, 76–77, 79–80, 82–87, 89–94
Solomon (Shlomo) son of Samson (Shimshon), 1, 115
Speyer, 1–3, 24–25, 42, 51, 61–62, 108, 112, 115, 148, 181, 196n47
St. Augustine, 322
St. Bartholomaeus Frankfurt Cathedral, 315
St. Bon, 135, 137, 140
St. George, 301
St. Odilo, 176
St. Trophime, 323
stone (quarrying), 176, 178, 190, 194–95, 202–4

stylus (Iron), 178, 197–200
Strasbourg, 52
students, 32n1, 57–58, 118, 119, 121, 149, 159–60, 163, 165, 260–61, 272, 320
Swabia, 106
synagogue, 2, 13, 24, 41, 45, 46, 147, 171, 178–80, 187–202, 205–6, 245, 260–67, 273, 275, 315, 320, 324, 329; as "Lesser Temple" 182, 186, 205

Taille, 127–32, 140; *Taille Judeorum,* 129, 133. *See also* taxes
tallit, 238
Takkanot (communal ordinances), 36, 37, 40–42
Talmud, 56, 163, 220–21nn33–35, 287–91, 319, 320
tariffs, 105–6, 108, 110. *See also* taxes
taverns, 151–54
taxes and taxation, 84–87, 104, 108, 129, 134, 138, 141
Temple, 181–86, 194, 195, 197n53, 203, 205, 207, 242, 245, 251, 271, 272, 332
territorialization, 74–77, 88, 91, 94
Terumat ha-Deshen. See Israel Isserlein
testimony, 40, 44–46. *See also* courts
Tetragrammaton, 289
textiles, 216–18
textile workers. *See* craftspeople
Thames River, 116
tolls, 103–13, 116, 119, 121–22; toll stations, 104–8, 110, 121
tombstones, 9, 15, 187, 196
Torah scroll, 320, 322, 323, 324, 325, 326
trade, 21, 104–6, 111–13, 119, 121, 125, 148, 151, 153, 155, 160–61, 166, 221
transportation, 104, 116–17, 120, 202–3
transubstantiation, 313. *See also* mass

travel, 35, 85, 101, 104–5, 108, 110–22, 145–47, 148–51, 164–66, 283, 315, 333–34
Trier, 90, 105–6, 111–12, 115–16
Trinkgeld, 84–86. *See also* tolls
Tzidkiah b. Abraham, 153

Ulrich von Richental, 324

Vienna, 314
violence, 36–37, 39, 81–84, 86–87, 103, 117
Vltava, 112

Wandsbek, 55
water, 171, 191, 194, 203, 238, 285, 287, 291, 296, 298
weddings. *See* marriage
Weisenfels, 243
Wetterau, 74–75, 78, 80, 86–87
widows, 28, 51, 56–57, 61, 63–64, 158
wine, 34, 160, 241, 285, 287, 291, 296, 298. *See also* food
women's synagogue (Worms), 196–200
Worms synagogue, 177, 179–86, 188–92, 196–200, 205
Worms, 42, 61, 62, 66, 108, 112, 114–15, 117, 121–22, 162–64, 177, 178–200, 205–6, 265, 332
Würzburg, 61–62, 118

Xanten, 112

Yakhin and Boʻaz, 182, 205
Yehuda Haggadah, 230n18, 231, 248
Yiddish, 55, 67, 70, 292
Yohanan, (Talmudic rabbi), 287–88
Yom Kippur. *See* holidays, High Holidays

www.ingramcontent.com/pod-product-compliance
Lightning Source LLC
Chambersburg PA
CBHW050925240426
43668CB00021B/2432